studysync®

TEACHER'S EDITION

Facing Challenges

GRADE 6 | UNIT 3

studysync

studysync.com

Send all inquiries to:
BookheadEd Learning, LLC
610 Daniel Young Drive
Sonoma, CA 95476

1 2 3 4 5 6 7 8 9 LMN 20 19 18 17 16
A
2016 G6U3

studysync®

GRADE 6 UNITS

Turning Points

UNIT 1

Overview • Pacing Guide • Instructional Path
Extended Writing Project • Research • Full-Text Study

Ancient Realms

UNIT 2

Overview • Pacing Guide • Instructional Path
Extended Writing Project • Research • Full-Text Study

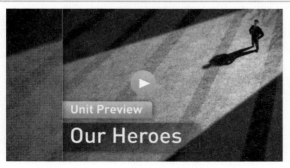

Facing Challenges

UNIT 3

Overview • Pacing Guide • Instructional Path
Extended Writing Project • Research • Full-Text Study

Our Heroes

UNIT 4

Overview • Pacing Guide • Instructional Path
Extended Writing Project • Research • Full-Text Study

Teacher's Edition

Welcome to StudySync

StudySync's comprehensive English Language Arts program for Grades 6-12 is a hybrid print and digital ELA solution. The program leverages cutting edge technology to create an engaging, relevant student and teacher experience. StudySync's multimedia content is available 24/7 from any desktop, tablet, or mobile device. In addition, the program's print resources allow for flexible, blended implementation models that fit the needs of every classroom.

StudySync's Core ELA curriculum was built from the ground up to fully align with the Common Core State Standards for English Language Arts. StudySync provides standards-based instruction that teachers can easily customize, scaffold, and differentiate to ensure all students are ready for college, career, and civic life in the 21st century.

STUDYSYNC TEACHER'S EDITION

The StudySync Teacher's Edition is designed to help you understand, pace, plan, and deliver the StudySync Core ELA curriculum to your students. In this **Teacher's Edition** you will find:

1 A list of StudySync Materials available in both your digital teacher account and this print Teacher's Edition.

2 A guide to StudySync's Core ELA Curriculum and additional content.

3 An overview of StudySync Teacher Tools and ideas and inspirations to help you get started today.

4 Resources for each Core ELA Unit in your grade:

Unit Overviews A big picture look at the key texts and skills.

Pacing Guides A day-to-day plan for integrating all Unit content from the Instructional Path, Extended Writing Project, Research, and Full-text Study with hints for reteaching and shortcuts.

Instructional Path Detailed Lesson Plans for each First Read, Skill, Close Read, and Blast.

Extended Writing Project Detailed Lesson Plans for each Extended Writing Project.

Research A teacher's guide to delivering the Research Project.

Full-text Study A Full-text Reading Guide with key passage explications, vocabulary, discussion and close reading questions.

DESIGNED FOR TODAY'S CLASSROOMS

StudySync combines the best of print and digital resources to meet you where you are and take you where you want to be—allowing low-tech and high-tech classrooms to take full advantage of StudySync's **rigor, relevance, and flexibility.**

RIGOR AND RELEVANCE

StudySync engages students with a learning experience that reflects the ways they experience the world by providing multiple opportunities for collaboration, social interaction, and exposure to rich media and thousands of classic and contemporary texts.

In addition, StudySync challenges students and helps them meet rigorous academic expectations with:

- Access to diverse characters and points of view with an expansive digital library, searchable by grade level and Lexile®-level.
- Close reading instruction with various levels of text complexity.
- In-depth studies of canonical and contemporary texts, representing all genres including literary and informational.
- Multiple opportunities for developing foundational language and literacy skills, all while building content knowledge and helping students make meaning.
- Practice and application of analytical writing to sources, with prompts and rubrics tied to the CCSS.

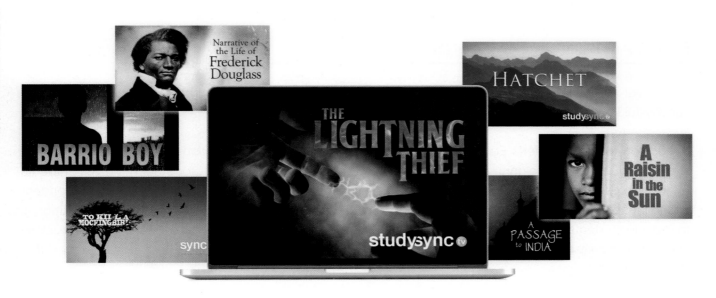

FLEXIBILITY

PRINT AND DIGITAL OPTIONS

Whichever format is right for your classroom—digital, print, or a combination of both, StudySync provides a successful learning experience for all students.

In addition to this Teacher's Edition, a *Student Reading and Writing Companion* is also available to allow students to complete assignments on or off line. This consumable handbook for students gives students printed access to all readings in a Core ELA Unit's instructional path, including First Reads, text-dependent Think questions, Skills lessons, Close Reads and writing prompts. The purpose of the student print support is to provide students with close reading opportunities so they may continue through the course successfully even without daily access to digital. *Please see page xi for a full overview of all StudySync materials available in both print and digital.*

MULTIPLE IMPLEMENTATION MODELS

Whether you are using blended instruction, a flipped classroom, or a traditional format, StudySync provides the flexibility to meet your instructional needs. For example, you can:

- Use print options in conjunction with a projector to engage students in a whole-class discussion regarding a text, an assignment, or a StudySync® TV video.

- Have students work in pairs, small groups, or individually to read, annotate, and answer think questions. Students can work on a single computer or shared devices; alternatively they can annotate directly in their student workbooks.

- Schedule time in computer labs for students to bring their Reading & Writing Companions and submit writing online and complete peer reviews.

Specific examples of using StudySync for whole-group, small-group, and individual instruction are provided on page *xxx* of this guide.

TIPS TO DIFFERENTIATE

Classrooms have a mix of interests, learning styles, and skill levels. Integrating technology makes it easier for teachers to better differentiate and personalize instruction without substantially adding to their workload.

StudySync allows teachers to customize their lessons and to:

- Scaffold assignments based on students' interests and reading abilities
- Make assignments and choose texts based on Lexile®-levels
- Access an extensive library of 6–12 content, texts, and excerpts
- Target specific learning objectives, skills, and Common Core Standards
- Tailor instruction to whole-class, small group, or individual needs
- Offer access support—including audio support, closed captioning, and vocabulary support

CUSTOMIZING YOUR CURRICULUM

With StudySync, you can build the kind of program you've always wanted to teach.
You have the ability to:

- Assign a Library text with the existing prompt or write your own
- Modify assignments for differentiated learning levels
- Access Skills Lessons separately from the Units and assign as stand-alone lessons, or pair with another text of your choosing
- Customize assessments by creating your own rubrics and peer review prompts

Leverage StudySync's online platform and peer review system with **your own content** by:

- Creating your own writing assignments
- Adding your own Library items to your account, including images and videos

COLLABORATION AMONG TEACHERS

StudySync facilitates collaboration by allowing you to share teacher-created content, rubrics, modified assignments, and new library items with other educators in your subscription. Have a rubric used specifically by your district? Have an assignment that every English teacher in your department will be utilizing? These only need to be created once, helping teachers save time and focus on working together.

SUCCESS FOR ALL LEARNERS

StudySync supports students every step of the way. Students experience a seamless online experience for reading and writing, submitting assignments, and writing and receiving reviews with tools that encourage close reading and critical thinking. Students access their assignments and then can view completed work and reviews received in their own online "binder."

Support for All Levels of Learners

- Grade and Lexile®-leveled filters for Digital Library of texts
- Access Path for EL support
- Differentiated learning tools including customizable groups, prompts, and rubrics
- Print materials for work offline

Online Learning Tools

- Collaborative learning platform with online student binders and social learning network
- Online teacher and anonymous peer review platform
- Online test practice similar to PARCC, Smarter Balanced, and other high-stakes test formats

Audio/Visual Resources

- Audio narration of text
- Audio text highlight option
- Online annotation tool
- Closed Captioning of video resources
- Engaging StudySync® TV & SkillsTV videos

Teacher's Edition

PROFESSIONAL DEVELOPMENT

StudySync's Professional Development is on target and ongoing. Our Professional Development Platform in ConnectED and the Teacher Homepage tab within StudySync provide online learning resources that support classroom implementation and instruction and connect explicitly to the standards. All audiovisual, multimedia, and technology resources include suggestions for appropriate implementation and use.

The **Professional Development course** provides an extensive overview of StudySync as well as support for implementing key instructional strategies in the English Language Arts classroom. The **Teacher Homepage** provides access to digital resources and up-to-date articles on "What's New" with StudySync features and content, plus "Ideas and Inspirations," with tips from featured StudySync users and the StudySync Curriculum team.

Review the Professional Development guides and videos within the StudySync Professional Development Implementation course in your ConnectED account and the content on your Teacher Homepage. Then turn to StudySync's Getting Started Guide to begin!

Teacher's Edition

STUDYSYNC MATERIALS

	Digital Teacher Account	Print Teacher's Edition	Digital Student Account	Student Reading & Writing Companion
Scope and Sequences	●			
Grade Level Overviews	●			
Core ELA Unit Overviews	●	●		
Core ELA Unit Pacing Guides	●	●		
Complete Lesson Plans	●	●		
Core Handouts	●			
Access Handouts	●			
Text Selections and Lessons	●		●	●
Reading Skill Lessons	●		●	
Blast Lessons	●		●	
Extended Writing Project Lessons	●		●	●
Writing Skill Lessons	●		●	●
Research Project Guide	●	●		
Full-text Reading Guide	●	●		
End-of-Unit & End-of-Course Digital Assessments	●		●	
Printable Assessments	●			

CORE ELA UNITS

StudySync's Core ELA curriculum consists of 4 **Core ELA Units** per grade. Each unit covers 45 days of instruction for a total of 180 days of instruction at each grade. A complete **Scope and Sequence** outlines standards coverage for each grade, and **Grade Level Overviews** provide teachers a more in-depth look at the reading and writing instruction in each unit. **Pacing Guides** offer detailed 45-day plans for delivering each unit's content.

Each Core ELA Unit is organized around a unique theme and essential question that challenges students to examine texts through an engaging, challenging lens. Each unit contains five key components:

1. Overview

2. Instructional Path

3. Extended Writing Project

4. Research

5. Full-text Study

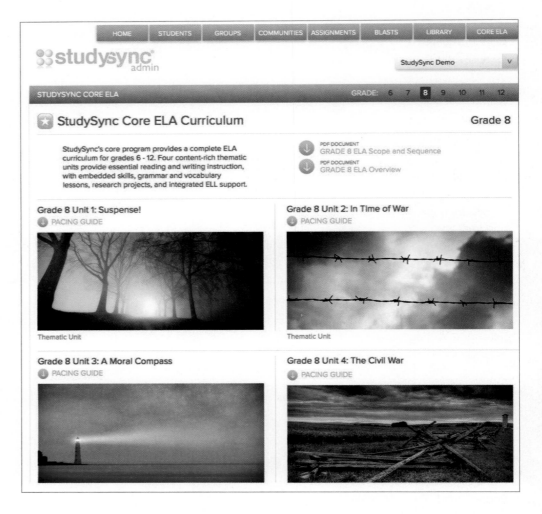

Teacher's Edition

OVERVIEW

The Overview of each Core ELA Unit provides a video preview and an introduction to the unit. The Overview also contains lists of readings, key Skills, standards, and other important general information about the unit.

PACING GUIDE

Pacing Guides provide a 45-day plan with day-to-day guidance for implementing each Core ELA Unit. They outline when and how to incorporate instruction from the Instructional Path, Extended Writing Project, Research Project, and Full-text Study. An additional Pacing Guide column helps teachers draw connections between the Full-text Study and the shorter text selections in the Instructional Path.

Pacing Guides also offer ideas for substituting lessons, revisiting difficult concepts, creating multidisciplinary strands of instruction, and designing independent reading programs. These guides show teachers how to bring StudySync's wealth of resources together to create dynamic, engaging learning environments for their students.

DAY	INSTRUCTIONAL PATH	EXTENDED WRITING PROJECT	RESEARCH PROJECT	FULL-TEXT STUDY	CONNECTING FULL-TEXT STUDY TO THEMATIC UNIT INSTRUCTIONAL PATH LESSONS
23	**SKILL** Media			*Harriet Tubman: Conductor on the Underground Railroad* Chapter 5 "Flight" **COMPARE** to *Old Plantation Days*	
24	**CLOSE READ** *Harriet Tubman: Conductor on the Underground Railroad*	**EXTENDED WRITING PROJECT** Literary Analysis		*Harriet Tubman: Conductor on the Underground Railroad* Chapter 6 "The Underground Road"	
25	**FIRST READ:** *The People Could Fly: American Black Folktales*			*Harriet Tubman: Conductor on the Underground Railroad* Chapter 7 "'Shuck this Corn'"	**LINK** to *Harriet Tubman: Conductor on the Underground Railroad* – Ask students to consider the premise of the folktale and discuss why the ability to fly like a bird would be so attractive to African American slaves. In what way does Harriet Tubman help slaves to "fly"?
26	**SKILL** Compare and Contrast	**EXTENDED WRITING PROJECT** Prewrite		*Harriet Tubman: Conductor on the Underground Railroad* Chapter 8 "Mint A Becomes Harriet"	
27	**CLOSE READ** *The People Could Fly: American Black Folktales*	**SKILL** Thesis Statement		*Harriet Tubman: Conductor on the Underground Railroad* Chapter 9 "The Patchwork Quilt"	**LINK** to *Harriet Tubman: Conductor on the Underground Railroad* – How does Harriet Tubman's marriage to John Tubman keep her a "caged bird"? How is this ironic given John's status?

Teacher's Edition

INSTRUCTIONAL PATH

The Instructional Path of each Core ELA Unit contains ten to twelve texts and/or text excerpts from a variety of genres and text types. Program authors, Douglas Fisher, Ph.D. and Timothy Shanahan, Ph.D., developed the instructional routines around these texts to support best practices in reading instruction.

Instruction around texts begins with a First Read lesson. First Read Lesson Plans include think alouds to help teachers model key vocabulary and comprehension skills for students before they read. Students read and annotate texts using either their digital accounts or their print Student Reading and Writing Companions, and First Read lessons conclude with a series of text-dependent Think questions that challenge students to provide textual evidence to support their understanding of the text.

At least three First Reads in every unit also include a StudySync® TV episode, one of the hallmarks of the program. Lessons with StudySync® TV contain additional metacognitive questions in which students reexamine short clips from the video to analyze how students in the model discussion construct meaning and express themselves effectively using academic vocabulary and discussion skills.

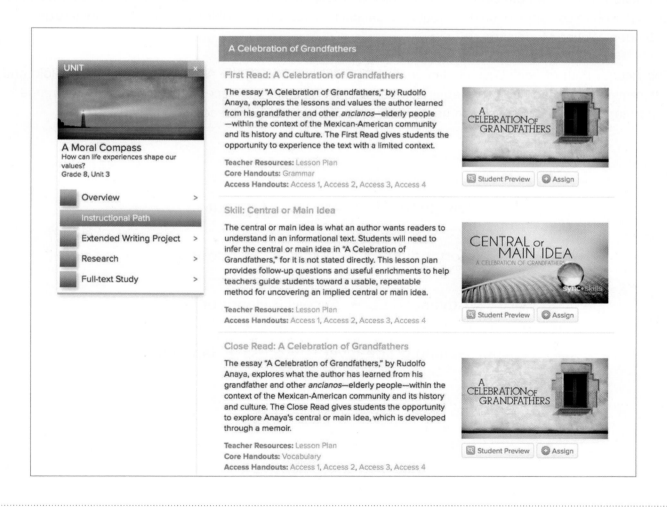

Reading Skill lessons follow First Reads, and apply the Gradual Release of Responsibility Model to deliver explicit instruction that helps students master key skills and reading strategies. Over the course of a unit, students will complete two to three of these lessons each week, offering teachers many opportunities to formatively assess student mastery and growth.

Close Read lessons culminate the instructional reading routine. Close Read lessons begin with an emphasis on vocabulary instruction as students refine or confirm their analyses of vocabulary from the First Read. Close Read lessons then challenge students to apply skills and reading strategies as they reread and annotate the text in preparation for writing their own short-constructed responses.

StudySync Blasts, the fourth lesson type found in the Instructional Path, typify the program's commitment to creating an engaging, twenty-first century context for learning. Each Blast is a short reading and writing lesson with its own research topic and driving question to which students respond in 140 characters or less.

Every assignment in the Instructional Path includes an in-depth Lesson Plan, available to teachers in their digital teacher account and this print Teacher's Edition, with both a Core Path and an Access Path of instruction. The Core Path contains the regular instructional routines that guide students toward mastery. Many lessons also contain Core Handouts—Grammar mini-lessons, Graphic Organizers, Vocabulary quizzes, or Student Writing Models.

The Access Path of each Lesson Plan contains guidance for using the Access Handouts to scaffold and differentiate instruction to insure equity and access for all students. Access Handouts provide a range of important scaffolds for English Learners and Approaching grade-level readers.

Beginner EL	➜ Access 1 Handout
Intermediate EL	➜ Access 2 Handout
Advanced EL	➜ Access 3 Handout
Approaching grade-level	➜ Access 4 Handout

EXTENDED WRITING PROJECT

Writing is an integral part of StudySync's Core ELA curriculum. The curriculum features comprehensive instruction in narrative, informative/explanatory, and argumentative writing forms, and in a wide variety of modes, including full-length essays and narratives, short constructed responses, peer reviews, Blasts, and the digital annotations of texts.

Each unit contains an Extended Writing Project (EWP) that focuses on one of the three primary writing forms and is woven into the instructional fabric of the unit. By the end of the year, each student generates a full-length narrative, informative/explanatory essay, literary analysis (in argumentative form), and an argumentative essay.

Numerous writing Skill lessons in each EWP provide instruction on skills essential to every form. EWP lessons contain Lesson Plans, Core Handouts, and Access Handouts that follow the same conventions as lessons in the Instructional Path.

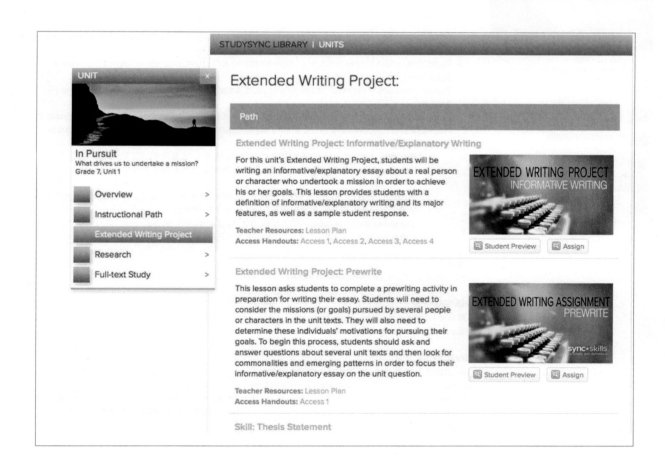

RESEARCH

In addition to the short research students complete in Blast assignments, each Core ELA Unit also contains an in-depth research project in which students explore a new angle of the unit's theme and essential question. This research project is fully integrated into the Pacing Guide, and builds on and complements the unit's key skills. Research projects deepen content knowledge, allow students to read more widely, and offer students the opportunity to present their claims and findings in a variety of formats that address key speaking and listening standards.

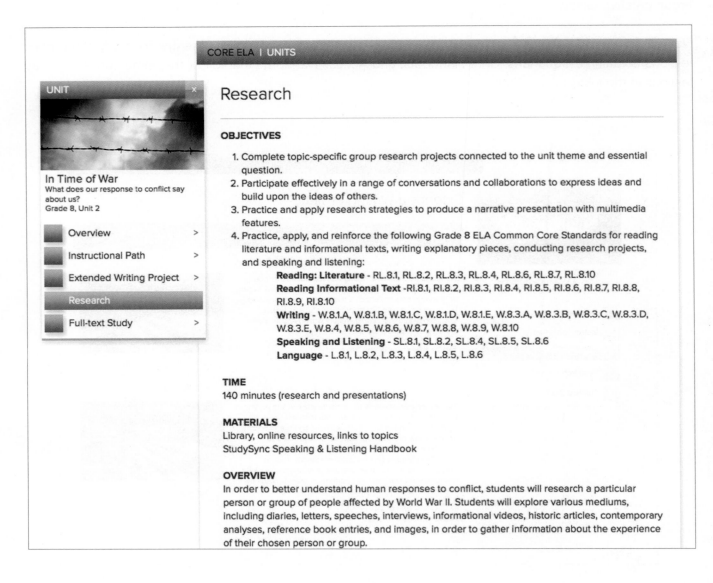

CORE ELA | UNITS

UNIT   x

In Time of War
What does our response to conflict say about us?
Grade 8, Unit 2

Overview   >

Instructional Path   >

Extended Writing Project   >

Research

Full-text Study   >

Research

OBJECTIVES

1. Complete topic-specific group research projects connected to the unit theme and essential question.
2. Participate effectively in a range of conversations and collaborations to express ideas and build upon the ideas of others.
3. Practice and apply research strategies to produce a narrative presentation with multimedia features.
4. Practice, apply, and reinforce the following Grade 8 ELA Common Core Standards for reading literature and informational texts, writing explanatory pieces, conducting research projects, and speaking and listening:
   Reading: Literature - RL.8.1, RL.8.2, RL.8.3, RL.8.4, RL.8.6, RL.8.7, RL.8.10
   Reading Informational Text -RI.8.1, RI.8.2, RI.8.3, RI.8.4, RI.8.5, RI.8.6, RI.8.7, RI.8.8, RI.8.9, RI.8.10
   Writing - W.8.1.A, W.8.1.B, W.8.1.C, W.8.1.D, W.8.1.E, W.8.3.A, W.8.3.B, W.8.3.C, W.8.3.D, W.8.3.E, W.8.4, W.8.5, W.8.6, W.8.7, W.8.8, W.8.9, W.8.10
   Speaking and Listening - SL.8.1, SL.8.2, SL.8.4, SL.8.5, SL.8.6
   Language - L.8.1, L.8.2, L.8.3, L.8.4, L.8.5, L.8.6

TIME
140 minutes (research and presentations)

MATERIALS
Library, online resources, links to topics
StudySync Speaking & Listening Handbook

OVERVIEW
In order to better understand human responses to conflict, students will research a particular person or group of people affected by World War II. Students will explore various mediums, including diaries, letters, speeches, interviews, informational videos, historic articles, contemporary analyses, reference book entries, and images, in order to gather information about the experience of their chosen person or group.

FULL-TEXT STUDY

Each Core ELA Unit contains an anchor text. An excerpt of this anchor text is included alongside other literature and informational texts in the Instructional Path. This anchor text is the recommended Full-text Study for the unit and the Pacing Guide for each unit provides teachers a recommended schedule for reading this text alongside the excerpts in the Instructional Path. The Pacing Guide also contains helpful hints to help teachers make direct connections between sections of the anchor text and lessons from the Core ELA Unit.

The Full-text Study Reading Guide supports the close reading of the complete anchor text. Reading guide lessons preview key vocabulary words and include close reading questions. Each Full-text Study Reading Guide section identifies a key passage that will help teachers guide students through an exploration of the essential ideas, events, and character development in the anchor text. This passage will also serve as the jumping off point from which students will engage in their own StudySync® TV-style group discussion.

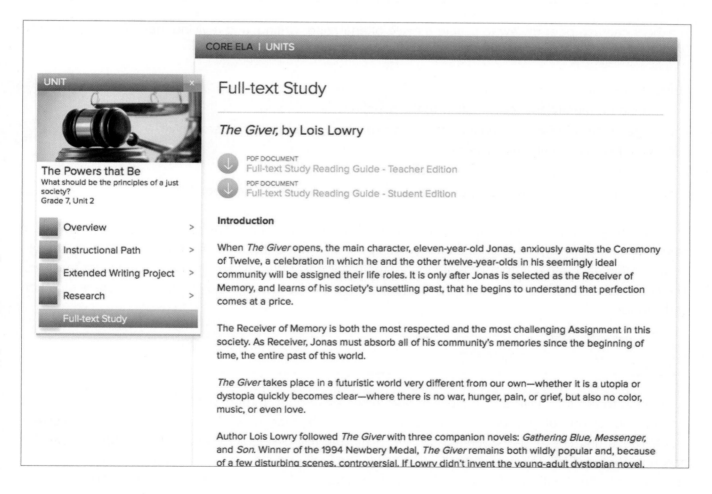

CORE ELA | UNITS

UNIT ×

The Powers that Be
What should be the principles of a just society?
Grade 7, Unit 2

Overview	>
Instructional Path	>
Extended Writing Project	>
Research	>
Full-text Study	

Full-text Study

The Giver, by Lois Lowry

PDF DOCUMENT
Full-text Study Reading Guide - Teacher Edition

PDF DOCUMENT
Full-text Study Reading Guide - Student Edition

Introduction

When *The Giver* opens, the main character, eleven-year-old Jonas, anxiously awaits the Ceremony of Twelve, a celebration in which he and the other twelve-year-olds in his seemingly ideal community will be assigned their life roles. It is only after Jonas is selected as the Receiver of Memory, and learns of his society's unsettling past, that he begins to understand that perfection comes at a price.

The Receiver of Memory is both the most respected and the most challenging Assignment in this society. As Receiver, Jonas must absorb all of his community's memories since the beginning of time, the entire past of this world.

The Giver takes place in a futuristic world very different from our own—whether it is a utopia or dystopia quickly becomes clear—where there is no war, hunger, pain, or grief, but also no color, music, or even love.

Author Lois Lowry followed *The Giver* with three companion novels: *Gathering Blue, Messenger,* and *Son.* Winner of the 1994 Newbery Medal, *The Giver* remains both wildly popular and, because of a few disturbing scenes, controversial. If Lowry didn't invent the young-adult dystopian novel,

ASSESSMENT

FORMATIVE ASSESSMENT

StudySync supports all forms of assessment. Teachers provide feedback on student writing, using either the ready-made Common Core-aligned rubrics in the program or their own customized rubrics created in StudySync. Lesson plans point teachers toward minute-to-minute formative assessment opportunities. Students self-assess and peer review regularly. First Reads, Skills, Close Reads, and Extended Writing Project process steps offer medium cycle formative assessment opportunities for students and teachers to chart progress toward key learning outcomes.

ANONYMOUS PEER REVIEW

Teachers can use peer review to initiate a cycle of analyzing, writing, and revising that turns students into skilled writers and critical thinkers.

Students learn to:
- Respond frequently and meaningfully to the texts they are reading.
- Engage in multiple forms of writing, including expository, narrative, and persuasive.
- Provide timely, anonymous critiques of other students' writing.
- Thoughtfully analyze and revise their work.
- Write to an authentic audience they know will be reading their work immediately.

StudySync capitalizes on the collective intelligence in a classroom by leveraging the valuable voices of students in the learning process. The anonymous peer review feedback helps students take an active role in supporting each other in the development of their skill sets. Peer review is not anonymous for teachers. They have a window into all student work in order to mediate the process and provide appropriate direction and support.

SUMMATIVE ASSESSMENT

In addition to the formative assessment opportunities embedded throughout StudySync, each Core ELA Unit includes an end-of-unit summative assessment and each grade level includes an end-of-course assessment. These unit and end-of-course tests are located in the Online Assessment tool in the ConnectED account. They can be delivered digitally or in print. They offer robust reporting options, including tracking student proficiency with the Common Core State Standards. This assessment format provides important practice for online standardized tests for students.

ADDITIONAL CONTENT

To go along with the Core ELA curriculum, StudySync continually provides new and additional content that allows teachers to easily customize and differentiate curriculum. The Library, Blasts, Skills, Full-text and other units, and other additional resources provide teachers thousands of extra lessons to go along with the Core ELA curriculum and make StudySync a dynamic, twenty-first century content solution in their classrooms.

LIBRARY

The extensive StudySync digital library consists of more than 1,000 texts and excerpts with supporting digital tools and lesson materials for close reading and critical writing assignments.

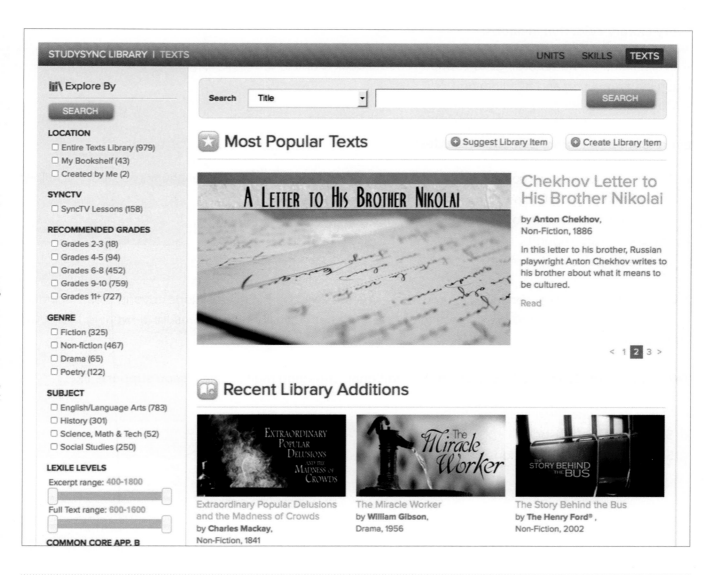

The StudySync Library is an ever-expanding resource that grows to fit the needs of all teachers. Looking for a passage of Twain's non-fiction to teach alongside *The Adventures of Huckleberry Finn*? Want to provide your students background on the political turmoil of 1960s America? Need a place to send students as a jumping off point for their own literary explorations? The StudySync Library is your answer.

To facilitate easy searching, in addition to title, author, keyword, topic, and genre searches, all texts in the Library can also be sorted by:

- Lexile®-level
- Genre
- Common Core Appendix B exemplars
- StudySync® TV Library items
- Publication date

Every Library selection includes:

- Professional audio recordings to support readers of all levels and develop speaking and listening skills
- Online annotation and highlighting
- Common Core-aligned writing prompts

Every Core ELA Library selection includes:

- An Audio Text Highlight tool that breaks texts into grammatical and syntactical chunks as students follow along with the authentic audio
- Auto-graded quizzes to formatively assess student reading comprehension
- Key vocabulary supports
- Text-dependent Think questions

As the StudySync Library continues to grow, these features will expand to selections beyond those included in the Core ELA program to provide teachers even greater flexibility and options for designing their own curriculum.

Texts with StudySync® TV lessons include additional, engaging multimedia lesson supports like:

- Movie trailer-like Previews
- StudySync® TV episodes
- Short-answer Think questions

BLASTS

In addition to the Blasts embedded in the Core ELA Units, StudySync digital teacher accounts house an ever-growing index with hundreds of Blasts that explore contemporary issues and other high-interest topics. StudySync releases new Blasts every school day, staying on top of all the latest news and providing fresh content to help teachers create engaging, relevant classrooms.

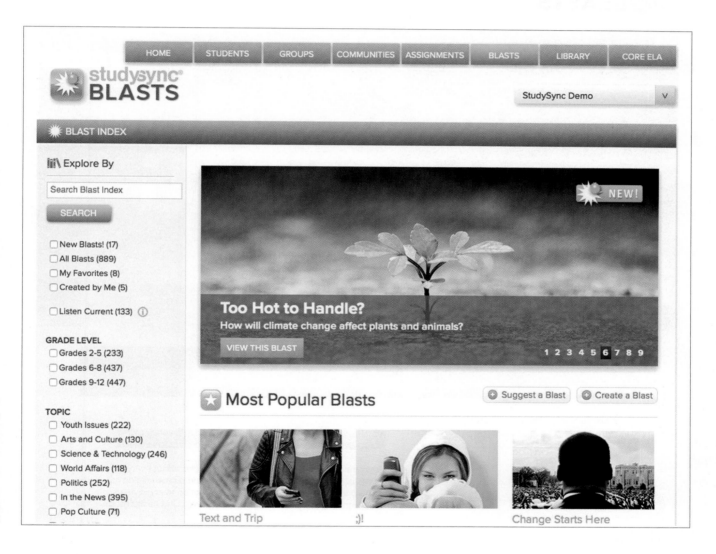

Students respond to the short informational texts and driving questions with 140-character or less Blast responses that allow them to practice clear, concise writing. The peer review platform allows students to read and respond to one another's Blasts, creating a social learning environment that teachers can easily mediate and monitor. Teachers may even elect to join the StudySync National Blast Community which enables students to read and respond to the Blasts of students from all over the United States.

Teachers can easily differentiate weekly Blasts by choosing to target any of the three Lexile® versions to students. Teachers even have the option to use the StudySync platform to create their own Blasts.

Teachers may also choose to select **Listen Current** Blasts. These weekly Blasts feature a background-building radio story to capture students' attention and help build key listening skills.

SKILLS

StudySync Skill lessons instruct students on the key reading, writing, and language skills and strategies necessary for mastery of the Common Core State Standards. The Skills index in every StudySync digital teacher account allows teachers to search for Skills lessons by grade level, topic, or keyword.

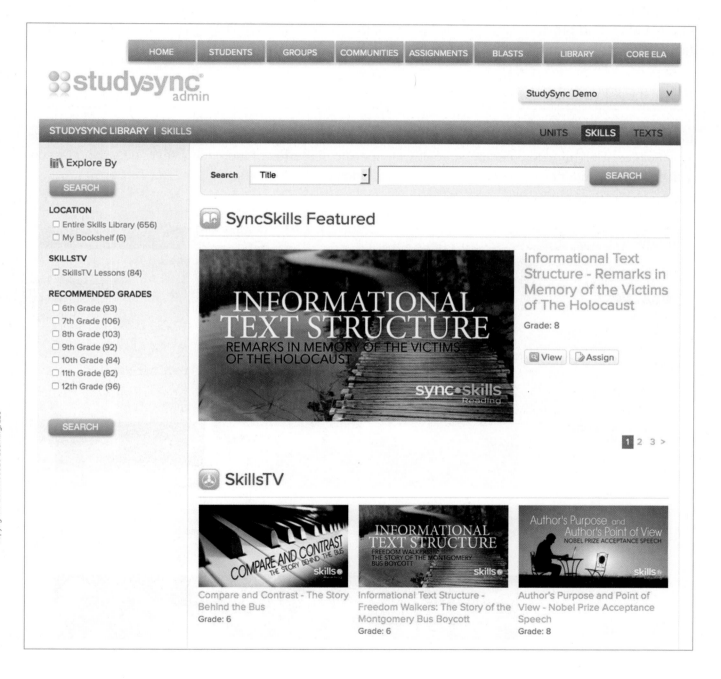

Skill lessons apply the Gradual Release of Responsibility Model. First, students learn the definition of the skill or strategy they'll be applying and watch a Concept Definition video in which students define and break down the key components of a skill or strategy. Next, teachers guide students through a "we do" portion of the lesson, facilitating discussion with follow-up questions from the lesson plan. Many Skills lessons contain SkillsTV videos in which students dramatize the application of a particular skill or strategy.

Lastly, students apply their new knowledge to short questions that ask students to both demonstrate mastery of a standard and provide textual evidence to support their understanding. Teachers receive immediate feedback on these short, formative assessments.

FULL-TEXT UNITS

Each text selected for a Full-text Study in the Core ELA Units also contains a corresponding Full-text Unit. This Full-text Unit provides readings to pair with specific passages of the anchor text and writing lessons that challenge students to compare anchor texts to additional selections.

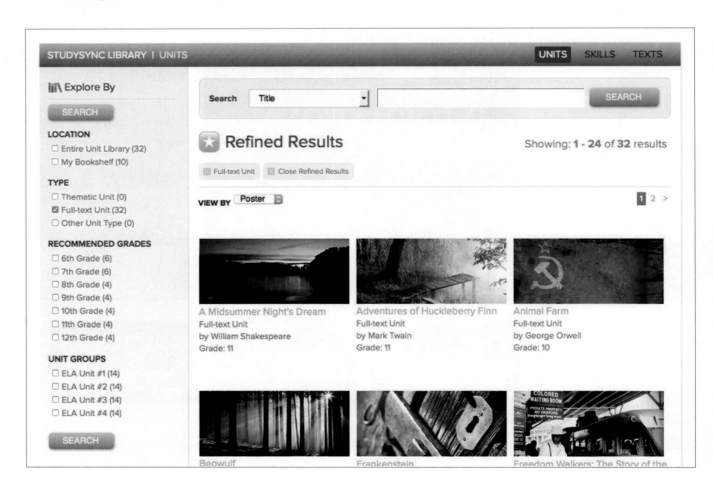

These Full-text Units are not a part of a grade level's 180 days of instruction, however teachers may wish to draw from them to incorporate materials from other disciplines or develop an alternative, novel-based approach to instruction.

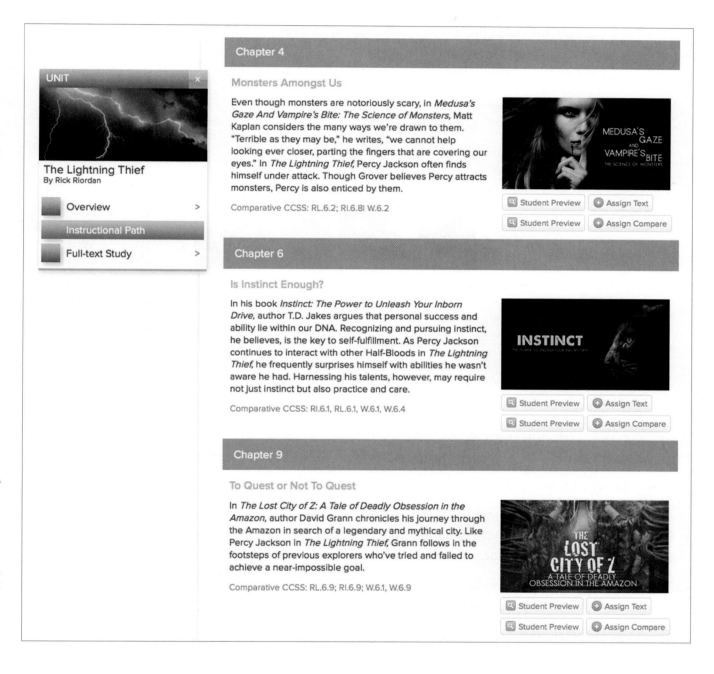

UNIT ✕

The Lightning Thief
By Rick Riordan

Overview >

Instructional Path

Full-text Study >

Chapter 4

Monsters Amongst Us

Even though monsters are notoriously scary, in *Medusa's Gaze And Vampire's Bite: The Science of Monsters*, Matt Kaplan considers the many ways we're drawn to them. "Terrible as they may be," he writes, "we cannot help looking ever closer, parting the fingers that are covering our eyes." In *The Lightning Thief*, Percy Jackson often finds himself under attack. Though Grover believes Percy attracts monsters, Percy is also enticed by them.

Comparative CCSS: RL.6.2; RI.6.8I W.6.2

🔍 Student Preview ⊕ Assign Text
🔍 Student Preview ⊕ Assign Compare

Chapter 6

Is Instinct Enough?

In his book *Instinct: The Power to Unleash Your Inborn Drive*, author T.D. Jakes argues that personal success and ability lie within our DNA. Recognizing and pursuing instinct, he believes, is the key to self-fulfillment. As Percy Jackson continues to interact with other Half-Bloods in *The Lightning Thief*, he frequently surprises himself with abilities he wasn't aware he had. Harnessing his talents, however, may require not just instinct but also practice and care.

Comparative CCSS: RI.6.1, RL.6.1, W.6.1, W.6.4

🔍 Student Preview ⊕ Assign Text
🔍 Student Preview ⊕ Assign Compare

Chapter 9

To Quest or Not To Quest

In *The Lost City of Z: A Tale of Deadly Obsession in the Amazon*, author David Grann chronicles his journey through the Amazon in search of a legendary and mythical city. Like Percy Jackson in *The Lightning Thief*, Grann follows in the footsteps of previous explorers who've tried and failed to achieve a near-impossible goal.

Comparative CCSS: RL.6.9; RI.6.9; W.6.1, W.6.9

🔍 Student Preview ⊕ Assign Text
🔍 Student Preview ⊕ Assign Compare

OTHER UNITS

In addition to Core ELA and Full-text Units, StudySync offers teachers a wide range of English Learner, Literature, and Composition Units from which to choose. In the ever-growing Units sections of the Library, teachers will find instructional content that allows them to further customize and differentiate curriculum to suit the unique needs of their students.

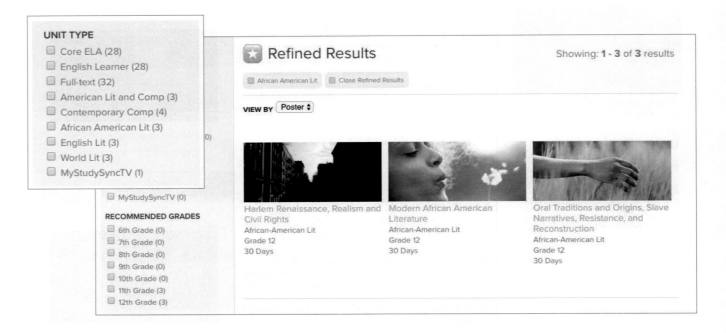

ADDITIONAL RESOURCES

- **Grade Level Assessments** documents contain printable versions of end-of-unit and end-of-course assessments for each grade.

- **Placement and Diagnostic Assessments** aid initial evaluation of student skills to decide on an appropriate instructional level for the student.

- **Foundational Skills** covers phonics, decoding, word recognition, and fluency to help build the skills that lead to students reading independently.

- **Speaking and Listening Handbook** addresses every Common Core ELA standard for speaking and listening and offers usable, repeatable methods and tools for helping students develop and master essential speaking and listening skills.

- **Grammar, Language and Composition Guide** provides additional instruction and practice that can be used for reteaching or preteaching.

- **Vocabulary Workbook** offers students additional opportunities to build and expand their vocabulary.

- **Spelling Workbook** teaches spelling patterns and concepts that apply to various word lists.

- **Standard English Learners Handbook** offers in-depth background information about different instructional routines that can be used with SELs to help them develop their Standard English and understand when it is appropriate to use it.

- **Language Transfers Handbook** provides cross linguistic transfer analysis to help teachers understand the language of students in their classroom.

- **Research-based Alignments** provides a summary of key research findings and recommendations for best practices of instruction in English Language Arts, focused on Reading, Writing, Speaking and Listening, Language, and Media and Technology. Following each section, alignment of the recommendations of the research to specific instruction within StudySync is provided.

- **The Glossary** offers basic summary of essential ELA terminology for each grade level.

Additional Resources

PDF DOCUMENT
Placement and Diagnostic Assessment

PDF DOCUMENT
Foundational Skills

PDF DOCUMENT
Speaking & Listening Handbook

PDF DOCUMENT
Grammar, Language, and Composition Guide

PDF DOCUMENT
Vocabulary Workbook

PDF DOCUMENT
Spelling Workbook

PDF DOCUMENT
Standard English Learners Handbook

PDF DOCUMENT
Language Transfers Handbook

PDF DOCUMENT
Research-base Alignments

PDF DOCUMENT
Student Glossary

PDF DOCUMENT
Teacher Glossary

DESIGN YOUR INSTRUCTION

As outlined above, StudySync provides a rich resource of materials for all ELA students and teachers. Our dynamic, ever-growing curriculum allows for teachers to customize instruction to meet their needs. Whether in a low-tech or high-tech environment, StudySync provides multiple opportunities for whole group, small group and individual instruction. Below are some specific examples of how teachers can integrate StudySync's key features into a variety of classroom contexts.

StudySync Content	Whole group	Small group or pairs	Individuals
Preview and/or Introduction	Project the multimedia Preview and view as a class. Read the Introduction as a class. Follow with a quick discussion about the images and information in the Preview and Introduction.	Have students turn and talk after watching the Preview and reading the Introduction. What images and information stood out? How did their interpretations differ?	Based on the Preview and Introduction, have students jot down predictions, questions, and/or inferences about the text.
First Read	Project a text on the screen. Model specific skills including using context clues to determine difficult vocabulary words, and using reading comprehension strategies to parse difficult passages.	Allow students to read and/or listen to the audio reading of the text in pairs or small groups, stopping to discuss thoughts and new vocabulary words as they annotate.	Students read and annotate the text, utilizing the audio or Audio Text Highlight feature as necessary. Alternatively, students can annotate in their print Companion.
StudySync® TV	Project the episode and view as a class. See the corresponding lesson plan for discussion prompts for specific sections of the episode.	Using prompts from the lesson plan, have students hold their own StudySync® TV discussions. Afterwards, briefly share with the whole class ideas that were discussed.	Ask students to jot down ideas from the StudySync® TV episode and their own discussions that might assist with their writing.
Think Questions	Think Questions may be discussed and answered as a class, using the text as support.	Think Questions may be discussed and answered in pairs or small groups before reviewing correct answers with the entire class.	Think Questions may be answered individually, using the text as support.

Teacher's Edition

Skills	Project the Concept Definition video and as a group read the definition of the Skill. If there is a SkillsTV video in the Model sections of the lesson, watch and discuss as a class.	Have students work in pairs or small groups to read through the text in the Model section, stopping throughout to discuss questions and ideas. Work your way around to each group to provide feedback.	Have students individually complete the mini-assessments that conclude Skills lessons. When all students are finished, project the questions and discuss correct answers.
Close Read	Review vocabulary analysis from the First Read. Ask students to compare their context analysis of vocabulary against the actual definitions. Review key skills students will apply in the Close Read.	Close Reads can occur individually or in small groups. If assigning Close Reads for small group work, have students discuss and explain their annotations to one another as they go.	Have students reread and annotate the text in order to complete the Skills Focus questions and prepare themselves for the writing prompt that follows.
Write	Discuss the prompt as a class, making sure students understand the directions and expectations. Display the rubric for the assignment as well.	Allow students time to brainstorm ideas or discuss the prompts with their peers, referring to the text, StudySync® TV episode, and/or previous discussions.	Students individually submit responses to the assigned prompt.
Peer Review	Remind students of your expectations for the peer review process, and inform them of specific directions for this assignment.	In pairs or small groups, have students discuss what they will look for in their peers' responses, based on the directions and rubric. What will an exemplar response include? Report ideas to the whole class.	Students complete peer reviews individually, using the guidelines established.
Blasts	As a class, hold a brief discussion about the prompt. After students read the Background information, discuss the Quikpoll and Number Crunch as a class. Ask students to make predictions on how their peers will answer the QuikPoll, and how the results might differ if answered by another class, age group, etc.	Students should read the Background section in small groups and record notes in their handbooks. Have students discuss questions and ideas that came up as they read. Ask students to split up the Research Links, so that each student researches 2-3 sites and then reports the information back to their peers.	Students may read the Background information individually, as well as the information from several Research Links. After discussing the information with their peers, they should craft their 140-character response to the prompt and complete 5 or more peer reviews.

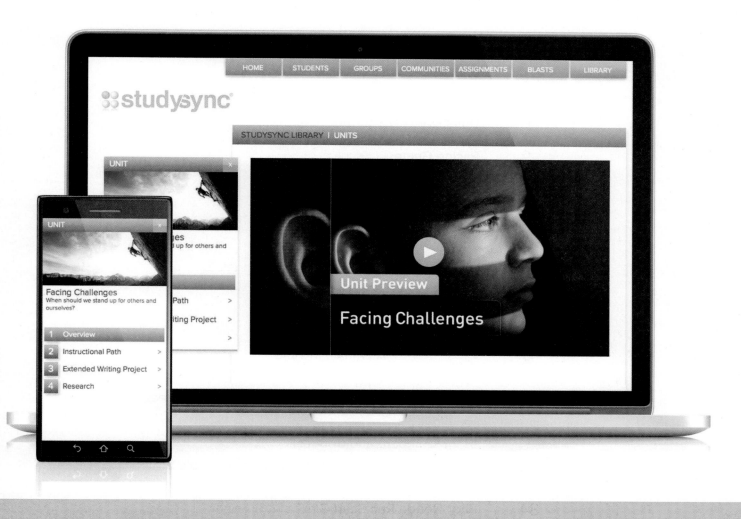

studysync®

Teacher's Edition

When should we stand up for others and ourselves?

Facing Challenges

Facing Challenges

OVERVIEW MATERIALS

INSTRUCTIONAL PATH

Please note that excerpts and passages in the StudySync® library, workbooks, and PDFs are intended as touchstones to generate interest in an author's work. The excerpts and passages do not substitute for the reading of entire texts, and StudySync® strongly recommends that teachers and students seek out and purchase the whole literary or informational work in order to experience it as the author intended. Links to online resellers are available in our digital library. In addition, complete works may be ordered through an authorized reseller by filling out and returning to StudySync® the order form enclosed in this workbook.

Teacher's Edition   3

EXTENDED WRITING PROJECT

RESEARCH

FULL-TEXT STUDY

Overview Materials

Facing Challenges

OVERVIEW

UNIT TITLE

Facing Challenges

UNIT DRIVING QUESTION

When should we stand up for others and ourselves?

UNIT OVERVIEW

Have you ever felt that you or someone else was treated unfairly? Perhaps you were accused of something you didn't do. Or maybe you witnessed a classmate being teased by another student in the hallway in between classes. When you experienced an injustice, did you feel the need to stand up for yourself or for another person? What motivated you to take a stance? Did your actions result in a positive outcome? Throughout history and literature, there have been real people and characters who have decided to take a stand against injustice and stand up for themselves, for another person, or for their community in an attempt to make a positive change.

In this Grade 6 unit, your students will explore through a variety of texts what motivates people to stand up for others and themselves, how they take a stand, and the outcomes of their actions. The unit begins with an excerpt from the novel *A Wrinkle in Time,* which showcases the bravery of two siblings who set out on a dangerous journey to find their father. Other selections share stories, past and present, of people who take a stance against injustice, including a selection that focuses on educator Leo Hart who stood up for "Okie" children during the Great Depression, an account of the efforts of Japanese Americans to prove their loyalty to the United States during World War II, and two sides of an argument about whether schools are doing enough to prevent bullying. Throughout this unit, students will explore the different reasons and ways in which people take a stance and, despite challenges, work hard to make a change for the better.

TEXTS

A Wrinkle in Time	Science Fiction
The Monsters Are Due on Maple Street	Drama
Red Scarf Girl	Memoir
I Am an American: A True Story of Japanese Internment	Informational
Roll of Thunder, Hear My Cry	Fiction
Children of the Dust Bowl: The True Story of the School at Weedpatch Camp	Informational

Copyright © BookheadEd Learning, LLC

The Circuit: Stories from the Life of a Migrant Child	Autobiographical Story
Les Misérables	Fiction
Jabberwocky	Poem
Bullying in Schools	Pro/Con Op-Ed

FULL-TEXT STUDY

Roll of Thunder, Hear My Cry
The Monsters Are Due on Maple Street (alternate)

EXEMPLAR TEXTS

A Wrinkle in Time
Roll of Thunder, Hear My Cry
Jabberwocky

ASSIGNMENT TYPES

Blasts: 9
First Reads: 10
Reading Skills: 13
Close Reads: 10
Extended Writing Project Prompts: 5
Writing Skills: 5

STANDARDS FOCUS

RL.6.2, RL.6.3, RL.6.4, RL.6.5, RL.6.6, RL.6.7, RL.6.9
RI.6.2, RI.6.3, RI.6.4, RI.6.5, RI.6.6, RI.6.7, RI.6.8
W.6.3.A, W.6.3.B, W.6.3.C, W.6.3.D, W.6.3.E, W.6.4, W.6.5, W.6.7, W.6.10
SL.6.1.A, SL.6.1.B, SL.6.1.C, SL.6.1.D, SL.6.2, SL.6.3, SL.6.4, SL.6.5, SL.6.6
L.6.1.A, L.6.1.C, L.6.1.D, L.6.1.E, L.6.2.A, L.6.3.A, L.6.4.A, L.6.4.B, L.6.4.C, L.6.5.C

KEY READING SKILLS

Plot
Media
Compare and Contrast
Informational Text Elements

Connotation and Denotation
Author's Purpose and Author's Point of View
Story Structure
Central or Main Idea
Point of View
Theme
Tone
Arguments and Claims

KEY GRAMMAR SKILLS

First Read: I Am an American - Possessive Pronouns
First Read: Roll of Thunder, Hear My Cry - Understanding Dialect
First Read: Les Miserables - Recognizing and Correcting Vague Pronouns
Extended Writing Project: Narrative Techniques and Sequencing - Restrictive and Nonrestrictive Elements
Extended Writing Project: Revise - Revising Dialogue
Extended Writing Project: Publish - Pronoun-Antecedent Agreement (Number and Gender)

KEY WRITING SKILLS

Audience and Purpose
Organize Narrative Writing
Descriptive Details
Introduction
Narrative Techniques and Sequencing
Conclusion
Style

EXTENDED WRITING PROJECT

As students make their way through the unit, they will read about characters and real people who have chosen to stand up against an injustice in order to make a difference, and will learn about the effects the action had on the person, on others, or on a community. The Extended Writing Project for this unit helps students showcase their knowledge through a well-constructed fictional narrative about a person who chooses to stand up to help someone else or to make a bad situation better. Small, manageable tasks lead students through the prewriting, planning, drafting, revising, and editing/proofreading/publishing steps of the writing process, while skill lessons offer modeling and instruction related to the specific mode of writing.

studysync®

GRADE 6 UNIT 3: FACING CHALLENGES

PURPOSE

This pacing guide will help you utilize the wealth of resources offered in each StudySync Core ELA unit. The pacing guide weaves lessons from every segment of this Core ELA unit: the Instructional Path, Extended Writing Project, Research Project, and Full-text Study.

The pacing guide presents a suggested plan to cover all content in this unit. You may cover all of these lessons in class, or you may decide to divide the assignments between in-class work and homework. Of course, no one understands your students' needs like you do, and one of the key benefits of StudySync is the ease with which you can adapt, alter, eliminate, or reorganize lessons to best meet the needs of your students. The Shortcuts and Additional Activities section at the end of this pacing guide contains recommendations to help in that regard.

ORGANIZATION

The pacing guide divides the unit into 45 days. Instructional days often have more than a single task. For example, all of the activities on row 1 are suggested to be covered on the first instructional day. Pacing is based on an assumption of 50-minute instructional days, but since schedules vary from school to school you may need to modify the suggested pacing to fit your unique needs.

The column labeled "Full-text Study Connections" often identifies other texts in the StudySync Library that complement the chapter in the Full-text Study students are reading on a particular day. Though these comparative texts are not considered part of the 45 days of Core ELA instruction for this unit, they are listed in the pacing guide in case you would like to include additional texts as part of this unit.

There are no activities or lessons planned for the final two days of the unit, which are dedicated to assessment.

CORE ELA UNIT

DAY	INSTRUCTIONAL PATH	EXTENDED WRITING PROJECT	RESEARCH PROJECT	FULL-TEXT STUDY	FULL-TEXT STUDY CONNECTIONS
1	**UNIT PREVIEW**		**SPEAKING & LISTENING HANDBOOK** "Research Using Various Media" Section		
2	**BLAST** Facing Challenges		**RESEARCH PROJECT PART I** Break students into small groups and assign each group a topic to research (see list of topics under Research tab) and begin research (in class and/or online).		
3	**FIRST READ** *A Wrinkle In Time*		**RESEARCH PROJECT PART I CONT.** Students should continue to research.		
4	**SKILL** Plot		**RESEARCH PROJECT PART I CONT.** Students should continue to research.	*Roll of Thunder, Hear My Cry* Chapter 1 **COMPARE** to *Delta Blues – Getting To Know Mississippi* OR *Simeon's Story: An Eyewitness Account of the Kidnapping of Emmett Till*	**LINK** to *Roll of Thunder, Hear My Cry –* Chapter 1 of the novel introduces the main characters and hints at the problems that will drive the plot forward. What problems are revealed in this chapter? What predictions can students make about the plot and what will happen in the story?

DAY	INSTRUCTIONAL PATH	EXTENDED WRITING PROJECT	RESEARCH PROJECT	FULL-TEXT STUDY	FULL-TEXT STUDY CONNECTIONS
5	**CLOSE READ** *A Wrinkle In Time*		**RESEARCH PROJECT PART II** Groups should work collaboratively (in class and/or online) on a presentation to present their information to the class.		
6	**FIRST READ** "The Monsters Are Due on Maple Street"		**RESEARCH PROJECT PART II CONT.** Students should continue working to create their presentations.	*Roll of Thunder, Hear My Cry* Chapter 2 **COMPARE** to "The Lynching"	**LINK** to *Roll of Thunder, Hear My Cry* – In "The Monsters Are Due on Maple Street" suspicion and fear fuel the progression of the plot. Suspicion and fear are also present in Chapter 2 of the novel. Ask students to compare the two texts: 1) Who is suspicious of whom and why? 2) What are people afraid of and why? 3) How do suspicion and fear fuel the plot?
7	**SKILL** Media		**RESEARCH PROJECT PART II CONT.** Students should continue working to create their presentations.		
8	**SKILL** Compare and Contrast		**SPEAKING & LISTENING HANDBOOK** "Presentation Skills" **RESEARCH PROJECT PART III** Allow a couple of groups to present for the class.	*Roll of Thunder, Hear My Cry* Chapter 3	**LINK** to *Roll of Thunder, Hear My Cry* – Reading a television script is entirely different from reading a novel. Different types of texts introduce characters, setting, and plot in different ways. Ask students to compare and contrast these two texts to identify similarities and differences. Ask them to evaluate how the reader learns about characters in each type of text.

DAY	INSTRUCTIONAL PATH	EXTENDED WRITING PROJECT	RESEARCH PROJECT	FULL-TEXT STUDY	FULL-TEXT STUDY CONNECTIONS
9	**CLOSE READ** "The Monsters Are Due on Maple Street"		**RESEARCH PROJECT PART III CONT.** Allow a couple of groups to present for the class.		
10	**FIRST READ** *Red Scarf Girl*		**RESEARCH PROJECT PART III CONT.** Allow a couple of groups to present for the class.	*Roll of Thunder, Hear My Cry* Chapter 4	**LINK** to *Roll of Thunder, Hear My Cry* – The struggle to maintain one's honor is evident in both *Red Scarf Girl* and Chapter 4 of the novel. Give students time to discuss how Ji-Li's honor and integrity are tested in this excerpt. Then ask them to draw parallels to the novel, discussing how the characters in *Roll of Thunder, Hear My Cry* also struggle to maintain honor and integrity.
11	**SKILL** Informational Text Elements				
12	**SKILL** Connotation and Denotation			*Roll of Thunder, Hear My Cry* Chapter 5 **COMPARE** to *Rosa Parks: My Story*	**LINK** to *Roll of Thunder, Hear My Cry* – Writers often use words with connotations to reveal information about how characters are feeling. Ask students to look closely at the start of Chapter 4 and identify words with emotional associations that help the reader to better understand how the children are feeling after hearing about the bus incident.
13	**CLOSE READ** *Red Scarf Girl*				

DAY	INSTRUCTIONAL PATH	EXTENDED WRITING PROJECT	RESEARCH PROJECT	FULL-TEXT STUDY	FULL-TEXT STUDY CONNECTIONS
14	**BLAST** Lost Generation			*Roll of Thunder, Hear My Cry* Chapter 6 **COMPARE** to *The Warmth of Other Suns* and *The People Could Fly: American Black Folktales*	**LINK** to *Roll of Thunder, Hear My Cry* – In the Lost Generation Blast, students learn about the lives of children during China's Cultural Revolution. Ask students to consider what they've learned about the lives of African American children growing up in the South during the 1930s. Brainstorm information as a class.
15	**FIRST READ** *I Am an American: A True Story of Japanese Internment*				
16	**SKILL** Author's Purpose and Author's Point of View			*Roll of Thunder, Hear My Cry* Chapter 7 **COMPARE** to *The Color of Water: A Black Man's Tribute To His White Mother*	**LINK** to *Roll of Thunder, Hear My Cry* – Ask students to reread the "Author's Note" at the start of the novel. What do they learn about Mildred Taylor's purpose in writing this novel? What insight does this note give the reader into Taylor's point of view as a writer?
17	**SKILL** Media				

DAY	INSTRUCTIONAL PATH	EXTENDED WRITING PROJECT	RESEARCH PROJECT	FULL-TEXT STUDY	FULL-TEXT STUDY CONNECTIONS
18	CLOSE READ *I Am an American: A True Story of Japanese Internment*			*Roll of Thunder, Hear My Cry* Chapter 8	LINK to *Roll of Thunder, Hear My Cry* – In Chapter 8 Papa tells Cassie, "There are things you can't back down on, things you gotta take a stand on. But it's up to you to decide what them things are." Ask students to consider this quote in relation to the excerpt from *I Am an American*. How did Japanese Americans stand up for themselves after the bombing of Pearl Harbor?
19	BLAST Dorothea Lange: Voice of the Downtrodden	EXTENDED WRITING PROJECT Narrative Writing			
20	FIRST READ *Roll of Thunder, Hear My Cry*			*Roll of Thunder, Hear My Cry* Chapter 9 COMPARE to *Men We Reaped*	
21	SKILL Story Structure	EXTENDED WRITING PROJECT Prewrite			
22	CLOSE READ *Roll of Thunder, Hear My Cry*			*Roll of Thunder, Hear My Cry* Chapter 10	
23	BLAST Tomato/Tomahto: Dialects and Accents				

DAY	INSTRUCTIONAL PATH	EXTENDED WRITING PROJECT	RESEARCH PROJECT	FULL-TEXT STUDY	FULL-TEXT STUDY CONNECTIONS
24	**FIRST READ** *Children of the Dust Bowl: The True Story of the School at Weedpatch Camp*	**BLAST** Audience and Purpose		*Roll of Thunder, Hear My Cry* Chapter 11 **COMPARE** to *A Mission from God*	**LINK** to *Roll of Thunder, Hear My Cry* – After reading the excerpt from *Children of the Dust Bowl*, ask students to compare the stereotypes about "Okie kids" with the stereotypes about African American children during 1930s. How were they similar and/or different? How did these stereotypes impact both populations of children?
25	**SKILL** Central or Main Idea	**SKILL** Organize Narrative Writing		*Roll of Thunder, Hear My Cry* Chapter 12 **COMPARE** to "I Am Prepared to Die"	**LINK** to *Roll of Thunder, Hear My Cry* – In the SyncTV episode, Ben states that the central or main idea in a text is "the key point the author is trying to make." After reading the last chapter in *Roll of Thunder, Hear My Cry*, ask students to identify the key point Mildred Taylor was trying to make in this novel.
26	**CLOSE READ** *Children of the Dust Bowl: The True Story of the School at Weedpatch Camp*				
27	**FIRST READ** *The Circuit: Stories from the Life of a Migrant Child.*	**SKILL** Descriptive Details			
28	**SKILL** Point of View				

DAY	INSTRUCTIONAL PATH	EXTENDED WRITING PROJECT	RESEARCH PROJECT	FULL-TEXT STUDY	FULL-TEXT STUDY CONNECTIONS
29	CLOSE READ — *The Circuit: Stories from the Life of a Migrant Child*	EXTENDED WRITING PROJECT — Plan			
30	BLAST — Down with the King	SKILL — Introduction			
31	FIRST READ — *Les Misérables*				
32	SKILL — Theme				
33	CLOSE READ — *Les Misérables*	SKILL — Narrative Techniques and Sequencing			
34	BLAST — Wage Rage; FIRST READ — "Jabberwocky"				
35	SKILL — Tone	SKILL — Conclusion/Story Ending			
36	CLOSE READ — "Jabberwocky"				

DAY	INSTRUCTIONAL PATH	EXTENDED WRITING PROJECT	RESEARCH PROJECT	FULL-TEXT STUDY	FULL-TEXT STUDY CONNECTIONS
37		**EXTENDED WRITING PROJECT** Draft			
38	**FIRST READ** "Bullying in Schools"	**BLAST** Style			
39	**SKILL** Arguments and Claims				
40	**CLOSE READ** "Bullying in Schools"				
41		**EXTENDED WRITING PROJECT** Revise			
42	**BLAST** Slowly But Surely				
43		**EXTENDED WRITING PROJECT** Edit/Proofread/Publish			
44	**ASSESSMENT** StudySync Grade 6 Unit 3 Assessment				

DAY	INSTRUCTIONAL PATH	EXTENDED WRITING PROJECT	RESEARCH PROJECT	FULL-TEXT STUDY	FULL-TEXT STUDY CONNECTIONS
45	**ASSESSMENT** StudySync Grade 6 Unit 3 Assessment				

SHORTCUTS AND ADDITIONAL ACTIVITIES

Shortcuts

In a perfect world, teachers would have time to cover everything, but most teachers feel like they are in a race against the bell. There is never enough time to cover everything. If you find yourself short on time, there are places where you can trim a StudySync Unit to ensure you are covering the most important parts. Here are some suggestions for how you can shorten this unit to fit in the time you have.

1. **Replace the Research Project with a Crowdsourcing Activity:** Instead of a 9-day research project, you can make the research component of this unit an informal exploration using a crowdsourcing activity. To facilitate a crowdsourcing assignment, break students into groups, give each group a question or research topic, and allow them time to research using computers or devices to generate information about their topic. Then allow them to share what they have learned with the class by writing their information on the board or posting it to a shared Padlet Wall (or other online collaborative space).

2. **Eliminate Repeated Media Skill Lessons:** Each unit focuses on developing specific skills. Some of these skills are repeated throughout the unit to ensure students have plenty of practice with those skills. As the old adage says, "practice makes perfect!" That said, if you are in a rush and looking to cut some of the content in a unit, you can eliminate one or two of these skill lessons and feel confident your students will still be exposed to the information they need about media.

3. **Content Cuts:** There are several different types of texts presented in a unit – excerpts from novels, nonfiction readings, short stories, and poems. If you are running out of time, you may want to eliminate a StudySync selection that focuses on a similar type of text as a previous lesson. For example, *Children of the Dust Bowl: The True Story of the School at Weedpatch Camp* and *I Am an American: A True Story of Japanese Internment* are both excerpts from informational texts that focus on people's lives during particular moments in American history.

Supportive Materials for Other Disciplines

The Full-text Unit for *Roll of Thunder, Hear My Cry* contains several texts that link to history curriculum. *Red Scarf Girl* is Ji-Li Jiang's memoir about being raised in Communist China during a period of intense persecution of people whom the government considered anti-revolutionary. The excerpt from *I Am an American: A True Story of Japanese Internment* examines the causes and effects of Japanese internment in the United States after the bombing of Pearl Harbor during World War II. The excerpt from *Children of the Dust Bowl: The True Story of the School at Weedpatch Camp* describes the experiences of migrant children from Oklahoma who settle in California during the Dust Bowl.

The Thematic Unit also contains several titles that provide more historical context for the novel *Roll of Thunder, Hear My Cry.* In *Simeon's Story: An Eyewitness Account of the Kidnapping of Emmett Till,* Simeon Wright describes what it was like to farm as a black sharecropper in the Jim Crow South. In *The Warmth of Other Suns,* journalist Isabel Wilkerson tells the history of African Americans who migrated from the rural southern United States to the Northeast, Midwest, and West to escape racial oppression and pursue economic and social opportunity.

In addition to these texts from the Thematic Unit and Full-text Unit for *Roll of Thunder, Hear My Cry,* there are StudySync Blasts that complement this unit. The "Group Dynamics" Blast examines the challenges of human interactions; while the "Friends Forever" Blast asks the question, "What role does race play in your friendships?" The "Change Starts Here" explores whether elected leaders or civilians have more power to create change. Each Blast assignment includes a "Research links" section that includes a wide array of resources that provide students with a deeper understanding of the topic.

Suggestions for Further and Independent Reading

Students will find a variety of reading choices among the informational texts presented in the Full-text Unit for *Roll of Thunder, Hear My Cry*. Ted Gioia's *Delta Blues: The Life and Times of the Mississippi Masters Who Revolutionized American Music* provides context for the setting of the Logans' story. *The Warmth of Other Suns: The Epic Story of America's Great Migration* by Isabel Wilkerson gives the perspective of those black families who remained in the Deep South, like the Logans, willing to endure racist violence as the cost of owning their land. Two books take up the theme of family: *The Color of Water: A Black Man's Tribute To His White Mother* by James McBride, and *Men We Reaped: A Memoir by Jesmyn Ward*.

Students looking for independent reading on such *Roll of Thunder, Hear My Cry* topics as the Great Depression, the Jim Crow South, and the Logan family, will have many titles to choose from. Mildred D. Taylor has developed the Logans through a series of nine novels, of which *Roll of Thunder, Hear My Cry* is the second. Before it are *The Land* and *Song of the Trees*. After it are *Let the Circle Be Unbroken*, *The Friendship*, *Mississippi Bridge*, *The Road to Memphis*, and *The Well: David's Story*. Christopher Paul Curtis won a Newbery Medal for his black urban novel of the Great Depression, *Bud, Not Buddy*. Two nonfiction titles use oral history to tell the living story of the Depression and Jim Crow laws: Studs Terkel's *Hard Times: An Oral History of the Great Depression*, and *Remembering Jim Crow: African Americans Tell About Life in the Segregated South* by William H. Chafe and Raymond Gavins.

Difficult Concepts

In 6th grade, students must "determine the meaning of words and phrases as they are used in a text, including figurative and connotative meanings; analyze the impact of a specific word choice on meaning and tone" (RL.6.4). However, tone is a more subtle concept than plot or character, which can make it challenging for students to identify in a text. It's crucial that students develop this skill because tone can be equally important in gaining an understanding and appreciation of a text. There is only one Tone Skill Lesson in this unit, but teachers can spend extra time reviewing the Tone Skill Lesson for "Jabberwocky" with students. Teachers can then repeat the process of analyzing word choice to determine tone with "Bullying in Schools." This text has a point and counterpoint, so students can analyze the word choice and sentence structure to identify the tone of each argument. In addition, teachers can provide extra practice with a wide range of texts by searching StudySync Library Skill Index for additional skill lessons that target this concept. Ideally, teachers should select skill lessons below the current grade level for additional practice to ensure the texts are accessible.

In 6th grade, students should be able to "compare and contrast the experience of reading a story, drama, or poem to listening to or viewing an audio, video, or live version of the text, including contrasting what they 'see' and 'hear' when reading the text to what they perceive when they listen or watch" (RL.6.7). Learning how to compare and contrast different media versions of the same text can be challenging for students. However, it's crucial that students appreciate how medium affects plot events, settings, characters, and the overall message communicated in a text. The Media Skill Lesson on "The Monsters Are Due on Maple Street" focuses on the differences between the print version of a drama and the television adaptation. Teachers can spend extra time walking students through this Media Skill Lesson by playing the clips in class and discussing the way the television adaptation impacts elements of the plot, setting, and characters. Instead of simply showing clips, teachers can show the entire episode and pause periodically to discuss the differences between the script and the television adaptation. Then the second Media Skill Lesson on *I Am an American: A True Story of Japanese Internment* will provide students with additional practice comparing a text with a video.

Read Aloud Selection

"Jabberwocky," Lewis Carroll's nonsensical poem about a brave boy's heroic quest makes use of invented language, rhyme, repetition of sounds, and punctuation to establish and maintain the poem's fanciful tone. Listening to the poem will help students recognize how tools such as inflection, volume, phrasing, and tone of voice bring Carroll's magical kingdom and its mysterious creatures to life. By reading the poem aloud, students have an opportunity to practice using expression, intonation, phrasing, punctuation, and pacing to find a personal connection with Carroll's words and themes.

Instructional Path

Facing Challenges

BLAST:
Facing Challenges

OVERVIEW

To develop a focus for this unit, students will examine ways that people address both small and large injustices. Students will learn about a young girl who helped animals at an animal shelter and will consider how Dr. Martin Luther King, Jr. and Rosa Parks worked against larger injustices. Research links explore other examples of people standing up for their rights and the rights of others.

OBJECTIVES

1. Explore background information about ways people can stand up for their own rights, the rights of others, and the rights of animals.
2. Research using the hyperlinks to learn about other examples of people standing up for their rights, including non-violent protests, food banks, animal shelters, and the civil rights movement.
3. Participate effectively in a range of conversations and collaborations to express ideas and build upon the ideas of others.

ELA Common Core Standards:
Reading: Informational Text - RI.6.1
Writing - W.6.1.A, W.6.5, W.6.6
Speaking & Listening - SL.6.1.A, SL.6.1.B, SL.6.1.C, SL.6.1.D

RESOURCES

Access 1 handout (Beginner)
Access 2 handout (Intermediate)
Access 4 handout (Approaching)

TITLE/DRIVING QUESTION

Core Path	Access Path
Discuss. As a class, read aloud the title and driving question for this Blast. These correspond to the title/driving question for the unit as a whole. Ask students what they already know about standing up for themselves and others. Taking into account the ideas of their classmates, do they have a sense of how people decide to do this? Remind students that they should not immediately reply to this question. They'll be returning to this question and responding after they've read the Background and some of the Research Links.	**English Learners All Levels** **Discuss a Visual.** Have students view photographs of the top ten non-violent protesters: http://tinyurl.com/ox6rjj7. Explain how the protestors in the photographs are in the act of standing up for themselves and others. Discuss how the photographs represent someone facing a challenge, prompting students with questions such as: • What is happening in each photo? • What emotion is revealed in each photo? How do you think these people feel? • What challenge do you think the people in the photographs are facing? How do you know? • What might they be standing up for?
Draft. In their notebooks or on scrap paper, have students draft their initial responses to the driving question. This will provide them with a baseline response that they will be developing as they gain more information about the topic in the Background and Research Links sections of the assignment.	**Beginner & Intermediate** **Draft with Sentence Frame.** When drafting their initial response to the driving question, have students refer to this Blast sentence frame on their Access 1 and 2 handouts: • People decide when to stand up for others or themselves by _____. Point out these two key features of the sentence frame: 1. The introductory clause "people decide when to stand up for others or themselves" borrows language directly from the Blast driving question to provide a response. 2. Ask students to make special note of the word "by" because it requires students to add supporting evidence for their claim.

BACKGROUND

Core Path	Access Path
Read. Have students read the Blast background to provide context for the driving question.	**Beginner & Intermediate** **Read with Support.** Have students read the Blast background to provide context for the driving question. When they encounter unfamiliar words or phrases, have students refer to the Blast Glossary on their Access 1 and 2 handouts. If there are unfamiliar words that are not included in their glossary, encourage students to check a dictionary or online reference tool, like http://tinyurl.com/6ytby. **Approaching** **Read and Summarize.** Have students read the Blast background to provide context for the driving question. As they read, ask students to complete the fill in the blank summary of the background provided on their Access 4 handout. When they encounter unfamiliar words or phrases, have students refer to the Blast Glossary on their Access 4 handout.
Discuss. Pair students and have them discuss the following questions. Makes sure students follow the rules for collegial discussions. 1. What are some ways people have stood up for themselves or others? (Rosa Parks didn't give up her seat on the bus; Isabel donated to PAWS.) 2. How did Rosa Parks influence the civil rights movement? (By not giving up her seat, she stood up for the rights of black people all over the nation.) 3. How did Isabel stand up for the rights of animals? (She donated money to PAWS, which protects animals; she asked for donations instead of birthday presents.) 4. What are some other ways we can stand up for ourselves or others? (We can try to prevent people from picking on or bullying others; we can point out racism or sexism; we can get help for injured animals.)	**Beginner** **Discuss.** Pair Beginning with Advanced (or Beyond) students and have them use the dialogue starter on their Access 1 handout to discuss the topic. Advise them to return to the dialogue and switch roles if they get stuck. **Intermediate** **Discuss.** Pair Intermediate with Advanced (or Beyond) students and have them use the dialogue starter on their Access 2 handout to discuss the topic. Advise them to return to the dialogue and switch roles if they get stuck. If their conversation is progressing smoothly, encourage them to continue the discussion beyond the dialogue starter sheet. They can expand their conversations to discuss other examples of historical figures, celebrities, or family members who have stood up for themselves or others.

Core Path	Access Path
Brainstorm. Remind students about the Driving Question for this Blast: How do people decide when to stand up for others or themselves? In their notebooks, ask students to make two columns, one for themselves, and one for others. Have them fill in things they've done or could do to stand up for themselves; then things they have done or could do to stand up for others. Here's a short example of how this might look: | Myself	Others
The time I told my friend when she said something that hurt my feelings; I could point out examples of sexism.	I could volunteer at an animal shelter; the time I told the teacher when I saw someone being bullied.		

RESEARCH LINKS

Core Path	Access Path
Examine and Explore. Before asking students to explore the research links, use these activities and questions to guide their exploration: 1. What's the most important thing to look for when you click on any of these links? (You should look for examples of how people decide when to stand up for themselves or others.) 2. Ask students to look at the link, "Top 10 Non-Violent Protests." What do you think non-violent protests have to do with the driving question for this Blast, "How do people decide when to stand up for others or themselves?" (Non-violent protests are a good way for people to stand up for their rights, and to show that they want change on a large scale.)	

Copyright © BookheadEd Learning, LLC

Core Path	Access Path
3. Why do you think links on food banks are included? (Helping to feed people who don't have enough to eat is a way of standing up for them.) 4. Have students read the article, "Food Banks Expand Beyond Hunger." As a class, discuss how education and farming are relevant to the driving question. (Educating people might help them stand up for themselves. Teaching them about farming might empower them to take care of themselves and others.)	

	Extend
	Research, Discuss and Present.
	
	1. Assign each group one link to explore in depth.
	2. Ask them to discuss the information:
	  a. What are the key points?
	  b. What inferences did you make as you read?
	  c. What did you learn about this "big idea" from reading this research?
	  d. How did this help you to better understand the topic?
	  e. What questions does your group have after exploring this link?
	3. Allow students time to informally present what they learned.

	Extend **Tech Infusion** **Share.** As students explore the links, allow them to crowdsource their findings using a backchannel tool like TodaysMeet (http://tinyurl.com/psef72j). Students can post the research they find individually or in groups to share with the class.

QUIKPOLL

Core Path	Access Path
Participate. Answer the poll question. Have students discuss their reasons for their answers. Students should refer to evidence from the Background and research links to defend their answer.	

NUMBER CRUNCH

Core Path	Access Path
Predict, Discuss, and Click. Remind students to click on the number to reveal the information. Ask them if they thought this number might be higher or lower, and why they thought so.	

CREATE YOUR BLAST (140 CHARACTERS)

Core Path	Access Path
Blast. Ask students to write their Blast responses in 140 characters or less.	**Beginner** **Blast with Support.** Have students refer back to the sentence frame on their Access 1 handout that they used to create their original Blast draft. Ask them to use this frame to write and enter their final Blast. **Intermediate** **Blast with Support.** Have students attempt to draft their Blast without the sentence frame on their Access 2 handout. If students struggle to compose their Blast draft without the sentence frame, remind them to reference it for support. **Beyond** **Write a Claim.** Ask students to use their answer to the poll question to write a strong claim that could be used as the foundation for a piece of argumentative writing.

Core Path	Access Path
	Once students have written their claims, ask them to read the claims to a small group of their peers. This activity will provide them practice writing claims, as well as expose them to claims written by their peers.
Review. After students have completed their own Blasts, ask them to review the Blasts of their peers and provide feedback.	**Extend** **Discuss.** As a whole class or in groups, identify a few strong blasts and discuss what made those responses so powerful. As a group, analyze and discuss what characteristics make a blast interesting or effective.
	Extend **Revise.** Resend a second version of this Blast assignment to your students and have them submit revised versions of their original Blasts. Do the same responses make the Top 10? How have the answers improved from the first submissions?

FIRST READ:
A Wrinkle in Time

OVERVIEW

The science fiction novel *A Wrinkle in Time*, by Madeleine L'Engle, follows the quest of three children who search for a missing father across time and get caught up in a battle between good and evil. The First Read gives students the opportunity to experience the text with a limited context.

OBJECTIVES

1. Perform an initial reading of a text and demonstrate comprehension by responding to short analysis and inference questions with textual evidence.
2. Practice defining vocabulary words using context.
3. Participate effectively in a range of conversations and collaborations to express ideas and build upon the ideas of others.

   ELA Common Core Standards:
   Reading: Literature - RL.6.1, RL.6.4, RL.6.10
   Speaking & Listening - SL.6.1.A, SL.6.1.B, SL.6.1.C, SL.6.1.D, SL.6.2
   Language - L.6.4.A, L.6.4.B, L.6.4.D

RESOURCES

Access 1 handout (Beginner)

Access 2 handout (Intermediate)

Access 3 handout (Advanced)

Access 4 handout (Approaching)

Teacher's Edition

ACCESS COMPLEX TEXT

In this excerpt from Chapter 7 of *A Wrinkle in Time,* Meg, Charles Wallace, and Calvin encounter a red-eyed man who communicates telepathically and is capable of mind control. Students are asked to analyze the relationship between character and plot. To help students master this skill, use the following suggestions to provide scaffolded instruction for a close reading of the more complex features of this text:

- **Connection of Ideas** - To analyze the relationship between character and plot, students must look for the ways in which the decisions and actions of the characters alter or advance the events of the plot and how the characters themselves change in response to events and to one another. Since character and plot are revealed through dialogue and narration, students must be able to connect details and make inferences.

- **Sentence Structure** - Much of the red-eyed man's dialogue is not directly attributed to him. Students must infer the speaker from the surrounding dialogue and narration. In addition, several of the sentences in the narration are long and complicated, with multiple clauses and phrases. This may present problems for some students.

- **Specific Vocabulary** - Some students may have difficulty with unfamiliar words, words with multiple meanings, and unusual constructions, such as "once ten is ten."

1. INTRODUCTION

Core Path	Access Path
Watch. As a class, watch the video preview of *A Wrinkle in Time*.	**English Learners All Levels & Approaching** **Fill in the Blanks.** Ask students to use their Access 1, 2, 3, and 4 handouts to fill in the blanks of the transcript for the preview's voiceover as they watch the preview along with their classmates. Correct answers are located at the end of the lesson plan online.

Core Path	Access Path
Read. Individually or as a class, read and discuss the Introduction for *A Wrinkle in Time*. The introduction provides context for the excerpt taken from Chapter 7.	**English Learners All Levels & Approaching** **Read and Listen.** Ask students to read and listen to the introduction for *A Wrinkle in Time*. Have them refer to the Introduction Glossary on their Access 1, 2, 3, and 4 handouts for definitions of key vocabulary terms. If there are unfamiliar words that are not included in their glossary, encourage students to check a dictionary or online reference tool, like http://tinyurl.com/6ytby.
Access Prior Knowledge. Explain that telepathy is the communication of thoughts or ideas from mind to mind without the use of words or other sensory clues. 1. Ask students if they've read any books or seen any movies or television shows that present examples of telepathy. Have them name examples. 2. Discuss whether students believe telepathy exists, and the reasons for their opinions. 3. Then, lead students to discuss the possible benefits and drawbacks that might accompany an ability to communicate mind-to-mind without verbal and nonverbal clues. 4. List students' ideas on the board.	**Beginner** **Complete and Discuss the Chart.** Pair Beginning and more proficient (Beyond) readers. Rather than discussing examples of telepathy in books and movies, have these groups complete the chart on the Access 1 handout that asks students to consider what advantages and drawbacks of telepathy might be. Have the pairs generate ideas, discuss the chart, and complete it together. **Intermediate & Advanced** **Complete and Discuss the Chart.** Pair Intermediate and Advanced students, and rather than discussing examples of telepathy in books and movies, have these groups complete the chart on the Access 2 and 3 handouts that ask students to consider what advantages and drawbacks of telepathy might be. Have the pairs generate ideas, discuss the chart, and complete it together. **Approaching** **Draw Responses.** 1. First, ask students to imagine that they have had an encounter with a telepathic person. Allow students to work in pairs if they wish. 2. Have students create a comic strip of three or four frames showing themselves and their actions in such a situation. 3. After they've finished their comic strips, ask students to fill in the Complete the Chart exercise on the Access 4 handout.

Copyright © BookheadEd Learning, LLC

Core Path	Access Path
	Extend **Discuss the Introduction.** After reading the introduction, use the information provided to facilitate a prereading discussion to get students thinking about the events and themes in *A Wrinkle in Time*. • What is time travel? • Why does the idea of time travel appeal to some people? • If you could travel backward or forward in time, where would you go and why?
	Extend **Analyze and Discuss a Quotation.** "Restriction of free thought … is the most dangerous of all subversions" (Supreme Court Justice William O. Douglas). • What do you think this quotation means? • Do you agree with this quotation? Why or why not? • Why might the sinister force that controls Camazotz want to "merge [the] … thoughts" of the children with his? • Are you able to think of any examples in history, film, or literature where leaders have tried to gain power by controlling communication, speech, or free thought? Name and explain.

2. READ

Core Path	Access Path
Make Predictions about Vocabulary. There are five bold vocabulary words in the text. As students read the text, ask them to make predictions about what they think each bold vocabulary word means based on the context clues in the sentence. If you are in a low-tech classroom and students are reading from printed copies or a projected text, ask students to record predictions in their notes, so they can be easily referenced in class. If your students have access to technology, they can use the annotation tool to make their predictions.	**Note:** This exercise, which extends vocabulary instruction, should be completed when the class shifts from whole group instruction to individual work during the "Read and Annotate" exercise.

Make Predictions about Vocabulary. There are five bold vocabulary words in the text. As students read the text, ask them to make predictions about what they think each bold vocabulary word means based on the context clues in the sentence. If you are in a low-tech classroom and students are reading from printed copies or a projected text, ask students to record predictions in their notes, so they can be easily referenced in class. If your students have access to technology, they can use the annotation tool to make their predictions.

It might be helpful to model this practice for students before they begin reading. Either using the board or projecting the actual text, focus in on the phrase that uses the word "gallivanting":

- Abandoning his wife and his four little children to go gallivanting off on wild adventures of his own.

Model for the class how to use the overall structure and meaning of the phrase and the sentences around it, the word's position, or other clues to define the unfamiliar vocabulary word. In this case, point out these context clues:

1. Look at the structure of the phrase. The verbs are *abandoning* and *gallivanting*. We know that Meg's father abandons and goes gallivanting. From later in the phrase, we know that he also goes "off on wild adventures of his own." So "gallivanting" has something to do with the adventures Meg's father is having.

2. Now, let's think about the speaker's meaning. He is saying that instead of fulfilling his family responsibilities, Meg's father goes on adventures. From the context of the sentences around this phrase, we know that he doesn't think that's a good thing.

Note: This exercise, which extends vocabulary instruction, should be completed when the class shifts from whole group instruction to individual work during the "Read and Annotate" exercise.

Beginner, Intermediate & Approaching Pair Practice.

1. Pair students with more proficient readers.

2. Give them an additional sentence that contains a new vocabulary word.

3. Ask the students to complete a Think Aloud using the teacher-led Make Predictions about Vocabulary activity as a model, while the proficient student actively listens.

4. The student should use the context clues in the sentence to try to determine the meaning of the new vocabulary word.

5. After the student has completed the Think Aloud and made a prediction about the word's meaning, allow time for the proficient reader to add his/her own thoughts and clarify any points of confusion.

6. Once they've completed this Think Aloud, encourage them to use a dictionary to confirm the definition of the new vocabulary word. Have them refer to the vocabulary listing on their Access 1, 2, and 4 handouts for definitions of key vocabulary terms in the text. Encourage them to add any additional vocabulary words or idioms they find in the text and look up definitions for those words and idioms online or in a dictionary.

Core Path	Access Path
3. What other words might work in this context? You might say that someone "goes off" having an adventure, or "running off," or "wandering off." So these are possible clues to the meaning of "gallivanting": it may mean "traveling" or "wandering."	
4. However, this word may have additional connotations or associations. The speaker suggests that Meg's father is doing something negative, irresponsible, and un-fatherly. So, "gallivanting" might more specifically mean "traveling or wandering from place to place, perhaps without care or regard for one's responsibilities."	

Model Reading Comprehension Strategy. Before students begin reading, model the reading comprehension strategy of rereading by using this Think Aloud that talks students through the first seven paragraphs of text. First, explain to your students that rereading is reading the passage again or going back to an earlier part of the selection to understand something that doesn't make sense.

Model for students how rereading will help them better comprehend the selection and help drive their discussions.

- When I read paragraphs 1, 3, and 5, I find a commonality. They are all composed of "number words" as Meg points out in paragraph 2.

- However, I'm not sure what they mean or why they are in the text. Rather than being confused or reading on without understanding, I can reread the text, this time more slowly, to help me determine meaning.

- "Once ten is ten. Once eleven is eleven. Once twelve is twelve." Wait, I think these are multiplication tables: 1 times 10 is 10. Let me check the other paragraphs. Yes, 2 times 1 is 2 and 2 times 4 is 8.

Note: This exercise, which extends vocabulary instruction, should be completed when the class shifts from whole group instruction to individual work during the "Read and Annotate" exercise.

Beginner, Intermediate & Approaching Apply Reading Comprehension Strategy.

1. Have students listen to the audio version of the excerpt from *A Wrinkle in Time* as they reread the excerpt. Ask students to record what they notice after having reread the text. Was there something they understood better after rereading it?

2. In pairs, ask students to discuss their lists. Did one student notice something different than another after having reread the text?

3. Call on pairs to share their thoughts with the class. Make a list of things noticed as a result of rereading.

Core Path	Access Path

Core Path

- Now that I know what the "number words" are, I need to reread again to figure out why the text begins with a recitation of multiplication facts.

- In paragraph 7, someone says that the kids have passed their "preliminary tests." So, the multiplication tables are part of a test. But, what kind of test? The answers are stated. Now, that I've reread to understand this part of the text, I can continue reading to find an answer to this question.

Read and Annotate. Have students independently read and annotate the excerpt. Ask students to use the annotation tool as they read to:

1. use context clues to analyze and determine the meaning of the bolded vocabulary terms

2. ask questions about passages of the text that may be unclear or unresolved

3. identify key information, events, characters, and connections between them

4. note unfamiliar vocabulary

5. capture their reactions to events in the text

Access Path

Beginner
Coach the Reading. While other students read, annotate, and discuss the text independently, work with Beginning students, listening to the audio of the text and pausing periodically or when any student has a question. Coach students in articulating their questions for the group and in highlighting and annotating the text. Have students use the Annotation Guide in the Access 1 handout to support them as they highlight and annotate the text.

For further support, ask questions about the text such as:

- Is there anything about the story that you don't understand?

- What do you think will happen to Meg, her brother, and her friend?

- Why do you think A Wrinkle in Time is the title of the story?

Intermediate
Listen to the Audio. Have these students listen to the audio of the text and use the definitions on the Access 2 handout to help them with words or idioms that may be unfamiliar. If students need help with annotating the text, have them use the Annotation Guide on the Access 2 handout. After working with the Beginning students, you may wish to check this group's progress and provide support as needed.

Core Path	Access Path
	Advanced **Pair with Proficient Peers.** Have Advanced students work with English proficient peers to read, annotate, and discuss the text. Have students use the Annotation Guide in the Access 3 handout to support them as they highlight and annotate the text. Encourage them to listen to the audio of the text if needed. **Approaching** **Use the Annotation Guide.** Have students use the Annotation Guide in the Access 4 handout to support them as they highlight and annotate the text.
Discuss. In small groups or pairs, have students discuss the questions and inferences they made while reading. To help facilitate discussions, refer to Collaborative Discussions in the Speaking & Listening Handbook. 1. What can readers know or infer about the man with red eyes? Reread to monitor your understanding of this character. (The man's features are blurry or distorted: "[Meg] was not sure what the face really looked like." The man is being controlled by another force: "it's coming through you. It isn't you." The man's mood changes from amused to angry throughout the scene. In the beginning, he chortles with delight. By the end, he speaks with "distinct menace.") 2. What are some characteristics of the relationship between Meg and Charles Wallace? Reread to monitor your understanding of this relationship. (Meg is protective of her little brother. She grabs Charles Wallace and pulls him away from the platform after he hits the man. She tackles Charles Wallace to keep him from being controlled by the man.)	**English Learners All Levels & Approaching** Use the extra time while on– and beyond–grade-level students are discussing their first reads of the text to work individually and in small groups with Approaching readers and English Learners as outlined on the previous page. Should those students complete their first reads quickly, integrate them into the on and beyond grade level discussion groups. Otherwise Approaching readers and English Learners will be given an opportunity to participate in text discussions with their peers later in the lesson.

Core Path	Access Path
3. What two views are presented of Meg's father? Reread to monitor your understanding of these points of view. (The man suggests that Meg's father has abandoned his family in favor of wild adventures of his own. Meg and Charles Wallace love their father and want to find him: we "want him because he's" our father.)	
	Extend **Tech Infusion** **Brainstorm.** Pair students and ask them to brainstorm what readers can infer about the man with "red eyes". Students who have access to a backchannel tool such as TodaysMeet (http://tinyurl.com/psef72j/) may enjoy brainstorming in that medium.
	Extend **Tech Infusion** **Interior Monologues.** Have students write interior monologues for Meg, Charles Wallace, or Calvin. What might each character say to him- or herself to fend off the mind-control advances of the red-eyed man? Ask volunteers to deliver their monologues in an open-mike style reading. Record students' performances and post them to your class YouTube channel.

3. SYNCTV

Core Path	Access Path
Watch. As a class, watch the SyncTV video on *A Wrinkle in Time*. Pause the video at these key moments to discuss the information with your students. Make sure students follow the rules for collegial discussions. Have students review and reflect on the ideas expressed, paraphrasing as necessary.	**Beginner & Intermediate** **Analyze the Discussion.** Have students use the Analyze the Discussion guide in the Access 1 and 2 handouts to identify key points in the discussion and the evidence the students use to determine those points. Sample answers are at the end of the lesson plan online.

Teacher's Edition

Core Path	Access Path
1. 0:32 - One of the students says that Camazotz was a bat god in ancient Mayan civilization. The name means "death bat." What type of setting might you associate with bats? What does this name suggest about the setting? 2. 1:32 - One of the students references Charles Wallace's line that "The spoken word is one of the triumphs of man." How do the children use the spoken word to triumph over the red-eyed man? 3. 6:52 - One student says that everybody on the planet is enslaved by the red-eyed man. What evidence suggests that the red-eyed man is trying to enslave the children?	**Advanced** **Analyze the Discussion.** Have students use the Analyze the Discussion exercise in the Access 3 handout to identify key points in the discussion and the evidence the students use to determine those points. Sample answers are at the end of the lesson plan online. **Approaching** **Analyze the Discussion.** Have students complete the chart on the Access 4 handout by listing textual evidence cited by the students in the video. Sample answers are at the end of the lesson plan online.

4. THINK

Core Path	Access Path
Answer and Discuss. Have students complete the Think questions and then use the peer review instructions and rubric to complete two peer reviews. Refer to the sample answers at the end of the lesson plan online to discuss responses with your students.	**Beginner & Intermediate** **Sentence Frames.** Have students use the Sentence Frames on the Access 1 and 2 handouts to support their responses to the Think questions. **Approaching** **Find the Evidence.** Have students use the Find the Evidence on the Access 4 handout to help them answer the Think questions.
SyncTV Style Discussion. Put students into heterogeneous small groups and give them a prompt to discuss. Have them model their discussions after the SyncTV episodes they have seen. Stress the importance of using academic language correctly and citing textual evidence in their conversations to support their ideas. To help students prepare for, strategize, and evaluate their discussions, refer to the Collaborative Discussions section of the Speaking & Listening Handbook.	**Beginner & Intermediate** **Use Sentence Frames.** Have these students use the sentence frames on Access handouts 1 and 2 to help them participate in the discussion. **Approaching** **Use Think Questions.** Remind these students to refer back to their answers to the Think questions to help them participate in the group discussion.

Core Path	Access Path
Discussion prompts:	

Core Path:

Discussion prompts:

1. How do the characters of Meg, Charles Wallace, and Calvin each respond to the red-eyed man? Is the different approach that each character takes effective given the situation? Why or why not?

2. How does staying focused on the goal of finding their father help Meg and Charles Wallace deal with the fear and uncertainty that confronts them?

Have students review the key ideas expressed, demonstrating an understanding of multiple perspectives through reflection and paraphrasing.

You may wish to have students create a video or audio recording of their SyncTV-Style Discussion.

Access Path:

Extend
Use Traits to Classify Government. Lead students to list the traits of the leader of Camazotz and Camazotz itself.

- Record these traits on the board.
- Then, form student groups. Present student groups with the forms of government listed below and have students quickly research the traits of each using print or digital sources.
  - democracy
  - republic
  - monarchy
  - aristocracy
  - dictatorship
- Ask students to make claims regarding the government of Camazotz.
- In writing, students should explain their acceptance or rejection of each type of government based on textual evidence.
- Have each group present its findings to the class.
- Discuss similarities and differences among the ideas of different groups.

SKILL:
Plot

OVERVIEW

Identifying how characters both influence and react to plot events is key to understanding a story. This lesson plan provides follow-up questions and useful enrichments to help teachers guide students toward a usable, repeatable method for identifying relationships between character and plot.

OBJECTIVES

1. Learn the definition of plot.
2. Practice using concrete strategies for identifying relationships between character and plot.
3. Participate effectively in a range of conversations and collaborations to express ideas and build upon the ideas of others.

ELA Common Core Standards:
Reading: Literature - RL.6.1, RL.6.3, RL.6.4
Speaking & Listening - SL.6.1.A, SL.6.1.B, SL.6.1.C, SL.6.2

RESOURCES

Access 1 handout (Beginner)
Access 2 handout (Intermediate)
Access 3 handout (Advanced)
Access 4 handout (Approaching)

1. DEFINE

Core Path	Access Path
Watch. Watch the Concept Definition video on plot with your students. Make sure your students write down the definition of plot and understand its basic components: beginning, middle, and end. Also make sure that they note which elements interact with each other to shape the plot, including characters, dialogue, and setting. (For further understanding, ask students to think of another story or fable and analyze its plot elements.) Pause the video at these key moments to discuss the information with your students:	**English Learners All Levels & Approaching** **Match.** Have students complete the matching exercise on the Access 1, 2, 3, and 4 handouts as they watch the video. Correct answers are located at the end of the lesson plan online.

Core Path (continued)

1. 1:00 – Besides dialogue, what other elements can a story use to reveal actions, character and decisions? What if a story contains little or no dialogue?

2. 1:46 – Does plot shape character, or does character shape plot? Or both? Discuss.

3. 2:04 – Must all stories contain a resolution? Why or why not? Is there a difference between a "resolution" and a "happy ending"?

Read and Discuss. After watching the Concept Definition video, have students read the definition of plot. Either in small groups or as a whole class, use these questions to engage students in a discussion about plot.

Make sure students follow the rules for collegial discussions.

1. What usually happens at the beginning of a story? (The plot presents a problem that the characters have to solve.)

2. What role can dialogue play in shaping a plot? (Dialogue is often a crucial element. It can influence characters' actions and decisions and reveal information the characters might otherwise not know. Dialogue can also raise questions that drive the story toward its resolution.)

Access Path (continued)

Beginner & Approaching
Complete a Chart. To prepare students to participate in the discussion, have them complete the chart on the Access 1 and 4 handouts as they read the definition. Correct answers are located at the end of the lesson plan online.

Intermediate & Advanced
Discuss Prompts. To help these students participate in the discussion, prompt them with questions that can be answered with a few words, such as:

- What is a plot? (a series of events that introduce, develop, and resolve a problem)

- Who are the people who resolve a problem? (characters)

- Can you think of a story you have read that has a strong plot? (Answers will vary.)

Core Path	Access Path
3. Typically, how does the plot affect the characters as they work to solve the problem? (The characters may undergo changes as they respond to rising tension.)	**Beyond** **Discuss.** Have students select a book they've read and describe the plot. Compile a list of examples. Have students discuss how the plot of each work affects what the reader learns about the characters. How might a switch in plot affect not only what the reader learns, but how much he or she enjoys the story?
	Extend **Tech Infusion** **Diagram It.** After watching the video, ask student pairs to create diagrams that illustrate the relationship between plot and character. Students should include examples from film or literature to support their ideas. Ask volunteers to present their diagrams to the class. Discuss similarities and differences among students' diagrams. Students may create print or digital diagrams (www.popplet.com).

2. MODEL

Core Path	Access Path
Read and Annotate. Have students independently read the Model section. As they read, ask students to use the annotation tool to: • highlight key points • ask questions • mark relationships between character and plot • identify places where the Model applies the strategies laid out in the Identification and Application section	**Note:** During this portion of the lesson, instruction shifts from whole group to individual work. Use this time to work one-on-one or in small groups with, Beginning, Intermediate, Advanced, and Approaching students.

Please note that excerpts and passages in the StudySync® library, workbooks, and PDFs are intended as touchstones to generate interest in an author's work. The excerpts and passages do not substitute for the reading of entire texts, and StudySync® strongly recommends that teachers and students seek out and purchase the whole literary or informational work in order to experience it as the author intended. Links to online resellers are available in our digital library. In addition, complete works may be ordered through an authorized reseller by filling out and returning to StudySync® the order form enclosed in this workbook.

Teacher's Edition  **43**

Core Path	Access Path
	Beginner & Intermediate **Coach the Reading.** Work with these students (either individually or in small groups) to fill out the Guided Reading questions on the Access 1 and 2 handouts. Have Beginning students refer to the Model Glossary on the Access 1 handout to help them determine the meaning of difficult words (note: provide the Access 1 handout glossary to Intermediate students if necessary). Let students know they'll use these answers to help participate in the discussion about the Model. Correct answers for this exercise are located at the end of the lesson plan online. **Advanced** **Identify Evidence.** Provide these students with the same instructions to read and annotate as on-grade level and Beyond students. In addition, ask Advanced students to complete the Identify Evidence exercise on the Access 3 handout. Let students know that they'll use these answers to help participate in the discussion about the Model. Sample answers for this exercise are located at the end of the lesson plan online. **Approaching** **Guided Reading.** Have students complete the Guided Reading questions on the Access 4 handout as they read. Let them know that they'll use these answers to help participate in the discussion about the Model. Sample answers for this exercise are located at the end of the lesson plan online.

Core Path	Access Path
Discuss. After students read the Model text, use these questions to facilitate a whole group discussion that helps students understand how to identify the relationship between character and plot in the passage:	

1. How does the Model for this passage go about explaining the children's problem? (Meg identifies the problem: "The only reason we are here is because we think our father is here." Meg and Charles's father has disappeared. The children are trying to solve the problem of his disappearance by looking for him.)

2. What is one strategy that the Model uses to reveal plot events and character reactions? (The Model examines the dialogue and notes that Meg learns information she doesn't know based on what the red-eyed man says. He confirms that he knows something about Meg's father's whereabouts. This information influences Meg to stay on her current course of action.)

3. What other strategy does the Model use to analyze a relationship between character and plot? (The model explains how Meg's interaction with the red-eyed man, and the red-eyed man's preference for wordless communication, help trigger the next plot event: Charles Wallace's surprising action.)

4. How do the plot events affect Charles Wallace and escalate the tension? (The Model notes that the confrontation between the children and the red-eyed man begins to change Charles Wallace: he shifts from confident defiance to uncharacteristic fear.)

3. YOUR TURN

Core Path	Access Path
Assess and Explain. Have students answer the comprehension questions to test for understanding. Share the explanations for Parts A and B (located online) with your students.	
	Extend **Discuss**. Before students respond to the questions, discuss with them how the change from defiance to fear in Charles Wallace advances the plot. Ask: Why does Charles Wallace choose to strike the red-eyed man—to overcome his fear and reassert his defiance, to show his frustration with the man's games, to demonstrate that he is smarter than the man, or some other reason? Make sure that students support all responses with textual evidence.
	Extend **Tech Infusion** **Send an E-mail.** Have students write e-mails in the voice of Meg or Charles Wallace to their mother to explain the progress they have made in locating their father. Have students explain events and how their characters have reacted to these events as well as the ensuing results. Students may send these e-mails to another class studying the same text. These students may respond in the voice of Meg and Charles Wallace's mother.

CLOSE READ:
A Wrinkle in Time

OVERVIEW

Madeleine L'Engle's science fiction novel *A Wrinkle in Time* follows the quest of three children who search for a missing father across time and get caught up in a battle between good and evil. The Close Read gives students the opportunity to analyze the ways in which the actions and responses of the characters both shape and are shaped by the plot.

OBJECTIVES

1. Complete a close reading of a passage of literature.
2. Practice and apply concrete strategies for identifying the relationship between plot and character.
3. Participate effectively in a range of conversations and collaborations to express ideas and build upon the ideas of others.
4. Prewrite, plan, and produce clear and coherent writing in response to a prompt.

ELA Common Core Standards:
Reading: Literature - RL.6.1, RL.6.3, RL.6.4, RL.6.10
Writing - W.6.2.A, W.6.2.D, W.6.2.E, W.6.4, W.6.5, W.6.6, W.6.10
Speaking & Listening - SL.6.1.A, SL.6.1.B, SL.6.1.C, SL.6.1.D, SL.6.6
Language - L.6.4.A, L.6.4.C, L.6.4.D

RESOURCES

A Wrinkle in Time Vocabulary handout

Access 1 handout (Beginner)

Access 2 handout (Intermediate)

Access 3 handout (Advanced)

Access 4 handout (Approaching)

1. INTRODUCTION

Core Path	Access Path
Define and Compare. Project the vocabulary words and definitions onto the board or provide students with handouts so they can copy the vocabulary into their notebooks. Suggest that students consult general and specialized reference materials, both print and digital, to compare the precise meaning of a specific word with their initial vocabulary predictions from the First Read. Review words that students defined incorrectly to understand why they were unable to use context clues to develop usable definitions.	**Beginner & Intermediate** **Complete the Sentences.** Have students complete the sentence frames on the Access 1 and 2 handouts using the vocabulary words. Point out that some of the words are in the questions and some will be in the answers. Sample answers are located at the end of the lesson plan online. **Advanced & Beyond** **Write in Journals.** Have students write a journal entry using all of their vocabulary words. Remind them to write sentences that communicate the meaning of the words they are using. **Approaching** **Graphic Organizer.** To support students in comparing their vocabulary predictions with the correct meanings, have them complete the graphic organizer on the Access 4 handout to record the vocabulary words, their initial analysis, and the definitions. Then have them write sentences using the words.
Review. Have students complete the fill in the blank vocabulary worksheet for this selection. Answers for the worksheet are listed at the end of the lesson plan online.	
	Extend **Tech Infusion** **Create.** Create online flashcards for the vocabulary using Quizlet (http://tinyurl.com/4gj6tz) or StudyBlue (http://tinyurl.com/6aqluw7).

Core Path	Access Path
	Extend **Create.** Form small groups and ask students to list with descriptions a series of "preliminary" tests that the red-eyed man might use to "bore" into the minds of "impressionable" children who have been caught "gallivanting" across the universe in search of a missing father. Ask each group to present selected entries to the class.

2. READ

Core Path	Access Path
Model Close Reading. Project the text onto the board and model a close reading of several paragraphs using the annotation strategies mentioned below. While modeling annotation strategies, make notes that tie the text to the focus skill and demonstrate what students are looking for as they read. Here is some guidance for you as you annotate for your students: • As the Skills lesson makes clear, plot events affect character responses and changes, and character responses and changes affect plot events. • In paragraphs 4–7, we see how character responses affect the plot. Calvin and Meg regain control of their thoughts, which prompts the red-eyed man to end the series of "preliminary tests." • In paragraphs 37–39, we see how a plot event creates a character response. The red-eyed man has hypnotized Charles Wallace. Meg responds with a "flying tackle" to bring Charles Wallace back to his senses. • In describing how the plot unfolds as a series of episodes, we must always examine the interplay between characters and events, noting how each serves as a driving force in moving the plot toward resolution.	

Core Path	Access Path
Read and Annotate. Read the Skills Focus questions as a class, so your students know what they should pay close attention to as they read. Then have students read and annotate the excerpt. Ask students to use the annotation tool as they read to:	**Note:** While on–grade level students are reading and annotating, work one-on-one or in small groups with Beginning, Intermediate, Advanced, and Approaching students to support them as they read and annotate the text.

Core Path (continued):

1. respond to the Skills Focus section
2. ask questions
3. make connections
4. identify key themes, events, characters, and details
5. note unfamiliar vocabulary
6. capture their reaction to the ideas and examples in the text

As they reread the text, remind students to use the comprehension strategy of Rereading that they learned in the First Read.

Access Path (continued):

Beginner & Intermediate
Summarize and Analyze the Text. Work with these students to complete the Summarize and Analyze the Text exercise on the Access 1 and 2 handouts (note: the sentence frames for Intermediate students on the Access 2 handout contain fewer scaffolds). They will then use the completed sentence frames to help them analyze and annotate the text. Encourage students to use the completed sentence frames to answer the Skills Focus questions. Refer to the sample Skills Focus answers online to help them complete the sentence frames and annotate the text.

Advanced
Work in Pairs. Pair these students with more proficient English speakers to work together on analyzing and annotating the text to complete the Skills Focus questions. If these students need more support, have them use the Summarize and Analyze the Text exercise on the Access 3 handout as they work with their more proficient peers.

Approaching
Summarize the Text. Have these students discuss and complete the Summarize the Text exercise on the Access 4 handout and use their summary to help them analyze and annotate the text by completing the Skills Focus questions. Correct answers for the summary are at the end of the lesson plan online. Also refer to the sample Skills Focus answers to aid students with their annotations.

Core Path	Access Path
Discuss. After students have read the text, use the sample responses to the Skills Focus questions online to discuss the reading and the process of making connections between plot and character. Make sure that students have acquired and accurately use academic-specific words and phrases related to the skill, and demonstrate a command of formal English appropriate to the discussion.	**Extend** **Pair and Share.** In small, heterogeneous groups or pairs, ask students to share and discuss their annotations with a focus on the plot presented in the selection. You can provide students with these questions to guide their discussion: 1. Even though this reading is an excerpt, how can you tell that the plot is moving forward? (There are several events and the characters are faced with a problem. The excerpt includes a lot of dialogue. The characters and their interactions ultimately push the plot forward.) 2. When Meg asks the red-eyed man about her father, what kind of language does she use? (Meg uses polite language and asks if the red-eyed man could please help her. She asks him several times in several ways, but she is always polite.) 3. How and when does Meg stand up for Charles Wallace? (Meg stands up for Charles Wallace by tackling him to break the red-eyed man's spell.)
	Extend **Tech Infusion** **Create.** Ask students to create collages of Meg's, Charles Wallace's, or Calvin's mind during this encounter with the red-eyed man. One part of the collage should focus on moments when the red-eyed man has control of the character's mind. The other part of the collage should focus on moments when the character regains control of his or her mind. Tell students to make the connection between character responses or changes and plot events clear. Students may use images and words taken from magazines as well as the text. Alternatively, they can use an online tool, such as Glogster (http://tinyurl.com/ydeyklq) or Google Drawing, to create virtual collages with a mix of text and media. Invite students to present their collages for the class, explaining why they selected particular words and images.

Please note that excerpts and passages in the StudySync® library, workbooks, and PDFs are intended as touchstones to generate interest in an author's work. The excerpts and passages do not substitute for the reading of entire texts, and StudySync® strongly recommends that teachers and students seek out and purchase the whole literary or informational work in order to experience it as the author intended. Links to online resellers are available in our digital library. In addition, complete works may be ordered through an authorized reseller by filling out and returning to StudySync® the order form enclosed in this workbook.

Teacher's Edition   51

3. WRITE

Core Path	Access Path
Prewrite and Plan. Read the prompt as a class and ask students to brainstorm about how and why the children take stands against the red-eyed man. Focus on how the children's actions and reactions affect the plot. Students can brainstorm together either as a class or in small groups to begin planning their responses. Remind your students to look at the excerpt and their annotations to find textual evidence to support their ideas.	**Beginner & Intermediate** **Answer and Discuss.** Have students complete the prewriting questions on the Access 1 and 2 handouts and then explain their answers to a partner before they write. Explain to students that when they answer a question—such as *How do the children stand up for themselves?*—they need to include a detail, example, or quote from the text that supports the statement. For example, students could include the first line, "Charles Wallace darted forward and hit the man as hard as he could," which reveals that he defended himself and the others. **Approaching** **Answer Prewriting Questions.** Have students complete the prewriting questions on the Access 4 handout to summarize their thoughts before they write.
	Extend **Tech Infusion** **Self-Assess.** Before students begin their peer reviews, invite them to discuss previous experiences they have had in reviewing their peers' writing. What strategies have they used? Which strategies worked well, and which worked less well? What do they expect to focus on as they review their classmates' writing? Use a voice recording app (Voice Memo on the iPhone or Smart Voice Recorder for Androids) or VoiceThread (http://tinyurl.com/4m389hy) to capture students' ideas.
Discuss. Project these instructions for the peer review onto the board and review them with your class, so they know what they are looking for when they begin to provide their classmates with feedback: • How well does the writer explain the impact the children's actions have on the plot?	

Core Path	Access Path
• What textual evidence does the writer provide to support his or her analysis? • How well does the writer demonstrate the connection between the textual evidence and his or her analysis? • How successfully does the writer maintain a formal style and use clear, precise language to examine and inform readers about this event in the story? • What specific suggestions can you make to help improve the writer's response to the prompt? • What things does this response do especially well? After you've looked at the peer review instructions, review the rubric with students before they begin writing. Allow time for students briefly to pose and discuss any questions they may have about the peer review instructions and rubric. Tell students how many peer reviews they will need to complete once they submit their writing.	
Write. Ask students to complete the writing assignment maintaining a formal style and using precise language in their explanations. They should include strong textual evidence to support their responses. Once they have completed their writing, they should click "Submit."	
Review. Once students complete their writing assignment, they should submit substantive feedback to two peers. Students should use their peers' feedback to improve their writing.	

OVERVIEW

The science fiction teleplay "The Monsters Are Due on Maple Street," by Rod Serling, examines the dreadful effects of fear and suspicion on a neighborhood community. The First Read gives students the opportunity to experience the text with a limited context.

OBJECTIVES

1. Perform an initial reading of a text and demonstrate comprehension by responding to short analysis and inference questions with textual evidence.
2. Practice defining vocabulary words using context, as well as Greek and Latin roots and affixes.
3. Participate effectively in a range of conversations and collaborations to express ideas and build upon the ideas of others.

ELA Common Core Standards:
Reading: Literature - RL.6.1, RL.6.3, RL.6.4, RL.6.10
Speaking & Listening - SL.6.1.A, SL.6.1.B, SL.6.1.C, SL.6.2
Language - L.6.4.A, L.6.4.B, L.6.4.D

RESOURCES

Access 1 handout (Beginner)

Access 2 handout (Intermediate)

Access 3 handout (Advanced)

Access 4 handout (Approaching)

ACCESS COMPLEX TEXT

Because this excerpt from "The Monsters Are Due on Maple Street" is a script for a teleplay, it may present special challenges for students. In addition, students are asked to make comparisons across media and between texts. Use the following suggestions to provide scaffolded instruction for a close reading of the more complex features of this text:

- **Organization** - Because this excerpt is from a teleplay, the end product is meant to be viewed, not read. The script is designed to provide producers, directors, and actors with dialogue and to help them determine visual elements such as setting, costuming, facial expressions, and body language. Students may have difficulty integrating the dialogue and the stage directions.

- **Genre** - Students are asked to compare and contrast different media versions of "The Monsters Are Due on Maple Street" to see how the change in medium creates changes in plot, character, or setting. They are also asked to compare and contrast how the authors of "The Monsters Are Due on Maple Street" and *A Wrinkle in Time* approach the theme of characters confronting a possible monster from another planet or outer space. To make either of these comparisons, students have to identify and analyze relevant details and make inferences.

- **Specific Vocabulary** - Some students may have difficulty with figures of speech, such as "walk right over you," "tip your hand," or "hanging judge."

1. INTRODUCTION

Core Path	Access Path
Read and Discuss. Individually or as a class, read the introduction for "The Monsters Are Due on Maple Street." The introduction provides context for the excerpts taken from Acts I and II. Afterward, discuss the introduction as a class.	**English Learners All Levels & Approaching Read and Define.** Ask students to read the introduction for "The Monsters Are Due on Maple Street." Have them refer to the Introduction Glossary on their Access 1, 2, 3, and 4 handouts for definitions of key vocabulary terms. If there are unfamiliar words that are not included in their glossary, encourage students to check a dictionary or online reference tool, like http://tinyurl.com/6ytby.

Please note that excerpts and passages in the StudySync® library, workbooks, and PDFs are intended as touchstones to generate interest in an author's work. The excerpts and passages do not substitute for the reading of entire texts, and StudySync® strongly recommends that teachers and students seek out and purchase the whole literary or informational work in order to experience it as the author intended. Links to online resellers are available in our digital library. In addition, complete works may be ordered through an authorized reseller by filling out and returning to StudySync® the order form enclosed in this workbook.

Teacher's Edition   55

Core Path	Access Path
	English Learners All Levels & Approaching Make Predictions. Have students work cooperatively in pairs. Based on the introduction, ask students to make predictions about the events they expect to happen in this text. Ask students to use their Access 1, 2, 3, and 4 handouts to fill in predictions. The handout helps guide their predictions. Encourage students to predict, based on their understanding of how they would feel in the same situation.
Build Background. Before or after students read the excerpts, explain that some of the lessons are built around clips from the actual television program. These clips correspond to the scripted excerpts. Wherever students are asked to watch a clip, a specific time code is provided for it. You may choose to have the class watch only the clips assigned in a lesson, or you may choose to have students watch the television episode in its entirety. The links for all three parts of the episode can be accessed on the lesson plan online: Part I http://www.teachertube.com/video/monsters-are-due-1-232706 Part 2 http://www.teachertube.com/video/monsters-part-2-234819 Part 3 http://www.teachertube.com/video/monsters-part-3-234821 Should you choose to have students watch the full episode, you may wish to preview it yourself first. Whether students watch the full episode or only clips, be sure to alert them in advance of their viewing that the episode contains violence. You may want to be specific about the type of violence that takes place so that students are prepared for the tragic incident. While this teleplay addresses universal themes regarding the effects of fear and suspicion on a group, it includes references that are bound by the time period in which it was written.	**English Learners All Levels & Approaching Build Background.** Pair students with more proficient (Beyond) readers to research time-related topics. Ask students to think about these questions to guide their research: *The Twilight Zone* 1. What types of events were shown in *The Twilight Zone*? 2. Would *The Twilight Zone* be a popular show today? Why or why not? Fifth columnist 1. What was a fifth columnist? 2. Why was the fifth columnist important to this text? Hanging judge 1. What is a hanging judge? 2. Why was a hanging judge used in this text? Kangaroo court 1. What is a kangaroo court? 2. Why is the idea of a kangaroo court used in this text? Firing squad 1. What is a firing squad?

Core Path	Access Path
In pairs or small groups, ask students to research the following references. Assign each pair or group a topic to investigate: • *The Twilight Zone* • fifth columnist • hanging judge • kangaroo court • firing squad • ham radio set • search warrant Students may record their findings in simple graphic organizers that provide space for the questions: *Who, What, Where, When, Why,* and *How.* Have each group present its findings to the class. Post these organizers for easy reference as students read and discuss the teleplay.	2. Do you think that a firing squad is a fair and just punishment? Why or why not? Ham radio set 1. What is a ham radio set? 2. In what type of situation would a ham radio set be most beneficial? Search warrant 1. When is a search warrant issued? 2. How might a search warrant be beneficial?
	Extend **Tech Infusion** **Map a Concept.** Provide students with printed web graphic organizers. Alternatively, students may create digital concept maps using Popplet (http://tinyurl.com/6z3snff). In the center circle, have students write the word "monster." In the radiating circles, instruct students to write words or phrases and draw images that define the term. Encourage students to think about the word in both literal and figurative ways. Ask volunteers to present selected ideas to the class. Lead the class to develop a definition for the term that is inclusive of students' ideas.
	Extend **Analyze and Discuss a Quotation.** "Collective fear stimulates herd instinct, and tends to produce ferocity toward those who are not regarded as members of the herd" (Bertrand Russell). • What do you think this quotation means? • Do you agree with this quotation? Why or why not? • In what ways is fear an emotion that spreads like a virus from person to person?

2. READ

Core Path	Access Path

Make Predictions about Vocabulary. There are five bold vocabulary words in the text. As students read the text, ask them to make predictions about what they think each bold vocabulary word means based on the context clues in the sentence. If you are in a low-tech classroom and students are reading from printed copies or a projected text, ask students to record predictions in their notes, so they can be easily referenced in class. If your students have access to technology, they can use the annotation tool to make their predictions.

It might be helpful to model this practice for students before they begin reading. Either using the board or projecting the actual text, focus in on the sentence that uses the word "dense":

- "I'm surprised at you, Charlie. How come you're so dense all of a sudden? ... Who do I talk to? I talk to monsters from outer space. I talk to three-headed green men who fly over here in what look like meteors."

Model for the class how to use the overall structure and meaning of the sentence and the sentences around it, the word's position, and other clues to define the unfamiliar vocabulary word. In this case, point out these context clues:

1. We can look at the structure of the sentence to figure out how this multiple meaning word is being used. The word "dense" is used in the sentence to describe Charlie. Because the word is being used to describe a person, we know that "dense" is an adjective.

2. We know that one meaning for "dense" is "thick." The word comes from the Latin root *dens,* meaning "thick," and this meaning comes out in phrases such as *dense fog*, but it is clear that this is not the meaning used in the selection. Charlie is not physically thicker than anyone else.

Note: This exercise, which extends vocabulary instruction, should be completed when the class shifts from whole group instruction to individual work during the "Read and Annotate" exercise.

Beginner, Intermediate & Approaching Pair Practice.

1. Pair students with more proficient readers.

2. Give them an additional sentence that contains a new vocabulary word.

3. Ask the students to complete a Think Aloud using the teacher-led Make Predictions about Vocabulary activity as a model, while the proficient student actively listens.

4. The student should use the context clues in the sentence to try to determine the meaning of the new vocabulary word.

5. After the student has completed the Think Aloud and made a prediction about the word's meaning, allow time for the proficient reader to add his/her own thoughts and clarify any points of confusion.

6. Once they've completed this Think Aloud, encourage them to use a dictionary to confirm the definition of the new vocabulary word. Have them refer to the vocabulary listing on their Access 1, 2, and 4 handouts for definitions of key vocabulary terms in the text. Encourage them to add any additional vocabulary words or idioms they find in the text and look up definitions for those words and idioms online or in a dictionary.

Core Path	Access Path
3. We can look at what Charlie says to Steve in the sentences before the word appears as clues to the meaning of "dense." Charlie asks questions, and we can see that he is trying to understand the purpose of Steve's radio. 4. Steve responds by stating that he is "surprised" at Charlie's questions and asks why he is so "dense all of a sudden." Therefore, we can determine that "dense" in this context likely means "unable to understand."	

Core Path	Access Path
Model Reading Comprehension Strategy. Before students begin reading, model the reading comprehension strategy of Visualizing by using this Think Aloud that talks students through the first few lines of text. First explain to your students that visualizing is forming a mental picture of something as you read, and using new details from the text to add to or change the mental images you have created. Model for students how visualizing will help them better comprehend the selection and help drive their discussions. • This text is a teleplay, and it is written to be viewed, not read. Producers, directors, and actors read the script carefully and visualize it or see it in their minds' eye so that they can make decisions about visual elements such as setting, costuming, facial expressions, body language, and so forth. • When I read the first few lines, I read like a producer, director, or actor. I visualize the characters, setting, and action to help me better understand the story. • In Goodman's first line, he says, "You keep your distance" all of you." This line tells me that Goodman faces a crowd. I read that he tells them to keep their distance, and so I visualize that they are close to him and that he is uncomfortable with their nearness. To show this feeling, Goodman may back up or hold up his hands to reinforce his message.	**Note:** This exercise, which extends vocabulary instruction, should be completed when the class shifts from whole group instruction to individual work during the "Read and Annotate" exercise. **Beginner, Intermediate & Approaching** **Apply Reading Comprehension Strategy.** 1. Have Beginning and Intermediate students listen to the audio version of the excerpt from "The Monsters Are Due on Maple Street" via the following link: http://tinyurl.com/lzxommb. As they listen to the audio recording, ask them to draw or sketch a picture of what they see in their minds as they visualize the story. Encourage them to include as much detail as possible in the time allowed. 2. Once they have listened to the audio version and created a picture or series of pictures based on what they heard, pair students with more proficient readers and ask them to describe what they drew and why. Why did they include particular images and/or colors? 3. Allow pairs time to discuss the pictures. Were there any details from the text that were not included in the picture? If so, encourage them to add details to the drawing based on their conversations.

Core Path	Access Path
• The first stage direction mentions a front porch. Now, I can visualize where to place Goodman and the crowd. They are in front of a house with a porch, perhaps in a neighborhood.	

Core Path	Access Path
Read and Annotate. Have students independently read and annotate the excerpt. Ask students to use the annotation tool as they read to: 1. use context clues, and the meanings of Greek or Latin roots and affixes, if possible, to analyze and determine the meaning of the bolded vocabulary terms 2. ask questions about passages of the text that may be unclear or unresolved 3. identify key information, events, characters, and connections between them 4. note unfamiliar vocabulary 5. capture their reaction to the events in the text	**Beginner** **Coach the Reading.** While other students read, annotate, and discuss the text independently, work with Beginning students. Read the text aloud and pause periodically or when any student has a question. Coach students in articulating their questions for the group and in highlighting and annotating the text. Have students use the Annotation Guide in the Access 1 handout to support them as they highlight and annotate the text. For further support, ask questions about the text such as: • What did you learn about the mysterious figure? • Is there anything about the story that you don't understand? • How did the crowd make the situation worse? **Intermediate** **Group Reading.** In small groups, have these students read the text and use the definitions on the Access 2 handout to help them with words or idioms that may be unfamiliar. If students need help with annotating the text, have them use the Annotation Guide on the Access 2 handout. After working with the Beginning students, you may wish to check this group's progress and provide support as needed. **Advanced** **Pair with Proficient Peers.** Have Advanced students work with English proficient peers to read, annotate, and discuss the text. Have students use the Annotation Guide in the Access 3 handout to support them as they highlight and annotate the text.

Core Path	Access Path
	Approaching **Use the Annotation Guide.** Have students use the Annotation Guide in the Access 4 handout to support them as they highlight and annotate the text.
Discuss. In small groups or pairs, have students discuss the questions and inferences they made while reading. Make sure students follow the rules for collegial discussions: Refer to Collaborative Discussions in the Speaking & Listening Handbook. 1. Why do the neighbors think that Goodman's insomnia is suspect? (Because they see Goodman go out on his porch at night and he is looking at the sky. They think he may be waiting for something to happen or someone from another world to appear.) 2. As the excerpt from Act II approaches conclusion, the stage directions describe the arrival of a "figure." How do you visualize the setting? (Answers will vary, but may include nighttime on a quiet street, with a crowd of neighbors watching as the outline of a figure comes toward them in the dark.) How does visualizing help you better understand the scene? (Answers will vary, but may include that it helps with understanding the neighbors' fear.) 3. What does Charlie say to try to excuse or justify his act of terrible violence? (He says he didn't know who the figure was and that he would never have hurt anyone he knew, that he was only trying to protect his home.) 4. What is the writer's point of view about those excuses? (The writer thinks they are invalid; Charlie has acted as a member of a mob driven by groundless fears. Next, they turn on Charlie.)	**English Learners All Levels & Approaching** Use the extra time while on– and beyond– grade level students are discussing their first reads of the text to work individually and in small groups with Approaching readers and English Learners as outlined on the previous page. Should those students complete their first read quickly, integrate them into the on– and beyond– grade level discussion groups. Otherwise, Approaching readers and English Learners will be given an opportunity to participate in text discussions with their peers later in the lesson.

Copyright © BookheadEd Learning, LLC

Core Path	Access Path
	Extend **Interpret Figures of Speech.** Draw students' attention to the following line: "You'd let whatever's out there walk right over us, wouldn't yuh?" Ask: *Does Charlie literally mean that Steve would let the mysterious monster walk across the body of everyone in the neighborhood, or does Charlie mean something else, and if so, what?* Then lead students in a discussion in which they determine that Steve, according to Charlie, would let the mysterious monster take advantage of the group's weaknesses and treat them all badly or harm them. Explain that "to walk over" someone is an example of an idiom, or a phrase that takes on a meaning that is separate from the literal meanings of the individual words. The idiom "to walk over" someone generally means to treat someone badly or in a thoughtless way.

3. THINK

Core Path	Access Path
Answer and Discuss. Have students complete the Think questions and then use the peer review instructions and rubric to complete two peer reviews. Refer to the sample answers at the end of the lesson plan online to discuss responses with your students.	**Beginner & Intermediate** **Sentence Frames.** Have students complete the Sentence Frames exercise on the Access 1 and 2 handouts to support their responses to the Think questions. **Approaching** **Find the Evidence.** Have students complete the Find the Evidence exercise on the Access 4 handout to help them identify the evidence needed to answer the Think questions.

Core Path	Access Path
	Extend **Debate.** Present students with an issue from the text that can be debated. Allow students to debate the issue as a class or in smaller groups. Debate prompts: 1. The monster in "The Monsters Are Due on Maple Street" is more frightening than the monster in the excerpt from *A Wrinkle in Time*. 2. There were steps Steve could have taken to quiet the mob and to get everyone to go home.
	Extend **Write and Support Opinions.** Ask students each to write a paragraph that clearly states his or her position in relation to the topic that was debated. Ask students to read their paragraphs to a small group of peers. Then have each group discuss whether the writers presented their opinions in a convincing way.

Please note that excerpts and passages in the StudySync® library, workbooks, and PDFs are intended as touchstones to generate interest in an author's work. The excerpts and passages do not substitute for the reading of entire texts, and StudySync® strongly recommends that teachers and students seek out and purchase the whole literary or informational work in order to experience it as the author intended. Links to online resellers are available in our digital library. In addition, complete works may be ordered through an authorized reseller by filling out and returning to StudySync® the order form enclosed in this workbook.

Teacher's Edition   **63**

OVERVIEW

By comparing and contrasting different media versions of the same text, such as the print version of a drama to its adaptation on television, students can gain an appreciation of how medium affects plot events, settings, characters, and the overall message communicated in a text. This lesson plan provides follow-up questions and useful enrichments to help teachers guide students toward a usable, repeatable method for comparing and contrasting media with text.

OBJECTIVES

1. Learn the definition of media.
2. Practice using concrete strategies for comparing and contrasting media with text.
3. Participate effectively in a range of conversations and collaborations to express ideas and build upon the ideas of others.

ELA Common Core Standards:
Reading: Literature - RL.6.1, RL.6.3, RL.6.7
Writing - W.6.4, W.6.6
Speaking & Listening - SL.6.1.A, SL.6.1.B, SL.6.1.C, SL.6.2

RESOURCES

Access 1 handout (Beginner)
Access 2 handout (Intermediate)
Access 3 handout (Advanced)
Access 4 handout (Approaching)

1. DEFINE

Core Path	Access Path
Watch. Watch the Concept Definition video on media with your students. Have your students write down the definition of "media" and consider the many different kinds of media, as well as the role of technology in the dissemination of information. Pause the video at these key moments to discuss the information with your students:	**English Learners All Levels & Approaching** **Match.** Have students complete the Match exercise on the Access 1, 2, 3, and 4 handouts as they watch the video. Correct answers are located at the end of the lesson plan online.
1. 0:30 – "Media" refers to methods of communication, but what do we mean when we say "the media"? What does this term encompass? From which forms of media do you get most of your news, entertainment, etc.?	
2. 0:36 – How has technology influenced the three basic forms of communication (spoken, written, visual)? Does all communication still fall into these three basic categories, or are there new forms that have been created?	
3. 0:43 – Think about modern forms of media, including Twitter, Facebook, Instagram, etc. How are language, form, and audience experience different for each? Discuss.	
Read and Discuss. After watching the Concept Definition video, have students read the definition of media. Either in small groups or as a whole class, use these questions to engage students in a discussion about media. Make sure students follow the rules for collegial discussions.	**Beginner & Approaching** **Finish the Sentences.** Have these students complete the sentence frames on the Access 1 and 4 handouts as they read the definition of media. Have them use the completed sentence frames to help them participate in the discussion. Correct answers for this exercise are located at the end of the lesson plan online.
1. What are the original media of communication? How is each unique? (speech, which is heard, so tone and inflection affect message; drawing, which is visual, so color, line, and shape affect message; and writing, which is textual, so word choice and style affect message)	**Intermediate & Advanced** **Discuss Prompts.** To help these students participate in the discussion, prompt them with questions that can be answered with a few words, such as:
2. How did advancements in technology affect communication in the 19th century? (Photography provided visuals, while the telegraph and the telephone added the element of speed to communication.)	• What are some different types of media? (television, phone, camera, radio, etc.) • What types of activities can you do on a Smartphone? (text, chat, tweet, surf, etc.)

Please note that excerpts and passages in the StudySync® library, workbooks, and PDFs are intended as touchstones to generate interest in an author's work. The excerpts and passages do not substitute for the reading of entire texts, and StudySync® strongly recommends that teachers and students seek out and purchase the whole literary or informational work in order to experience it as the author intended. Links to online resellers are available in our digital library. In addition, complete works may be ordered through an authorized reseller by filling out and returning to StudySync® the order form enclosed in this workbook.

Teacher's Edition   65

Core Path	Access Path
3. How do stories and ideas change as they are translated from one medium to another? (A writer might use sensory details to describe a face or a sound, while a filmmaker conveys the same information with a camera shot or a sound effect.)	• What different types of media have you used this week? (Answers will vary, but may include: television, phone, etc.) **Beyond** **Discuss.** Have students discuss how media has changed due to the invention of the smartphone and tablet computer. Has it improved media? If so, how? How have these inventions changed people's behavior?
	Extend **Tech Infusion** **Freewrite.** After watching the video, ask students to freewrite in their journals about the language and the user experience of a modern form of media. For example, what is the language of Twitter? Describe the experience of communicating via Twitter. Ask students to consider the following questions about the medium they choose to guide their writing: • What are the advantages and disadvantages of this form of communication? • How do the features of this medium affect communication? • Suggest that students post excerpts from their entries via the medium they choose to analyze. Have them report any responses they receive to the class.

2. MODEL

Core Path	Access Path
Read and Annotate. Have students independently read the Model section. As they read, ask students to use the annotation tool to: • highlight key points • ask questions	**Note:** During this portion of the lesson, instruction shifts from whole group to individual work. Use this time to work one-on-one or in small groups with Beginning, Intermediate, Advanced, and Approaching students.

Core Path	Access Path
• identify places where the Model applies the strategies laid out in the Identification and Application section **Note to teacher:** The links in this lesson plan are to parts two and three of "The Monsters Are Due on Maple Street." These parts of the episode can be accessed on the lesson plan online: Part I http://www.teachertube.com/video/monsters-are-due-1-232706 Part 2 http://www.teachertube.com/video/monsters-part-2-234819	**Beginner & Intermediate** **Coach the Reading.** Work with these students (either individually or in small groups) to fill out the guided reading questions on the Access 1 and 2 handouts. Have students refer to the Model Glossary on the Access 1 and 2 handouts to help them determine the meaning of difficult words. Let students know they'll use these answers to help participate in the discussion about the Model. Sample answers for this exercise are located at the end of the lesson plan online. **Advanced** **Guided Reading.** Have students complete the guided reading questions on the Access 3 handout as they read. Let them know that they'll use these answers to help participate in the discussion about the Model. Sample answers for this exercise are located at the end of the lesson plan online. **Approaching** **Group Guided Reading.** In small groups, have students complete the guided reading questions on the Access 4 handout as they read. Let them know that they'll use these answers to help participate in the discussion about the Model. Sample answers for this exercise are located at the end of the lesson plan online.
Discuss. After students read the Model text, use these questions to facilitate a whole group discussion that helps students understand how to compare and contrast the print passage with the televised version: 1. How does the Model compare and contrast textual visualizations with visual perceptions and features? (The Model notes a setting difference between the teleplay and the television show. Then, the model draws conclusions about the causes of these differences based on the features of the visual medium.)	

Please note that excerpts and passages in the StudySync® library, workbooks, and PDFs are intended as touchstones to generate interest in an author's work. The excerpts and passages do not substitute for the reading of entire texts, and StudySync® strongly recommends that teachers and students seek out and purchase the whole literary or informational work in order to experience it as the author intended. Links to online resellers are available in our digital library. In addition, complete works may be ordered through an authorized reseller by filling out and returning to StudySync® the order form enclosed in this workbook.

Teacher's Edition   **67**

Core Path	Access Path
2. How does the Model justify the differences between events in the print version and events in the televised version of the text? (The Model rationalizes that because the scene takes place during the day, the porch light flickering on and off would barely be noticeable to the characters in the televised version, but the car starting on its own startles the crowd. So replacing the light with the self-starting car has a greater impact on the characters and audiences, fueling the idea that there is a monster.)	
3. What is a question the Model suggests readers should ask as they continue to compare and contrast the text and television version? (Answers will vary, but may include "How is the role of the audience potentially different in each version?")	
4. What can finding the answer to this question reveal about texts presented in multiple media forms? (By comparing and contrasting media, readers can better understand how different elements of a medium affect the meaning or the message of the story and the audience's interpretation of the message.)	
	Extend **Tech Infusion** **Listen to Another Medium.** Listen to all of "The Monsters Are Due on Maple Street" via the following link: http://tinyurl.com/q9rvnao. During the listening, have students complete print or digital triple Venn diagrams using Creately (http://tinyurl.com/dk8xvq) to compare and contrast the experiences of reading, viewing, and listening to the story. Students should include in their diagrams contrasts of visualizations while reading with perceptions during watching or listening.

3. YOUR TURN

Core Path	Access Path
Assess and Explain. Have students answer the comprehension questions to test for understanding. Share the explanations for Parts A and B (located online) with your students.	**English Learners All Levels & Approaching** Ask students to work in pairs to practice answering comprehension questions. Use the first two questions from the test. Do a Think Aloud model showing students how to answer a comprehension question.
	Extend **Tech Infusion** **Direct the Scene.** Have students write stage directions and production notes for the way Les Goodman should deliver the line: "That's what I'd like to know" and the way that the image of him should be shot for a video production. Students may record their ideas in print or digital concept maps using Popplet (http://tinyurl.com/4dlp3se). To begin, lead students to discuss Les's possible meanings by asking the following questions: • Does he become part of the crowd, accusing Charlie of something? • Does he gloat over Charlie now that Charlie is going through the same experience that Les does at the beginning of the text? • Does he make a genuine request for information that would explain the events on Maple Street? Explain that before they begin writing, the students need to make decisions about the purpose of Les's statement within the context of the overall plot. Then they need to choose facial expressions, vocal tones, gestures and body language, and camera shots and angles that will convey these meanings to an audience.

Please note that excerpts and passages in the StudySync® library, workbooks, and PDFs are intended as touchstones to generate interest in an author's work. The excerpts and passages do not substitute for the reading of entire texts, and StudySync® strongly recommends that teachers and students seek out and purchase the whole literary or informational work in order to experience it as the author intended. Links to online resellers are available in our digital library. In addition, complete works may be ordered through an authorized reseller by filling out and returning to StudySync® the order form enclosed in this workbook.

Teacher's Edition  69

OVERVIEW

Comparing and contrasting stories in different forms or genres is key to understanding varying perspectives on significant topics and universal themes. This lesson plan provides follow-up questions and useful enrichments to help teachers guide students toward a usable, repeatable method for comparing and contrasting texts.

OBJECTIVES

1. Learn the definition of compare and contrast.
2. Practice using concrete strategies for comparing and contrasting.
3. Participate effectively in a range of conversations and collaborations to express ideas and build upon the ideas of others.

ELA Common Core Standards:
Reading: Literature - RL.6.1, RL.6.3, RL.6.9
Writing - W.6.4, W.6.6
Speaking & Listening - SL.6.1.A, SL.6.1.B, SL.6.1.C, SL.6.2

RESOURCES

Access 1 handout (Beginner)

Access 2 handout (Intermediate)

Access 3 handout (Advanced)

Access 4 handout (Approaching)

1. DEFINE

Core Path	Access Path
Watch. Watch the Concept Definition video on compare and contrast with your students. Make sure students understand the different components of comparing and contrasting. Pause the video at these key moments to discuss the information with your students:	**English Learners All Levels & Approaching** **Match.** Have students complete the Match exercise on the Access 1, 2, 3, and 4 handouts as they watch the video. Correct answers are located at the end of the lesson plan online.

1. 0:16 – In addition to the example in the video, what are some other things you can compare and contrast? Why do you think people like to compare and contrast things?
2. 1:34 – When is it helpful to compare and contrast two (or more) different texts, or characters within a text? How does this help to make you a more active reader?
3. 1:58 – What do you think we gain by comparing a character's actions or choices to our own? How do you respond differently to a character who has more in common with you, versus a character who is different?

Core Path	Access Path
Read and Discuss. After watching the Concept Definition video, have students read the definition of compare and contrast. Either in small groups or as a whole class, use these questions to engage students in a discussion about comparing and contrasting. Make sure students follow the rules for collegial discussions.	**Beginner & Approaching** **Complete a Chart.** To prepare students to participate in the discussion, have them complete the chart on the Access 1 and 4 handouts as they read the definition of compare and contrast. Correct answers are located at the bottom of the lesson plan online.

1. What does it mean to compare? (to say how two or more items are similar)
2. What does it mean to contrast? (to say how two or more items are different)
3. Which do you think is easier to do when reading: compare or contrast? Explain your choice. (Answers will vary.)
4. What kinds of comparisons and contrasts do you make regularly? How do they help you in your daily life? (Answers will vary.)

Intermediate & Advanced
Discuss Prompts. To help these students participate in the discussion, prompt them with questions that can be answered with a few words, such as:

- What is an example from your life when you compare things? (deciding on what to eat for lunch)
- When you read, what can comparing things help you do? (understand two characters; understand how two texts approach a theme)

Core Path	Access Path
5. What is the value of comparing and contrasting two mediums? (to understand what two characters may have in common; to understand how two mediums treat the same theme or topic)	**Beyond** **Discuss.** Have students select two books they've read and compare them in terms of characters, themes, and genres. Compile a list of examples. Discuss comparisons as a class.
	Extend **Tech Infusion** **Brainstorm.** Using a whiteboard or a Padlet Wall (http://tinyurl.com/aedptok), create a Venn diagram to lead students in comparing and contrasting the theme of two familiar texts in different genres or forms.

2. MODEL

Core Path	Access Path
Read and Annotate. Have students independently read the Model section. As they read, ask students to use the annotation tool to: • highlight key points • ask questions • identify places where the Model applies the strategies laid out in the Identification and Application section	**Note:** During this portion of the lesson, instruction shifts from whole group to individual work. Use this time to work one-on-one or in small groups with Beginning, Intermediate, Advanced, and Approaching students. **Beginner, Intermediate, & Approaching** **Summarize the Discussion.** In pairs, have students watch the Concept Definition video again and complete the Summarize the Discussion exercise on the Access 1, 2, and 4 handouts as they watch the video. Sample answers for this exercise are located at the end of the lesson plan online. **Advanced** **Summarize the Discussion.** Have students complete the Summarize the Discussion exercise on the Access 3 handout. If students need to, have them watch the Concept Definition video again to complete the exercise. Sample answers for this exercise are located at the end of the lesson plan online.

Core Path	Access Path
Discuss. After students read the Model text, use these questions to facilitate a whole group discussion that helps students understand how to compare and contrast two texts:	

1. In what way does the Model claim that *A Wrinkle in Time* and "The Monsters Are Due on Maple Street" are similar? (Both deal with the idea of confronting a monster and the challenges it presents.)

2. What difference does the Model go on to explore? (looking at the differences in the way the monster or alleged monster is described and how the characters in each text respond)

3. How does this Model analyze this in the first text? (In *A Wrinkle in Time*, the monster takes a human form. Although the children are "unsure exactly what the face really looked like," the monster is a very real being in the context of the novel.)

4. How does this Model analyze the second text? (In the teleplay, "The Monsters Are Due on Maple Street," the characters never actually see the monster, and there is no actual evidence that a monster exists at all. It is fear that drives residents to believe a monster actually is among them.)

5. What other differences does the Model present? (It also addresses the character action and reaction in each text. The characters face their fears very differently. In *A Wrinkle in Time*, the children stand up to the monster, the red-eyed man. In "The Monsters Are Due on Maple Street," the neighbors react to their fears by becoming suspicious and turning against one another. This results in tragic consequences.)

6. How does the Model conclude the comparison and contrast? (The model suggests that the texts provide insight into a similar theme.)

Please note that excerpts and passages in the StudySync® library, workbooks, and PDFs are intended as touchstones to generate interest in an author's work. The excerpts and passages do not substitute for the reading of entire texts, and StudySync® strongly recommends that teachers and students seek out and purchase the whole literary or informational work in order to experience it as the author intended. Links to online resellers are available in our digital library. In addition, complete works may be ordered through an authorized reseller by filling out and returning to StudySync® the order form enclosed in this workbook.

Teacher's Edition   73

Core Path	Access Path
	Extend **Tech Infusion** **Visualize.** Divide the class into two groups and provide each student with drawing paper and markers. Alternatively, students may draw digitally using Google Drawings (http://tinyurl.com/mtddzfx). Ask one half of the class to draw images that represent the monster found in *A Wrinkle in Time*. Ask the other half of the class to draw images that represent the monster found in "The Monsters Are Due on Maple Street." Have students post the images from *A Wrinkle in Time* together on one side of a board and the images from "The Monsters Are Due on Maple Street" together on the other side of a board. Lead the class to discuss similarities and differences between the images on the two sides of the board. End the discussion by leading students to conclude what lessons they are able to learn about the idea of monsters within the individual, within a community, and in the world.

3. YOUR TURN

Core Path	Access Path
Assess and Explain. Have students answer the comprehension questions to test for understanding. Share the explanations for Parts A and B (located online) with your students.	
	Extend **Tech Infusion** **Blog the Theme.** Have students post blog entries about why mind control or the lack of free thought is dangerous for people. Students should also cite textual evidence to suggest positive means and negative means for fighting against such forces. Encourage students to use the kind of informal, personal voice that bloggers often use. Students may wish to work in pairs.

OVERVIEW

The science fiction teleplay "The Monsters Are Due on Maple Street," by Rod Serling, examines the dreadful effects of fear and suspicion on a neighborhood community. The Close Read gives students the opportunity to compare and contrast theme and experience across media and genre.

OBJECTIVES

1. Complete a close reading of a passage of literature.
2. Practice and apply concrete strategies for comparing and contrasting texts in different media and genre.
3. Participate effectively in a range of conversations and collaborations to express ideas and build upon the ideas of others.
4. Prewrite, plan, and produce clear and coherent writing in response to a prompt.

   ELA Common Core Standards:

   Reading: Literature - RL.6.1, RL.6.2, RL.6.3, RL.6.4, RL.6.7, RL.6.9, RL.6.10

   Writing - W.6.1.A, W.6.1.B, W.6.4, W.6.5, W.6.6, W.6.8, W.6.9.A, W.6.10

   Speaking & Listening - SL.6.1.A, SL.6.1.B, SL.6.1.C, SL.6.1.D, SL.6.6

   Language - L.6.4.A, L.6.4.B, L.6.4.C, L.6.4.D

RESOURCES

"The Monsters Are Due on Maple Street" Vocabulary handout

"The Monsters Are Due on Maple Street" Graphic organizer

Access 1 handout (Beginner)

Access 2 handout (Intermediate)

Access 3 handout (Advanced)

Access 4 handout (Approaching)

Please note that excerpts and passages in the StudySync® library, workbooks, and PDFs are intended as touchstones to generate interest in an author's work. The excerpts and passages do not substitute for the reading of entire texts, and StudySync® strongly recommends that teachers and students seek out and purchase the whole literary or informational work in order to experience it as the author intended. Links to online resellers are available in our digital library. In addition, complete works may be ordered through an authorized reseller by filling out and returning to StudySync® the order form enclosed in this workbook.

Teacher's Edition   75

1. INTRODUCTION

Core Path	Access Path
Define and Compare. Project the vocabulary words and definitions onto the board or provide students with handouts so they can copy the vocabulary into their notebooks. Suggest that students consult general and specialized reference materials, both print and digital, to compare the precise meaning of a specific word with their initial vocabulary predictions from the First Read. Review words that students defined incorrectly to understand why they were unable to use context clues to develop usable definitions.	**Beginner & Intermediate** **Complete the Sentences.** Have students complete the sentence frames on the Access 1 and 2 handouts using the vocabulary words. Correct answers are located at the end of the lesson plan online. **Advanced & Beyond** **Write.** Form student pairs and assign each pair a vocabulary word. Ask them to create three quiz questions using this frame: Which shows [*incriminate, insomnia, dense*]: _____ or _____? One example should exemplify the word and the other example should exemplify the word's opposite. Encourage students to create examples that are engaging and fun. Have each pair ask its questions aloud to the class and have volunteers respond and explain their thinking. **Approaching** **Graphic Organizer.** To support students in comparing their vocabulary predictions with the correct meanings, have them complete the graphic organizer on the Access 4 handout to record the vocabulary words, their predictions, and the definitions. Then have them write sentences using the words.
Review. Have students complete the fill in the blank vocabulary worksheet for this selection. Answers for the worksheet are listed at the end of the lesson plan online.	

Core Path	Access Path
	Extend **Tech Infusion** **Write.** Using the noun forms of the vocabulary words ("incrimination," "idiosyncrasy," "insomnia"), have students write short narratives that feature personified main characters whose names are the vocabulary words, one word per student. For example, students might begin with a line such as this one: *As Incrimination gazed into the bathroom mirror; she wondered what she would be told she is guilty of doing today. . . .*The vocabulary words "dense" and "contorted" should appear in sentences in the narrative once each: *Incrimination contorted her face in horror at the police officer's claim.* Remind students to develop their characters through sensory description and dialogue. Ask volunteers to read aloud their passages in an open-mike style reading by adapting their speech to the context and task, and using appropriate eye contact, adequate volume, and clear pronunciation. Record students' readings and post them to your class YouTube channel.
	Extend **Act.** Form small student groups. Have students write short skits about a person incriminating another for doing something. Tell students to incorporate the vocabulary words into the dialogue. Ask each group to perform its skit for the class.

Please note that excerpts and passages in the StudySync® library, workbooks, and PDFs are intended as touchstones to generate interest in an author's work. The excerpts and passages do not substitute for the reading of entire texts, and StudySync® strongly recommends that teachers and students seek out and purchase the whole literary or informational work in order to experience it as the author intended. Links to online resellers are available in our digital library. In addition, complete works may be ordered through an authorized reseller by filling out and returning to StudySync® the order form enclosed in this workbook.

Teacher's Edition   77

2. READ

Core Path	Access Path
Model Close Reading. Project the text onto the board and model a close reading of the first few lines using the annotation strategies mentioned below. While modeling annotation strategies, make notes that tie the text to the focus skills and demonstrate what students are looking for as they read. Here is some guidance for you as you annotate for your students:	

- As the Skills lessons that precede this text make clear, media and genre affect the ways in which authors convey messages, meanings, and themes.

- In paragraph 4, Steve introduces the theme of the monster through dialogue. He defines a monster as something "different than us."

- Remember that in *A Wrinkle in Time,* the idea of the monster—something undefinable—is introduced through sensory detail and narration: "she was not sure what the face really looked like, whether it was young or old, cruel or kind, human or alien."

- In all cases, the monster is not a physical three-headed green man as Steve references at one point, but something intangible, different, and undefinable. It is these qualities of formlessness, difference, and indefinability that cause the characters to feel fear and then succumb to it or rise above it.

- The way in which the characters from both genres (novel and teleplay) choose to confront their fears will have an impact on their lives.

Core Path	Access Path
Read and Annotate. Read the Skills Focus questions as a class, so your students know what they should pay close attention to as they read. Then have students read and annotate the excerpt. Ask students to use the annotation tool as they read to: 1. respond to the Skills Focus section 2. ask questions 3. make connections 4. identify key themes, events, characters, and details 5. note unfamiliar vocabulary 6. capture their reaction to the ideas and examples in the text As they reread the text, remind students to use the comprehension strategy of Visualizing that they learned in the First Read.	**Note:** While on–grade level students are reading and annotating, work one-on-one or in small groups with Beginning, Intermediate, Advanced and Approaching students to support them as they read and annotate the text. **Beginner & Intermediate** **Summarize and Analyze the Text.** Work with these students to complete the sentence frames on the Access 1 and 2 handouts. They will then use the completed sentence frames to help them analyze and annotate the text as they answer the Skills Focus questions. Refer to the sample Skills Focus answers to help them complete the sentence frames and annotate the text. **Advanced** **Work in Pairs.** Pair these students with more proficient English speakers to work together on analyzing and annotating the text to complete the Skills Focus questions. If these students need more support, have them use the Summarize and Analyze the Text exercise on the Access 3 handout as they work with their more proficient peers. **Approaching** **Summarize the Text.** Have these students discuss and complete the text summary on the Access 4 handout. Encourage students to use their summary to help them analyze and annotate the text and to help them answer the Skills Focus questions. Correct answers for the summary are at the end of the lesson plan online. Also refer to the sample Skills Focus answers to aid students with their annotations.

Core Path	Access Path
Discuss. After students have read the text, use the sample responses to the Skills Focus questions online to discuss the reading and the process of comparing and contrasting mediums and text forms: Make sure that students have acquired and accurately use academic-specific words and phrases related to the skill, and demonstrate a command of formal English appropriate to the discussion.	**Extend** **Pair and Share.** In small, heterogeneous groups or pairs, ask students to share and discuss their annotations with a focus on the point of view presented in the selection. You can provide students with these questions to guide their discussion: 1. What type of figure do you imagine when the shadow approaches? Some think it is an alien, Tommy claims it is the monster. 2. How do the neighbors' fears add to the climax of the story? Because everyone is afraid of the monster and eerie things happen, everyone is very jumpy and skittish at the end of the excerpt. 3. In what way does fear turn all people into children? The people don't really have good reasons for being suspicious of others. They are jumping to conclusions without thinking clearly.
	Extend **Tech Infusion** **Make and Revise Storyboards.** Have pairs of students carefully watch five to ten paragraphs of the text as they are portrayed in the television clip and create print or digital storyboards of the scenes as they were shot, including the placement of actors, props, setting details, light and camera angles, sound effects, and so on. Then have students use alternative text colors and boxes to mark and revise the storyboard to better represent their visions of the scene based on the text alone. Have volunteers present selected entries to the class. Then lead students to discuss the process of translating what readers "see" and "hear" when they read to a visual medium such as film. Which elements cross mediums easily? Which do not and why? What strategies do filmmakers use to solve these problems?

Core Path	Access Path
	Extend **Tech Infusion** **Compare and Contrast.** Ask students to create side-by-side print or digital images of the monsters in *A Wrinkle in Time* and "The Monsters Are Due on Maple Street." Students may choose to include words, phrases, or text quotations in their drawings. Then, have students create Venn diagrams using Google Drawings (http://tinyurl.com/k53lde2) to compare and contrast the two monsters. Have volunteers present selected entries from their work to the class.

3. WRITE

Core Path	Access Path
Prewrite and Plan. Read the prompt as a class and ask students to brainstorm about similarities and differences in the questions characters ask in the excerpts from the novel and the teleplay, and what the questions reveal about the theme of seeking the truth. Students can brainstorm together either as a class or in small groups to begin planning their responses. Remind your students to look at the excerpts from both texts as well as at their annotations to find strong and relevant textual evidence to support their ideas. Students should also view the television clips again as needed to respond to the prompt.	**Beginner & Intermediate** **Answer and Discuss.** Have students complete the prewriting questions on the Access 1 and 2 handouts and then explain their answers to a partner before they write. Explain to students that when they answer a question, like *Why did the neighbors accuse Les of wrongdoing?* they need to include a detail, example or quote from the text that supports the statement. **Approaching** **Answer Prewriting Questions.** Have students complete the prewriting questions on the Access 4 handout to summarize their thoughts before they write.
	Extend **Organize.** Encourage students to complete Venn diagrams (See Resources) to organize their ideas before they type their responses. Students should use the circles to compare and contrast the two versions of "The Monsters Are Due on Maple Street."

Core Path	Access Path
Discuss. Project these instructions for the peer review onto the board and review them with your class, so they know what they are looking for when they begin to provide their classmates with feedback:	

- What similarities in the characters' questions does the writer cite? What differences?
- What does the writer's comparison reveal about the theme of seeking the truth?
- How do the excerpts from the novel and teleplay treat this theme similarly? Differently?
- What evidence from the text and the television episode does the writer provide to support his or her claim or claims?
- What specific suggestions will help the writer improve the response?
- What elements of this response are written especially well?
- Be sure to tell the writer what he or she does well and what he or she needs to improve. Remember that your comments are most useful when they are specific and constructive.

After you've looked at the peer review instructions, review the rubric with students before they begin writing. Allow time for students briefly to pose and discuss any questions they may have about the peer review instructions and rubric. Tell students how many peer reviews they will need to complete once they submit their writing.

Write. Ask students to complete the writing assignment using textual evidence chosen from the novel excerpt and the teleplay, as well as evidence from the television episode, to support their responses. Once they have completed their writing, they should click "Submit."

Core Path	Access Path
Review. Once students complete their writing assignments, they should submit substantive feedback to two peers. Students should use their peers' feedback to improve their writing.	
Note to teacher: The links for all three parts of "The Monsters Are Due on Maple Street" are provided on the lesson plan online: Part I http://www.teachertube.com/video/monsters-are-due-1-232706 Part 2 http://www.teachertube.com/video/monsters-part-2-234819 Part 3 http://www.teachertube.com/video/monsters-part-3-234821	

FIRST READ:
Red Scarf Girl

OVERVIEW

Ji-Li Jiang was born and raised in Communist China during a period of intense persecution of people whom the government considered anti-revolutionary—including her family. In this excerpt from her memoir *Red Scarf Girl*, Jiang portrays the fear and the ethical dilemma she faced in having to choose between her family and the demands of her country. The First Read gives students the opportunity to experience the text with a limited context.

OBJECTIVES

1. Perform an initial reading of a text and demonstrate comprehension by responding to short analysis and inference questions with textual evidence.
2. Practice defining vocabulary words using context.
3. Participate effectively in a range of conversations and collaborations to express ideas and build upon the ideas of others.

ELA Common Core Standards:
Reading: Informational - RI.6.1, RI.6.3, RI.6.4, RI.6.10
Speaking & Listening - SL.6.1.A, SL.6.1.B, SL.6.1.C, SL.6.2
Language - L.6.4.A, L.6.4.B, L.6.5.B

RESOURCES

Access 1 handout (Beginner)

Access 2 handout (Intermediate)

Access 3 handout (Advanced)

Access 4 handout (Approaching)

ACCESS COMPLEX TEXT

In this excerpt from *Red Scarf Girl,* Ji-Li Jiang is being interrogated by people from her father's theater group about her father's landlord past and supposed crimes against the Cultural Revolution. To grasp what is happening to Jiang and to understand her emotions, students must interpret historical and cultural references and look for deeper more sinister meanings for words and phrases that normally carry mild connotations. Use the following suggestions to provide scaffolded instruction for a close reading of the more complex features of this text:

- **Organization** – *Red Scarf Girl* is a memoir. Like many memoirs, it includes dialogue as well as first-person narration. Students need to draw details from both the dialogue and narration to understand the relationships between individuals, events, and ideas.

- **Specific Vocabulary** – Many words, such as *comrades,* or *study session,* had special connotations during the Chinese Cultural Revolution. Students will need to consider these connotations while reading. In addition, the memoir does not always provide exact details about the study session. Students will need to consider the shades of meaning of various words to understand what is happening and how Ji-Li Jiang feels.

- **Prior Knowledge** – The focus on Chinese culture during a specific period in history may present special challenges for students. Many students may lack prior knowledge of the Chinese Communist Party and events surrounding the Cultural Revolution.

1. INTRODUCTION

Core Path	Access Path
Read. Individually or as a class, read the Introduction for *Red Scarf Girl*. The introduction provides context for the excerpt.	**English Learners All Levels** **Fill in the Blanks.** Have students listen to the audio of the introduction. As they listen, ask them to use their Access 1, 2, and 3 handouts to fill in the blanks and complete the transcript. Answers are located at the end of this lesson plan online.

Please note that excerpts and passages in the StudySync® library, workbooks, and PDFs are intended as touchstones to generate interest in an author's work. The excerpts and passages do not substitute for the reading of entire texts, and StudySync® strongly recommends that teachers and students seek out and purchase the whole literary or informational work in order to experience it as the author intended. Links to online resellers are available in our digital library. In addition, complete works may be ordered through an authorized reseller by filling out and returning to StudySync® the order form enclosed in this workbook.

Teacher's Edition   85

Core Path	Access Path
Build Background. In pairs or small groups, ask students to use devices to research Communist China. You may want to assign each group a topic to investigate, including: • Revolution in China: the facts • Who was Mao Zedong? • What happened to those who opposed Mao? • How were people educated during the Revolution? If you are in a low-tech classroom, you can provide photocopies of materials on Communist China for students to read and discuss. Have each group present their findings. You may wish to have groups create a video recording of their presentations.	**English Learners All Levels & Approaching True or False.** Pair students and have them complete the matching activity on Mao Zedong on their Access 1, 2, 3, and 4 handouts using the help of research materials. When they are done, have students share their findings with other groups. Encourage them to discuss what they understand about Mao and what life was like under his rule.
	Extend **Discuss the Introduction.** After reading the introduction, use the information provided to facilitate a prereading discussion to get students thinking about the events and themes in *Red Scarf Girl*. 1. What is "persecution?" 2. What are some examples of persecution? Have you ever felt persecuted in some way? 3. How might the persecution of someone who grew up in a dictatorship compare to the persecution you've experienced?

2. READ

Core Path	Access Path
Make Predictions about Vocabulary. There are five bold vocabulary words in the text. As students read the text, ask them to make predictions about what they think each vocabulary word means based on the clues in the sentence. If you are in a low tech classroom and students are reading from printed copies or a projected text, ask students to write predictions in their notes for use in class. If your students have access to technology, they can use the annotation tool to make their predictions.	**Note:** This exercise, which extends vocabulary instruction, should be completed when the class shifts from whole group instruction to individual work during the "Read and Annotate" exercise.

Make Predictions about Vocabulary. There are five bold vocabulary words in the text. As students read the text, ask them to make predictions about what they think each vocabulary word means based on the clues in the sentence. If you are in a low tech classroom and students are reading from printed copies or a projected text, ask students to write predictions in their notes for use in class. If your students have access to technology, they can use the annotation tool to make their predictions.

Consider modeling making predictions about vocabulary before students begin reading. At the board or by projecting the passage text, focus in on the sentence that uses the word "testify":

- We want you to testify against your father at the struggle meeting.

Model for the class how to use the meaning of the sentence and nearby words and sentences, the word's position in the sentence, and other clues to define the vocabulary word. Point out these context clues:

1. We can look at the structure of the sentence to figure out what part of speech "testify" is. It's in the clause, "We want you to testify." The subject of the clause is "We" and the verb with "We" is "want." So what do "We" "want"? They want someone to "testify." That sounds like an action—a verb.

2. Next we ask what kind of action "testify" is. This is the time to look for context clues. One clue is "against your father." Testifying is something you can do against—and maybe for—someone. And it's going to happen at a meeting. What do people do at a meeting? They speak. It sounds like "testify" means "to speak for or against someone, formally."

Access Path

Note: This exercise, which extends vocabulary instruction, should be completed when the class shifts from whole group instruction to individual work during the "Read and Annotate" exercise.

Beginner, Intermediate & Approaching Pair Practice.

1. Pair students with more proficient readers.

2. Give them an additional sentence that contains a new vocabulary word.

3. Ask the students to complete a Think Aloud using the teacher-led Make Predictions about Vocabulary activity as a model, while the proficient student actively listens.

4. The student should use the context clues in the sentence to try to determine the meaning of the new vocabulary word.

5. After the student has completed the Think Aloud and made a prediction about the word's meaning, allow time for the proficient reader to add his/her own thoughts and clarify any points of confusion.

6. Once they've completed this Think Aloud, encourage them to use a dictionary to confirm the definition of the new vocabulary word. Have them refer to the vocabulary listing on their Access 1, 2, and 4 handouts for definitions of key vocabulary terms in the text. Encourage them to add any additional vocabulary words or idioms they find in the text and look up definitions for those words and idioms online or in a dictionary.

Core Path	Access Path
3. "Testify" also seems like it might be related to words such as "testimony" or "testament." Both of those words also suggest something official or formal: testimony is the statement someone gives in court; the books of the Bible are called testaments. This is further evidence that "testify" might mean speaking or making a statement, formally.	

Model Reading Comprehension Strategy. Before students begin reading, model the reading comprehension strategy of making, confirming, and revising predictions. Use this Think Aloud to talk students through the first three paragraphs of text. Begin by explaining that making, confirming, and revising predictions consists of saying what you think might happen next in the text; then, reading ahead to see if you were right or not; then, if you weren't right, changing your prediction of what will happen later, based on the new details you just read.

Model for students how making, confirming, and revising predictions will help them comprehend and discuss the selection.

- When I read the first paragraph, I see that the narrator is entering something called a study session. What's going to happen at this study session? I predict she's going to study a school subject.

- I read the next action that occurs. Oh, she's not studying a school subject! It sounds like something much more serious! She thinks about her family being "exposed," and having "no pride left," and no longer being "educable."

- This calls for a revision of my prediction. Based on what the Chairman tells Ji-Li, and what Ji-Li thinks, my new prediction is that Ji-Li is going to face a big problem that will threaten her family and her education.

Note: This exercise, which extends vocabulary instruction, should be completed when the class shifts from whole group instruction to individual work during the "Read and Annotate" exercise.

Beginner, Intermediate & Approaching
Apply Reading Comprehension Strategy.

1. Have students listen to the audio version of the excerpt from *Red Scarf Girl*. As they listen to the audio, pause the recording after paragraph 3. Instruct them to write one sentence predicting who the characters are and what will happen during the conversation.

2. Resume the audio, pausing periodically to allow students to write a new sentence underneath, refining their previous predictions. Offer guidance to help them notice clues in the events, descriptions, and dialogue.

3. Once they have finished listening to the audio, have them write one final sentence, summarizing the text.

4. Pair students with more proficient readers and ask them to discuss the differences between their initial predictions and their final summaries. Which predictions changed and which stayed the same? What clues were the most important? Encourage groups to share their findings with the class, and point out strategies that they may have used without realizing it.

Core Path	Access Path
Read and Annotate. Have students independently read and annotate the excerpt. Ask students to use the annotation tool as they read to: 1. use context clues to analyze and determine the meaning of the bolded vocabulary terms 2. ask questions about passages of the text that may be unclear or unresolved 3. identify key information, events, individuals, and connections between them 4. note unfamiliar vocabulary 5. capture their reaction to the events in the text	**Beginner** **Coach the Reading.** While other students read, annotate, and discuss the text independently, work with Beginning students, listening to the audio of the text and pausing periodically or when any student has a question. Coach students in articulating their questions for the group and in highlighting and annotating the text. Have students use the Annotation Guide in the Access 1 handout to support them as they highlight and annotate the text. For further support, ask questions about the text such as: • Is there anything about the story that you don't understand? • What do you think will happen to Ji-Li? • What does the excerpt tell you about Mao and the Cultural Revolution? **Intermediate** **Listen to the Audio.** Have these students listen to the audio of the text and use the definitions on the Access 2 handout to help them with words or idioms that may be unfamiliar. If students need help with annotating the text, have them use the Annotation Guide on the Access 2 handout. After working with the Beginning students, you may wish to check this group's progress and provide support as needed. **Advanced** **Pair with Proficient Peers.** Have Advanced students work with English proficient peers to read, annotate, and discuss the text. Have students use the Annotation Guide in the Access 3 handout to support them as they highlight and annotate the text. Encourage them to listen to the audio of the text if needed. **Approaching** **Use the Annotation Guide.** Have students use the Annotation Guide in the Access 4 handout to support them as they highlight and annotate the text.

Core Path	Access Path
Discuss. In small groups or pairs, have students discuss the questions and inferences they made while reading. Make sure students follow the rules for collegial discussions: Refer to Collaborative Discussions in the Speaking & Listening Handbook.	**English Learners All Levels & Approaching** Use the extra time while on– and beyond–grade level students are discussing their first reads of the text to work individually and in small groups with Approaching readers and English Learners as outlined on the previous page. Should those students complete their first reads quickly, integrate them into the on– and beyond–grade level discussion groups. Otherwise English Learners and Approaching readers will be given an opportunity to participate in text discussions with their peers later in the lesson.

Core Path:

1. What details of life in Communist China during Ji-Li's girlhood does the text provide? (Students could be confronted and threatened in school by Party officials; the Party punished people who had opinions it didn't like.)

2. What is upsetting to Ji-Li about her meeting with the Chairman and the other adults? (She is put on the spot about either denouncing her father or being disgraced.)

3. What were your predictions? How accurate were they? What revisions, if any, did you make to your predictions? (Students' answers will vary depending upon the predictions they made.)

Access Path:

Extend Tech Infusion
Reporters. After students have read the memoir, invite them to imagine that they are fellow students of Ji-Li's who are reporters for the school newspaper. Have them write news stories reporting on what happened during Ji-Li's meeting with the Chairman and the others. Make sure students include the following elements:

- A headline that vividly sums up the event in no more than six words

- A lead paragraph that provides the most important basic information about the event—information that answers questions such as *Who, What, Where, When,* and *Why.*

- Two or more paragraphs of additional factual detail that fill in the event

- Accurate dialogue spoken at the meeting

Use a voice recording app (Voice Memo on the iPhone or Smart Voice Recorder for Androids) to have students read their news stories aloud. Encourage them to read in lively, clear, newscaster-type voices.

3. THINK

Core Path	Access Path
Answer and Discuss. Have students complete the Think questions and then use the peer review instructions and rubric to complete two peer reviews. Refer to the sample answers at the end of the lesson plan online to discuss responses with your students.	**Beginner & Intermediate** **Sentence Frames.** Have students use the Sentence Frames on the Access 1 and 2 handouts to support their responses to the Think questions. If necessary, distribute sentence frames to Advanced students as well. **Approaching** **Find the Evidence.** Have students use Find the Evidence on the Access 4 handout to help them identify the evidence needed to answer the questions.
	Extend **Debate.** Present students with an issue from the text that can be debated. Allow students to debate the issue as a class or in smaller groups. Debate prompts: 1. Should Ji-Li condemn her father or refuse to condemn him? 2. Could experiences like the ones in this memoir ever happen in the United States?

Please note that excerpts and passages in the StudySync® library, workbooks, and PDFs are intended as touchstones to generate interest in an author's work. The excerpts and passages do not substitute for the reading of entire texts, and StudySync® strongly recommends that teachers and students seek out and purchase the whole literary or informational work in order to experience it as the author intended. Links to online resellers are available in our digital library. In addition, complete works may be ordered through an authorized reseller by filling out and returning to StudySync® the order form enclosed in this workbook.

Teacher's Edition   91

OVERVIEW

When students feel overwhelmed by the information in a text, they can break the text down into its basic elements, such as events, ideas, individuals, facts, and details, in order to focus on them individually and make meaningful inferences among them. This lesson plan provides follow-up questions and useful enrichments to help teachers guide students toward a usable, repeatable method for recognizing informational text elements.

OBJECTIVES

1. Learn the definition of informational text elements.
2. Practice using concrete strategies for identifying informational text elements.
3. Participate effectively in a range of conversations and collaborations to express ideas and build upon the ideas of others.

ELA Common Core Standards:
Reading: Informational - RI.6.1, RI.6.3
Speaking & Listening - SL.6.1.A, SL.6.1.B, SL.6.1.C, SL.6.2

RESOURCES

Red Scarf Girl Graphic organizer
Access 1 handout (Beginner)
Access 2 handout (Intermediate)
Access 3 handout (Advanced)
Access 4 handout (Approaching)

1. DEFINE

Core Path	Access Path
Watch. Watch the Concept Definition video on informational text elements with your students. Make sure your students are familiar with all the different elements shared in the video—including details, events, people, and ideas—as well as how these elements may interact over the course of a text. Pause the video at these key moments to discuss the information with your students:	**English Learners All Levels & Approaching** **Match.** Have students complete the matching exercise on the Access 1, 2, 3, and 4 handouts as they watch the video. Answers are located at the end of this lesson plan online.

Core Path

1. 0:25 – Before people wrote things down, how do you think they remembered and communicated information? What challenges might have led to the development of a written language?

2. 0:50 – Do you think there are any similarities between the elements of fictional and informational texts? What are they? Compare and contrast the two forms.

3. 1:20 – For what reasons might an author "leave out" various events in an informational text? How does this challenge our understanding of certain facts or events? What can we do as readers to broaden our understanding of a topic or event?

Core Path

Read and Discuss. After watching the Concept Definition video, have students read the definition of informational text elements. Either in small groups or as a whole class, use these questions to engage students in a discussion about elements of informational text. Make sure students follow the rules for collegial discussions.

1. How does knowing the genre of an informational text give you a better idea of which text elements might be important?

2. A memoir is one kind of informational text that focuses on an individual and provides details about his or her life and character. What are some others? What informational texts like this have we read in class already this year?

Access Path

Beginner & Approaching
Complete a Chart. To prepare students to participate in the discussion, have them complete the chart on the Access 1 and 4 handouts as they read the definition. The correct answers are located on the lesson plan online.

Intermediate & Advanced
Discuss Prompts. To help these students participate in the discussion, prompt them with questions that can be answered with a few words, such as:

- A memoir is a kind of informational text that focuses on what? (one person's memories)

- What type of information does an informational text discuss? (people, places, and/or things)

Core Path	Access Path
3. Can you think of a time when you used one of the strategies described to help you analyze text elements in an informational text?	• What is another type of informational text you have read this year? (Answers will vary.) **Beyond** **Discuss.** Have students select a nonfiction book they've read and describe its genre. Compile a list of examples. Have students discuss how the genre of each work affects what the reader learns about. How might a switch in genre affect not only what the reader learns, but how much he or she enjoys the information?
	Extend **Tech Infusion** **Brainstorm.** After watching the video, ask students to list nonfiction works they have read about individuals. Have them brainstorm events and facts from those individuals' lives and inferences that they made based on those events and facts. Compile a class list of examples using a whiteboard or a Padlet Wall (http://tinyurl.com/n7l7cyy). You may wish to continue adding to this class list throughout the year.

2. MODEL

Core Path	Access Path
Watch. Ask students to take notes on the SkillsTV video on informational text elements in *Red Scarf Girl: A Memoir of the Cultural Revolution* as you watch together. Remind students to listen for the way the students use academic vocabulary related to the definition of informational text elements during their discussion. Pause the video at these key moments to discuss the information with your students: 1. 0:22 – What type of informational text is *Red Scarf Girl*? How does this detail help students understand the information presented?	**Beginner, Intermediate, & Approaching** **Analyze the Discussion.** Have students watch the video again and complete the chart on the Access 1, 2, and 4 handouts as they watch the video. Sample answers for this exercise are located at the end of the lesson plan online. **Advanced** **Journals.** Have students note in their journals the strategies the students in the SkillsTV video use to find informational text elements.

Copyright © Bookheaded Learning, LLC

Core Path	Access Path
2. 1:24 – How do Ji-Li Jiang's thoughts, words, and actions introduce and explain the events in the text? 3. 3:30 – From the events that Ji-Li Jiang describes, what inference can students make about why Party officials are now focusing their attention on her? What evidence from the text do they cite to help them make inferences?	
Read and Annotate. Have students independently read the Model section. As they read, ask students to use the annotation tool to: • highlight key events, facts, and details • ask questions • make inferences from the text • identify places where the Model applies the strategies laid out in the Identification and Application section on informational text elements	**Note:** During this portion of the lesson, instruction shifts from whole group to individual work. Use this time to work one-on-one or in small groups with Beginning, Intermediate, Advanced, and Approaching students. **Beginner & Intermediate** **Coach the Reading.** Work with these students (either individually or in small groups) to fill out the guided reading questions on the Access 1 and 2 handouts. Have Beginning students refer to the glossary on the Access 1 handout to help them determine the meaning of difficult words (note: provide the Access 1 handout glossary to Intermediate students if necessary). Let students know they'll use these answers to help participate in the discussion about the Model. Sample answers for this exercise are located at the end of the lesson plan online.
	Advanced **Identify Evidence.** Provide these students with the same instructions to read and annotate as on-grade level and Beyond students. In addition, ask Advanced students to complete the Identifying Evidence exercise on the Access 3 handout. Let students know that they'll use these answers to help participate in the discussion about the Model. Sample answers for this exercise are located at the end of the lesson plan online.

Core Path	Access Path
	Approaching **Guided Reading.** Have students complete the guided reading questions on the Access 4 handout as they read. Let them know that they'll use these answers to help participate in the discussion about the Model. Sample answers for this exercise are located at the end of the lesson plan online.

Discuss. After students read the Model text, use these questions to facilitate a whole group discussion that helps students understand how to find and analyze informational text elements of the passage:

1. How does the Model for this passage begin its analysis of informational text elements? (It focuses on the first event—the study session—and the facts and details that the text provides. It also looks at the meaning of the special term "study session.")

2. After finding the facts and details of the event, how does the Model look for deeper meaning? (The Model looks for the *how* and *why* of the event, such as why Ji-Li has been singled out for the study session.)

3. How does the Model use specific words and phrases in the text to make inferences about facts and details? (The Model uses words and phrases such as "filthy past" and "landlord family" in Thin-Face's dialogue as a way of explaining what the adults confronting Ji-Li have against her father and why her family has been singled out for investigation.)

4. What inference can be made from the information in the Model about why Ji-Li is being questioned? (Ji-Li's father's "mistakes," and his refusal to confess to them, have angered the Communist Party, and turned the Party's attention on Ji-Li. Several Party officials are pressuring Ji-Li to prove her loyalty to Chairman Mao by turning against her father.)

Core Path	Access Path
5. According to the Model, what does the text **not** explain? (It doesn't explain what Ji-Li's father's mistakes were and why they offended the Party.)	
	Extend **Talk Together.** Assign pairs of students to analyze the informational text elements presented in different sections of the passage: paragraphs 6–10; paragraphs 11–15; or paragraphs 16–18. Suggest that they reread the passage first, then consult the Model as they identify important facts and details. After students work through the event, encourage them to discuss how using the skill and the Model helped them better understand the text. Consider having students exchange ideas using Twitter (http://tinyurl.com/248s9m) or TodaysMeet (http://tinyurl.com/8ydulv4) during and after their talk.

3. YOUR TURN

Core Path	Access Path
Assess and Explain. Have students answer the comprehension questions to test for understanding. Share the explanations for Parts A and B (located online) with your students.	
	Extend **Share and Discuss.** Have students complete the Your Turn section in class. Poll students about their responses and, as a class, discuss the different strategies they used to determine the correct answers. Ask students which aspects of the questions they found hard, and how they solved the difficulty. Conduct your poll by asking your students to complete a handout with questions or using Poll Everywhere (http://tinyurl.com/5grl69) or Socrative (http://tinyurl.com/nfz427v).

Core Path	Access Path
	Extend **Find Evidence.** Have students, individually or in pairs, construct textual evidence charts to draw inferences based on the excerpt from *Red Scarf Girl* and to record facts and details that serve as evidence for their inferences. You can distribute copies of a blank chart for students to use (See Resources), or suggest that students use Google Drawings (http://docs.google.com/drawings) to make their charts.

Connotation and Denotation

OVERVIEW

Proficient readers become sensitive to the subtle differences in meaning between closely related words. Skillful writers choose the words that best match the shades of meaning, the nuances, that are intended. This lesson plan provides follow-up questions and useful enrichments to help teachers guide students toward a usable, repeatable method for analyzing the connotations and denotations of words and phrases.

OBJECTIVES

1. Learn the definition of connotation and denotation.
2. Practice using concrete strategies for identifying connotations and denotations.
3. Learn and practice using word relationships, including connotation and denotation, to further understand the meanings of words.
4. Participate effectively in a range of conversations and collaborations to express ideas and build upon the ideas of others.
5. Practice acquiring and using academic vocabulary correctly.

   ELA Common Core Standards:
   Reading: Informational - RI.6.1, RI.6.4
   Speaking & Listening - SL.6.1.A, SL.6.1.B, SL.6.1.C, SL.6.2
   Language - L.6.5.B, L.6.5.C, L.6.6

RESOURCES

Access 1 handout (Beginner)

Access 2 handout (Intermediate)

Access 3 handout (Advanced)

Access 4 handout (Approaching)

1. DEFINE

Core Path	Access Path
Watch. Watch the Concept Definition video on connotation and denotation with your students. Make sure students understand the different aspects of the connotations of words. Remind students to pay attention to the way the speakers use academic vocabulary to express ideas. Pause the video at these key moments to discuss the information with your students:	**English Learners All Levels & Approaching** **Match.** Have students complete the matching exercise on the Access 1, 2, 3, and 4 handouts as they watch the video. Answers are located at the end of the lesson plan online.

1. 0:20 – What does a word's "cultural connection" refer to? Can you think of a word (or words) which has a connotative meaning derived from a certain cultural connection? How did this particular connotative meaning come to exist?
2. 0:42 – Similar to the "child" example, brainstorm some other words with neutral denotations and place them in a context in which the connotation gives it a completely different meaning. How does the relationship between words work to create or clarify meaning?
3. 0:56 – Why do you think authors use words with specific connotations? Why don't they just state what they mean directly?

Core Path	Access Path
Read and Discuss. After watching the Concept Definition video, have students read the definition of connotation and denotation. Either in small groups or as a whole class, use these questions to engage students in a discussion about the connotations of words in texts. Make sure students follow the rules for collegial discussions and remind them to use their newly acquired academic vocabulary correctly.	**Beginner & Approaching** **Complete a Chart.** To prepare students to participate in the discussion, have them complete the chart on the Access 1 and 4 handouts as they read the definition. The correct answers are located on the lesson plan online.

1. Adjectives and adverbs are often chosen for the specific connotations that make them different from adjectives with similar denotations. What examples can you find in *Red Scarf Girl* of adjectives or adverbs that have strongly negative or positive shades of meaning?

Intermediate & Advanced
Discuss Prompts. To help these students participate in the discussion, prompt them with questions that can be answered with a few words, such as:

*   What other meanings do words have beyond the dictionary definition? (implied or associated meanings)

Core Path	Access Path
2. Synonyms for tones of voice or gestures often have a range of connotations. For example, the connotation of "stare" is different from the connotation of "look." What words for tones and gestures does Ji-Li Jiang use in *Red Scarf Girl*? What connotations do they have? Can you think of other synonyms for these words that would help clarify those connotations? 3. Can a word or phrase have negative shades of meaning—such as connoting a threat—even when the meanings of the words themselves are neutral or positive? Find examples of how the Party officials use language this way in *Red Scarf Girl*.	• What is the term for a word's literal meaning? (denotation) • What is the term for a word's meaning depending on the context? (connotation) **Beyond** **Discuss.** Have pairs of students discuss common phrases they know that demonstrate positive or negative connotations. Compile a list of examples. Have students analyze the connotations of each example. How might a word with a different connotation change the meaning in a particular context?
	Extend **Tech Infusion** **Brainstorm.** Have volunteers jot down groups of synonymous words, such as *thin/skinny/slender/scrawny.* Invite all students to supply additional synonyms and rank them in order from most positive to most negative. Follow up by composing sentences that show the connotations of each word. Have the class discuss how the connotations of the different synonyms affect the meaning or emotion of the sentence. Compile a class list of examples using a whiteboard or a Padlet Wall (http://tinyurl.com/n7l7cyy). Invite all students to add to the list.

2. MODEL

Core Path	Access Path
Read and Annotate. Have students independently read the Model section. As they read, ask students to use the annotation tool to: • highlight key points • ask questions	**Note:** During this portion of the lesson, instruction shifts from whole group to individual work. Use this time to work one-on-one or in small groups with Beginning, Intermediate, Advanced, and Approaching students.

Core Path	Access Path
<ul><li>gather vocabulary knowledge and use newly acquired academic vocabulary correctly</li><li>identify places where the Model applies the strategies laid out in the Identification and Application section on connotation and denotation</li><li>note relationships between words and their denotations or connotations</li></ul>	**Beginner & Intermediate** **Coach the Reading.** Work with these students (either individually or in small groups) to fill out the guided reading questions on the Access 1 and 2 handouts. Have Beginning students refer to the glossary on the Access 1 handout to help them determine the meaning of difficult words (note: provide the Access 1 handout glossary to Intermediate students if necessary). Let students know they'll use these answers to help participate in the discussion about the Model. Sample answers for this exercise are located at the end of the lesson plan online. **Advanced** **Identify Evidence.** Provide these students with the same instructions to read and annotate as on-grade level and Beyond students. In addition, ask Advanced students to complete the Identifying Evidence exercise on the Access 3 handout. Let students know that they'll use these answers to help participate in the discussion about the Model. Sample answers for this exercise are located at the end of the lesson plan online. **Approaching** **Guided Reading.** Have students complete the guided reading questions on the Access 4 handout as they read. Let them know that they'll use these answers to help participate in the discussion about the Model. Sample answers for this exercise are located at the end of the lesson plan online.

Core Path	Access Path
Discuss. After students read the Model text, use these questions to facilitate a whole group discussion that helps students understand connotation and denotation. Remind students they will use this vocabulary knowledge when considering a word or phrase important to comprehension or expression. To help facilitate a discussion, refer to Collaborative Discussions in the Speaking and Listening Handbook as you work through the questions:	

1. How does the Model introduce the difference between denotation and connotation? (It introduces the idea that writers of informational text make choices regarding certain words and phrases, in order to convey their ideas to readers. It distinguishes between a word's denotation, or dictionary meaning, and connotation, or shades of meaning.)

2. According to the Model, what major types of connotation do words usually have? (Words have positive or negative connotations. Remind students that some words may also have a neutral connotation.)

3. How does the Model identify the relationship between the author's word choice and the author's intent? (The author chooses a specific word, from among words with similar denotations, to convey her ideas to the reader. Because the author wishes to convey a particular meaning or emotion, choosing the correct word is important.)

4. What example does the Model give of a word in *Red Scarf Girl* that has an important connotation in context? How can the synonyms for this word help explain the writer's word choice? (The Model examines the connotation of the word *expose* within the context of the text. It discusses synonyms for *expose* that have more neutral connotations, and then compares them to the connotations of *expose*. The comparison illustrates that *expose* is the stronger word choice in the context.)

Please note that excerpts and passages in the StudySync® library, workbooks, and PDFs are intended as touchstones to generate interest in an author's work. The excerpts and passages do not substitute for the reading of entire texts, and StudySync® strongly recommends that teachers and students seek out and purchase the whole literary or informational work in order to experience it as the author intended. Links to online resellers are available in our digital library. In addition, complete works may be ordered through an authorized reseller by filling out and returning to StudySync® the order form enclosed in this workbook.

Teacher's Edition   103

Core Path	Access Path
5. In what context does the Model explain the denotation and connotation of the word *cold?* (The model examines the denotation and connotation of the word *cold* as it relates to the actions of the official named Thin-Face.)	
	Extend **Talk Together.** Assign pairs of students to reread portions of *Red Scarf Girl* containing two to four paragraphs. Tell them to read slowly and to pause and make a note when they come across a word that could have more than one connotation, or a word that has synonyms. The word may or may not be one that is important to the event described in the passage. Tell the pairs to discuss the connotations of the word in context and to suggest synonyms or alternate phrasings that might have had different connotations and emotional impact. Many words in the passage have possible synonyms or alternate phrasings that could make Ji-Li's situation feel either more dire and frightening, or less so, such as "mistakes" (paragraph 5), "reform" (paragraph 8), and "severe" (paragraph 17). Consider having students create screencasts of the talks using Educreations (http://tinyurl.com/k6wl3aw).

3. YOUR TURN

Core Path	Access Path
Assess and Explain. Have students answer the comprehension questions to test for understanding. Share the explanations for Parts A and B (located online) with your students.	

Core Path	Access Path
	Extend **Share and Discuss.** Have students complete the Your Turn section in class. Poll students about their responses and as a class discuss the different strategies they used to determine the correct answers. Ask students which aspects of the questions they found hard, and how they solved the difficulty. Conduct your poll by asking your students to complete a handout with questions or using Poll Everywhere (http://tinyurl.com/5grl69) or Socrative (http://tinyurl.com/nfz427v).
	Extend **Tech Infusion** **Create.** Have students use Google Drawing to draw details from *Red Scarf Girl* which include words that they think could have synonyms with different connotations. Under the drawing have students write the text sentence that contains the word. Then have students make a second drawing of the same subject, but as if the sentence used a different word with a different connotation—for instance, a word that made Thin-Face seem less threatening. Have students write the new sentence under that picture. Invite students to talk about how their drawings show the different connotations of the words.

OVERVIEW

The memoir *Red Scarf Girl*, by Ji-Li Jiang, relates the real-life experience of a girl in Communist China who was faced with the agonizing choice of whether to denounce her father for anti-Party activities or to defend him and risk probable retribution against her whole family, including herself. The Close Read gives students the opportunity to find informational text elements to take meaning from the passage, aided by understanding of the denotations and connotations of words and phrases.

OBJECTIVES

1. Complete a close reading of a passage from a memoir.
2. Practice and apply concrete strategies for identifying informational text elements and word relationships such as connotations and denotations.
3. Participate effectively in a range of conversations and collaborations to express ideas and build upon the ideas of others.
4. Prewrite, plan, and produce clear and coherent writing in response to a prompt.

   ELA Common Core Standards:
   Reading: Informational Text - RI.6.1, RI.6.3, RI.6.4, RI.6.10
   Writing - W.6.1.A, W.6.1.B, W.6.4, W.6.5, W.6.6, W.6.10
   Speaking & Listening -SL.6.1.A, SL.6.1.B, SL.6.1.C, SL.6.1.D, SL.6.6
   Language - L.6.4.A, L.6.4.C, L.6.4.D, L.6.5.B, L.6.5.C

RESOURCES

Red Scarf Girl Vocabulary handout

Access 1 handout (Beginner)

Access 2 handout (Intermediate)

Access 3 handout (Advanced)

Access 4 handout (Approaching)

1. INTRODUCTION

Core Path	Access Path
Define and Compare. Project the vocabulary words and definitions onto the board or provide students with handouts so they can copy the vocabulary into their notebooks. Suggest that students consult general and specialized reference materials, both print and digital, to compare the precise meaning of a specific word with their initial vocabulary predictions from the First Read. Review words that students defined incorrectly to understand why they were unable to use context clues to develop usable definitions.	**Beginner & Intermediate** **Complete the Sentences.** Have students complete the sentence frames on the Access 1 and 2 handouts using the vocabulary words. Point out that some of the words are in the questions and some will be in the answers. Correct answers are located at the end of the lesson plan online. **Advanced & Beyond** **Write in Journals.** Have students write a journal entry using all of their vocabulary words. Remind them to write sentences that communicate the meaning of the words they are using. **Approaching** **Graphic Organizer.** To support students in comparing their vocabulary predictions with the correct meanings, have them complete the graphic organizer on the Access 4 handout to record the vocabulary words, their initial analysis, and the definitions. Then have them write sentences using the words.
Review. Have students complete the fill in the blank vocabulary worksheet for this selection. Answers for the worksheet are listed at the end of the lesson plan online.	
	Extend **Tech Infusion** **Act and Record.** Break students into small groups, assign each group a vocabulary word, and ask them to design a short skit to demonstrate the meaning of the word for their peers. You may decide to assign each group two or more words, as the lesson's vocabulary work well together. If possible, record skits and post them to your class YouTube Channel, so they can be reviewed later.

Please note that excerpts and passages in the StudySync® library, workbooks, and PDFs are intended as touchstones to generate interest in an author's work. The excerpts and passages do not substitute for the reading of entire texts, and StudySync® strongly recommends that teachers and students seek out and purchase the whole literary or informational work in order to experience it as the author intended. Links to online resellers are available in our digital library. In addition, complete works may be ordered through an authorized reseller by filling out and returning to StudySync® the order form enclosed in this workbook.

Teacher's Edition  **107**

Core Path	Access Path
	Extend **Tech Infusion** **Create.** Create online flashcards for the vocabulary using Quizlet (http://quizlet.com) or StudyBlue (www.studyblue.com). **Extend** **Tech Infusion** **Monologue.** Have students create an interior monologue in Ji-Li's first-person voice, describing what she thinks during her "study session." Remind students to use their memory of their first reading of *Red Scarf Girl* to provide text elements, such as dialogue and descriptive details, for Ji-Li's monologue. Invite students to post their monologues on a class blog such as Pen.io (http://tinyurl.com/3edm9se), Blogger (http://tinyurl.com/e67d), or Edublogs (http://tinyurl.com/dygdcc5).

2. READ

Core Path	Access Path
Model Close Reading. Project the text onto the board and model a close reading of the opening paragraphs using the annotation strategies below and on the following page. While modeling the strategies, make notes that connect the text to the skills and demonstrate what students should focus on as they read. Here is some guidance for you as you model the skills: • As the Skills lesson on informational text elements shows, when we read a text we look closely at the events, individuals, ideas, and details that can help us understand what's happening and why. For example, the first paragraph tells us that Ji-Li is being ordered to sit in a chair for a "study session."	

Core Path	Access Path
• As the Skills lesson on denotation and connotation shows, readers can use the shades of meaning in words to help them understand what's happening and how the characters feel. The first four paragraphs don't provide exact detail about what occurs during a "study session," but the words that Ji-Li uses to describe the scene connote dread, such as "never imagined this," "expose my family," "no pride left," and "never be an educable child again." • In the passage, some words have special connotations in this context. For example, "comrades" generally means "friends," but in this context it means "fellow members of the Communist Party"—who may not be Ji-Li's friends at all. In addition, special connotations arise in this passage because the speakers often don't mean what they say, or because they are using mild words to connote major threats. For example, "nothing to worry about" connotes a great deal to worry about in this context. The harmless-sounding phrase "study session" doesn't imply getting together with some classmates to review lessons. It implies being confronted by a potentially very dangerous authority.	
Read and Annotate. Read the Skills Focus questions as a class, so your students know what they should pay close attention to as they read. Then have students read and annotate the memoir excerpt. Ask students to use the annotation tool as they read to: 1. respond to the Skills Focus section 2. ask questions 3. make connections 4. identify key information, examples, and details 5. note unfamiliar vocabulary	**Note:** While on-grade level students are reading and annotating, work one-on-one or in small groups with Approaching, Beginning, Intermediate, and Advanced students to support them as they read and annotate the text.

Please note that excerpts and passages in the StudySync® library, workbooks, and PDFs are intended as touchstones to generate interest in an author's work. The excerpts and passages do not substitute for the reading of entire texts, and StudySync® strongly recommends that teachers and students seek out and purchase the whole literary or informational work in order to experience it as the author intended. Links to online resellers are available in our digital library. In addition, complete works may be ordered through an authorized reseller by filling out and returning to StudySync® the order form enclosed in this workbook.

Teacher's Edition   109

Core Path	Access Path
6. note the connotations of words and their relationships to denotative meanings 7. capture their reaction to the ideas and examples in the text As they reread the text, remind students to use the comprehension strategy of Making, Confirming, and Revising Predictions that they learned in the First Read.	**Beginner & Intermediate** **Summarize and Analyze the Text.** Work with these students to complete the sentence frames on the Access 1 and 2 handouts (note: the sentence frames for Intermediate students on the Access 2 handout contain fewer scaffolds). They will then use the completed sentence frames to help them analyze and annotate the text by completing the Skills Focus questions. Refer to the sample Skills Focus answers to help them complete the sentence frames and annotate the text. **Advanced** **Work in Pairs.** Pair these students with more proficient English speakers to work together on analyzing and annotating the text to complete the Skills Focus questions. If these students need more support, have them use the Sentence Frames on the Access 3 handout as they work with their more proficient peers. **Approaching** **Summarize the Text.** Have these students discuss and complete the text summary on the Access 4 handout and use their summary to help them analyze and annotate the text by completing the Skills Focus questions. Correct answers for the summary are at the end of the lesson plan online. Also refer to the sample Skills Focus answers to aid students with their annotations.
Discuss. After students have read the text, use the sample responses to the Skills Focus questions online to discuss the reading and the process of searching for the ways to identify informational text elements and the relationships between the denotations and connotations of words in the text. Make sure that students have acquired and accurately use academic-specific words and phrases related to the skill, and demonstrate a command of formal English appropriate to the discussion.	**Extend** **Pair and Share.** In small, heterogeneous groups or pairs, ask students to share and discuss their annotations with a focus on the point of view presented in the selection. You can provide students with these questions to guide their discussion: 1. How can you tell the "study session" is very serious? (Thin-Face says that her father's problems are very serious and later speaks of a "struggle meeting".)

Copyright © BookheadEd Learning, LLC

Core Path	Access Path
	2. What does Thin-Face want Ji-Li to do? (He tries to convince her to testify against her father by using words with positive connotations and an anecdote to show that she would be doing good.) 3. What does Ji-Li think about her situation? (She feels "in a trap" and doesn't know what to do, but knows that she is in a difficult position either way.)
	Extend **Search for Denotations and Connotations.** Have students work collaboratively, using a combination of dictionaries, thesauruses, and/or mobile devices, to find a synonym for each vocabulary word. The groups should record the words and at least one synonym for each. Then have students discuss the connotations of each synonym and explain why the author chose the word in the text.
	Extend **Tech Infusion** **Write and Perform.** Ask students to write a dialogue between Ji-Li and her father, occurring that evening when Ji-Li tells her father about the study session. What basic information does Ji-Li share with him? What details does she report? Does she omit anything, and if so, why? How does her father respond—for example, does he ask her to defend him, or to condemn him, or to do what she decides is best? Tell students to choose words whose denotations and connotations express the characters' feelings. Have students record their performance on video and post them using a Padlet wall (http://tinyurl.com/n7l7cyy).

3. WRITE

Core Path	Access Path
Prewrite and Plan. Read the prompt as a class and ask students to brainstorm possible arguments for each side of the issue. Students can brainstorm together either as a class or in small groups to begin planning their responses. Remind your students to look at the memoir and their annotations to find informational text elements and analyze the connotations of specific words and phrases to support their ideas.	**Beginner & Intermediate** **Answer and Discuss.** Have students complete the prewriting questions on the Access 1 and 2 handouts and then explain their answers to a partner before they write. Explain to students that when they answer a question—such as *What arguments could be made for Ji-Li to condemn her father?*—they need to include a detail, example, or quote from the text that supports the statement. For example, students could include the first line, "He made serious mistakes," which reveals that is a reason for her to condemn her father. **Approaching** **Answer Prewriting Questions.** Have students complete the prewriting questions on the Access 4 handout to summarize their thoughts before they write.
	Extend **Organize.** As prewriting, encourage pairs of students to complete a two-column chart listing reasons for and against Ji-Li condemning her father. By working together, students can more easily evaluate which of their reasons are strongest and weakest, and thus decide which to include in their finished arguments.
Discuss. Project these instructions for the peer review onto the board and review them with your class, so they know what they are looking for when they begin to provide their classmates with feedback: • Did the writer give strong support for both sides of the argument? • What textual evidence did the writer use to support each side of the argument? Was this evidence convincing?	

Copyright © BookheadEd Learning, LLC

Core Path	Access Path
• Did the writer refer to the denotations or connotations of words and phrases to support the argument? Was this evidence convincing? • What thing(s) does this response do especially well? • Be sure to tell the writer what he or she did well and what he or she needs to work on. Remember that your comments are most useful when they are constructive. After you've looked at the peer review instructions, review the rubric with students before they begin writing. Allow time for students briefly to raise and discuss questions they may have about the peer review instructions and the rubric. Tell students how many peer reviews they will need to complete once they submit their writing.	
	Extend **Tech Infusion** **Self-Assess.** Before students begin their peer reviews, invite them to discuss previous experiences they have had in reviewing their peers' writing. What strategies have they used? Which strategies worked well, and which worked less well? What do they expect to focus on as they review their classmates' arguments about the memoir? Use a voice recording app (Voice Memo on the iPhone or Smart Voice Recorder for Androids) or VoiceThread (http://tinyurl.com/4m389hy) to capture students' ideas.
Write. Ask students to complete the writing assignment using textual evidence to support their answers. Once they have completed their writing, they should click "Submit."	
Review. Once students complete their writing assignment, they should submit substantive feedback to two peers. Students should use their peers' feedback to improve their writing.	

BLAST:
Lost Generation

OVERVIEW

In this blast, students will learn about the Chinese Cultural Revolution, including its causes, the role children played in the movement, and its effects on the country. Students will research the links below to explore more background on the Cultural Revolution, including the personal stories of people who grew up during that period.

OBJECTIVES

1. Explore background information about the role children played in China's Cultural Revolution.
2. Research using the hyperlinks to learn more about the revolution, along with peoples' personal accounts of their experiences during the Cultural Revolution.
3. Participate effectively in a range of conversations and collaborations to express ideas and build upon the ideas of others.

ELA Common Core Standards:
Reading: Informational Text - RI.6.1
Writing - W.6.1.A, W.6.5, W.6.6
Speaking & Listening - SL.6.1.A, SL.6.1.B, SL.6.1.C, SL.6.1.D, SL.6.2

RESOURCES

Access 1 handout (Beginner)

Access 2 handout (Intermediate)

Access 4 handout (Approaching)

Teacher's Edition

TITLE/DRIVING QUESTION

Core Path	Access Path
Discuss. As a class, read aloud the title and driving question for this Blast. Ask students what they already know about the Cultural Revolution. How did it come about? Taking into account ideas generated by their classmates, do they have a sense of the role children played? Remind students that they should not immediately reply to this question. They'll be returning to this question and responding after they've read the Background and some of the Research Links.	**English Learners All Levels** **Discuss a Visual.** Have students view a photograph of children in China, such as the ones at: http://tinyurl.com/nu6m4yo. Discuss how the picture represents children in China during the Cultural Revolution, prompting students with questions such as: • What is happening in this photo? • What emotion is revealed in the picture? How do you think this person feels? • How do you think this person's life was during this time? • What do you think they feel about the politics of their country? • What do you think they want from their government?
Draft. In their notebooks or on scrap paper, have students draft their initial responses to the driving question. This will provide them with a baseline response that they will be altering as they gain more information about the topic in the Background and Research Links sections of the assignment.	**Beginner & Intermediate** **Draft with Sentence Frame.** When drafting their initial response to the driving question, have students refer to this Blast sentence frame on their Access 1 and 2 handouts: • Children were important to China's Cultural Revolution because they _____. Point out these two key features of the sentence frame: 1. The introductory clause "Children were important to China's Cultural Revolution" borrows language directly from the Blast driving question to provide a response. 2. Ask students to make special note of the word "because," since it asks students to explain.

BACKGROUND

Core Path	Access Path
Read. Have students read the Blast background to provide context for the driving question.	**Beginner & Intermediate** **Read with Support.** Have students read the Blast background to provide context for the driving question. When they encounter unfamiliar words or phrases, have students refer to the glossary on their Access 1 and 2 handouts. If there are unfamiliar words that are not included in their glossary, encourage students to check a dictionary or online reference tool, like http://tinyurl.com/3qe7. **Approaching** **Summarize the Text.** Have students read the Blast background to provide context for the driving question. As they read, ask students to complete the fill in the blank summary of the background provided on their Access 4 handouts. When they encounter unfamiliar words or phrases, have students refer to the glossary on their Access 4 handouts.
Discuss. Either in small groups or as a whole class, use these questions to spur discussion among your students about the Background information. Make sure students follow the rules for collegial discussions. 1. Why did Mao Zedong feel that China needed to "purify its intent" toward communism? (Because people were slipping toward capitalism, owning land and profiting from businesses.) 2. How were younger generations involved in the Cultural Revolution? (They spearheaded it by informing on their parents and elders. They were sent to be educated by peasants on farms.) 3. What happened at the end of the Cultural Revolution? (China became chaotic again, with different factions of the Red Guard vying for power and the economy failing.)	**Beginner & Intermediate** **Discuss.** Pair Beginning and Intermediate with Advanced (or Beyond) students and have them use the dialogue starter on their Access 1 and 2 handouts to discuss the topic. Advise them to return to the dialogue and switch roles if they get stuck. If their conversation is progressing smoothly, encourage them to continue the discussion beyond the dialogue starter sheet. They can expand their conversations to discuss other examples of revolutionary movements or historical dictatorship.

Core Path	Access Path
4. What does *brainwashed* mean? How was it used in the Cultural Revolution? (Brainwashing is when one person or people try to completely change the viewpoint, ideas, and philosophy of another person or people. During the Cultural Revolution, children were brainwashed into betraying their parents and going along with the Red Guard.)	

Brainstorm. Ask students to make two columns in their notebook, one for Chinese children during the Cultural Revolution, and one for Chinese adults. Have them think of problems that were faced by each group.

Here's an example of what that might look like:

Children	Adults
worried about betraying their parents, getting sent to labor camps or to work on farms; no more access to education	worried about being betrayed by their children, getting sent to labor camps or prisons, had to make sure not to be seen as intellectuals

RESEARCH LINKS

Core Path	Access Path
Examine and Explore. Before asking students to explore the research links, use these activities and questions to guide their exploration: 1. Which links would you use to read about specific people's personal stories about the Cultural Revolution? ("China's 'Lost Generation' Recall Hardships of the Cultural Revolution," "One Woman's Journey From Chinese Labor Camp to Top American Tech Entrepreneur," and "My Youth in China")	**English Learners All Levels & Approaching** Ask students to work in pairs as they explore the research links. Have students note any vocabulary they do not understand. They can also note any questions they have about the research.

Please note that excerpts and passages in the StudySync® library, workbooks, and PDFs are intended as touchstones to generate interest in an author's work. The excerpts and passages do not substitute for the reading of entire texts, and StudySync® strongly recommends that teachers and students seek out and purchase the whole literary or informational work in order to experience it as the author intended. Links to online resellers are available in our digital library. In addition, complete works may be ordered through an authorized reseller by filling out and returning to StudySync® the order form enclosed in this workbook.

Teacher's Edition   117

Core Path	Access Path
2. What do you think we can learn from these personal accounts? (We might be able to learn more about the specific ways people's lives were changed by the Cultural Revolution.) 3. Why do you think a link about the cultural history of China is included? (It might give the Cultural Revolution more historical context; it might be helpful to know more about what happened before and after the revolution so we can better understand it.) 4. Read "Reasons for the Cultural Revolution." What positive thing was Mao trying to achieve with the Cultural Revolution? (He wanted the value of physical labor and mental labor to be equal.) Do you think that was a worthwhile effort? Why or why not?	

QUIKPOLL (UP TO 5 ANSWERS)

Core Path	Access Path
Participate. Answer the poll question. Have students discuss their reasons for their answers. Students should refer to evidence from the background and research links to support their answer.	

NUMBER CRUNCH

Core Path	Access Path
Predict, Discuss, and Click. Before students click on the number, break them into pairs and have them make predictions about what they think the number is related to. After they've clicked the number, ask students if they are surprised by the revealed information.	

CREATE YOUR BLAST (140 CHARACTERS)

Core Path	Access Path
Blast. Ask students to write their Blast response in 140 characters or less.	**Beginner** **Blast with Support.** Have students refer back to the sentence frame on their Access 1 handout that they used to create their original Blast draft. Ask them to use this frame to write and enter their final Blast. **Intermediate** **Blast with Support.** Have students attempt to draft their Blast without the sentence frame on their Access 2 handout. If students struggle to compose their Blast draft without the sentence frame, remind them to reference it for support. **Beyond** **Write a Claim.** Ask students to use their answer to the poll question to write a strong claim that could be used as the foundation for a piece of argumentative writing. Once students have written their claims, ask them to read the claims to a small group of their peers. This activity will provide them practice writing claims, as well as expose them to claims written by their peers.
Review. After students have completed their own Blasts, ask them to review the Blasts of their peers and provide feedback.	**Extend** **Discuss.** As a whole class or in groups, identify a few strong blasts and discuss what made those responses so powerful. As a group, analyze and discuss what characteristics make a blast interesting or effective.
	Extend **Revise.** Resend a second version of this Blast assignment to your students and have them submit revised versions of their original Blasts. Do the same responses make the Top 10? How have the answers improved from the first submissions?

Copyright © BookheadEd Learning, LLC

I Am an American: A True Story of Japanese Internment

OVERVIEW

The informational text *I Am an American: A True Story of Japanese Internment,* by Jerry Stanley, examines the causes and effects of Japanese internment in the U.S. after the bombing of Pearl Harbor during World War II. The First Read gives students the opportunity to experience the text with a limited context.

OBJECTIVES

1. Perform an initial reading of a text and demonstrate comprehension by responding to short analysis and inference questions with textual evidence.
2. Practice defining vocabulary words using context.
3. Learn and practice strategies for using possessive pronouns correctly.
4. Participate effectively in a range of conversations and collaborations to express ideas and build upon the ideas of others.

ELA Common Core Standards:
Reading: Informational Text - RI.6.1, RI.6.2, RI.6.3, RI.6.4, RI.6.10
Writing - W.6.7
Speaking & Listening - SL.6.1.A, SL.6.1.C, SL.6.2, SL.6.5
Language - L.6.1.A, L.6.4.A, L.6.4.B, L.6.4.C, L.6.5.B

RESOURCES

Grammar handout: Possessive Pronouns
Access 1 handout (Beginner)
Access 2 handout (Intermediate)
Access 3 handout (Advanced)
Access 4 handout (Approaching)

ACCESS COMPLEX TEXT

In this excerpt from Chapter 2 of *I Am an American: A True Story of Japanese Internment*, author Jerry Stanley explores how the fear that Japan might invade the west coast during World War II led the government to force more 100,000 Japanese Americans into internment camps. To help students understand Stanley's point of view on how this happened, use the following suggestions to provide scaffolded instruction for a close reading of the more complex features of this text:

- **Purpose** - Stanley's overall purpose is to inform and his point of view is one of criticism for the people who acted on false information. To understand the author's purpose and point of view, students will need to analyze how the author uses organizational structure, words, and images to convey information.

- **Connection of Ideas** - The author uses a chronological organization so that students can see how circumstances for the Issei and Nisei changed as events in the war raised new fears. Students will need to trace events and make connections between details in the text in order to understand how and why the government's and public's stand on Japanese Americans changed over time. In addition, students are asked to compare and contrast Stanley's account of events with a video interview with Jimmie Kanaya, a Japanese American who helped his parents move into an internment camp. Students will need to be able to draw connections between these two sources in order to understand how the video adds to their understanding of events.

- **Prior Knowledge** - The text assumes a general understanding of the events of World War II, the terms *Issei* and *Nisei*, and the geography of the Pacific. Students may lack adequate knowledge in these areas.

1. INTRODUCTION

Core Path	Access Path
Read and Listen. Individually or as a class, read and listen to the Introduction for *I Am an American: A True Story of Japanese Internment*. The introduction provides context for the excerpt taken from Chapter 2.	**English Learners All Levels & Approaching Read and Listen.** Ask students to read and listen to the introduction for *I Am an American: A True Story of Japanese Internment*. Have them refer to the vocabulary listing on their Access 1, 2, 3, and 4 handouts for definitions of key vocabulary terms. If there are unfamiliar words that are not included in their glossary, encourage students to check a dictionary or online reference tool, like http://tinyurl.com/6ytby.

Core Path	Access Path
	Approaching **Summarize.** Ask students to use their Access 4 handout to fill in the blanks of the Introduction summary with their classmates. Answers are located at the end of this lesson plan online. Have them refer to the glossary for definitions of key vocabulary terms. If there are unfamiliar words that are not included in their glossary, encourage students to check a dictionary or online reference tool, like http://tinyurl.com/6ytby.
Build Background. The text assumes a general understanding of the events of World War II with which students may not be familiar. In pairs or small groups, ask students to research textual and multimedia references. Assign each group a topic to investigate. Make sure students follow the rules for collegial discussions. 1. "Issei" and "Nisei": What do these terms mean, and how might the use of these terms have served to isolate Japanese Americans from other citizens during World War II? 2. Pearl Harbor: What happened here and why? 3. War Bonds: What are they, and how does buying them show patriotism? 4. Tokyo: Where is it, and why might it be a desirable target for the U.S. during World War II? 5. San Francisco, Los Angeles, and Seattle: Where are these cities, and why did many of the Japanese American demonstrations take place in these cities? 6. Japanese American Citizens League: What is it, and what was its purpose during World War II?	**Beginner & Approaching** **Complete and Discuss the Chart.** Pair Beginning and Approaching students with more proficient (Beyond) readers. Have these groups complete the "Imagine" exercise on the Access 1 and 4 handouts that asks students to consider what their own responses would be in the situation described. Have the pairs generate ideas, discuss the chart, and complete it together. **Intermediate & Advanced** **Complete and Discuss the Chart.** Pair Intermediate and Advanced students, and have them complete the "Imagine" exercises on the Access 2 and 3 handouts that ask students to consider what their own responses would be in a situation like the one that Japanese American faced early in World War II. Have the pairs generate ideas, discuss the chart, and complete it together.

Core Path	Access Path
7. Guam, Hong Kong, Manila, Singapore: Where are these places, and why did Japanese victories here cause the U.S. to fear a west coast invasion? Students may record their findings in print or digital graphic organizers and present them to the class. Each group may also include multimedia components and visual displays as part of their presentations. Remind students to use appropriate eye contact, adequate volume, clear pronunciation, and appropriate gestures when presenting orally. You may wish to have groups create a video recording of their presentations.	
	Extend **Analyze and Discuss a Quotation.** "We saw all these people behind the fence, looking out, hanging onto the wire, and looking out because they were anxious to know who was coming in. But I will never forget the shocking feeling that human beings were behind this fence like animals [crying]. And we were going to also lose our freedom and walk inside of that gate and find ourselves … cooped up there … when the gates were shut, we knew that we had lost something that was very precious; that we were no longer free" (Mary Tsukamoto). Lead students in a discussion of this quote. • What setting does Tsukamoto describe? • Why does Tsukamoto call freedom "precious"? • Why might the narrator compare the people in the camp to animals?

2. READ

Core Path	Access Path
Make Predictions about Vocabulary. There are five bold vocabulary words in the text. As students read the text, ask them to make predictions about what they think each bold vocabulary word means based on the context clues in the sentence. If you are in a low tech classroom and students are reading from printed copies or a projected text, ask students to record predictions in their notes, so they can be easily referenced in class. If your students have access to technology, they can use the annotation tool to make their predictions.	**Note:** This exercise, which extends vocabulary instruction, should be completed when the class shifts from whole group instruction to individual work during the "Read and Annotate" exercise.

Core Path (continued):

It might be helpful to model this practice for students before they begin reading. Either using the board or projecting the actual text, focus in on the sentence that uses the word "sabotage":

- He ordered the Federal Bureau of Investigation to arrest approximately 16,000 enemy aliens suspected of espionage or sabotage, but within weeks he released two-thirds of them.

Model for the class how to use the overall structure and meaning of the sentence and the sentences around it, the word's position, and other clues to define the unfamiliar vocabulary word. In this case, point out these context clues:

1. Look at the structure of the sentence. What word appears to be a synonym for "sabotage"? ("espionage") Yes, but "espionage" may be an unfamiliar word, too. Let's look at the rest of the sentence. What is the result for people who are suspected of espionage or sabotage? (They are arrested.) So, we know that these words describe something illegal.

Access Path (continued):

Beginner, Intermediate & Approaching Pair Practice.

1. Pair students with more proficient readers.

2. Give them an additional sentence that contains a new vocabulary word.

3. Ask the students to complete a Think Aloud using the teacher-led Make Predictions about Vocabulary activity as a model, while the proficient student actively listens.

4. The student should use the context clues in the sentence to try to determine the meaning of the new vocabulary word.

5. After the student has completed the Think Aloud and made a prediction about the word's meaning, allow time for the proficient reader to add his/her own thoughts and clarify any points of confusion.

6. Once they've completed this Think Aloud, encourage them to use a dictionary to confirm the definition of the new vocabulary word. Have them refer to the vocabulary listing on their Access 1, 2, and 4 handouts for definitions of key vocabulary terms in the text. Encourage them to add any additional vocabulary words or idioms they find in the text and look up definitions for those words and idioms online or in a dictionary.

Core Path	Access Path
2. Notice that if we keep reading, the word "sabotage" appears several more times in this text: "the report blamed the disaster [Pearl Harbor] on ... Japanese sabotage"; "Although the report of Japanese sabotage on Hawaii was totally false, newspaper writers and radio broadcasters began warning of the danger of Japanese sabotage on the west coast." Here, Japanese Americans are accused of helping the Japanese bomb Pearl Harbor in Hawaii, which is not only illegal, but something done on purpose.	
3. We know that "sabotage" means something illegal and we have an example of an alleged act of sabotage. Therefore, we can determine that "sabotage" means "an illegal act of destruction." Checking in a dictionary reveals that it means "destroying or damaging something so that it does not work correctly."	

Model Reading Comprehension Strategy. Before students begin reading, model the reading comprehension strategy of summarizing by using this Think Aloud that talks students through the first paragraph of text. First explain to your students that summarizing is selecting, organizing, and synthesizing the most important elements of a text to restate in one's own words.

Model for students how summarizing will help them better comprehend the selection and help drive their discussions.

- When I read the first paragraph, I see a sequence word, "After," so I know that I'm reading about a sequence of events. First, the Japanese bombed Pearl Harbor. After this event, Japanese Americans tried to show their loyalty to the U.S. by engaging in mass demonstrations of loyalty.

- The text gives many examples of these mass demonstrations, but I don't need to list them all in a summary. I'll select just two or three to include, such as buying war bonds and donating blood.

Note: This exercise, which extends vocabulary instruction, should be completed when the class shifts from whole group instruction to individual work during the "Read and Annotate" exercise.

Beginner, Intermediate & Approaching
Apply Reading Comprehension Strategy.

1. Have students listen to the audio version of the excerpt from I Am an American. As they listen to the audio recording, pause the recording periodically and allow students the opportunity to summarize, in their own words, what is happening. Instruct them to write a one-sentence summary whenever you pause the recording.

2. Once they have listened to the audio version and periodically summarized what they heard, pair students with more proficient readers and ask them to share what they summarized and why. Why did they include particular details and leave others out?

Please note that excerpts and passages in the StudySync® library, workbooks, and PDFs are intended as touchstones to generate interest in an author's work. The excerpts and passages do not substitute for the reading of entire texts, and StudySync® strongly recommends that teachers and students seek out and purchase the whole literary or informational work in order to experience it as the author intended. Links to online resellers are available in our digital library. In addition, complete works may be ordered through an authorized reseller by filling out and returning to StudySync® the order form enclosed in this workbook.

Teacher's Edition   **125**

Core Path	Access Path
• I notice that these demonstrations took place in Seattle, San Francisco and Los Angeles, which are west coast cities. I will include this information in a summary. • Finally, I notice that one example of the demonstrations was a telegram to the president. This act seems important so I will include it in my summary, as well. • By selecting, organizing, and synthesizing this information, I have made sure that I understand it and I'm more likely to remember it for future situations, such as tests, essays, or discussions.	3. Allow pairs time to discuss their summaries. Were there any details from the text that were not included in either summary? If so, encourage them to add details to the summaries based on their conversations.

Core Path	Access Path
Read and Annotate. Have students read and annotate the excerpt. Ask students to use the annotation tool as they read to: 1. use context clues to analyze and determine the meaning of the bolded vocabulary terms 2. ask questions about passages of the text that may be unclear or unresolved 3. identify key information, events, ideas, and connections between them 4. note unfamiliar vocabulary 5. capture reactions to the events and ideas in the text	**Beginner** **Coach the Reading.** While other students read, annotate, and discuss the text independently, work with Beginning students, listening to the audio of the text and pausing periodically or when any student has a question. Coach students in articulating their questions for the group and in highlighting and annotating the text. Have students use the Annotation Guide on the Access 1 handout to support them as they highlight and annotate the text. For further support, ask questions about the text such as: • Is there anything about the reading that you don't understand? • What do you think will happen to the Japanese American community? • Why do you think the author chose the title *I Am an American*? **Intermediate** **Listen to the Audio.** Have these students listen to the audio of the text and use the definitions on the Access 2 handout to help them with words or idioms that may be unfamiliar. If students need help with annotating the text, have them use the Annotation Guide on the Access 2 handout. After working with the Beginning students, you may wish to check this group's progress and provide support as needed.

Core Path	Access Path
	Advanced **Pair with Proficient Peers.** Have Advanced students work with English proficient peers to read, annotate, and discuss the text. Have students use the Annotation Guide in the Access 3 handout to support them as they highlight and annotate the text. Encourage them to listen to the audio of the text if needed. **Approaching** **Use the Annotation Guide.** Have students use the Annotation Guide on the Access 4 handout to support them as they highlight and annotate the text.
Discuss. In small groups or pairs, have students discuss the questions and inferences they made while reading. Make sure students follow the rules for collegial discussions: Refer to Collaborative Discussions in the Speaking & Listening Handbook. 1. How does noting that the text is organized in chronological or time sequence help readers summarize? (Readers may organize a summary in the same way, as a series of chronological events: Pearl Harbor → FBI Investigations → Military Losses in the Pacific → Media propaganda → Internment.) 2. In addition to a sequence of events, the text cites cause-and-effect relationships. How might recognizing this text structure help readers summarize? (Readers may organize a summary in the same way, as a series of causes and effects: Pearl Harbor, losses in the Pacific, and media propaganda led to Japanese internment.) 3. Readers may also note that the text assigns blame for Japanese internment to government and military leaders as well as to the media. How might recognizing the responsibilities of these parties help readers summarize? (Readers may highlight these groups in a summary structured by cause and effect: Government investigations, military losses in the Pacific, and media warnings of Japanese sabotage on the west coast led to Japanese internment.)	**English Learners All Levels & Approaching** Use the extra time while on–and beyond–grade level students are discussing their first reads of the text to work individually and in small groups with Approaching readers and English Learners as outlined above. Should those students complete their first reads quickly, integrate them into the on–and beyond–grade level discussion groups. Otherwise, English Learners and approaching readers will be given an opportunity to participate in text discussions with their peers later in the lesson. **Beyond** **Tech Infusion** **Brainstorm.** Pair students and ask them to brainstorm ways that the Japanese Americans affected by the internment program could respond to their treatment. Students who have access to a backchannel tool such as TodaysMeet (http://tinyurl.com/nogqjow) may enjoy brainstorming in that medium.

Please note that excerpts and passages in the StudySync® library, workbooks, and PDFs are intended as touchstones to generate interest in an author's work. The excerpts and passages do not substitute for the reading of entire texts, and StudySync® strongly recommends that teachers and students seek out and purchase the whole literary or informational work in order to experience it as the author intended. Links to online resellers are available in our digital library. In addition, complete works may be ordered through an authorized reseller by filling out and returning to StudySync® the order form enclosed in this workbook.

Teacher's Edition   **127**

Core Path	Access Path
(G) **Grammar, Usage, and Mechanics.** Distribute the StudySync grammar handout on possessive pronouns. Review with students the use of possessive pronouns as explained in the handout. Then, have students complete the practice exercise. (Answers for the practice exercise appear at the end of the lesson plan online.) Finally, encourage students to apply what they have learned by analyzing the use of possessive pronouns in *I Am an American: A True Story of Japanese Internment.* Ask students:	**Beginner & Intermediate** **Work with the Teacher.** Remind these students that pronouns are words that can be used to represent other, more specific nouns. For example, the pronoun *he* can stand in for a person with a proper name such as *Jim* or *Pablo*.

Core Path

1. Reread the first sentence of paragraph 2. What possessive pronoun is used in this sentence? (our) What is the pronoun's antecedent? (Japanese American Citizens League) What items in the sentence are possessed by the pronoun? (the first use of *our* refers to *cooperation*, the second to *country*)

2. Is the pronoun in the previous example singular or plural? (plural) Explain what this choice indicates about the pronoun's antecedent. (The pronoun is not referring to the Japanese American Citizens League as a single organization, but instead is referring to all those represented by the League.)

3. Rewrite the following sentence from paragraph 3 so that it uses a standalone possessive pronoun: "This is their country."("This country is theirs.")

4. Identify the possessive pronoun in the last sentence of paragraph 4. (their) How does this pronoun help explain why the Nisei were considered loyal citizens? (It indicates that the parents of the Nisei had done nothing to aid Japan.)

Access Path

Possessive pronouns are those that indicate possession of something. For example, instead of *Jim's hat* or *Pablo's shoe*, one could say "his hat" or "his shoe."

Write the following sentence on the board: *Julie's book is missing.*
Ask: *What pronoun could you replace* Julie's *with? (her)*

Then work with students to recognize other pairs of nouns and possessive pronouns, such as *we/our* and *them/their.*

Advanced & Beyond
Extend the Search. Challenge these students to work in pairs or small groups to find examples of pronouns and possessive pronouns in the text.

Approaching
Analyze an Example. If students need more support identifying possessive pronouns, call their attention to these words in paragraph 2: *we pledge our fullest cooperation to you, and to our country.* Ask: *Which word is a possessive pronoun?* Remind students that possessive pronouns indicate that someone possesses something. Ask: *Which word in the quotation indicates that?*

3. THINK

Core Path	Access Path
Answer and Discuss. Have students complete the Think questions and then use the peer review instructions and rubric to complete two peer reviews. Refer to the sample answers at the end of the lesson plan online to discuss responses with your students.	**Beginner & Intermediate** **Sentence Frames.** Have students use the Sentence Frames on the Access 1 and 2 handouts to support their responses to the Think questions. If necessary, distribute sentence frames to Advanced students as well. **Advanced** **Justice Served.** Have students use the chart on their Access 3 handout to help them think about the themes of the reading and identify the evidence needed to answer the questions. **Approaching** **Find the Evidence.** Have students use Find the Evidence on the Access 4 handout to help them identify the evidence needed to answer the questions.
	Extend **Debate.** Present students with an issue from the text that can be debated. Allow students to debate the issue as a class or in smaller groups. Debate prompts: • In a time of war, it is right to condemn or intern a whole group of people? • If the government made a mistake in interning Japanese Americans, what are these people and their families owed?
	Extend **Tech Infusion** **Blog.** Have pairs of students use a blogging tool such as Edublogs (http://tinyurl.com/dygdcc5) or Blogger (http://tinyurl.com/5x8z) to write a blog entry about the responsibilities of media in wartime. Students may cite textual evidence, describing the role of the media in Japanese internment during World War II.

Copyright © BookheadEd Learning, LLC

OVERVIEW

Determining the author's purpose and author's point of view in an informational text is a key to analyzing the credibility of the information and forming one's own opinions about a subject. This lesson plan provides follow-up questions and useful enrichments to help teachers guide students toward a usable, repeatable method for uncovering author's purpose and author's point of view.

OBJECTIVES

1. Learn the definitions of author's purpose and author's point of view.
2. Practice using concrete strategies for identifying and analyzing author's purpose and author's point of view.
3. Participate effectively in a range of conversations and collaborations to express ideas and build upon the ideas of others.

ELA Common Core Standards:
Reading: Informational Text - RI.6.1, RI.6.4, RI.6.6
Speaking & Listening - SL.6.1.A, SL.6.1.B, SL.6.1.C, SL.6.2, SL.6.5

RESOURCES

Access 1 handout (Beginner)

Access 2 handout (Intermediate)

Access 3 handout (Advanced)

Access 4 handout (Approaching)

1. DEFINE

Core Path	Access Path
Watch. Watch the Concept Definition video on author's purpose and author's point of view with your students. Make sure students understand why it's critical to know an author's purpose or point of view when trying to unlock the meaning of a text. Pause the video at these key moments to discuss the information with your students:	**Beginner & Approaching** **Match.** Have students complete the matching exercise on the Access 1 and 4 handouts as they watch the video. Answers are located at the end of the lesson plan online.
1. 1:00 – Can you think of any other purpose (or purposes) an author might have? How does genre affect purpose; i.e., how might the purpose of a fiction text differ from that of an informational text? How might it stay the same?	**Intermediate & Advanced** **Complete a Chart.** Have pairs of students complete the chart on their Access 2 and 3 handouts based on the Concept Definition video. Encourage students to expand the discussion with ideas of their own.
2. 1:18 – Are there any other elements of a text that might offer clues into an author's purpose or point of view? What are some additional resources we can use if we're having trouble deciphering the purpose or point of view?	
3. 2:03 – Why don't authors of fiction or poetry state their purposes clearly in the same way a politician or an essayist might?	

Core Path	Access Path
Read and Discuss. After watching the Concept Definition video, have students read the definition of author's purpose and point of view. Either in small groups or as a whole class, use these questions to engage students in a discussion about author's purpose and point of view:	**Beginner & Approaching** **Find the Purpose.** To prepare students to participate in the discussion, have them complete the chart on the Access 1 and 4 handouts with the correct author's purpose as they read the definition. The correct answers are located at the end of the lesson plan online.
• How does an author's point of view reveal purpose? (An author makes choices about how and what information to include, which helps to reveal his purpose.)	
• How might the words "healthiest" and "taste best" reveal a positive point of view toward organic farming? (These words have positive connotations; as a result, they make organic farming sound more appealing to readers and indicate that the author believes it is beneficial.)	**Intermediate & Advanced** **Discuss Prompts.** To help these students participate in the discussion, prompt them with questions that can be answered with a few words, such as: • What purpose does the author have to write *I Am an American*? (inform; explain)

Copyright © BookheadEd Learning, LLC

Core Path	Access Path
• What words might reveal a negative point of view toward organic farming? (Answers will vary: "expensive," "trendy," or "imperfect.")	• What does it mean for an author to have a point of view? (An author has ideas and/or opinions about his or her subject, such as the importance of a historical event.)
	Beyond **Discuss.** Have students think of something they've read in which the author expresses a clear point of view. Compile a list of examples. Have students discuss how the point of view of each work affects what the reader learns about the subject of the writing. How might a switch in point of view affect what the reader learns?
	Extend **Tech Infusion** **Graph It.** After watching the video, have pairs or groups of students design and create graphic organizers to help them analyze author's purpose and point of view. Students can use resources such as Bubbl.us (http://tinyurl.com/34u5mr) or Teach-nology (http://tinyurl.com/4u5xb). Recommend that students include spaces for the following topics: • comparison and contrast • language and word choice • facts and statistics • figurative language • any other topics that students determine Have students present their organizers to the class. Lead the class to choose one organizer for reproduction that all will use to analyze the text.

2. MODEL

Core Path	Access Path
Read and Annotate. Have students independently read the Model section. As they read, ask students to use the annotation tool to: • highlight key points • ask questions • identify places where the Model applies the strategies laid out in the Identification and Application section	**Note:** During this portion of the lesson, instruction shifts from whole group to individual work. Use this time to work one-on-one or in small groups with Beginning, Intermediate, Advanced, and Approaching students. **Beginner & Intermediate** **Coach the Reading.** Work with these students (either individually or in small groups) to fill out the guided reading questions on the Access 1 and 2 handouts. Have Beginning students refer to the glossary on the Access 1 handout to help them determine the meaning of difficult words. (note: Provide the Access 1 handout glossary to Intermediate students if necessary.) Let students know they'll use these answers to help participate in the discussion about the Model. Sample answers for this exercise are located at the end of the lesson online plan. **Advanced** **Identify Evidence.** Provide these students with the same instructions to read and annotate as on-grade level and Beyond students. In addition, ask Advanced students to complete the Identifying Evidence exercise on the Access 3 handout. Let students know that they'll use these answers to help participate in the discussion about the Model. Sample answers for this exercise are located at the end of the lesson plan online. **Approaching** **Guided Reading.** Have students complete the guided reading questions on the Access 4 handout as they read. Let them know that they'll use these answers to help participate in the discussion about the Model. Sample answers for this exercise are located at the end of the lesson plan online.

Please note that excerpts and passages in the StudySync® library, workbooks, and PDFs are intended as touchstones to generate interest in an author's work. The excerpts and passages do not substitute for the reading of entire texts, and StudySync® strongly recommends that teachers and students seek out and purchase the whole literary or informational work in order to experience it as the author intended. Links to online resellers are available in our digital library. In addition, complete works may be ordered through an authorized reseller by filling out and returning to StudySync® the order form enclosed in this workbook.

Teacher's Edition   133

Core Path	Access Path
Discuss. After students read the Model text, use these questions to facilitate a whole group discussion that helps students understand how to analyze author's purpose and point of view in the passage:	

1. How does the Model define the author's purpose? (The model acknowledges that the title of this nonfiction text points at a sequence of events intended to inform readers.)

2. How does the Model identify clues that reveal the author's point of view? (In the course of analyzing the way the text is structured, the Model points out a contrast between a quotation and an action by the same man. This contrast presents Biddle in a negative light, which suggests that the author does not approve of Biddle or his actions on behalf of the U.S. government.)

3. How does the Model move on to confirm its initial assessment of the author's point of view? (The Model points out another contrast between facts and actions. This contrast confirms the author's negative point of view toward Japanese internment and assigns blame for this event.)

4. According to the Model, how does determining the author's point of view clarify a purpose for reading? (The Model explains that readers can consider the author's viewpoint as they read in order to determine whether or not they agree with it and why.)

Core Path	Access Path
	Extend **Tech Infusion** **Analyze Point of View.** Have pairs of students use print or digital two-column graphic organizers (http://tinyurl.com/k53lde2) to analyze the author's point of view. In the left column, have students write the three groups to whom the author assigns blame for the error of Japanese internment: California Hotheads, the media, and the military. In the right column, have students write questions and comments for the author regarding his presentation of each party's role in the events. Ask volunteers to present selected entries from their charts to the class. Then, lead the class to discuss whether the author's point of view is credible and why.

3. YOUR TURN

Core Path	Access Path
Assess and Explain. Have students answer the comprehension questions to test for understanding. Share the explanations for Parts A and B (located online) with your students.	
	Extend **Tech Infusion** **Blog a Reaction.** Have students use Kidblog (http://tinyurl.com/cun9ae3) or Edublogs (http://tinyurl.com/ytgznw) to post blog entries in reaction to the signing of Executive Order No. 9066 from the points of view of Japanese Americans. Encourage students to use the informal, personal voice that bloggers often use. Students may wish to work in pairs.

OVERVIEW

Determining how to use media in conjunction with a text can be challenging for students. This lesson plan provides follow-up questions and useful enrichments to help teachers guide students toward a usable, repeatable method for using media to enhance understanding of a text.

OBJECTIVES

1. Learn the definition of media.
2. Practice using concrete strategies for evaluating media.
3. Participate effectively in a range of conversations and collaborations to express ideas and build upon the ideas of others.

ELA Common Core Standards:
Reading: Informational Text - RI.6.1, RI.6.6, RI.6.7
Speaking & Listening - SL.6.1.A, SL.6.1.B, SL.6.1.C, SL.6.2

RESOURCES

Access 1 handout (Beginner)

Access 2 handout (Intermediate)

Access 3 handout (Advanced)

Access 4 handout (Approaching)

1. DEFINE

Core Path	Access Path
Watch. Watch the Concept Definition video on media with your students. Have your students write down the definition of "media" and consider the many different kinds of media, as well as the role of technology in the dissemination of information. Pause the video at these key moments to discuss the information with your students: 1. 0:26 – How is a photograph a method of communication? What type of message is communicated? How does the audience receive and interpret the message? 2. 0:36 – In what ways have the traditional media of speech, writing, and visuals been incorporated into new forms of social media such as Twitter or Facebook? 3. 1:10 – How might the experience of receiving and interpreting the joke the girl tells change if the joke was conveyed through a different medium?	**Beginner & Approaching** **Match.** Have students complete the matching exercise on the Access 1 and 4 handouts as they watch the video. Answers are located at the end of the lesson plan online. **Intermediate & Advanced** **Complete a Chart.** Have pairs of students complete the chart on their Access 2 and 3 handouts based on the Concept Definition video. Encourage students to expand the discussion with ideas of their own.
Read and Discuss. After watching the Concept Definition video, have students read the definition of media. Either in small groups or as a whole class, use these questions to engage students in a discussion about media. Make sure students follow the rules for collegial discussions. • How might the explosion of media options in the 19th century have affected the ways in which historical events were recorded and published? • Historical information may be presented in a variety of media through the points of view of primary and secondary sources. In what ways might different media affect the public's understanding of historical events? • How has the explosion of social media, where information can be posted moments after an event, affected the recording and understanding of modern historical events?	**Beginner & Approaching** **Audience or Communicator?** To prepare students to participate in the discussion, have them complete the chart about media on the Access 1 and 4 handouts as they read the definition. The correct answers are located at the end of the lesson plan online. **Intermediate & Advanced** **Discuss Prompts.** To help these students participate in the discussion, prompt them with questions that can be answered with a few words, such as: • What are two types of media from which you get important information? (Internet, TV, etc.) • What are some differences between those types? (Answers will vary, but should reflect direct student experience of the two types.) • Does either form of media seem better or more useful than the other? Explain. (Answers will vary.)

Core Path	Access Path
	Beyond **Discuss.** Have students compare two or more types of media and their differences. Are they equally trustworthy? Is there a type of media students do not trust in terms of accuracy or truthfulness? If so, why?
	Extend **Analyze the Medium and the Message.** Form student groups and provide each group with different media reports on a current topic or issue: print news story, online newspaper or magazine article, tweet, and a blog, for example. Ask each group to analyze its sample(s) using the following focus questions: • What is the medium and what are its unique features? • How is the topic presented within the medium—factual or editorial? formal or informal? graphic elements or no? and so on. • What is your reaction to the content? Is this reaction dictated by the information or the unique features of the medium or both? Explain. Students can record their responses in print or digital graphic organizers.

2. MODEL

Core Path	Access Path
Read and Annotate. Have students independently read the Model section. As they read, ask students to use the annotation tool to: • highlight key points • ask questions • identify places where the Model applies the strategies laid out in the Identification and Application section	**Note:** During this portion of the lesson, instruction shifts from whole group to individual work. Use this time to work one-on-one or in small groups with Beginning, Intermediate, Advanced, and Approaching students.

Copyright © BookheadEd Learning, LLC

Core Path	Access Path
Note: This Media lesson utilizes a video from the National WWII Museum archive. That link is provided to students in the lesson and can be viewed from your teacher account using the "Student Preview" button in the Instructional Path online. A copy of the URL is also provided here for your convenience: http://tinyurl.com/pyqcsjv.	**Beginner & Intermediate** **Coach the Reading.** Work with these students (either individually or in small groups) to fill out the guided reading questions on the Access 1 and 2 handouts. Have Beginning students refer to the glossary on the Access 1 handout to help them determine the meaning of difficult words. (note: Provide the Access 1 handout glossary to Intermediate students if necessary.) Let students know they'll use these answers to help participate in the discussion about the Model. Sample answers for this exercise are located at the end of the lesson online plan. **Advanced** **Identify Evidence.** Provide these students with the same instructions to read and annotate as on-grade level and Beyond students. In addition, ask Advanced students to complete the identifying evidence exercise on the Access 3 handout. Let students know that they'll use these answers to help participate in the discussion about the Model. Sample answers for this exercise are located at the end of the lesson plan online. **Approaching** **Guided Reading.** Have students complete the guided reading questions on the Access 4 handout as they read. Let them know that they'll use these answers to help participate in the discussion about the Model. Sample answers for this exercise are located at the end of the lesson plan online.

Discuss. After students read the Model text, use these questions to facilitate a whole group discussion that helps students understand how to relate media about the same topic to the passage:

1. What's the first step this Model uses in analyzing the textual medium? (It identifies information that is not included as part of the text.)

Core Path	Access Path
2. What observation does the Model make about this omission? (The Model notes that it leaves the readers in the same position as Roosevelt, without personal knowledge or firsthand accounts of Japanese living in America.) 3. What does the Model do next? (It identifies a source of the missing information in the form of a video interview.) 4. What is one way that the Model differentiates between the two forms of media? (The text is a secondary source, while the video is a primary source.) 5. What other questions might you ask when comparing different media other than those in the Model? (What is the most effective way to convey historical information?) 6. How do the two media in the Model work together to provide the audience with information about a historical event? (The two media provide different points of view or perspectives regarding the event, making the audience's understanding of the event richer.)	
	Extend **Tech Infusion** **Concept Map.** Pair students and have them read transcripts of Executive Order No. 9066 online (http://tinyurl.com/nfmb9jb). If necessary, help students to paraphrase pertinent sections of text. Then, have students prepare concept maps with "Executive Order No. 9066" written in the center circle. (Students can use Bubbl.us [http://tinyurl.com/yceu2jg] or Google Drawings [http://tinyurl.com/mtddzfx] to create their maps online.) In each of the radiating circles, have students respond to the following: • What is Jerry Stanley's point of view and why does Stanley choose to express his point of view in textual form? • What is Jimmie Kanaya's point of view and why does Kanaya choose to express his point of view in the form of a video interview?

Core Path	Access Path
	• What is the point of view of President Roosevelt and why does he choose to express his point of view in the form of an executive order? Have volunteer pairs present selected entries from their diagrams to the class. Then, lead the class to discuss how the different media work together to develop students' understanding of the topic.

3. YOUR TURN

Core Path	Access Path
Assess and Explain. Have students answer the comprehension questions to test for understanding. Share the explanations for Parts A and B (located online) with your students.	
	Extend **Interpret Figures of Speech.** Ask students to recall the idiom "under one's breath" used in the video interview. Explain that the phrase is figurative. A figure of speech is a phrase that has a meaning separate from the meanings of its individual words. To say something "under one's breath," is to say it quietly in hopes that others cannot hear one's exact words. Ask if students know of any other examples. Use "keep an eye on something" as an example to spur further discussion.

OVERVIEW

Jerry Stanley's informational text *I Am an American: A True Story of Japanese Internment* examines the causes and effects of Japanese internment in the U.S. after the bombing of Pearl Harbor during World War II. The Close Read gives students the opportunity to analyze the text and apply their understanding of author's purpose, point of view, and media.

OBJECTIVES

1. Complete a close reading of an informational text.
2. Practice and apply concrete strategies for identifying author's purpose and point of view and comparing and contrasting different forms of media.
3. Participate in conversations and collaborations to express ideas and build upon the ideas of others.
4. Prewrite, plan, and produce clear and coherent writing in response to a prompt.

ELA Common Core Standards:
Reading: Informational Text - RI.6.1, RI.6.3, RI.6.4, RI.6.6, RI.6.7, RI.6.10
Writing - W.6.4, W.6.5, W.6.6, W.6.10
Speaking & Listening - SL.6.1.A, SL.6.1.B, SL.6.1.C, SL.6.1.D, SL.6.6
Language - L.6.4.A, L.6.4.C, L.6.4.D

RESOURCES

I Am an American: A True Story of Japanese Internment Vocabulary handout
I Am an American: A True Story of Japanese Internment Graphic organizer
Access 1 handout (Beginner)
Access 2 handout (Intermediate)
Access 3 handout (Advanced)
Access 4 handout (Approaching)

1. INTRODUCTION

Core Path	Access Path
Define and Compare. Project the vocabulary words and definitions onto the board or provide students with handouts so they can copy the vocabulary into their notebooks. Suggest that students consult general and specialized reference materials, both print and digital, to compare the precise meaning of a specific word with their initial vocabulary predictions from the First Read. Review words that students defined incorrectly to understand why they were unable to use context clues to develop usable definitions.	**Beginner & Intermediate** **Complete the Sentences.** Have students complete the sentence frames on the Access 1 and 2 handouts using the vocabulary words. Point out that some of the words are in the questions and some will be in the answers. Sample answers are located at the end of the lesson plan online. **Advanced & Beyond** **Write in Journals.** Have students write a journal entry using all of their vocabulary words. Remind them to write sentences that communicate the meaning of the words they are using. **Approaching** **Graphic Organizer.** To support students in comparing their predictions with the correct meanings, have them complete the graphic organizer on the Access 4 handout to record the vocabulary words, their initial analysis, and the definitions. Then have them write sentences using the words.
Review. Have students complete the fill in the blank vocabulary worksheet for this selection. Answers for the worksheet are listed at the end of the lesson plan online.	
	Extend **Tech Infusion** **Create.** Using iPad or Android art apps, have students create signs that Japanese American demonstrators might have carried at one of the mass demonstrations of loyalty following the bombing of Pearl Harbor. Tell students to incorporate vocabulary words into the text and to include graphics as well. Have students present their signs to the class.

Please note that excerpts and passages in the StudySync® library, workbooks, and PDFs are intended as touchstones to generate interest in an author's work. The excerpts and passages do not substitute for the reading of entire texts, and StudySync® strongly recommends that teachers and students seek out and purchase the whole literary or informational work in order to experience it as the author intended. Links to online resellers are available in our digital library. In addition, complete works may be ordered through an authorized reseller by filling out and returning to StudySync® the order form enclosed in this workbook.

Teacher's Edition   143

Core Path	Access Path
	Extend **Tech Infusion** **Link Words to History.** Form student groups and assign each group one of the following words: "demonstrations," "internment," "sabotage." Have students conduct research to find other examples of each word in U.S. or world history. Students may record their findings in print or digital graphic organizers. Have each group share selected entries with the class.

2. READ

Core Path	Access Path
Model Close Reading. Project the text onto the board and model a close reading of the text using the annotation strategies mentioned below and on the following page. While modeling annotation strategies, make notes that tie the text to the focus skills and demonstrate what students should be looking for as they read. Here is some guidance for you as you annotate with your students: • As the Skills lessons on Author's Purpose and Author's Point of View and Media that precede this text make clear, all media—including text and video—are produced with purpose. Elements such as structure, words, and images convey an author's, a speaker's, or a producer's point of view in achieving this purpose. The unique features of any particular medium may affect some of these intentions or choices. Often, two media on the same topic will help an audience develop a broad understanding of a topic or issue.	

Core Path	Access Path
• Focusing on the text, the author's use of sequence words and phrases, such as "After Pearl Harbor" (in paragraph 1) and "At first" (in paragraph 3) reveal one purpose (to inform). However, as we discover the author's point of view on the subject (criticism of those who acted negatively based on false information), another purpose may be revealed later, in paragraph 8 (to explain the causes of Japanese internment): "Although the charge of Japanese sabotage on Hawaii was totally false, newspaper writers and radio broadcasters began warning of the danger of Japanese sabotage on the west coast." • Finally, we may note that the author says in the final paragraph that order 9066 "never mentioned the Japanese by name." We have to go to the video to find the names and faces of people affected by the order. Then, we can integrate this information to develop our understanding of the topic as well as analyze how we are affected by the elements of each medium.	

Read and Annotate. Read the Skills Focus questions as a class, so your students know what they should pay close attention to as they read. Then have students read and annotate the excerpt. Ask students to use the annotation tool as they read to: 1. respond to the Skills Focus section 2. ask questions 3. make connections 4. identify key information, examples, events, and details 5. note unfamiliar vocabulary 6. capture their reaction to the ideas and examples in the text As they reread the text, remind students to use the comprehension strategy of Summarizing that they learned in the First Read.	**Note:** While on–grade level students are reading and annotating, work one-on-one or in small groups with Beginning, Intermediate, Advanced, and Approaching students to support them as they read and annotate the text. **Beginner & Intermediate** **Summarize and Analyze the Text.** Work with these students to complete the sentence frames on the Access 1 and 2 handouts (note: the sentence frames for Intermediate students on the Access 2 handout contain fewer scaffolds). They will then use the completed sentence frames to help them analyze and annotate the text by completing the Skills Focus questions. Refer to the sample Skills Focus answers to help them complete the sentence frames and annotate the text.

Core Path	Access Path
	Advanced **Work in Pairs.** Pair these students with more proficient English speakers to work together on analyzing and annotating the text to complete the Skills Focus questions. If these students need more support, have them use the Sentence Frames on the Access 3 handout as they work with their more proficient peers. **Approaching** **Summarize the Text.** Have these students discuss and complete the text summary on the Access 4 handout and use their summary to help them analyze and annotate the text by completing the Skills Focus questions. Correct answers for the summary are at the end of the lesson plan online. Also refer to the sample Skills Focus answers to aid students with their annotations.
Discuss. After students have read the text, use the sample responses to the Skills Focus questions online to discuss the reading and the process of analyzing the author's purposes and points of view and comparing and contrasting the text with the video interview. Make sure that students have acquired and accurately use academic-specific words and phrases related to the skill, and demonstrate a command of formal English appropriate to the discussion.	**Extend** **Pair and Share.** In small, heterogeneous groups or pairs, ask students to share and discuss their annotations with a focus on the point of view presented in the selection. You can provide students with these questions to guide their discussion: 1. What purpose might an author have in writing an informational text such as this? Would an author choose to write about a subject he or she thinks is unimportant? (Answers will vary, but an author will presumably think their subject is important and it is worth informing others about it.) 2. Why might the author of *I Am an American* think that the internment of Japanese Americans during World War II is an important story? Cite specific textual evidence to support your answer. (Answers will vary, but might refer to the disruption of the lives of so many people.) 3. What points of view may have inspired the authors of the text and the video? (Answers will vary, but might refer to explaining the story historically, and illustrating a personal story.)

Core Path	Access Path
	Extend **Tech Infusion** **Identify Causes and Effects.** Ask students, either individually or in small groups, to create print or digital cause and effect graphic organizers to record the causes and effects of Japanese internment as presented in the text and the video interview. Ask volunteers to present selected entries to the class. Lead the class to discuss whether there are any possible causes or effects that have been omitted from the presentations.

3. WRITE

Core Path	Access Path
Prewrite and Plan. Read the prompt as a class and ask students to brainstorm about how the text and the video each reflects varying purposes and points of view, and how each sheds light on the issue of standing up or standing down in the face of conflict. Students can brainstorm together either as a class or in small groups to begin planning their responses. Remind your students to look at the excerpt and their annotations to find textual evidence to support their ideas. In addition, have students think about how the information in the video interview combined with the text helps them develop an understanding of the topics and issues.	**Beginner & Intermediate** **Answer and Discuss.** Have students complete the prewriting questions on the Access 1 and 2 handouts and then explain their answers to a partner before they write. Explain to students that when they answer a question, they need to include a detail, example, or quote from the text that supports the statement. **Approaching** **Answer Prewriting Questions.** Have students complete the prewriting questions on the Access 4 handout to summarize their thoughts before they write.

Please note that excerpts and passages in the StudySync® library, workbooks, and PDFs are intended as touchstones to generate interest in an author's work. The excerpts and passages do not substitute for the reading of entire texts, and StudySync® strongly recommends that teachers and students seek out and purchase the whole literary or informational work in order to experience it as the author intended. Links to online resellers are available in our digital library. In addition, complete works may be ordered through an authorized reseller by filling out and returning to StudySync® the order form enclosed in this workbook.

Teacher's Edition   **147**

Core Path	Access Path
	Extend **Organize Ideas.** Distribute a blank Venn diagram to students. (See Resources) Have students use the Venn diagrams to compare and contrast the text with the video interview in terms of purpose and point of view. Then model for students how to use the collected data to draw conclusions and state ideas. For example, in the case of Japanese internment, Stanley's text and Kanaya's interview show that the result was the same for those who did or did not stand up to false accusations of sabotage.
	Extend **Evaluate a Writing Sample.** Project a writing sample on the board and have students identify the elements of writing that are strong, as well as those that are weak or in need of improvement. Alternatively, you can give students photocopies of a writing sample to collaboratively evaluate. After students have had an opportunity to evaluate student samples, have them generate and share with the class strategies to use as they complete their peer reviews to ensure they are substantive.

Discuss. Project these instructions for the peer review onto the board and review them with your class, so they know what they are looking for when they begin to provide their classmates with feedback:

- How does this essay help you understand how the two media convey purpose and point of view?

- How does the writer explain the similarities and differences in the two media?

- How does the writer address the issue of standing up or standing down in the face of conflict?

- What supporting evidence does the writer provide from the text and the video?

- What elements does this response address especially well?

Core Path	Access Path
• Be sure to tell the writer what aspects of the response work well, as well as where additional work is needed. Remember that your comments are most useful when they are specific and constructive. After you've looked at the peer review instructions, review the rubric with students before they begin writing. Allow time for students briefly to pose and discuss any questions they may have about the peer review instructions and the rubric. Tell students how many peer reviews they will need to complete once they submit their writing.	
Write. Ask students to complete the writing assignment using textual evidence to support their responses. Once they have completed their writing, they should click "Submit."	
Review. Once students complete their writing assignment, they should submit substantive feedback to two peers. Students should use their peers' feedback to improve their writing.	

Dorothea Lange: Voice of the Downtrodden

OVERVIEW

To enhance understanding of *I Am an American* and to add context, students will learn about the acclaimed photojournalist Dorothea Lange and how she photographed the people of the Dust Bowl and the Japanese internment camps during World War II. Research links provide additional background information for students to explore Dorothea Lange's work as well as the Dust Bowl and Japanese internment camps.

OBJECTIVES

1. Explore background information about Dorothea Lange and photojournalism.
2. Research using the hyperlinks to learn more about Dorothea Lange and the people she photographed.
3. Participate effectively in a range of conversations and collaborations to express ideas and build upon the ideas of others.

ELA Common Core Standards:

Reading: Informational Text - RI.6.1
Writing - W.6.1.A, W.6.1.B, W.6.5, W.6.6
Speaking & Listening - SL.6.1.A, SL.6.1.B, SL.6.1.C, SL.6.1.D, SL.6.2

RESOURCES

Access 1 handout (Beginner)

Access 2 handout (Intermediate)

Access 4 handout (Approaching)

TITLE/DRIVING QUESTION

Core Path	Access Path
Discuss. As a class, read aloud the title and driving question for this Blast. Ask students what they already know about photojournalism. Do they have any ideas about how photojournalists can help stand up for others? Remind students that they should not immediately reply to this question. They'll be returning to this question and responding after they've read the Background and some of the Research Links.	**English Learners All Levels & Approaching** **Brainstorm.** Provide students with the definition of a photojournalist: "someone who communicates news or stories through photographs." Then ask students to complete the Brainstorm chart on their Access 1, 2, and 4 handouts to generate details they can use in the class discussion. Prior to the class discussion, have students discuss their charts in small groups.
Draft. In their notebooks or on scrap paper, have students draft their initial responses to the driving question. This will provide them with a baseline response that they will be altering as they gain more information about the topic in the Background and Research Links sections of the assignment.	**Beginner & Intermediate** **Draft with Sentence Frame.** When drafting their initial response to the driving question, have students refer to this Blast sentence frame on their Access 1 and 2 handouts: • Photojournalists can help stand for others by telling stories that _____. Point out these two key features of the sentence frame: 1. The introductory clause "Photojournalists can help stand for others" borrows language directly from the Blast driving question to provide a response. 2. Ask students to make special note of the conjunction *that*, which requires students to expand upon the Blast.

Please note that excerpts and passages in the StudySync® library, workbooks, and PDFs are intended as touchstones to generate interest in an author's work. The excerpts and passages do not substitute for the reading of entire texts, and StudySync® strongly recommends that teachers and students seek out and purchase the whole literary or informational work in order to experience it as the author intended. Links to online resellers are available in our digital library. In addition, complete works may be ordered through an authorized reseller by filling out and returning to StudySync® the order form enclosed in this workbook.

Teacher's Edition   **151**

BACKGROUND

Core Path	Access Path
Read. Have students read the Blast background to provide context for the driving question.	**Beginner & Intermediate** **Read with Support.** Have students read the Blast background to provide context for the driving question. When they encounter unfamiliar words or phrases, have students refer to the Blast Glossary on their Access 1 and 2 handouts. If there are unfamiliar words that are not included in their Blast Glossary, encourage students to check a dictionary or online reference tool, like http://tinyurl.com/3qe7. **Approaching** **Read and Summarize.** Have students read the Blast background to provide context for the driving question. As they read, ask students to complete the fill in the blank summary of the background provided on their Access 4 handout. When they encounter unfamiliar words or phrases, have students refer to the glossary on their Access 4 handout.
Discuss. Pair students and have them discuss the following questions. Make sure students follow the rules for collegial discussions. 1. Who was Dorothea Lange? (a photojournalist born in 1895 who photographed people in the Dust Bowl and the Japanese internment camps) 2. What did Dorothea do when she saw the effects of the Great Depression in her own neighborhood? (She went out and photographed people on bread lines and in labor strikes.) How do you think that might have been helpful? (Some who might not have known how bad it was for those people could have been inspired to help; she helped draw attention to their struggle.) 3. What was the Dust Bowl? (The name given to the Great Plains region that was affected by a severe drought, causing hunger and poverty.) 4. Why did Dorothea Lange photograph Japanese internment camps? (She wanted to show the injustices the prisoners faced along with racial and civil rights issues.)	**Beginner** **Discuss.** Pair Beginning with Advanced (or Beyond) students and have them use the dialogue starter on their Access 1 handout to discuss the topic of photojournalism. Advise them to return to the dialogue and switch roles if they get stuck. **Intermediate** **Discuss.** Pair Intermediate with Advanced (or Beyond) students and have them use the dialogue starter on their Access 2 handout to discuss the topic. Advise them to return to the dialogue and switch roles if they get stuck. If their conversation is progressing smoothly, encourage them to continue the discussion beyond the dialogue starter sheet. They can expand their conversations to discuss other examples of how photojournalists can help stand for others.

Core Path	Access Path
Brainstorm. Remind students about the Driving Question for this Blast: How can photojournalists help stand up for others? In their notebooks, ask students to make a list of ways Dorothea Lange helped stand up for others. Here's a short example of how this might look: • showed people the injustice that went on inside Japanese internment camps • showed what was happening to people living in the Dust Bowl • showed the labor strikes and bread lines in San Francisco during the Great Depression	

RESEARCH LINKS

Core Path	Access Path
Examine and Explore. Before asking students to explore the research links, use these activities and questions to guide their exploration: 1. Why do you think it's important to read background information on the Dust Bowl? (This will help give context to Dorothea Lange's work, and help us understand what she wanted people to see.) 2. Why do you think links to Dorothea's photographs are included? (The links show what her work actually looked like, as well as what the places talked about in the Background were like.) 3. Ask students to read the essay, "Why is Photojournalism Important?" Why is photojournalism sometimes dangerous? (Photojournalists sometimes have to go to dangerous places, such as war zones.) 4. What's the most important thing to look out for in any research link you click on? (examples of how photojournalists can help stand up for others)	

Please note that excerpts and passages in the StudySync® library, workbooks, and PDFs are intended as touchstones to generate interest in an author's work. The excerpts and passages do not substitute for the reading of entire texts, and StudySync® strongly recommends that teachers and students seek out and purchase the whole literary or informational work in order to experience it as the author intended. Links to online resellers are available in our digital library. In addition, complete works may be ordered through an authorized reseller by filling out and returning to StudySync® the order form enclosed in this workbook.

Teacher's Edition 153

Core Path	Access Path

	Research, Discuss, and Present.
	
	1. Assign each group one link to explore in depth.
	2. Ask them to discuss the information:
	
	    a. What are the key points?
	    b. What inferences did you make as you read?
	    c. What did you learn about this "big idea" from reading this research?
	    d. How did this help you to better understand the topic?
	    e. What questions does your group have after exploring this link?
	
	Allow students time to informally present what they learned.

	Extend **Tech Infusion** **Share.** As students explore the links, encourage them to keep track of their thoughts using an online journal like Penzu (http://tinyurl.com/lwuy989). Students can share their thoughts with others.

QUIKPOLL

Core Path	Access Path
Participate. Answer the poll question. Have students use information from the background and research links to explain their answers.	

NUMBER CRUNCH

Core Path	Access Path
Predict, Discuss, and Click. Before students click on the number, break them into pairs and have them make predictions about what they think the number is related to. After they've clicked the number, ask students if they are surprised by the revealed information.	

CREATE YOUR BLAST (140 CHARACTERS)

Core Path	Access Path
Blast. Ask students to write their Blast response in 140 characters or less.	**Beginner** **Blast with Support.** Have students refer back to the sentence frame on their Access 1 handout that they used to create their original Blast draft. Ask them to use this frame to write and enter their final Blast. **Intermediate** **Blast with Support.** Have students attempt to draft their Blast without the sentence frame on their Access 2 handout. If students struggle to compose their Blast draft without the sentence frame, remind them to reference it for support. **Beyond** **Write a Claim.** Ask students to use their answer to the poll question to write a strong claim that could be used as the foundation for a piece of argumentative writing. Once students have written their claims, ask them to read the claims to a small group of their peers. This activity will provide them practice writing claims, as well as expose them to claims written by their peers.

Please note that excerpts and passages in the StudySync® library, workbooks, and PDFs are intended as touchstones to generate interest in an author's work. The excerpts and passages do not substitute for the reading of entire texts, and StudySync® strongly recommends that teachers and students seek out and purchase the whole literary or informational work in order to experience it as the author intended. Links to online resellers are available in our digital library. In addition, complete works may be ordered through an authorized reseller by filling out and returning to StudySync® the order form enclosed in this workbook.

Teacher's Edition   **155**

Core Path	Access Path
Review. After students have completed their own Blasts, ask them to review the Blasts of their peers and provide feedback.	**Extend** **Discuss.** As a whole class or in groups, identify a few strong blasts and discuss what made those responses so powerful. As a group, analyze and discuss what characteristics make a blast interesting or effective.
	Extend **Revise.** Resend a second version of this Blast assignment to your students and have them submit revised versions of their original Blasts. Do the same responses make the Top 10? How have the answers improved from the first submissions?

OVERVIEW

The novel *Roll of Thunder, Hear My Cry,* by Mildred D. Taylor, excitingly and movingly shows the shared suffering and love within an African American farming family in Mississippi during the Great Depression of the 1930s. The First Read gives students the opportunity to experience the text with a limited context.

OBJECTIVES

1. Perform an initial reading of a text and demonstrate comprehension by responding to short analysis and inference questions with textual evidence.
2. Practice defining vocabulary words using context.
3. Learn and practice strategies for recognizing and understanding variations from standard English.
4. Participate effectively in a range of conversations and collaborations to express ideas and build upon the ideas of others.

   ELA Common Core Standards:
   Reading: Literature - RL.6.1, RL.6.3, RL.6.4, RL.6.10
   Writing - W.6.7
   Speaking & Listening - SL.6.1.A, SL.6.1.B, SL.6.1.C, SL.6.1.D, SL.6.2, SL.6.6
   Language - L.6.1.E, L.6.4.A, L.6.4.B, L.6.4.C, L.6.4.D

RESOURCES

Grammar handout: Understanding Dialect

Access 1 handout (Beginner)

Access 2 handout (Intermediate)

Access 3 handout (Advanced)

Access 4 handout (Approaching)

Please note that excerpts and passages in the StudySync® library, workbooks, and PDFs are intended as touchstones to generate interest in an author's work. The excerpts and passages do not substitute for the reading of entire texts, and StudySync® strongly recommends that teachers and students seek out and purchase the whole literary or informational work in order to experience it as the author intended. Links to online resellers are available in our digital library. In addition, complete works may be ordered through an authorized reseller by filling out and returning to StudySync® the order form enclosed in this workbook.

Teacher's Edition   **157**

ACCESS COMPLEX TEXT

While students may find the characters in this excerpt from Mildred D. Taylor's *Roll of Thunder, Hear My Cry* accessible, the novel's story structure and its historic nature may be challenging. To help students get the most out of the story, use the following suggestions to provide scaffolded instruction for a close reading of the more complex features of this text:

- **Organization** - Taylor structures the text so that it unfolds chronologically through a sequence of events that present a conflict and a resolution. The problems the Logans and their neighbors face, and the solutions they seek, drive the plot. Nine-year-old Cassie Logan is the narrator of the story, and she describes what is happening around her. Have students note how the author cleverly devises ways for Cassie to learn about events in her household. Students will need to be able to ask and answer *who, what, where*, and *how* question to analyze plot events and the story's framework.

- **Connection of Ideas** - Because plot events are revealed through dialogue, students need to make connections between what the characters say and how events and the characters' reactions to those events drive the plot forward.

- **Prior Knowledge** - The story is directly tied to its setting. Students may not know about the racial and economic inequalities of sharecropping or the grave effects of the Great Depression on African American small landowners and sharecroppers. This may make it difficult for students to understand the significance of Thurston Wallace's power over the characters in the story.

- **Sentence Structure** - Students may find the use of dialect challenging. As students read the story, have them note any variations from standard English. Then, as a class, discuss the meanings of the specific words and phrases, analyzing what the dialect reveals about characters, and what it contributes to the story.

1. INTRODUCTION

Core Path	Access Path
Watch. As a class, watch the video preview of *Roll of Thunder, Hear My Cry*.	**English Learners All Levels & Approaching** **Fill in the Blanks.** Ask students to use their Access 1, 2, 3, and 4 handouts to fill in the blanks of the transcript for the preview's voiceover as they watch the preview along with their classmates. Answers are located at the end of this lesson plan online. Some students may want to watch the video to focus on it and then watch a second time and complete handouts during the second viewing.
Read. Individually or as a class, read and listen to the Introduction for *Roll of Thunder, Hear My Cry*. The introduction provides context for the excerpt, which is taken from Chapter 9.	**English Learners All Levels & Approaching** **Read and Listen.** Ask students to read and listen to the introduction for *Roll of Thunder, Hear My Cry*. Have them refer to the vocabulary listing on their Access 1, 2, 3, and 4 handouts for definitions of key vocabulary terms. If there are unfamiliar words that are not included in their glossary, encourage students to check a dictionary or online reference tool, like http://tinyurl.com/3qe7.
Build Background Knowledge. Tell students that the Great Depression was a period in American history, during the 1930s, when poverty became widespread, unemployment soared, and thousands of family farms failed. Conditions for African Americans in the South had long been worse than for whites in general, and that remained true during the Depression. Assign groups of students to find out more about the Great Depression and about racial discrimination in the South in that era. Questions for students to investigate might include: 1. When did the Depression begin and end? What were the major events that prompted it to do so? 2. What was sharecropping? 3. What were the major crops grown in the South during the Depression? 4. What were Jim Crow laws? Cite examples of what they did.	**Beginner & Intermediate** **Research.** Pair readers with more proficient readers to research the Great Depression, the Deep South, and Jim Crow laws. Ask Beginning and Intermediate students to refer to their Access 1 and 2 handouts to complete the sentence frames that will help them guide their research on what life was like in the 1930s. **Advanced & Approaching** **Research Guide Questions.** Pair these students together so that the Advanced students can help Approaching students research the Great Depression. Ask students to first answer the Research Guide Questions on the Access 3 and 4 handouts to guide their research.

Please note that excerpts and passages in the StudySync® library, workbooks, and PDFs are intended as touchstones to generate interest in an author's work. The excerpts and passages do not substitute for the reading of entire texts, and StudySync® strongly recommends that teachers and students seek out and purchase the whole literary or informational work in order to experience it as the author intended. Links to online resellers are available in our digital library. In addition, complete works may be ordered through an authorized reseller by filling out and returning to StudySync® the order form enclosed in this workbook.

Teacher's Edition   **159**

Core Path	Access Path
Have small groups research information online or in print sources available in your school. Remind students that their research should include relevant facts, definitions, and other concrete details. Students should use precise language and domain specific vocabulary. They should provide a strong conclusion for their research. Invite each group to deliver their presentation orally. Remind students to use appropriate eye contact, adequate volume, and clear pronunciation when presenting. You might want to compile all the information on a Google Docs (http://tinyurl.com/u7u9k) or TitanPad (http://tinyurl.com/24pyy9m) document for students to refer to during their study of *Roll of Thunder, Hear My Cry*.	
	Extend **Tech Infusion** **Interactive Photo Search.** During the Depression, the U.S. government's Farm Security Administration hired some of America's best photographers to chronicle the lives of people affected by the crisis. About 170,000 photos are gathered at the Yale University database Photogrammar (http://tinyurl.com/kr7krmf). These amazing images paint a picture of the time period. Supervise students as they click to the interactive map (http://tinyurl.com/khc5leh), which allows viewers to search for photos by specific photographers in county-size areas of the states. The darker the shading of the area, the more photos available. Clicking on an area on the map provides the area's name and the number of photos, with a link to a page to view them. On that page, clicking on a thumbnail photo results in an enlargement accompanied by bibliographical information, including the photo's specific location and date.

Core Path	Access Path
	Invite students to browse photos of Southeastern states, such as Alabama, Mississippi, Georgia, Louisiana, and Florida. They can also pull down the All Photographers menu to search for photographers by name, and collate photographers with geographical areas. Three eminent names to search for are Jack Delano, Gordon Parks, and Marion Post Wolcott. Students can annotate and share their photo discoveries by using Diigo (http://tinyurl.com/g5uja).

2. READ

Core Path	Access Path
Make Predictions about Vocabulary. Five vocabulary words are boldfaced in the text. As students come to each word, have them predict its meaning, using context clues from the sentence and elsewhere in the text. If you are in a low-tech classroom and students are reading from printed copies or a projected text, ask students to write their predictions in their notes. If your students have access to technology, they can use the annotation tool.	**Note:** This exercise, which extends vocabulary instruction, should be completed when the class shifts from whole group instruction to individual work during the "Read and Annotate" exercise.
	Beginner, Intermediate & Approaching Pair Practice.
Before students begin reading, you may want to model using sentence structure to predict word meanings. Either using the board or projecting the actual text, focus on the sentence that uses the word "overshadow":	1. Pair students with more proficient readers.
	2. Give them an additional sentence that contains a new vocabulary word.
• "Them other trees all around. . . they're a lot bigger and they take up more room and give so much shade they almost overshadow that little ole fig."	3. Ask the students to complete a Think Aloud using the teacher-led Make Predictions about Vocabulary activity as a model, while the proficient student actively listens.
	4. The student should use the context clues in the sentence to try to determine the meaning of the new vocabulary word.
	5. After the student has completed the Think Aloud and made a prediction about the word's meaning, allow time for the proficient reader to add his/her own thoughts and clarify any points of confusion.

Core Path	Access Path
Model for the class how to use the structure and meaning of the sentence and the sentences around it, the word's position, and other clues to define the unfamiliar vocabulary word. In this case, point out these context clues:	6. Once they've completed this Think Aloud, encourage them to use a dictionary to confirm the definition of the new vocabulary word. Have them refer to the vocabulary listing on their Access 1, 2, and 4 handouts for definitions of key vocabulary terms in the text. Encourage them to add any additional vocabulary words or idioms they find in the text and look up definitions for those words and idioms online or in a dictionary.

Core Path (continued):

1. In this long sentence, let's focus first on the clause that "overshadow" belongs to. The structure of the clause shows that "overshadow" is a verb—an action—that "they"—the trees—perform. The bigger trees overshadow the smaller fig tree.

2. The sentence provides a word-picture. We can visualize it to get an idea of what "overshadow" means. There's a group of trees, and the fig is small and the others are big. We can imagine that the other trees tower over the fig tree. They block the sunlight from reaching it. They literally put it in the shade.

3. There are other clues in the sentence from the text. For example, the word "shade," is also used. The word "overshadow" contains "over." The trees in this sentence stand *over* the fig and shade it. We can infer that to overshadow something is to be bigger than it is, so that it suffers by comparison. It seems less significant.

4. If we replace the word "overshadow" in the sentence with our definition, it still makes sense in context. So that's one clue that our definition is close to correct. Then, we can confirm the meaning by looking up "overshadow" in the dictionary.

Core Path	Access Path
Model Reading Comprehension Strategy. Before students begin reading, model the comprehension strategy of rereading by using this Think Aloud that talks students through the first paragraph of text. First explain to your students that rereading is going over a passage that you have read in order to clarify your understanding of events, facts, and details.	**Note:** This exercise, which extends vocabulary instruction, should be completed when the class shifts from whole group instruction to individual work during the "Read and Annotate" exercise.

Core Path

Explain to students how rereading will help them better comprehend the selection and help drive their discussions.

- Sometimes even good readers misread a word or words. In the first paragraph, it took me a couple of readings to get the names of Christopher-John and Little Man straight in my mind.

- Sometimes a complicated action, such as an action that involves more than two characters, is hard to keep track of without rereading. In the first paragraph, Cassie grabs the iron bell before Christopher-John or Little Man can claim it. Then she runs to the back porch and calls Papa, Mr. Morrison, and Stacey in from the fields. Papa, Mr. Morrison, and Stacey wash up. Then Mama joins Papa at the end of the porch. That's a lot in one short paragraph. As I reread it, I made a mental list of who was doing what. After I'd reread the paragraph twice, I had a clear picture of the scene in my mind.

Read and Annotate. Have students independently read and annotate the excerpt. Ask students to use the annotation tool as they read to:

1. use context clues to analyze and determine the meaning of the bolded vocabulary terms

2. ask questions about passages of the text that may be unclear or unresolved

3. identify key events, characters, and connections between them

4. note unfamiliar vocabulary

5. capture reactions to characters and events

Access Path

Beginner, Intermediate & Approaching Apply.

1. Have students listen to the audio version of the excerpt from *Roll of Thunder, Hear My Cry.* As they listen to the audio recording, ask them to listen carefully to the last paragraph.

2. Have students listen again to the audio of the last paragraph as if they were rereading as in the comprehension model. Then have students complete the Apply exercise on the Access 1, 2, and 4 handouts.

3. Have students discuss the handouts. Have them share how the second listen helped them to complete the handouts.

Beginner
Coach the Reading. While other students read, annotate, and discuss the text independently, work with Beginning students, listening to the audio of the text and pausing periodically or when any student has a question. Coach students in articulating their questions for the group and in highlighting and annotating the text. Have students use the Annotation Guide on the Access 1 handout to support them as they highlight and annotate the text.

For further support, ask questions about the text such as:

- Is there anything about the story that you don't understand?

- What do you think will happen to Cassie and her family?

- How does the time period affect the Logan family?

Please note that excerpts and passages in the StudySync® library, workbooks, and PDFs are intended as touchstones to generate interest in an author's work. The excerpts and passages do not substitute for the reading of entire texts, and StudySync® strongly recommends that teachers and students seek out and purchase the whole literary or informational work in order to experience it as the author intended. Links to online resellers are available in our digital library. In addition, complete works may be ordered through an authorized reseller by filling out and returning to StudySync® the order form enclosed in this workbook.

Teacher's Edition   **163**

Core Path	Access Path
	Intermediate **Listen to the Audio.** Have these students listen to the audio of the text and use the Text Glossary definitions on the Access 2 handout to help them with words or idioms that may be unfamiliar. If students need help with annotating the text, have them use the Annotation Guide on the Access 2 handout. After working with the Beginning students, you may wish to check this group's progress and provide support as needed. **Advanced** **Pair with Proficient Peers.** Have Advanced students work with English proficient peers to read, annotate, and discuss the text. Have students use the Annotation Guide in the Access 3 handout to support them as they highlight and annotate the text. Encourage them to listen to the audio of the text if needed. **Approaching** **Use the Annotation Guide.** Have students use the Annotation Guide on the Access 4 handout to support them as they highlight and annotate the text.
Discuss. In small groups or pairs, have students discuss the questions and inferences they made while reading. Make sure students follow the rules for collegial discussions. For help with these rules, refer to Collaborative Discussions in the Speaking & Listening Handbook. 1. Who are the members of the family? (Nine-year-old Cassie Logan is the narrator; her Mama and Papa and her brothers Christopher-John, Little Man, and Stacey make up the family.) 2. Why do Mr. Lanier and Mr. Avery visit Cassie's family? (They are neighbors, who are sharecroppers, and they have previously agreed to join Papa in the boycott of Thurston Wallace's store, but because of economic pressures they are backing out of the boycott.)	**English Learners All Levels & Approaching** Use the extra time while on- and beyond-grade level students are discussing their first reads of the text to work individually and in small groups with Approaching readers and English Learners as outlined above. Should those students complete their first reads quickly, integrate them into the on- and beyond-grade level discussion groups. Otherwise, Approaching readers and English Learners will be given an opportunity to participate in text discussions with their peers later in the lesson.

Core Path	Access Path
3. Why does Papa tell Cassie about the fig tree? (He uses the description of the fig tree as a kind of parable to teach Cassie about the importance of never giving up.) 4. How did rereading the text help you find answers to the above questions? (Answer will vary.)	

Core Path	Access Path
(G) Grammar, Usage, and Mechanics. Distribute the StudySync handout on dialect. Review with students that dialect is a variation in the standard form of a language and is spoken by people belonging to a specific group or region. Tell students that dialects can have their own grammar, vocabulary, and syntax (or rules for word order), and these may be different from or similar to standard English. For additional information and instruction on recognizing and understanding non-standard English, refer to the StudySync Standard English Learners Handbook online. Explain that dialect can be a helpful tool in determining more about a story's setting, by evoking a time and place, or a character's background. Mildred Taylor uses dialect of the Mississippi countryside to help readers imagine the setting of this story and the sounds of the characters' voices. Review the instruction on the handout with students before they complete the practice exercise. (Answers for the practice exercise appear at the end of this lesson plan online.) Finally, encourage students to apply what they have learned by analyzing the use of dialect in *Roll of Thunder, Hear My Cry*. Ask students: 1. Reread paragraph 10. Explain how you can determine the meaning of Papa's words, "Well, look-a-here!" (The words are similar to "look here" or "look at this," and the fact Papa is pointing out the food that Mama and Cassie have prepared for dinner confirms this meaning.)	**Beginner & Intermediate** **Work with the Teacher.** Remind these students that dialect in this story helps tell the reader the time period (1930s) and setting (Deep South). Work with students to identify examples of dialect in the excerpt. Then have students write the formal English of the dialect expression. **Advanced & Beyond** **Extend the search.** Challenge these students to work in pairs or small groups to find the dialect in the excerpt. Then challenge students to review other stories that use dialect. Authors who use dialect in their stories are Joel Chandler Harris, Mary Ann Rodman, Paul Laurence Dunbar (poet), and John Steptoe. Students can share examples of dialect with the class. **Approaching** **Analyze an Example.** If students need more support identifying dialect, reread paragraph 10 with students. Point out the dialect, "Well, look-a-here." Have students rewrite the dialect in formal English. Encourage students to find other examples of dialect in the excerpt. Pairs can rewrite the examples they find.

Core Path	Access Path
2. What do you notice about the amount of dialect in the previous paragraphs? (There is very little dialect used in paragraphs 1–9.) Why might that be? (In these first few paragraphs, Mama and Papa are having a serious discussion. In paragraph 10, Papa shifts into dialect as he tries to make the conversation more lighthearted.) 3. Cassie, the narrator of the story, does not use dialect in her narration. How does her use of standard English to tell the story affect the way readers might perceive her? (The lack of dialect might indicate that Cassie has grown up to be more educated than some of the other characters, or that she has left the region. It might also indicate that she is telling the story as an adult, long after the events have happened. It separates her narrator's voice from her childhood voice.)	
	Extend **Use Vocabulary.** After students have read the text, invite them to compose sentences that use the words, in contexts other than the context of the novel excerpt. This group of vocabulary words is readily generalizable to many contexts. Students may either write their sentences and read them aloud, or compose the sentences orally, as you prefer.
	Extend **Tech Infusion** **Record.** Use a voice recording app (Voice Memo for the iPhone or Smart Voice Recorder for Androids) or VoiceThread (http://tinyurl.com/amd9w2) to preserve students' sentences in the above vocabulary activity.

3. SYNCTV

Core Path	Access Path
Watch. As a class, watch the SyncTV video on *Roll of Thunder, Hear My Cry*. Pause the video at these key moments to discuss the information with your students. Make sure students follow the rules for collegial discussions. Have students review and reflect on the ideas expressed, paraphrasing as necessary. 1. 0:33 – Tora says, "Everyone must have been under a lot of pressure." What pressures is Cassie's family under? 2. 2:40 – Chris says, "But then Cassie puts the food on the table and everything seems alright again." Do you agree that "everything seems alright" at that point? Explain what you think is "alright" and what you think is not—Chris likes the fact that Papa explains the family's problems to Cassie. Christina doesn't agree. Which student do you agree with, and why?	**Beginner & Intermediate** **Analyze the Discussion.** Have students use the "Analyze the Discussion" guide on the Access 1 and 2 handouts to identify key points in the discussion and the evidence the students use to determine those points. Sample answers are at the end of this lesson plan online. **Advanced** **Identify the Turning Points.** Have students discuss and complete the chart on the Access 3 handout, referring back to the SyncTV video as needed to clarify their answers. Sample answers appear at the end of this lesson plan online. **Approaching** **Analyze the Discussion.** Have students complete the chart on the Access 4 handout by listing textual evidence cited by the students in the video. Sample answers are at the end of this lesson plan online.
	Extend **Tech Infusion.** **Record.** Ask one student in each group to videotape their conversation. They can upload their videos to YouTube, share them via Google Drive, or email them to you for review. They can also play the video back and critique their own conversations to continually improve.

Please note that excerpts and passages in the StudySync® library, workbooks, and PDFs are intended as touchstones to generate interest in an author's work. The excerpts and passages do not substitute for the reading of entire texts, and StudySync® strongly recommends that teachers and students seek out and purchase the whole literary or informational work in order to experience it as the author intended. Links to online resellers are available in our digital library. In addition, complete works may be ordered through an authorized reseller by filling out and returning to StudySync® the order form enclosed in this workbook.

Teacher's Edition   **167**

4. THINK

Core Path	Access Path
Answer and Discuss. Have students complete the Think questions and then use the peer review instructions and rubric to complete two peer reviews. Refer to the sample answers at the end of this lesson plan online to discuss responses with your students.	**Beginner & Intermediate** **Sentence Frames.** Have students use the Sentence Frames on the Access 1 and 2 handouts to support their responses to the Think questions. If necessary, distribute sentence frames to Advanced students as well. **Approaching** **Find the Evidence.** Have students use Find the Evidence on the Access 4 handout to help them identify the evidence needed to answer the questions.
SyncTV Style Discussion. Put students into heterogeneous small groups and give them a prompt to discuss. Remind them to model their discussions after the SyncTV episodes they have seen, being sure to use language appropriate to this task. Stress the importance of citing textual evidence in their conversations to support their ideas. To help students prepare for, strategize, and evaluate their discussions, refer to the Collaborative Discussions section of the Speaking & Listening Handbook. Discussion prompts: 1. Why does this excerpt create tension for the reader even though it contains little action? 2. What is the main action that occurs in this excerpt? What causes it? What might its results be? Have students review the key ideas expressed, demonstrating an understanding of multiple perspectives through reflection and paraphrasing. You may wish to have students create a video or audio recording of their SyncTV-Style Discussion.	**Extend** **Tech Infusion.** **Create.** Have students draw the scene in the excerpt, including the porch setting and all the characters. Have students label the characters with their names. Also have students write brief descriptions of the characters and what roles they play in the excerpt. Have one or more volunteers display their drawings to the class and read their text aloud. Invite students to post their creations on a Padlet wall (http://tinyurl.com/aedptok).

Copyright © BookheadEd Learning, LLC

Story Structure

OVERVIEW

Determining the structure of a work of fiction is key to understanding the plot, and thus the themes and characters. This lesson plan provides follow-up questions and useful enrichments to help teachers guide students toward a usable, repeatable method for uncovering story structure.

OBJECTIVES

1. Learn the definition of story structure.
2. Practice using concrete strategies for analyzing story structure.
3. Participate effectively in a range of conversations and collaborations to express ideas and build upon the ideas of others.

ELA Common Core Standards:
Reading: Literature - RL.6.1, RL.6.5
Speaking & Listening - SL.1.A, SL.6.1.B, SL.6.1.C, SL.6.2

RESOURCES

Roll of Thunder, Hear My Cry Graphic organizer

Access 1 handout (Beginner)

Access 2 handout (Intermediate)

Access 3 handout (Advanced)

Access 4 handout (Approaching)

1. DEFINE

Core Path	Access Path
Watch. Watch the Concept Definition video on story structure with your students. Make sure students write down and understand the basic components of story structure: not only beginning, middle, and end, but also trigger, climax, and denouement. Pause the video at these key moments to discuss the information with your students:	**English Learners All Levels & Approaching** **Fill in the Blanks.** Have students complete the Fill in the Blanks exercise on the Access 1, 2, 3, and 4 handouts as they watch the video. Answers are located at the end of the lesson plan online.

1. 0:30 – Does the same basic story structure apply to movies and TV shows? Think of a film or a TV show you've seen and break it down to determine if this general framework applies to storytelling in a different medium.

2. 0:48 – Think of an example of a "trigger" from a novel you've read, or a film or TV show you've seen. Share your example. When does the trigger usually occur? What elements must be in place before this can happen?

3. 1:35 – Why would an author choose to tell a story out of linear order? When do you think a non-linear narrative is a good storytelling choice, and when might it be unnecessary? Share some examples.

Read and Discuss. After watching the Concept Definition video, have students read the definition of story structure. Either in small groups or as a whole class, use these questions to engage students in a discussion about story structure. Make sure students follow the rules for collegial discussions.

1. Think of a movie, television show, or book you like. How are the stories you like best usually structured? Do they vary? What kind of structure do you like best?

2. Which stories that you have read or viewed have had a memorable climax? What was there about it that made it memorable?

3. How does understanding how a story is structured help you to better understand it?

Beginner & Approaching
Complete a Chart. To prepare students to participate in the discussion, have them complete the chart on the Access 1 and 4 handouts as they read the definition. The correct answers are located at the end of the lesson plan online.

Intermediate & Advanced
Discuss Prompts. To help these students participate in the discussion, prompt them with questions that can be answered with a few words, such as:

- What is story structure? (the framework writers use to develop events of the plot)

- How does a character-driven novel work? (the story is told from the point of view of one character)

- What are some other ways a story can be driven? (by humor or suspense)

Core Path	Access Path
	Beyond **Discuss.** Have students select a book they've read and describe its story structure. Compile a list of examples. Have students discuss how the different kinds of story structures work in the novels listed. Why did the authors pick a specific kind of story structure to tell their story?
	Extend **Tech Infusion** **Blast.** Create a Blast and ask students to "blast out" the definition of story structure in their own words. Encourage students to compare and contrast their definitions so that they can clarify and elaborate on their understanding of story structure.

2. MODEL

Core Path	Access Path
Watch. Ask students to take notes on the SkillsTV video on story structure in *Roll of Thunder, Hear My Cry*, as you watch together. Remind students to listen for the way the students use academic vocabulary related to the definition of story structure during their discussion. Pause the video at these key moments to discuss the information with your students: 1. 0:16 – What do students learn about the Logan family at the beginning of the story? 2. 0:44 – During their conversation on the porch, what do Papa and Mama discuss? How does Mama react to the information Papa reveals? How does their dialogue contribute to the development of the plot? 3. 2:14 – How do the students respond to Mama's question? Is it an indication of trouble to come? How does the information fit into the overall structure of the text and help move the plot forward?	**Beginner & Intermediate** **Analyze the Discussion.** Have students watch the Model video and complete the chart on the Access 1 and 2 handouts as they watch the video. Sample answers for this exercise are located at the end of the lesson plan online. **Advanced** **Journals.** Have students note in their journals the strategies the students in the SkillsTV video use to find the story structure. **Approaching** **Analyze the Discussion.** Have students watch the Model video and complete the chart on the Access 4 handout as they watch the video. Sample answers for this exercise are located at the end of the lesson plan online.

Please note that excerpts and passages in the StudySync® library, workbooks, and PDFs are intended as touchstones to generate interest in an author's work. The excerpts and passages do not substitute for the reading of entire texts, and StudySync® strongly recommends that teachers and students seek out and purchase the whole literary or informational work in order to experience it as the author intended. Links to online resellers are available in our digital library. In addition, complete works may be ordered through an authorized reseller by filling out and returning to StudySync® the order form enclosed in this workbook.

Teacher's Edition   171

Core Path	Access Path
Read and Annotate. Have students independently read the Model section. As they read, ask students to use the annotation tool to: • highlight key points • ask questions • identify places where the Model applies the strategies laid out in the Identification and Application section on story structure	**Note:** During this portion of the lesson, instruction shifts from whole group to individual work. Use this time to work one-on-one or in small groups with Beginning, Intermediate, Advanced, and Approaching students. **Beginner & Intermediate** **Coach the Reading.** Work with these students (either individually or in small groups) to fill out the guided reading questions on the Access 1 and 2 handouts. Have Beginning students refer to the glossary on the Access 1 handout to help them determine the meaning of difficult words. (note: Provide the Access 1 handout glossary to Intermediate students if necessary.) Let students know they'll use these answers to help participate in the discussion about the Model. Sample answers for this exercise are located at the end of the lesson plan online. **Advanced** **Identify Evidence.** Provide these students with the same instructions to read and annotate as on-grade level and Beyond students. In addition, ask Advanced students to complete the Identifying Evidence exercise on the Access 3 handout. Let students know they'll use these answers to help participate in the discussion about the Model. Sample answers for this exercise are located at the end of the lesson plan online. **Approaching** **Guided Reading.** Have students complete the guided reading questions on the Access 4 handout as they read. Let them know that they'll use these answers to help participate in the discussion about the Model. Sample answers for this exercise are located at the end of the lesson plan online.

Core Path	Access Path
Discuss. After students read the Model text, use these questions to facilitate a whole group discussion that helps students understand how to find and analyze story structure in the passage:	

Core Path

Discuss. After students read the Model text, use these questions to facilitate a whole group discussion that helps students understand how to find and analyze story structure in the passage:

1. What is story structure? (Story structure is the framework the author uses to organize his or her ideas.)

2. What elements of story structure does the Model discuss first? (It explains that the author organizes the text so that it unfolds through a series of plot events.)

3. What other element of story structure does the Model discuss? (The Model explains that conflict and resolution help move a plot forward.)

4. What question words does the Model use in order to understand and analyze story structure? (It explains to readers that asking *who, what,* and *where* questions can help them analyze events of the plot; asking *how* questions can help them analyze the story's framework.)

5. According to the Model, what does the use of tension usually add to a story? (Tension is often used by an author to build suspense or excitement in a story. In this Model, the author's use of tension emphasizes Mama's concern over the possibility that Thurston Wallace's plan may lead to racial unrest.)

Access Path

Extend
Tech Infusion
Discuss. Have students use a backchannel tool such as TodaysMeet (http://tinyurl.com/8ydulv4) or Twitter (http://tinyurl.com/3667fa) to share questions that they have about the Model and to suggest answers to each other's questions. Monitor the communications so that you will be able to answer questions about story structure that confuse students or that they leave unresolved.

3. YOUR TURN

Core Path	Access Path
Assess and Explain. Have students answer the comprehension questions to test for understanding. Share the explanations for Parts A and B (located online) with your students.	
	Extend **Tech Infusion** **Share and Discuss.** Have students complete the Your Turn section in class. Poll students about their responses, and as a class discuss the strategies students used to find the answers. Ask students which aspects of the questions they found hard and how they solved the difficulty. Conduct your poll either by using Poll Everywhere (http://tinyurl.com/3zyw33) or Socrative (http://tinyurl.com/3bxbjpt). If you are in a low-tech classroom, give students a paper handout with questions.
	Extend **Tech Infusion** **Chart the Story Structure.** Have students complete graphic organizers showing the story structure of the excerpt from *Roll of Thunder, Hear My Cry* divided into Beginning, Middle, and Ending. Within each of those three boxes, students should list the events of the narrative in the order in which they are shown in the text. Have students add indications of time, such as "the next day" or "after school is out," when the text provides them for a scene. This can be done through crowdsourcing using Google Docs (http://tinyurl.com/u7u9k) so that a large number of students can contribute their understanding of the story structure. If you are in a low-tech classroom, provide the blank chart as a handout (See Resources) and write an exemplar finished chart on the board or project it. After the class's chart is finished, invite students to talk about how analyzing the structure helped them understand the excerpt.

Copyright © BookheadEd Learning, LLC

CLOSE READ:
Roll of Thunder, Hear My Cry

OVERVIEW

The novel *Roll of Thunder, Hear My Cry*, by Mildred D. Taylor, plunges students into the midst of the problems and joys of an African American family in Mississippi in the 1930s. The Close Read gives students the opportunity to identify elements of story structure and analyze its impact on the work.

OBJECTIVES

1. Complete a close reading of a passage of literature.
2. Practice and apply concrete strategies for identifying story structure.
3. Practice and apply strategies for recognizing and understanding variations from standard English.
4. Participate effectively in a range of conversations and collaborations to express ideas and build upon the ideas of others.
5. Prewrite, plan, and produce clear and coherent writing in response to a prompt.

   ELA Common Core Standards:
   Reading: Literature - RL.6.1, RL.6.2, RL.6.3, RL.6.4, RL.6.5, RL.6.10
   Writing - W.6.2.B, W.6.4, W.6.5, W.6.6, W.6.10
   Speaking & Listening - SL.6.1.A, SL.6.1.B, SL.6.1.C, SL.6.1.D, SL6.6
   Language - L.6.1.E, L.6.4.A, L.6.4.B, L.6.4.C, L.6.4.D

RESOURCES

Roll of Thunder, Hear My Cry Vocabulary handout

Access 1 handout (Beginner)

Access 2 handout (Intermediate)

Access 3 handout (Advanced)

Access 4 handout (Approaching)

1. INTRODUCTION

Core Path	Access Path
Define and Compare. Project the vocabulary words and definitions onto the board or provide students with handouts so they can copy the vocabulary into their notebooks. Suggest that students consult general and specialized reference materials, both print and digital, to compare the precise meaning of a specific word with their initial vocabulary predictions from the First Read. Review words that students defined incorrectly to understand why they were unable to use context clues to develop usable definitions.	**Beginner & Intermediate** **Complete the Sentences.** Have students work in groups to complete the sentence frames on the Access 1 and 2 handouts using the vocabulary words. Point out that some of the words are in the questions and some will be in the answers. Sample answers are located at the end of this lesson plan online. **Advanced & Beyond** **Write in Journals.** Have students write a journal entry using all of their vocabulary words. Remind them to write sentences that communicate the meaning of the words they are using. **Approaching** **Graphic Organizer.** To support students in comparing their predictions with the correct meanings, have them complete the graphic organizer on the Access 4 handout to record the vocabulary words, their initial analysis, and the definitions. Then have them write sentences using the words.
Review. Have students complete the fill in the bank vocabulary worksheet for this selection. Answers for the worksheet are listed at the end of the lesson plan online.	

Core Path	Access Path
	Extend **Tech Infusion** **Picture Vocabulary Quiz.** Invite students to choose one vocabulary word apiece without telling anyone. Then have them create artwork to visually represent their word using Google Drawing, an iPad or Android art app, or paper and traditional tools such as crayons or pencils. Have students form groups of three to five. Within each group, each student should be given a turn to stand up and show his or her vocabulary drawing without revealing the word it represents. The other members of the group then try to guess the word. If time allows, invite students to discuss how hard or easy the various words, and the various drawings, were to guess.
	Extend **Tech Infusion** **Write.** Have students, independently or in pairs, compose a paragraph that uses three or more of the five vocabulary words. The paragraph may be based on the excerpt from *Roll of Thunder, Hear My Cry*, but does not have to be. Encourage students to use their imaginations freely in selecting topics and settings for their paragraphs and using the words in clever but accurate ways. For example, a word such as "mortgage" might suggest a modern suburban setting, while the word "imprisoned" might suggest being trapped in a cave. Have students share their paragraphs in an online journal using Penzu (http://tinyurl.com/lwuy989) and see the many original ways they have used the words. Have students confirm each other's correct use of the words.

Please note that excerpts and passages in the StudySync® library, workbooks, and PDFs are intended as touchstones to generate interest in an author's work. The excerpts and passages do not substitute for the reading of entire texts, and StudySync® strongly recommends that teachers and students seek out and purchase the whole literary or informational work in order to experience it as the author intended. Links to online resellers are available in our digital library. In addition, complete works may be ordered through an authorized reseller by filling out and returning to StudySync® the order form enclosed in this workbook.

Teacher's Edition   **177**

Core Path	Access Path
	Extend **Retell and Discuss.** To enhance students' appreciation of story structure, have different students in turn retell the exposition, the trigger, the rising action, the climax, and the denouement (or more simply, the beginning, middle, and ending) of the excerpt from *Roll of Thunder, Hear My Cry*, based on their reading. Brief character descriptions should be part of the retelling. Then use one or more of the following questions to prompt students to discuss their reactions to the excerpt and their expectations about rereading it: • Do you remember certain scenes or parts of the story better than others? Which ones? Why do you think that is? • What would you like to understand better about the story when you read it this time? • As you read the story this time, what aspects of the plot structure and of the characters are you going to pay most attention to? Explain.

2. READ

Core Path	Access Path
Model Close Reading. Project the text onto the board and model a close reading of the first few paragraphs using the annotation strategies mentioned below. While modeling annotation strategies, make notes that tie the text to the focus skill and demonstrate what students are looking for as they read. Here is some guidance for you as you annotate for your students: • As the Skills lesson that precedes this text shows, a story has a structure, or organization. A given sentence or section of the story might advance the plot, develop a character, rearrange the time sequence of the narrative, create or alter a mood, add tension or suspense—or a combination of those. In the excerpt from *Roll of Thunder, Hear My Cry*, the first paragraph, or exposition, introduces the setting and characters.	

Core Path	Access Path
• A shift from one passage to another, such as from narrative to dialogue, may signal a transition. The excerpt from *Roll of Thunder, Hear My Cry* contains several separate conversations. They vary by characters and by topic. The first conversation begins with the third paragraph of the excerpt. • In this story, several characters use a variation on standard English called a dialect. When readers recognize dialect or other variations, they should pause and be sure they understand exactly what is being said, and consider what the use of dialect might reveal about a character or setting. • It's a good idea for a reader to pause after noticing when a passage ends, and review what it was about. This can help give the reader a sense of how that particular passage relates to what has come before and what will come after. Analyzing this will help students to understand how each sentence or passage fits into the overall structure of the text and helps to develop the story's plot. For example, the line, ". . . right now I've got better things to think about," shows the reader that the dialogue between Papa and Mama is ending. It's a good place to pause and ask, "What was this section about?"	
Read and Annotate. Read the Skills Focus questions as a class, so your students know what they should pay close attention to as they read. Then have students read and annotate the excerpt. Ask students to use the annotation tool as they read to: 1. respond to the Skills Focus section 2. ask questions 3. make connections 4. identify key themes. events, characters, and details	**Note:** While on-grade level students are reading and annotating, work one-on-one or in small groups with Beginning, Intermediate, Advanced and Approaching students to support them as they read and annotate the text.

Please note that excerpts and passages in the StudySync® library, workbooks, and PDFs are intended as touchstones to generate interest in an author's work. The excerpts and passages do not substitute for the reading of entire texts, and StudySync® strongly recommends that teachers and students seek out and purchase the whole literary or informational work in order to experience it as the author intended. Links to online resellers are available in our digital library. In addition, complete works may be ordered through an authorized reseller by filling out and returning to StudySync® the order form enclosed in this workbook.

Teacher's Edition   179

Core Path	Access Path
5. note unfamiliar vocabulary 6. note variations from standard English 7. capture their reaction to the ideas and events in the text As they reread the text, remind students to use the comprehension strategy of Rereading that they learned in the First Read.	**Beginner & Intermediate** **Summarize and Analyze the Text.** Work with these students to complete the sentence frames on the Access 1 and 2 handouts (note: the sentence frames for Intermediate students on the Access 2 handout contain fewer scaffolds). They will then use the completed sentence frames to help them analyze and annotate the text by completing the Skills Focus questions. Refer to the sample Skills Focus answers to help them complete the sentence frames and annotate the text. **Advanced** **Work in Pairs.** Pair these students with more proficient English speakers to work together on analyzing and annotating the text to complete the Skills Focus questions. If these students need more support, have them use the Sentence Frames on the Access 3 handout as they work with their more proficient peers. **Approaching** **Summarize the Text.** Have these students discuss and complete the text summary on the Access 4 handout and use their summary to help them analyze and annotate the text by completing the Skills Focus questions. Correct answers for the summary are at the end of this lesson plan online. Also refer to the sample Skills Focus answers to aid students with their annotations.
Discuss. After students have read the text, use the sample responses to the Skills Focus questions at the end of the lesson plan online to discuss the reading and the process of searching for ways to identify story structure. Make sure that students have acquired and accurately use academic-specific words and phrases related to the skill, and demonstrate a command of formal English appropriate to the discussion.	**Extend** **Pair and Share.** In small groups or pairs, ask students to share and discuss their annotations with a focus on story structure and how an author organizes, or structures, the text. You can provide students with questions to guide their discussion: 1. In this excerpt, which elements of the story's structure do you feel were most compelling? Why? (Answers will vary, but might include the dialogue and interactions between family members.) Quote parts of the text that you especially liked.

Core Path	Access Path
	2. Do you feel that any element of this story's structure was ineffective or unnecessary? (Answers will vary.) Identify it and support your view with reasons and textual evidence.
	3. Imagine that you are the author, and somewhere in this excerpt you want to insert an extra section—a flashback. What would it show? Where in the excerpt would it go? In what ways do you think this addition would enhance the text? (Answers will vary.)
	Extend Tech Infusion **Discuss the Unit Question.** Remind students of the unit question, "How do people decide when to stand up for others and themselves?" Using Socrative (http://tinyurl.com/8544k4p) or Poll Everywhere (http://tinyurl.com/3zyw33) to poll students on the following question: "Should Papa take a stand by boycotting Thurston Wallace's store, or not?" Share the results of the poll and invite students to discuss the reasons for their answers.

3. WRITE

Core Path	Access Path
Prewrite and Plan. Divide students into groups to read the prompt and discuss story structure. Invite them to begin by discussing the structure of the excerpt from *Roll of Thunder, Hear My Cry*. Suggest that they use the example of this excerpt to brainstorm how understanding story structure helps them understand fiction overall. Remind them to examine the use of language, including variations on standard English. Students can brainstorm together either as a class or in small groups to begin planning their responses. Remind them to mention specific story elements from the excerpt and details from their annotations to support their ideas.	**Beginner & Intermediate** **Answer and Discuss.** Have students complete the prewriting questions on the Access 1 and 2 handouts and then explain their answers to a partner before they write. Explain to students that when they answer a question—such as *How does story structure help you understand the characters and plot in* Roll of Thunder, Hear My Cry?—they need to include a detail, example, or quote from the text that supports the statement. For example, students could include the first line, "Don't keep anything from me, David. If there's trouble, I want to know," which reveals that there are problems the family will have to face.

Please note that excerpts and passages in the StudySync® library, workbooks, and PDFs are intended as touchstones to generate interest in an author's work. The excerpts and passages do not substitute for the reading of entire texts, and StudySync® strongly recommends that teachers and students seek out and purchase the whole literary or informational work in order to experience it as the author intended. Links to online resellers are available in our digital library. In addition, complete works may be ordered through an authorized reseller by filling out and returning to StudySync® the order form enclosed in this workbook.

Core Path	Access Path
	Approaching **Answer Prewriting Questions.** Have students complete the prewriting questions on the Access 4 handout to summarize their thoughts before they write.
	Extend **Tech Infusion** **Organize.** You may want to allow students to use Google Docs (http://tinyurl.com/u7u9k) or TitanPad (http://tinyurl.com/kla4kmd) to build a shared document of prewriting notes, including points such as: • What are the major structural elements of the excerpt from *Roll of Thunder, Hear My Cry*? • What are my understandings of each element? • What would be a good thesis, or main idea, for my essay about story structure? • What two or three supporting points about story structure should this essay include? • What scenes could be connected to those ideas? Ask students to write their responses individually.
	Extend **Reflect.** After students have had an opportunity to evaluate peer samples, invite them to discuss their experiences of the review process. Ask them to consider the following points: • What did they learn about writing? • What did they learn about reviewing other writers' work? • What did they learn about having their own work read by their peers? Encourage students to share particular pieces of feedback that they found helpful or unhelpful.

Core Path	Access Path
Discuss. Project these instructions for the peer review onto the board and review them with your class, so they know what they are looking for when they begin to provide their classmates with feedback: • How has this response helped you understand an author's choice about story structure? • Does the writer refer to specific events and characters in the text? Does the writer connect those to the story's structure in a clear way? • Has the writer identified examples of dialect and other language variations used by characters, and explained their relevance? • Has the writer cited specific evidence from the text to support his or her ideas? • What thing(s) does this response do especially well? • Remember that your comments are most useful when they are constructive. After you've looked at the peer review instructions, review the rubric with students before they begin writing. Allow time for students briefly to pose and discuss any questions they may have about the peer review instructions and the rubric. Tell students how many peer reviews they will need to complete once they submit their writing.	
Write. Ask students to complete the writing assignment using textual evidence to support their answers. Once they have completed their writing, they should click "Submit."	
Review. Once students complete their writing assignment, they should submit substantive feedback to two peers. Students should use their peers' feedback to improve their writing.	

Please note that excerpts and passages in the StudySync® library, workbooks, and PDFs are intended as touchstones to generate interest in an author's work. The excerpts and passages do not substitute for the reading of entire texts, and StudySync® strongly recommends that teachers and students seek out and purchase the whole literary or informational work in order to experience it as the author intended. Links to online resellers are available in our digital library. In addition, complete works may be ordered through an authorized reseller by filling out and returning to StudySync® the order form enclosed in this workbook.

Teacher's Edition 183

BLAST:
Tomato/Tomahto: Dialects and Accents

OVERVIEW

To provide context for some of the dialogue in *Roll of Thunder, Hear My Cry,* students will learn about dialect and why an author might choose to use it, with a focus on Mark Twain's "The Celebrated Jumping Frog of Calaveras County." Research links explore more about accents and dialects, including audio examples of several American dialects.

OBJECTIVES

1. Explore background information about what dialect is and why an author might choose to use it, with a focus on Mark Twain's "The Celebrated Jumping Frog of Calaveras County" as an example.
2. Research using the hyperlinks to learn more about dialects, including audio examples.
3. Participate effectively in a range of conversations and collaborations to express ideas and build upon the ideas of others.

ELA Common Core Standards:

Reading: Informational Text - RI.6.1
Writing - W.6.1.A, W.6.5, W.6.6
Speaking & Listening - SL.6.1.A, SL.6.1.B, SL.6.1.C, SL.6.1.D, SL.6.2
Language - L.6.1.E

RESOURCES

Access 1 handout (Beginner)

Access 2 handout (Intermediate)

Access 4 handout (Approaching)

TITLE/DRIVING QUESTION:

Core Path	Access Path
Discuss. As a class read aloud the title and driving question for this Blast. Ask students what they know about dialect, and other variations on standard English, already. Do they have a sense of why an author might choose to use dialect? Remind students that they should not immediately reply to this question. They'll be returning to this question and responding after they've read the Background and some of the Research Links.	**English Learners All Levels & Approaching Discuss a Recording.** Have students listen to a recording of "The Celebrated Jumping Frog of Calaveras County," such as the one at: http://tinyurl.com/kqp46tx. Or students might be familiar with Joel Chandler Harris and the "Uncle Remus" tales, which also use dialect. A recording of "Uncle Remus" is at http://tinyurl.com/l5teklw. Discuss how the recording uses dialect and how dialects gives the story a sense of time and place, prompting students with questions such as: • Why did the author use dialect? • How does dialect change or add to a story? • What is the difference between dialect and an accent? • What are some stories, movies, or songs that use dialect?
Draft. In their notebooks or on scrap paper, have students draft their initial responses to the driving question. This will provide them with a baseline response that they will be altering as they gain more information about the topic in the Background and Research Links sections of the assignment.	**Beginner & Intermediate** **Draft with Sentence Frame.** When drafting their initial response to the driving question, have students refer to this Blast sentence frame on their Access 1 and 2 handouts: • Authors sometimes write in dialect because _____. Point out these two key features of the sentence frame: 1. The sentence frame borrows language directly from the Blast driving question to provide a response. 2. The word "because" prompts students to provide evidence to support their response.

Please note that excerpts and passages in the StudySync® library, workbooks, and PDFs are intended as touchstones to generate interest in an author's work. The excerpts and passages do not substitute for the reading of entire texts, and StudySync® strongly recommends that teachers and students seek out and purchase the whole literary or informational work in order to experience it as the author intended. Links to online resellers are available in our digital library. In addition, complete works may be ordered through an authorized reseller by filling out and returning to StudySync® the order form enclosed in this workbook.

BACKGROUND:

Core Path	Access Path
Read. Have students read the Blast background to provide context for the driving question.	**Beginner & Intermediate** **Read with Support.** Have students read the Blast background to provide context for the driving question. When they encounter unfamiliar words or phrases, have students refer to the glossary on their Access 1 and 2 handouts. If there are unfamiliar words that are not included in their glossary, encourage students to check a dictionary or online reference tool, like http://tinyurl.com/3qe7. **Approaching** **Read and Summarize.** Have students read the Blast background to provide context for the driving question. As they read, ask students to complete the fill in the blank summary of the background provided on their Access 4 handout. When they encounter unfamiliar words or phrases, have students refer to the glossary on their Access 4 handout.
Discuss. Either in pairs, small groups, or as a whole class use these questions to spur discussion among your students about Background information. Make sure students follow the rules for collegial discussions. 1. What is dialect? (a variation of language used by a particular group of people of a particular place or time) 2. Why did Mark Twain use dialect in his short story "The Celebrated Jumping Frog of Calaveras County?" (to depict the personality and character of Samuel Wheeler, a garrulous storyteller, whose dialect would have been very common among the members of a western mining camp in the late 1800s) 3. What is the difference between *accent* and *dialect*? (*accent* is only about how words are pronounced, *dialect* also includes grammar and usage) 4. How can an author portray dialect in text? (by changing the spelling of some words and using different grammar)	**Beginner** **Discuss.** Pair Beginning with Advanced (or Beyond) students and have them use the dialogue starter on their Access 1 handout to discuss the topic. Advise them to return to the dialogue and switch roles if they get stuck. **Intermediate** **Discuss.** Pair Intermediate with Advanced (or Beyond) students and have them use the dialogue starter on their Access handout 2 to discuss the topic. Advise them to return to the dialogue and switch roles if they get stuck. If their conversation is progressing smoothly, encourage them to continue the discussion beyond the dialogue starter sheet. They can expand their conversations to discuss authors who use dialect, why they use it, and how it makes the story more interesting as well as the difference between accent and dialect.

Core Path	Access Path
(G) Grammar, Usage, and Mechanics. Review with students the purpose of dialect in text, including its effect on a reader's perception of a story's setting or characters. For additional resources on types of dialects and other non-standard English, refer to the StudySync Standard English Learners Handbook online.	

Then, encourage students to analyze the use of dialect in "The Celebrated Jumping Frog of Calaveras County."

1. Reread this sentence from the story: "Quicker'n you could wink, he'd spring straight up, and snake a fly off'n the counter there." What words or phrases are examples of regional dialect? ("spring straight up" and "snake a fly") What words or phrases are examples of accent? ("quicker'n" and "off'n")

2. Based on the excerpts you have heard so far, how might Twain's use of dialect impact the way a reader experiences the story? (It allows the reader to hear the characters' words as they would have actually said them; it adds humor to the story.)

3. In the story, Simon Wheeler's narrative recounting the tale of Jim Smiley is written completely in the dialect of a miner from the Old West. Suppose Twain had chosen to write this recount using standard English rather than dialect. How might the reading experience be different? (The reader might not fully understand or appreciate Simon Wheeler's personality; the tone of the story would be less humorous.)

Please note that excerpts and passages in the StudySync® library, workbooks, and PDFs are intended as touchstones to generate interest in an author's work. The excerpts and passages do not substitute for the reading of entire texts, and StudySync® strongly recommends that teachers and students seek out and purchase the whole literary or informational work in order to experience it as the author intended. Links to online resellers are available in our digital library. In addition, complete works may be ordered through an authorized reseller by filling out and returning to StudySync® the order form enclosed in this workbook.

Teacher's Edition 187

Core Path	Access Path
Brainstorm. Remind students about the Driving Question for this Blast: Why do authors sometimes write in dialect? Ask students to think about what they've learned about the differences and similarities between *accent* and *dialect*. Have them make a Venn diagram in their notebooks comparing the two concepts. Here's a short example of how that might look:	

Accent	Similarities	Dialect
doesn't affect grammar or usage; harder to convey in text	both affect the way speech sounds; both involve purposely misspelling words to convey in text	affects not only pronunciation but grammar and usage; can be portrayed in text

RESEARCH LINKS:

Core Path	Access Path
Examine and Explore. Before asking students to explore the research links, use these activities and questions to guide their exploration: 1. Ask students to look at "Uses and Abuses of Dialect." What are some of the pitfalls of using dialect in your writing? (It can make your writing hard to read; it can alienate some readers.) 2. What's the most important thing to look for in any research link you click on? (examples of how and why authors might use dialect)	

Core Path	Access Path
3. Explore "International Dialects of English Archive." Ask students to listen to an example of dialect from their own state. Do they think it sounds like the way they speak? (Answers will vary.) 4. Which link would you use to learn more about Mark Twain's use of dialect? ("The Dialects of Huckleberry Finn")	

	Extend
	Research, Discuss and Present.
	
	1. Assign each group one link to explore in depth.
	
	2. Ask them to discuss the information:
	
	   a. What are the key points?
	
	   b. What inferences did you make as you read?
	
	   c. What did you learn about this "big idea" from reading this research?
	
	   d. How did this help you to better understand the topic?
	
	   e. What questions does your group have after exploring this link?
	
	3. Allow students time to informally present what they learned.

	Extend **Tech Infusion** **Share.** As students explore the links, allow them to make videos compiling their findings, using a website like Animoto (http://tinyurl.com/2zj97a).

QUIKPOLL (UP TO 5 ANSWERS):

Core Path	Access Path
Participate. Answer the poll question. Have students discuss their reasons for their answers. Students should refer to evidence from the background and research links to defend their answer.	

NUMBER CRUNCH:

Core Path	Access Path
Predict, Discuss, and Click. Before students click on the number, break them into pairs and have them make predictions about what they think the number is related to. After they've clicked the number, ask students if they are surprised by the revealed information.	

CREATE YOUR BLAST (140 CHARACTERS):

Core Path	Access Path
Blast. Ask students to write their Blast response in 140 characters or less.	**Beginner** **Blast with Support.** Have students refer back to the sentence frame on their Access 1 handout that they used to create their original Blast draft. Ask them to use this frame to write and enter their final Blast. **Intermediate** **Blast with Support.** Have students attempt to draft their Blast without the sentence frame on their Access 2 handout. If students struggle to compose their Blast draft without the sentence frame, remind them to reference it for support. **Beyond** **Write a Claim.** Ask students to use their answer to the poll question to write a strong claim that could be used as the foundation for a piece of argumentative writing. Once students have written their claims, ask them to read the claims to a small group of their peers. This activity will provide them practice writing claims, as well as expose them to claims written by their peers.

Core Path	Access Path
Review. After students have completed their own Blasts, ask them to review the Blasts of their peers and provide feedback.	**Extend** **Discuss.** As a whole class or in groups, identify a few strong blasts and discuss what made those responses so powerful. As a group, analyze and discuss what characteristics make a blast interesting or effective.
	Extend **Revise.** Resend a second version of this Blast assignment to your students and have them submit revised versions of their original Blasts. Do the same responses make the Top 10? How have the answers improved from the first submissions?

Please note that excerpts and passages in the StudySync® library, workbooks, and PDFs are intended as touchstones to generate interest in an author's work. The excerpts and passages do not substitute for the reading of entire texts, and StudySync® strongly recommends that teachers and students seek out and purchase the whole literary or informational work in order to experience it as the author intended. Links to online resellers are available in our digital library. In addition, complete works may be ordered through an authorized reseller by filling out and returning to StudySync® the order form enclosed in this workbook.

Teacher's Edition 191

FIRST READ:
Children of the Dust Bowl: The True Story of the School at Weedpatch Camp

OVERVIEW

The informational text *Children of the Dust Bowl: The True Story of the School at Weedpatch Camp,* by Jerry Stanley, examines the experiences of migrant children from Oklahoma who settle in California during the Dust Bowl, and the work of one man who decides to stand up for them. The First Read gives students the opportunity to experience the text with a limited context.

OBJECTIVES

1. Perform an initial reading of a text and demonstrate comprehension by responding to short analysis and inference questions with textual evidence.
2. Practice defining vocabulary words using context and checking inferred definitions in context or a dictionary.
3. Participate effectively in a range of conversations and collaborations to express ideas and build upon the ideas of others.

   ELA Common Core Standards:
   Reading: Informational Text - RI.6.1, RI.6.2, RI.6.4, RI.6.10
   Speaking & Listening - SL.6.1.A, SL.6.1.B, SL.6.1.C, SL.6.2
   Language - L.6.4.A, L.6.4.B, L.6.4.D

RESOURCES

Access 1 handout (Beginner)

Access 2 handout (Intermediate)

Access 3 handout (Advanced)

Access 4 handout (Approaching)

ACCESS COMPLEX TEXT

These excerpts from *Children of the Dust Bowl: The True Story of the School at Weedpatch Camp* focus primarily on the plight of Okie children living in Kern County, California, during the 1930s. In addition to exploring the hostilities of Californians toward the Okies, Stanley discusses the efforts of Leo Hart to provide a school for the children. Students are asked to determine the author's central or main idea. Use the following suggestions to provide scaffolded instruction for a close reading of the more complex features of this text:

- **Connection of Ideas** - Stanley does not explicitly state the central idea in this selection. Instead, he leaves it to the reader to infer the most important ideas. Consequently, students need to decide what the text is mainly about and what the supporting details have in common.

- **Organization** - The selection is composed of excerpts from three chapters in *Children of the Dust Bowl*. Students will need to determine how the excerpts fit together in order to determine the author's central idea.

- **Specific Vocabulary** - Stanley uses many words with negative connotations when describing the reactions of Californians to the Okies. In addition, he makes the point that the term *Okies* took on a negative connotation over time. Students will need to pay attention to the connotation of words when finding supporting evidence for the author's main ideas.

- **Sentence Structure** - Sentences are complex, and some include direct quotes.

1. INTRODUCTION

Core Path	Access Path
Read. Individually or as a class, read the introduction for *Children of the Dust Bowl: The True Story of the School at Weedpatch Camp*. The introduction provides context for the excerpts taken from Chapters 4, 5, and 6.	**English Learners All Levels & Approaching Read and Discuss.** Ask students to read and discuss the introduction for *Children of the Dust Bowl: The True Story of the School at Weedpatch Camp*. Have them refer to the Introduction Glossary on their Access 1, 2, 3, and 4 handouts for definitions of key vocabulary terms. If there are unfamiliar words that are not included in their glossary, encourage students to check a dictionary or online reference tool, like http://dictionary.reference.com.

Please note that excerpts and passages in the StudySync® library, workbooks, and PDFs are intended as touchstones to generate interest in an author's work. The excerpts and passages do not substitute for the reading of entire texts, and StudySync® strongly recommends that teachers and students seek out and purchase the whole literary or informational work in order to experience it as the author intended. Links to online resellers are available in our digital library. In addition, complete works may be ordered through an authorized reseller by filling out and returning to StudySync® the order form enclosed in this workbook.

Teacher's Edition   193

Core Path	Access Path
Build Background. Because students may be unfamiliar with the period of the Dust Bowl, form small research groups. Provide each group with sticky notes and a map of the United States, focusing on the area between Oklahoma and California. Ask students to utilize print or digital resources to locate and mark the following places:	**Beginner & Intermediate** **Build Background.** Break students into small groups or pairs. Ask students to look at images of the Dust Bowl, such as the ones at: http://tinyurl.com/mg7lmnv. Ask students to discuss the images and what they think of the Dust Bowl. They can use their discussions as points for reference when they do their research.

Core Path

Build Background. Because students may be unfamiliar with the period of the Dust Bowl, form small research groups. Provide each group with sticky notes and a map of the United States, focusing on the area between Oklahoma and California. Ask students to utilize print or digital resources to locate and mark the following places:

- Prairies in northwestern Oklahoma and the panhandle
- Route 66
- San Joaquin Valley, California
- Los Angeles, California
- Arvin, California
- Kern County, California
- Arvin Farm Labor Camp or the Arvin Federal Government Camp or the Sunset Labor Camp (Weedpatch Camp)
- Vineland School District

Then, have students use the sticky notes to annotate the map using the following focus questions:

- Why did the Okies leave the prairies of Oklahoma?
- How long was the journey along route 66 between Oklahoma and California? What decision did Okies make when they reached Barstow, California?
- Who built the Arvin Farm Labor camp and for what purpose? Describe the camp.
- Who is John Steinbeck? What is the connection between Steinbeck's *The Grapes of Wrath* and the Arvin Farm Labor Camp?

Ask each group to present selected entries to the class. Lead the class to identify and discuss the causes and effects of the Okie migration during the Dust Bowl.

Access Path

Beginner & Intermediate

Build Background. Break students into small groups or pairs. Ask students to look at images of the Dust Bowl, such as the ones at: http://tinyurl.com/mg7lmnv. Ask students to discuss the images and what they think of the Dust Bowl. They can use their discussions as points for reference when they do their research.

Once students have completed their discussions, have them pair up with Advanced and Beyond students to do the research. Students might also be interested in listening to Woody Guthrie singing about the Dust Bowl, see: http://tinyurl.com/k5llfhb.

Approaching

Build Background. Break students into small groups. Ask to students to look at images of Dust Bowl, such as the ones at: http://tinyurl.com/mg7lmnv. Ask them to think about these questions:

- How would you describe the Dust Bowl?
- Why did people want to escape the Dust Bowl?
- How would you feel if migrating to California?

Students might also learn more about the Dust Bowl by listening to Woody Guthrie sing about it, see: http://tinyurl.com/k5llfhb.

Once they have reviewed the images and listened to the song, have them pair with Advanced students to conduct the research. They can use the images as their frame of reference.

Core Path	Access Path
	Beyond **Analyze and Discuss a Quotation.** "When a majority of the people are hungry and cold they will take by force what they need. And the little screaming fact that sounds through all history: repression works only to strengthen and knit the repressed" (John Steinbeck, *The Grapes of Wrath*). 1. What is repression? 2. What are some examples of repression in history? What is the outcome in each example? 3. What do you think this quotation means? 4. Do you agree with this quotation? Why or why not? Have students share their insights into the quote with the whole class.

2. READ

Core Path	Access Path
Make Predictions about Vocabulary. There are five bold vocabulary words in the text. As students read the text, ask them to make predictions about what they think each bold vocabulary word means based on the context clues in the sentence. If you are in a low-tech classroom and students are reading from printed copies or a projected text, ask students to record predictions in their notes, so they can be easily referenced in class. If your students have access to technology, they can use the annotation tool to make their predictions. It might be helpful to model this practice for students before they begin reading. Either using the board or projecting the actual text, focus in on the sentence that uses the word "epidemics": • For example, epidemics of disease in the Okievilles caused the health and sanitation budget for Kern County to double between 1935 and 1940.	**Note:** This exercise, which extends vocabulary instruction, should be completed when the class shifts from whole group instruction to individual work during the "Read and Annotate" exercise.

Please note that excerpts and passages in the StudySync® library, workbooks, and PDFs are intended as touchstones to generate interest in an author's work. The excerpts and passages do not substitute for the reading of entire texts, and StudySync® strongly recommends that teachers and students seek out and purchase the whole literary or informational work in order to experience it as the author intended. Links to online resellers are available in our digital library. In addition, complete works may be ordered through an authorized reseller by filling out and returning to StudySync® the order form enclosed in this workbook.

Teacher's Edition   **195**

Core Path	Access Path
Model for the class how to use the overall structure and meaning of the sentence and the sentences around it, the word's position, and other clues to define the unfamiliar vocabulary word. In this case, point out these context clues:	**Beginner, Intermediate & Approaching Pair Practice.**

Core Path

Model for the class how to use the overall structure and meaning of the sentence and the sentences around it, the word's position, and other clues to define the unfamiliar vocabulary word. In this case, point out these context clues:

- I can start by looking at the structure of the sentence. It says that the epidemics were "of disease," so I know that an epidemic can be connected to sickness.

- It also says the epidemics caused a big increase in the "health and sanitation budget." I know what health means, and if the health budget had to double, I can infer that many people were sick.

- If many people were sick, and had the disease, then "epidemics" must be "large outbreaks of disease."

- This definition makes sense if I plug it into the sentence in place of "epidemics." But to be sure, I can consult a dictionary. This shows me that "epidemic" does, in fact, mean "something affecting a large number of people or spreading widely, such as a disease." In this context, it seems like it's definitely referring to disease.

Model Reading Comprehension Strategy. Before students begin reading, model the reading comprehension strategy of asking and answering questions by using this Think Aloud that talks students through the first two paragraphs of text. First explain to your students that asking and answering questions is a strategy you can use before, during, and after you read a text; by asking questions and then searching for answers within that text, you engage with it and will better remember what you read.

Access Path

Beginner, Intermediate & Approaching Pair Practice.

1. Pair students with more proficient readers.

2. Give them an additional sentence that contains a new vocabulary word.

3. Ask the students to complete a Think Aloud using the teacher-led Make Predictions about Vocabulary activity as a model, while the proficient student actively listens.

4. The student should use the context clues in the sentence to try to determine the meaning of the new vocabulary word.

5. After the student has completed the Think Aloud and made a prediction about the word's meaning, allow time for the proficient reader to add his/her own thoughts and clarify any points of confusion.

6. Once they've completed this Think Aloud, encourage them to use a dictionary to confirm the definition of the new vocabulary word. Have them refer to the vocabulary listing on their Access 1, 2, and 4 handouts for definitions of key vocabulary terms in the text. Encourage them to add any additional vocabulary words or idioms they find in the text and look up definitions for those words and idioms online or in a dictionary.

Note: This exercise, which extends vocabulary instruction, should be completed when the class shifts from whole group instruction to individual work during the "Read and Annotate" exercise.

Core Path	Access Path
Model for students how asking and answering questions will help them better comprehend the selection and help drive their discussions.	**Beginner, Intermediate & Approaching** **Apply Reading Comprehension Strategy.**
• When I read the first paragraph, I have one important question: Why are some Californians and the media so hostile toward the Okies?	1. Have students read the first chapter excerpt. Invite them to identify what people say about the "Okies." What questions do the students have about what people are saying? Why do they think these people are saying these things? Have students write their responses. Next, have them write any questions they have about what they have read.
• As I read the second paragraph, I learn the answer to my question about why some Californians and the media are so hostile toward the Okies. This information gives rise to another question: Are the Okies really to blame for the circumstances, or are there larger forces at work? As I continue to read, I'll look for clues to help me answer this question.	2. Now have students read the second paragraph. Remind students this paragraph answers many questions about why the people were so hostile and angry at the migrants. Ask them to write down any questions they have about what might happen to the migrant children. Encourage students to answer their questions by looking for answers in the text.
	3. Allow pairs to read the third paragraph. Give them time to discuss the reading and their questions. Invite students to share how they found answers to their questions in the text. Ask them if they have any questions they'd like answered as they continue to read.
Read and Annotate. Have students independently read and annotate the excerpt. Ask students to use the annotation tool as they read to:	**Beginner** **Coach the Reading.** While other students read, annotate, and discuss the text independently, work with Beginning students, reading aloud the text and pausing periodically or when any student has a question. Coach students in articulating their questions for the group and in highlighting and annotating the text. Have students use the Annotation Guide in the Access 1 handout to support them as they highlight and annotate the text.
1. use context clues to analyze and determine the meaning of the bolded vocabulary terms	
2. ask questions about passages of the text that may be unclear or unresolved	
3. identify key information, events, ideas, and connections between them	
4. note unfamiliar vocabulary	
5. capture their reaction to events and ideas in the text	

Core Path	Access Path
	For further support, ask questions about the text such as:
	• Is there anything about the text that you don't understand?
	• What do you think happened to migrant children?
	• Do you think building a special school for the migrant children was a good idea? Why or why not?
	Intermediate
	Read Aloud and Discuss. Have these students take turns reading aloud the text and use the definitions on the Access 2 handout to help them with words or idioms that may be unfamiliar. If students need help with annotating the text, have them use the Annotation Guide on the Access 2 handout. After working with the Beginning students, you may wish to check this group's progress and provide support as needed.
	Advanced
	Pair with Proficient Peers. Have Advanced students work with English proficient peers to read, annotate, and discuss the text. Have students use the Annotation Guide in the Access 3 handout to support them as they highlight and annotate the text.
	Approaching
	Use the Annotation Guide. Have students use the Annotation Guide in the Access 4 handout to support them as they highlight and annotate the text.

Core Path	Access Path
Discuss. In small groups or pairs, have students discuss the questions and inferences they made while reading. Make sure students follow the rules for collegial discussions: Refer to Collaborative Discussions in the Speaking & Listening Handbook.	**English Learners All Levels & Approaching** Use the extra time while on-and beyond-grade level students are discussing their first reads of the text to work individually and in small groups with Approaching readers and English Learners as outlined on the previous page. Should those students complete their first reads quickly, integrate them into the on and beyond grade level discussion groups. Otherwise Approaching readers and English Learners will be given an opportunity to participate in text discussions with their peers later in the lesson.

1. How does Leo Hart view the Okies differently than many other Californians or the media? (He is sympathetic to their situation and objects to their mistreatment, "ridicule" and "rejection." He is concerned with helping the Okie children.)

2. What was Leo Hart's vision of a school for Okie children? (Leo Hart believes that the Okie school should reflect the needs of these particular students. He wants to provide a specific curriculum for them. He wants to create an environment that will help the Okie children feel "proud" about who they are.)

3. What were Hart's tactics for getting approval for the Okie school? (Hart's strategy was to make it seem as if he was doing the public school board president a favor by eliminating "overcrowding" in the schools. Instead, he was removing the Okie children so he could send them to a special school he was planning to create, just for them.)

4. What question did you have that you could find the answer to in the text? What question could you not find the answer to? (I wondered exactly how Leo Hart was going to help the Okie children. That answer was in the text. I also wondered what it was that made Hart so sympathetic to their situation. It seemed that he could especially relate to these children. I wondered if he faced some of the same problems growing up as they did. I could not find that specific answer in the text.)

Core Path	Access Path
	Extend **Tech Infusion** **Write.** Have students write journal entries from the points of view of students who attend Leo Hart's school. Tell students to use language and dialect that is appropriate for their characters. Ask volunteers to read aloud their entries in an open-mike style reading. You may record these readings and post them to the class YouTube channel.

3. THINK

Core Path	Access Path
Answer and Discuss. Have students complete the Think questions and then use the peer review instructions and rubric to complete two peer reviews. Refer to the sample answers at the end of this lesson plan online to discuss responses with your students.	**Beginner & Intermediate** **Sentence Frames.** Have students use the Sentence Frames on the Access 1 and 2 handouts to support their responses to the Think questions. If necessary, distribute sentence frames to Advanced students as well. **Approaching** **Find the Evidence.** Have students use Find the Evidence on the Access 4 handout to help them identify the evidence needed to answer the questions.
	Extend **Debate.** Provide students with the following sentence frame: • It was/was not a good idea for Leo Hart to further segregate the Okie children by placing them in a separate school because _____. Place students in pairs or groups with equal numbers of students who respond in the positive and in the negative. Ask each student to present his or her point of view for discussion. Have each pair or group present selected ideas to the class. Ask the class whether any points of view are changed as a result of the discussion and why.

Copyright © BookheadEd Learning, LLC

Central or Main Idea

OVERVIEW

Determining the central or main idea in a text is a key to understanding the author's purpose, structure, and message. This lesson plan provides follow-up questions and useful enrichments to help teachers guide students toward a usable, repeatable method for identifying the central or main idea.

OBJECTIVES

1. Learn the definition of central or main idea.
2. Practice using concrete strategies for identifying central or main idea.
3. Participate effectively in a range of conversations and collaborations to express ideas and build upon the ideas of others.

ELA Common Core Standards:
Reading: Informational Text - RI.6.1, RI.6.2
Speaking & Listening - SL.6.1.A, SL.6.1.B, SL.6.1.C, SL.6.1.D, SL.6.2

RESOURCES

Access 1 handout (Beginner)

Access 2 handout (Intermediate)

Access 3 handout (Advanced)

Access 4 handout (Approaching)

1. DEFINE

Core Path	Access Path
Watch. Watch the Concept Definition video on central or main idea with your students. Make sure students understand the definition of central or main idea, as well as how to write proper summaries. Pause the video at these key moments to discuss the information with your students: 1. 0:23 – Why is it necessary to have a central or main idea in an informational text? How might an informational text be different if there were no central or main idea within? 2. 0:43 – How do you determine the "key details" in a given text? What are a few strategies for figuring out which details in the text are more important than others? 3. 1:09 – Why is summarizing such an important study skill? How do we apply this skill outside of the classroom, as well?	**English Learners All Levels & Approaching Sentence Frames.** Have students complete the sentence frames on the Access 1, 2, 3, and 4 handouts as they watch the video. Correct answers are located at the end of the lesson plan online.
Read and Discuss. After watching the Concept Definition video, have students read the definition of central or main idea. Either in small groups or as a whole class, use these questions to engage students in a discussion about the central or main idea. Make sure students follow the rules for collegial discussions. 1. What is the central or main idea in a text? (The central or main idea is the most important point an author makes about a topic.) 2. How do supporting ideas and details help you determine the central or main idea? (Commonalities reveal the central or main idea.) 3. Why is it important to determine the central or main idea when reading nonfiction? (By determining the central or main idea, readers are able to understand what the focus of the text will be, the author's purpose, and message.)	**Beginner & Approaching** **Finish the Sentences.** To prepare students to participate in the discussion, have them complete the Finish the Sentences exercise on the Access 1 and 4 handouts as they read the definition of central or main idea. Correct answers are located at the end of the lesson plan online. **Intermediate & Advanced** **Discuss Prompts.** To help these students participate in the discussion, prompt them with questions that can be answered with a few words, such as: • What is the most important point an author makes about a topic? (the central or main idea) • What should you look for in supporting ideas and details? (commonalities) • What is the central idea of the last book or article that you read? (Answers will vary.)

Core Path	Access Path
	Beyond **Discuss.** Have students select a book they've read and describe its central idea. Compile a list of examples. Have students discuss how the central idea helps explain the topic. Why is it important to understand the central ideas in informational texts?
	Extend **Match the Information.** Provide student pairs with short informational texts and summaries of these texts. Have students cut and glue the texts into the left columns of two-column charts. Have students cut and glue the summaries into the right columns. Tell students to draw arrows between the two passages to show how information from the texts was translated into the summaries. Students should identify and label the central or main ideas as well as important supporting details. Make sure that students note that the summaries are written in original language and are generally shorter than the original texts.

2. MODEL

Core Path	Access Path
Read and Annotate. Have students independently read the Model section. As they read, ask students to use the annotation tool to: • highlight key points • ask questions • identify places where the Model applies the strategies laid out in the Identification and Application section	**Note:** During this portion of the lesson, instruction shifts from whole group to individual work. Use this time to work one-on-one or in small groups with Beginning, Intermediate, Advanced, and Approaching students.

Please note that excerpts and passages in the StudySync® library, workbooks, and PDFs are intended as touchstones to generate interest in an author's work. The excerpts and passages do not substitute for the reading of entire texts, and StudySync® strongly recommends that teachers and students seek out and purchase the whole literary or informational work in order to experience it as the author intended. Links to online resellers are available in our digital library. In addition, complete works may be ordered through an authorized reseller by filling out and returning to StudySync® the order form enclosed in this workbook.

Teacher's Edition   203

Core Path	Access Path
	Beginner & Intermediate
	Coach the Reading. Work with these students (either individually or in small groups) to fill out the Guided Reading questions on the Access 1 and 2 handouts. Have Beginning students refer to the Model Glossary on the Access 1 handout to help them determine the meaning of difficult words. (note: Provide the Access 1 handout Model Glossary to Intermediate students if necessary.) Let students know they'll use these answers to help participate in the discussion about the Model. Sample answers for this exercise are located at the end of the lesson plan online.
	Advanced
	Identify Evidence. Provide these students with the same instructions to read and annotate as on-grade level and Beyond students. In addition, ask Advanced students to complete the Identify Evidence exercise on the Access 3 handout. Let students know that they'll use these answers to help participate in the discussion about the Model. Sample answers for this exercise are located at the end of the lesson plan online.
	Approaching
	Guided Reading. Have students complete the Guided Reading questions on the Access 4 handout as they read. Let them know that they'll use these answers to help participate in the discussion about the Model. Sample answers for this exercise are located at the end of the lesson plan online.
Discuss. After students read the Model text, use these questions to facilitate a whole group discussion that helps students understand how to determine the central or main idea of the passage:	
1. To begin, how does this Model go about identifying the supporting details from the passages in chapter 4? (It identifies commonalities among details in chapter 4. The details focus on the many examples of negative treatment toward Okies.)	

Core Path	Access Path
2. How does this Model continue to determine the supporting details from the passages in chapter 5? (It identifies the commonalities among the details in chapter 5. Chapter 5 focuses on the educator Leo Hart, his anger about the way the Okie children were treated in the public schools, and his desire to help them.) 3. How does this Model identify the central idea of the text? (It notes a contrast between the negative treatment of the Okies described in chapter 4 and the positive attitude toward them shown by Leo Hart in chapter 5. The Model uses the supporting details from the passages in both chapters 4 and 5 to identify the central idea of the text.) 4. How does the Model create a summary? Why is summarizing a text important? (Identifying the central idea and supporting details can help readers summarize, or briefly retell, what the text is about. A summary uses original language and is free from personal opinions or judgments. Summarizing helps readers remember what they have read.)	
	Extend **Tech Infusion** **Use Graphic Organizers.** Have students use print or digital inverted pyramid graphic organizers to record important supporting details, identify commonalities, and write a summary of the central or main ideas for other informational texts on the subject of the Dust Bowl. Ask volunteers to present selected entries from their pyramids to the class. Prompt students to discuss how the use of graphic organizers helps them move from the words and ideas in whole texts to statements of central or main ideas.

Please note that excerpts and passages in the StudySync® library, workbooks, and PDFs are intended as touchstones to generate interest in an author's work. The excerpts and passages do not substitute for the reading of entire texts, and StudySync® strongly recommends that teachers and students seek out and purchase the whole literary or informational work in order to experience it as the author intended. Links to online resellers are available in our digital library. In addition, complete works may be ordered through an authorized reseller by filling out and returning to StudySync® the order form enclosed in this workbook.

Teacher's Edition   205

3. YOUR TURN

Core Path	Access Path
Assess and Explain. Have students answer the comprehension questions to test for understanding. Share the explanations for Parts A and B (located online) with your students.	
	Extend **Tech Infusion** **Analyze Character.** Before students respond to the questions, have them use print or digital web graphic organizers or open mind diagrams to create character charts for Leo Hart.
	Extend **Tech Infusion** **In Character.** Have student pairs write and perform dialogues of the telephone conversation between Leo Hart and school board president. Tell students to make sure that the dialogue illustrates language and character traits consistent with those presented in the text. You may record some of these performances and post them to the class YouTube channel.

Children of the Dust Bowl: The True Story of the School at Weedpatch Camp

OVERVIEW

The informational text *Children of the Dust Bowl: The True Story of the School at Weedpatch Camp,* by Jerry Stanley, examines the experiences of migrant children from Oklahoma who settle in California during the Dust Bowl and the work of one man who decides to stand up for them. The Close Read gives students the opportunity to determine the central or main idea of the text.

OBJECTIVES

1. Complete a close reading of a passage of informational text.
2. Practice and apply concrete strategies for identifying the central or main idea.
3. Participate effectively in a range of conversations and collaborations to express ideas and build upon the ideas of others.
4. Prewrite, plan, and produce clear and coherent writing in response to a prompt.

ELA Common Core Standards:

Reading: Informational Text - RI.6.1, RI.6.2, RI.6.3, RI.6.4, RI.6.6, RI.6.10

Writing - W.6.4, W.6.5, W.6.6, W.6.10

Speaking & Listening - SL.6.1.A, SL.6.1.B, SL.6.1.C, SL.6.1.D, SL.6.6

Language - L.6.4.A, L.6.4.C, L.6.4.D, L.6.5.C

RESOURCES

Children of the Dust Bowl: The True Story of the School at Weedpatch Camp Vocabulary handout

Access 1 handout (Beginner)

Access 2 handout (Intermediate)

Access 3 handout (Advanced)

Access 4 handout (Approaching)

1. INTRODUCTION

Core Path	Access Path
Define and Compare. Project the vocabulary words and definitions onto the board or provide students with handouts so they can copy the vocabulary into their notebooks. Suggest that students consult general and specialized reference materials, both print and digital, to compare the precise meaning of a specific word with their initial vocabulary predictions from the First Read. Review words that students defined incorrectly to understand why they were unable to use context clues to develop usable definitions.	**Beginner & Intermediate** **Complete the Sentences.** Have students complete the sentence frames on the Access 1 and 2 handouts using the vocabulary words. Point out that some of the words are in the questions and some will be in the answers. Correct answers are located at the end of this lesson plan online. **Advanced & Beyond** **Write in Journals.** Have students write a journal entry using all of their vocabulary words. Remind them to write sentences that communicate the meaning of the words they are using. **Approaching** **Graphic Organizer.** To support students in comparing their vocabulary predictions with the correct meanings, have them complete the graphic organizer on the Access 4 handout to record the vocabulary words, their initial analysis, and the definitions. Then encourage students to write sentences using the words.
Review. Have students complete the fill in the blank vocabulary worksheet for this selection. Correct answers for the worksheet are listed at the end of the lesson plan online.	
	Extend **Tech Infusion** **Create.** Have students create artworks to visually represent connections between pairs of vocabulary words, such as "rejection" and "opposition" or "epidemics" and "sanitation," using iPad or Android art apps.

Core Path	Access Path
	Extend **Tech Infusion** **Create.** Explain that the suffixes "-ion," "-tion," "-ation," and "-ition" all mean "act or process." Point out that the base words "reject" and "oppose" are verbs and that the added suffixes form nouns. Provide students with a list of verbs and have them add these suffixes to form nouns: (*act, add, assert, confess, exclaim, explain, interrupt, object, observe,* and so on). Then, have each student choose one word to feature in a print or digital word web that includes the following elements: base word and meaning; suffix and meaning; new word and meaning; and an original, contextual sentence. Have volunteers present their webs to the class.

2. READ

Core Path	Access Path
Model Close Reading. Project the text onto the board and model a close reading of the first paragraph using the annotation strategies mentioned below and on the following page. While modeling annotation strategies, make notes that tie the text to the focus skills and demonstrate what students are looking for as they read. Here is some guidance for you as you annotate for your students: • As the Skills lesson that precedes this text makes clear, authors of informational texts provide details that support the central or main idea. In communicating this information, authors choose words that have both denotations and connotations, which may reveal additional information regarding point of view or purpose.	

Core Path	Access Path
• In the first paragraph, there are many words with negative connotations. Let's highlight them: *ridicule, rejection, shame, scum, ignorant, filthy, shiftless, trash, dogs, alarmed, horde,* and *invades.* • All these negative words are no accident. The author has chosen them deliberately to reveal a point of view and as details that support a central idea. I might ask myself, what do all these negative words tell me about the point of view? What central idea do they help me understand? The idea that the "Okies" were viewed negatively and treated badly by a lot of people. • Later, in chapter 5, the author includes details that reveal his point of view about the educator Leo Hart. The words the author chooses to use here are positive ones: *like, caring, smile,* and *played.* I might ask myself, what do all these positive words tell me about the point of view? What central idea do they help me understand? The idea that Leo Hart cared about the Okie children and wanted to do something to help them get a good education and feel positively about themselves.	
Read and Annotate. Read the Skills Focus questions as a class, so your students know what they should pay close attention to as they read. Then have students read and annotate the excerpt. Ask students to use the annotation tool as they read to 1. respond to the Skills Focus section 2. ask questions 3. make connections 4. identify key information, examples, and ideas 5. note unfamiliar vocabulary 6. note variations from standard English 7. capture their reaction to the ideas and examples in the text	**Note:** While on–grade level students are reading and annotating, work one-on-one or in small groups with Beginning & Intermediate, Advanced, and Approaching students to support them as they read and annotate the text. **Beginner & Intermediate** **Summarize and Analyze the Text.** Work with these students to complete the sentence frames on the Access 1 and 2 handouts. Encourage students to then use the completed sentence frames to help them analyze and annotate the text so as to complete the Skills Focus questions. Refer to the sample Skills Focus answers to help them complete the sentence frames and annotate the text.

Core Path	Access Path
As they reread the text, remind students to use the comprehension strategy of Asking and Answering Questions that they learned in the First Read.	**Advanced** **Work in Pairs.** Pair these students with more proficient English speakers to work together on analyzing and annotating the text to complete the Skills Focus questions. If these students need more support, have them use the Summarize and Analyze the Text on the Access 3 handout as they work with their more proficient peers. **Approaching** **Summarize the Text.** Have these students discuss and complete the text summary on the Access 4 handout and use their summary to help them analyze and annotate the text by completing the Skills Focus questions. Correct answers for the summary are at the end of this lesson plan online. Also refer to the sample Skills Focus answers to aid students with their annotations.
Discuss. After students have read the text, use the sample responses to the Skills Focus questions at the bottom of this lesson plan online to discuss the reading and the process of searching for the central idea.	**Extend** **Pair and Share.** In small, heterogeneous groups or pairs, ask students to share and discuss their annotations with a focus on the central idea presented in the selection. You can provide students with these questions to guide their discussion: 1. How does the migration of the people from Oklahoma affect the people in California? Cite specific textual evidence to support your statements. (The people in California think that the "Okies" might take their jobs. "Californians were hostile to Okies because they competed with residents for jobs." Plus, to solve problems such as sanitation, the people in California have to pay higher taxes. The local teachers do not think the migrant children can learn. There is resentment and anger toward the "Okies.")

Core Path	Access Path
Make sure that students have acquired and accurately use academic-specific words and phrases related to the skill, and demonstrate a command of formal English appropriate to the discussion.	2. Why did the teachers treat the migrant children so poorly? Why does *rejection* describe how the children felt? Cite specific textual evidence to support your answer. (Student responses will vary, but may include that the children often could not read or write. Therefore the teachers assumed the students were stupid and could not learn. "Most teachers ignored the migrants, believing that Okie kids were too stupid to learn the alphabet." The other children made fun of the way the Okies dressed. The Okie children felt rejected.) 3. How did Leo Hart use the "excuse" of overcrowding as a solution to help the Okie children? (He used the idea of overcrowding to get the federal government to supply funds to build a new school for the Okie children. Hart used that reason to build a school where the Okie children could succeed and be treated fairly.)
	Extend **Tech Infusion** **Create.** Ask students to create print or digital illustrated maps of Weedpatch Camp by combining images of historical photographs with original drawings and textual quotations. Students may also add quotations from other primary or secondary sources. Tell students to utilize language and images to present contrasting points of view of the camp. For example, how did residents view the camp? How did the government view the camp? How did Californians view the camp? Ask volunteers to present their maps to the class.

Core Path	Access Path
	Extend **Tech Infusion** **Interview.** Form student groups of three and have each student assume one of the following roles: Leo Hart, School Board President, and Reporter. Tell students to imagine that a reporter from the evening news is doing a story about the new school at Weedpatch Camp. As part of the story, the reporter will interview Leo Hart and the School Board President. Have students prepare questions and answers for the interviews based on information and inferences from the text, as well as the reporter's introduction and conclusion to the story. As part of the story development, students should determine a central or main idea for the report as well as a point of view. Ask each group to present its news story to the class. Lead the class to identify and compare and contrast the varying main ideas and points of view presented. You may record these stories and post them to the class YouTube channel.

3. WRITE

Core Path	Access Path
Prewrite and Plan. Read the writing prompt as a class and ask students to brainstorm about Jerry Stanley's central idea in *Children of the Dust Bowl: The True Story of the School at Weedpatch Camp.* Students can brainstorm together either as a class or in small groups to begin planning their responses. Remind your students to look at the excerpt and their annotations to find textual evidence to support their ideas.	**Beginner & Intermediate** **Answer and Discuss.** Have students complete the prewriting questions on the Access 1 and 2 handouts and then explain their answers to a partner before they write. Explain to students that when they answer a question—such as *What is the author's central idea in* Children of the Dust Bowl: The True Story of the School at Weedpatch Camp?—they need to include a detail, example or quote from the text that supports the statement. For example, students could include the first line, "When they left Weedpatch Camp to find work, the Okies faced ridicule, rejection, and shame," which reveals that the Okies were not welcome in California and people resented them. Then the author explains that the feeling of rejection was greatest among the children, which sets the stage for the remainder of the excerpt.

Core Path	Access Path
	Approaching **Answer Prewriting Questions.** Have students complete the prewriting questions on the Access 4 handout to summarize their thoughts before they write.
	Extend **Tech Infusion** **Organize.** Before students begin writing, encourage them to use print or digital two-column charts to gather textual evidence. Tell them to label the left column "Oklahomans" and the right column "Leo Hart." Then, have them write the point of view of each regarding the Okie migration to California. Ask them to consider how these two contrasting points of view reveal the author's central or main ideas. Finally, have students gather and explain examples of the author's language that supports or reveals each point of view.
	Extend **Critique.** As students read and respond to the drafts of their peers, have them answer the following questions in writing: • According to the writer, what are the author's central or main ideas? • According to the writer, how does the author use language or word choice to reveal these central or main ideas? • What is one example of language the writer quotes from the text? • How does the writer use the central ideas and supporting details to write an objective summary? Give student reviewers the following guidance: if you are unable to find or understand information in the paper to answer any of these questions fully, then • ask the writer a question about something that is not clear, not well-explained, or missing from the writing.

Core Path	Access Path
	• make a specific suggestion for an idea or an example that the writer might include in the writing.
	• suggest that the writer reorder or resequence information to be more logical.
	• point out ways that the writer might connect information or make the relationships between information clearer for readers by using transitional words or phrases.
Discuss. Project these instructions for the peer review onto the board and review them with your class, so they know what they are looking for when they begin to provide their classmates with feedback: • How effectively has the writer identified the central idea that was developed over the course of *Children of the Dust Bowl: The True Story of the School at Weedpatch Camp*? • Has the writer provided textual evidence to explain how this central idea is conveyed through particular details? • Is the summary objective and free from personal opinions or judgments? • What parts of this response are done especially well? • Be sure to tell the writer what he or she does well and what he or she needs to work on. Remember that your comments are most useful when they are specific and constructive After you've looked at the peer review instructions, review the rubric with students before they begin writing. Allow time for students briefly to raise and discuss any questions they may have about the peer review instructions and the rubric. Tell students how many peer reviews they will need to complete once they submit their writing.	

Please note that excerpts and passages in the StudySync® library, workbooks, and PDFs are intended as touchstones to generate interest in an author's work. The excerpts and passages do not substitute for the reading of entire texts, and StudySync® strongly recommends that teachers and students seek out and purchase the whole literary or informational work in order to experience it as the author intended. Links to online resellers are available in our digital library. In addition, complete works may be ordered through an authorized reseller by filling out and returning to StudySync® the order form enclosed in this workbook.   Teacher's Edition   215

Core Path	Access Path
Write. Ask students to complete the writing assignment using textual evidence to support their responses. Once they have completed their writing, they should click "Submit."	
Review. Once students complete their writing assignments, they should submit substantive feedback to two peers. Students should use their peers' feedback to improve their writing.	

OVERVIEW

The story "The Circuit," by Francisco Jimenez, forms part of an autobiographical novel entitled *The Circuit: Stories from the Life of a Migrant Child.* The narrator, part of a family of migrant workers, tells of his experiences as a young immigrant to the United States, traveling ceaselessly and grabbing the few formal educational experiences available. The First Read gives students the opportunity to experience the text with a limited context.

OBJECTIVES

1. Perform an initial reading of a text and demonstrate comprehension by responding to short analysis and inference questions with textual evidence.
2. Practice defining vocabulary words using context.
3. Participate effectively in a range of conversations and collaborations to express ideas and build upon the ideas of others.

   ELA Common Core Standards:
   Reading: Literature - RL.6.1, RL.6.3, RL.6.4, RL.6.10
   Speaking & Listening - SL.6.1.A, SL.6.1.B, SL.6.1.C, SL.6.2
   Language - L.6.4.A, L.6.5.B

RESOURCES

Access 1 handout (Beginner)

Access 2 handout (Intermediate)

Access 3 handout (Advanced)

Access 4 handout (Approaching)

ACCESS COMPLEX TEXT

Through its rich first-person narration and limited dialogue, this excerpt from *The Circuit: Stories from the Life of a Migrant Child* helps students understand the emotional impact on a migrant child and his family of moving from farm to farm to pick fruits and vegetables. Use the following suggestions to provide scaffolded instruction for a close reading of the more complex features of this text.

- **Genre** – Because *The Circuit: Stories from the Life of a Migrant Child* is a collection of autobiographical stories, this excerpt is told from a first-person point of view. Students are asked to consider how this point of view impacts their understanding of the story. Students will need to analyze details in the story to determine the impact.

- **Connection of Ideas** - The first-person point of view of the selection also means that students can only know the thoughts of the narrator. They cannot directly know the thoughts of Roberto, Papá, or the other characters. Students must infer the thoughts of these characters through narration, dialogue, and actions.

- **Specific Vocabulary** - The author uses several Spanish phrases that are not translated. Non-Spanish speakers will need to use context clues, the assistance of Spanish speakers, or Spanish–English dictionaries to determine meanings.

1. INTRODUCTION

Core Path	Access Path
Read. Individually or as a class, read the Introduction for *The Circuit: Stories from the Life of a Migrant Child.* The introduction provides context for the excerpt from the chapter titled "The Circuit."	**English Learners All Levels & Approaching Read and Discuss.** Ask students to read and discuss the introduction for *The Circuit: Stories from the Life of a Migrant Child.* Have them refer to the vocabulary listing on their Access 1, 2, 3, and 4 handouts for definitions of key vocabulary terms. If there are unfamiliar words that are not included in their glossary, encourage students to check a dictionary or online reference tool, like http://tinyurl.com/6ytby.

Core Path	Access Path
Build Background. Tell students that the story they are about to read is based on the author's life. Explain that the author and thousands of other immigrants worked as migrant farm laborers. The wages were meager and their living conditions were substandard. One man in particular is known for his contribution to improving working conditions for the migrant farmers: Cesar Chavez. Have students conduct research on Chavez, identifying what he has done to improve the lives of thousands of people. You may also wish to have students search online for articles, images, or video clips that will help them better understand experiences shared by migrant agricultural workers like those they will read about in "The Circuit." Invite students to share their findings with the rest of the class. As a class or in small groups, generate a list (on the board or on paper) of students' impressions or questions based on their research. After compiling a list, discuss how students' impressions shape their expectations for what might happen in the story.	**Beginner & Intermediate** **Discuss Images.** Break students into small groups or pairs. Ask students to look at images of migrant workers, such as the ones at: http://tinyurl.com/l6y8yqf. Ask students to discuss the images and what life was like for a migrant worker. They can use their discussions as points of reference when they do their research. Once students have completed their discussions, have them pair up with Advanced and Beyond students to complete the research. **Approaching** **Discuss Images.** Break students into small groups. Ask students to look at images of migrant workers, such as the ones at: http://tinyurl.com/l6y8yqf. Ask them to think about these questions: • How would you describe the work of picking strawberries? • Why is it hard to keep moving to find work? • How would you feel if your family had to move each season?
	Extend **Tech Infusion** **Make Predictions.** Based on the introduction, ask students to make predictions about the events and ideas they would expect to encounter in this text. Have students share their predictions on a virtual note board such as Lino.it (http://tinyurl.com/ylewks3) or a backchannel tool such as TodaysMeet (http://tinyurl.com/8ydulv4).

2. READ

Core Path	Access Path
Make Predictions about Vocabulary. There are six bold vocabulary words in the text. As students read the text, ask them to make predictions about what they think each vocabulary word means based on the context clues in the sentence. If you are in a low-tech classroom and students are reading from printed copies or a projected text, ask students to record predictions in their notes, so they can be easily referenced in class. If your students have access to technology, they can use the annotation tool to make their predictions.	**Note:** This exercise, which extends vocabulary instruction, should be completed when the class shifts from whole group instruction to individual work during the "Read and Annotate" exercise.

<table>
<tr><td>

It might be helpful to model this for students before they begin reading. Either using the board or projecting the actual text, focus in on the sentence that uses the word "detect":

- He listened to the motor, tilting his head from side to side like a parrot, trying to detect any noises that spelled car trouble.

Model for the class how to use the overall structure and meaning of the sentence and the sentences around it, the word's position, and other clues to define the unfamiliar vocabulary word. In this case, point out these context clues:

1. Look at the position of the word in the sentence. The sentence says that Papá was "trying to detect" something. This tells us that "detect" is a verb—an action word. He's trying to do something.

2. What other words does "detect" remind you of? (Possible answers: detective, smoke detector) What do these words have in common? (They all involve looking for or noticing things.)

3. As Papá listens, he is "tilting his head from side to side like a parrot." Why might he be doing that? (The comparison to a parrot creates a vivid image of Papá's action. When people move their heads like this, they're often trying to alternate the ear through which they are listening. This suggests Papá is trying to listen very carefully.)

</td><td>

Beginner, Intermediate & Approaching Pair Practice.

1. Pair students with more proficient readers.

2. Give them an additional sentence that contains a new vocabulary word.

3. Ask the students to complete a Think Aloud using the teacher-led Make Predictions about Vocabulary activity as a model, while the proficient student actively listens.

4. The student should use the context clues in the sentence to try to determine the meaning of the new vocabulary word.

5. After the student has completed the Think Aloud and made a prediction about the word's meaning, allow time for the proficient reader to add his/her own thoughts and clarify any points of confusion.

</td></tr>
</table>

Core Path	Access Path
4. Papá is turning his head this way "trying to detect noises that spelled car trouble." Does it seem like those noises would be hard or easy to hear? (hard) So "detect" might involve listening for something that is hard to find. And it might have to do with more than just hearing, too, because the author doesn't use the word "hear," specifically. Combining these clues, we can infer that "detect" means something like "to find or uncover something."	6. Once they've completed this Think Aloud, encourage them to use a dictionary to confirm the definition of the new vocabulary word. Have them refer to the vocabulary listing on their Access 1, 2, and 4 handouts for definitions of key vocabulary terms in the text. Encourage them to add any additional vocabulary words or idioms they find in the text and look up definitions for those words and idioms online or in a dictionary.

Model Reading Comprehension Strategy. Before students begin reading, model the reading comprehension strategy of making, confirming, and revising predictions by using this Think Aloud that talks students through the first paragraph of text. First explain to your students that making, confirming, and revising predictions is trying to guess what's going to happen as the story goes on. You can predict using what you learn from the text itself and what you know about life and people. As you keep reading, you find out whether your predictions are confirmed—right—or wrong. If they're not confirmed, you can make new predictions based on the new information you've read.

Model for students how predicting will help them better comprehend the selection and help drive their discussions.

- When I read the first paragraph, I see that Francisco and his family have been picking strawberries, but that strawberry season is ending. I predict that the family won't have any more work.

- As I read further, I find that the family goes to a different farm and finds work there. So my first prediction isn't quite confirmed.

- I revise my prediction. Now, I predict the family will have to keep moving from farm to farm, staying at each farm just for a while until the growing season ends.

Note: This exercise, which extends vocabulary instruction, should be completed when the class shifts from whole group instruction to individual work during the "Read and Annotate" exercise.

Beginner, Intermediate & Approaching Apply Reading Comprehension Strategy.

1. Have students work in pairs and read the first two paragraphs of the excerpt. Then have them predict what they think will happen. They can write their predictions.

2. Next have them read the fourth paragraph. Have students list "clues" or textual evidence that help confirm their prediction. If they want to revise or change their prediction, have them list what makes them want to change or revise their prediction.

3. Allow pairs time to discuss the process of making predictions. Have them list text evidence, such as signal words (then, next, now), action words, or dialogue that helps them make predictions. Invite students to predict how the story will end. Save their predictions so they can compare it to the ending.

Please note that excerpts and passages in the StudySync® library, workbooks, and PDFs are intended as touchstones to generate interest in an author's work. The excerpts and passages do not substitute for the reading of entire texts, and StudySync® strongly recommends that teachers and students seek out and purchase the whole literary or informational work in order to experience it as the author intended. Links to online resellers are available in our digital library. In addition, complete works may be ordered through an authorized reseller by filling out and returning to StudySync® the order form enclosed in this workbook.

Teacher's Edition   221

Core Path	Access Path
Read and Annotate. Have students independently read and annotate the excerpt. Ask students to use the annotation tool as they read to: 1. use context clues to analyze and determine the meaning of the bolded vocabulary terms 2. ask questions about passages of the text that may be unclear or unresolved 3. identify key information, events, characters, and connections between them 4. note unfamiliar vocabulary 5. capture their reaction to the characters and events in the text	**Beginner** **Coach the Reading.** While other students read, annotate, and discuss the text independently, work with Beginning students, reading aloud the text and pausing periodically or when any student has a question. Coach students in articulating their questions for the group and in highlighting and annotating the text. Have students use the Annotation Guide on the Access 1 handout to support them as they highlight and annotate the text. For further support, ask questions about the text such as: • Is there anything about the story that you don't understand? • What do you think will happen to the narrator? • Reread the definition of *circuit*. Why is that a good word for the title? How does it connect to moving? **Intermediate** **Read the Text.** Have these students read the text and use the definitions on the Access 2 handout to help them with words or idioms that may be unfamiliar. Students may want to take turns reading the text aloud. If students need help with annotating the text, have them use the Annotation Guide on the Access 2 handout. After working with the Beginning students, you may wish to check this group's progress and provide support as needed.
	Advanced **Pair with Proficient Peers.** Have Advanced students work with English proficient peers to read, annotate, and discuss the text. Have students use the Annotation Guide on the Access 3 handout to support them as they highlight and annotate the text. Encourage them to listen to the audio of the text if needed. **Approaching** **Use the Annotation Guide.** Have students use the Annotation Guide on the Access 4 handout to support them as they highlight and annotate the text.

Core Path	Access Path
Discuss. In small groups or pairs, have students discuss the predictions and inferences they made while reading. Make sure students follow the rules for collegial discussions: Refer to Collaborative Discussions in the Speaking & Listening Handbook.	**English Learners All Levels & Approaching** Use the extra time while on— and beyond—grade level students are discussing their first reads of the text to work individually and in small groups with English Learners and Approaching readers as outlined on the previous page. Should those students complete their first reads quickly, integrate them into the on— and beyond—grade level discussion groups. Otherwise, English Learners and Approaching readers will be given an opportunity to participate in text discussions with their peers later in the lesson.

Core Path

1. Based on inferences you can make from the text, why does Francisco's family make their living by picking crops on one farm after another? (Francisco and his family are migrant workers. In order to earn a living and support themselves, the family must move frequently to take advantage of the work opportunities as different crops, with different growing seasons, are ready to be picked.)

2. Why doesn't Roberto go to school when Francisco does? (Roberto has to work during cotton season.) Why do you think that is? (Because Roberto is older, it's likely that he is stronger and able to do more heavy work than Francisco, and therefore is needed more in the fields.)

3. What can you infer about Mr. Lena from Francisco's description of him on the first morning of school? (Mr. Lena is kind and understanding. He tries to make Francisco feel included by asking him to read aloud. Then, as soon as he notices that Francisco is nervous, he assures him that he can read later.)

4. Describe one prediction you made as you read "The Circuit." How was your prediction confirmed or revised, and how did it help you better understand the story? (Answers will vary.)

Access Path

Tech Infusion
Beyond
Brainstorm. Pair students and ask them to brainstorm why school is so important to Francisco. Students who have access to a backchannel tool such as TodaysMeet (http://tinyurl.com/nogqjow) may enjoy brainstorming in that medium.

Core Path	Access Path
	Extend **Identify and Define.** After reading the text, compile a list of additional vocabulary words. Ask students to reference their annotations and share any vocabulary words that were unfamiliar. 1. As a class, compile a list of unknown words on the board. 2. In small groups, ask students to make predictions about what they think these words mean based on how they are used in the sentence. 3. Each group should work together using dictionaries or devices to define the words and write the definitions in their notebooks.

3. THINK

Core Path	Access Path
Answer and Discuss. Have students complete the Think questions and then use the peer review instructions and rubric to complete two peer reviews. Refer to the sample answers at the end of this lesson plan online to discuss responses with your students.	**Beginner & Intermediate** **Sentence Frames.** Have students use the Sentence Frames on the Access 1 and 2 handouts to support their responses to the Think questions. If necessary, distribute sentence frames to Advanced students as well. **Approaching** **Find the Evidence.** Have students use Find the Evidence on the Access 4 handout to help them identify the evidence needed to answer the questions.
	Extend **Debate.** Present students with an issue from the text that can be debated. Allow students to debate the issue as a class or in smaller groups. Debate prompts: 1. Does Francisco have a good life or a bad life? Support your opinion with textual evidence. 2. Should it be against the law to use migrant workers to pick crops? Why or why not?

Point of View

OVERVIEW

Determining the point(s) of view in a narrative is an important skill for students to acquire. Understanding the function and impact of a particular point of view in a text increases a reader's understanding of characters and events. This lesson plan provides follow-up questions and useful enrichments to help teachers guide students toward a usable, repeatable method for uncovering point of view.

OBJECTIVES

1. Learn the definition of point of view.
2. Practice using concrete strategies for identifying and analyzing point of view.
3. Participate effectively in a range of conversations and collaborations to express ideas and build upon the ideas of others.

ELA Common Core Standards:

Reading: Literature - RL.6.1, RL.6.6
Speaking & Listening - SL.6.1.A, SL.6.1.B, SL.6.1.C, SL.6.2

RESOURCES

Access 1 handout (Beginner)

Access 2 handout (Intermediate)

Access 3 handout (Advanced)

Access 4 handout (Approaching)

Please note that excerpts and passages in the StudySync® library, workbooks, and PDFs are intended as touchstones to generate interest in an author's work. The excerpts and passages do not substitute for the reading of entire texts, and StudySync® strongly recommends that teachers and students seek out and purchase the whole literary or informational work in order to experience it as the author intended. Links to online resellers are available in our digital library. In addition, complete works may be ordered through an authorized reseller by filling out and returning to StudySync® the order form enclosed in this workbook.

Teacher's Edition   225

1. DEFINE

Core Path	Access Path
Watch. Watch the Concept Definition video on point of view with your students. Make sure students understand the different components of point of view. Pause the video at these key moments to discuss the information with your students:	**English Learners All Levels & Approaching** **Match.** Have students complete the matching exercise on the Access 1, 2, 3, and 4 handouts as they watch the video. Answers are located at the end of this lesson plan online.

Core Path (continued):

1. 0:43 – Ben talks about second person reminding him of a hypnotist, but what are some other examples of second-person point of view that you can think of? What effect does the second person and the repetition of "you" have on readers or listeners?

2. 1:50 – What are the advantages and disadvantages for writers in using the different third-person point of view options? What considerations might a writer make before choosing an omniscient versus an objective narrator?

3. 2:25 – So how is character point of view, mentioned last in the video, distinguishable from the various types of first-, second-, and third-person point of view? What other elements go into a character's point of view?

Read and Discuss. After watching the Concept Definition video, have students read the definition of point of view. Either in small groups or as a whole class, use these questions to engage students in a discussion about point of view. Make sure students follow the rules for collegial discussions.

1. What are some examples of stories that typically feature a first-person point of view? What are some examples that typically feature a third-person point of view? (Answers will vary, but should include that autobiographical texts are usually first person, while biographical or informational texts are often third person.)

Access Path (continued):

Beginner & Approaching
Complete a Chart. To prepare students to participate in the discussion, have them complete the chart on the Access 1 and 4 handouts as they read the definition. The correct answers are located at the end of this lesson plan online.

Intermediate & Advanced
Discuss Prompts. To help these students participate in the discussion, prompt them with questions that can be answered with a few words, such as:

- In first-person point of view, the narrator is the same person as whom? (the main character)

- If the narrator tells the feelings of all the characters, what point of view is the author using? (third-person omniscient)

Core Path	Access Path
2. Why might an author choose to use one point of view over another? What are some advantages and disadvantages of each kind? (Answers will vary, but should include that often it depends on the genre of the text and the author's purpose in deciding to use either first person or third person.) 3. Think of the last story you read. How easy was it to determine the point of view of the story? What made it easy or difficult? (Answers will vary.)	• Can you think of a story you have read that has a third-person limited point of view? (Answers will vary.) **Beyond** **Discuss.** Have students select a book they've read and describe its point of view. Compile a list of examples. Have students discuss how the point of view of each work affects what the reader learns about the characters and plot. How might a switch in point of view affect not only what the reader learns, but how much he or she enjoys the story?
	Extend **Tech Infusion** **Poll.** Using polling software such as Socrative (http://tinyurl.com/8544k4p) or Poll Everywhere (http://tinyurl.com/5grl69), poll students as to whether they generally prefer first-person or third-person narratives. Then begin a discussion on students' reasons for their answers. Encourage students to reflect on the use of point of view based on their First Read of "The Circuit" and their previous reading of literary narratives.

2. MODEL

Core Path	Access Path
Read and Annotate. Have students independently read the Model section. As they read, ask students to use the annotation tool to: • highlight pronouns and other details that help identify Francisco as the narrator • note what Francisco knows and is able to report on and what he does not know and is thus not able to share	**Note:** During this portion of the lesson, instruction shifts from whole group to individual work. Use this time to work one-on-one or in small groups with Beginning, Intermediate, Advanced, and Approaching students.

Core Path	Access Path
• ask questions • identify places where the Model applies the strategies laid out in the Identification and Application section	**Beginner & Intermediate** **Coach the Reading.** Work with these students (either individually or in small groups) to fill out the guided reading questions on the Access 1 and 2 handouts. Have Beginning students refer to the glossary on the Access 1 handout to help them determine the meaning of difficult words. (note: Provide the Access 1 handout glossary to Intermediate students if necessary.) Let students know they'll use these answers to help participate in the discussion about the Model. Sample answers for this exercise are located at the end of the lesson plan online. **Advanced** **Identify Evidence.** Provide these students with the same instructions to read and annotate as on—grade level and Beyond students. In addition, ask Advanced students to complete the identifying evidence exercise on the Access 3 handout. Let students know that they'll use these answers to help participate in the discussion about the Model. Sample answers for this exercise are located at the end of the lesson plan online. **Approaching Guided Reading.** Have students complete the guided reading questions on the Access 4 handout as they read. Let them know that they'll use these answers to help participate in the discussion about the Model. Sample answers for this exercise are located at the end of the lesson plan online.

Discuss. After students read the Model text, use these questions to facilitate a whole group discussion that helps students understand how to analyze the point of view of the passage:

1. What hint does the Model use to begin thinking about the point of view of the passage? (The Model uses the fact that the passage comes from an autobiographical novel based on the life of author Francisco Jimenez.) What point of view does this hint at? (It hints at first-person point of view.)

Core Path	Access Path
2. How does the Model confirm the point of view of the passage? (It looks for first-person pronouns in the text.) What unusual aspect of the point of view does the Model identify? (It is not until the second paragraph of the text that the point of view from which the story will be told is identified.)	
3. The Model claims that telling the story from Francisco's point of view makes it more believable and compelling. Why do you think that might be the case? (Possible response: Since readers know that Jimenez lived through similar experiences as a child, they trust that Jimenez's account of Francisco's childhood experiences is accurate.)	
4. According to the Model, once a reader has confirmed that a passage is told from a first-person point of view, what can he or she expect? (While they might learn what other characters do and say, they will only be certain of the thoughts and feelings of the character who is telling the story.)	
5. What difference between the first-person viewpoint and the third-person omniscient viewpoint does the Model explain? (In the first-person point of view, the narrator is one of the characters in the story. The reader learns what the narrator thinks, sees, hears, or experiences because he tells them. What the narrator *can't* know is what the other characters are thinking. A third-person omniscient point of view would reveal most about the characters and events in the story. With this point of view, the narrator is all-seeing and all-knowing and can reveal the thoughts, feelings, and motives of any character.)	

Please note that excerpts and passages in the StudySync® library, workbooks, and PDFs are intended as touchstones to generate interest in an author's work. The excerpts and passages do not substitute for the reading of entire texts, and StudySync® strongly recommends that teachers and students seek out and purchase the whole literary or informational work in order to experience it as the author intended. Links to online resellers are available in our digital library. In addition, complete works may be ordered through an authorized reseller by filling out and returning to StudySync® the order form enclosed in this workbook.

Teacher's Edition   229

Core Path	Access Path
	Extend **Tech Infusion** **Rewrite Point of View.** Assign groups of students to rewrite the next to last paragraph of "The Circuit" (beginning, "One Friday during lunch hour"), with each group using a different point of view: third-person omniscient, third-person objective, third-person limited from Francisco's viewpoint, and Mr. Lema's first-person point of view. Have a member of each group read its revision aloud and post it on a shared online journal using Penzu (http://tinyurl.com/lwuy989), or a shared blog. Invite the class to post comments about the effectiveness of the new points of view.

3. YOUR TURN

Core Path	Access Path
Assess and Explain. Have students answer the comprehension questions to test for understanding. Share the explanations for Parts A and B (located online) with your students.	
	Extend **Tech Infusion** **Share and Discuss.** Have students complete the Your Turn section in class. Poll students about their responses, and as a class, discuss the different strategies they used to determine the correct answers. Ask students which aspects of the questions they found hard, and how they solved the difficulty. Conduct your poll by asking your students to complete a handout with questions or using Poll Everywhere (http://tinyurl.com/3zyw33) or Socrative (http://tinyurl.com/3bxbjpt).

Core Path	Access Path
	Extend **Tech Infusion** **Readers' Theater.** Have students conduct a Readers' Theater for any scene of "The Circuit" so that they can hear what the first-person voice adds to a story. Have students read consecutive passages, switching readers when they come to a new paragraph or to a new speaker of dialogue. Encourage students to use a voice that believably reflects Francisco. Use a voice recording app (Voice Memo on the iPhone or Smart Voice Recorder for Androids) or VoiceThread (http://tinyurl.com/amd9w2) to capture each group's discussion ideas. As students listen to the recording, invite them to discuss points at which the use of the first-person voice helps them understand or appreciate the story and characters.

The Circuit: Stories from the Life of a Migrant Child

OVERVIEW

The story "The Circuit," by Francisco Jimenez, forms part of a book of fictionalized reminiscences entitled *The Circuit: Stories from the Life of a Migrant Child*. The narrator, part of a family of migrant workers, tells of his experiences as a young immigrant to the United States, traveling ceaselessly and grabbing the few formal educational experiences available. The Close Read gives students the opportunity to analyze the use of first-person point of view and its impact on story elements.

OBJECTIVES

1. Complete a close reading of a passage of literature.
2. Practice and apply concrete strategies for identifying and analyzing point of view.
3. Participate effectively in a range of conversations and collaborations to express ideas and build upon the ideas of others.
4. Prewrite, plan, and produce clear and coherent writing in response to a prompt.

ELA Common Core Standards:
Reading: Literature - RL.6.1, RL.6.3, RL.6.4, RL.6.6, RL.6.10
Writing - W.6.2.A, W.6.2.B, W.6.4, W.6.5, W.6.6, W.6.9.A, W.6.10
Speaking & Listening - SL.6.1.A, SL.6.1.B, SL.6.1.C, SL.6.1.D, SL.6.6
Language - L.6.4.A, L.6.4.C, L.6.4.D

RESOURCES

The Circuit: Stories from the Life of a Migrant Child Vocabulary handout
The Circuit: Stories from the Life of a Migrant Child Graphic organizer
Access 1 handout (Beginner)
Access 2 handout (Intermediate)
Access 3 handout (Advanced)
Access 4 handout (Approaching)

1. INTRODUCTION

Core Path	Access Path
Define and Compare. Project the vocabulary words and definitions onto the board or provide students with handouts so they can copy the vocabulary into their notebooks. Suggest that students consult general and specialized reference materials, both print and digital, to compare the precise meaning of a specific word with their initial vocabulary predictions from the First Read. Review words that students defined incorrectly to understand why they were unable to use context clues to develop usable definitions.	**Beginner & Intermediate** **Complete the Sentences.** Have students complete the sentence frames on the Access 1 and 2 handouts using the vocabulary words. Point out that some of the words are in the questions and some will be in the answers. Answers are located at the end of this lesson plan online. **Advanced & Beyond** **Write in Journals.** Have students write a journal entry using all of their vocabulary words. Remind them to write sentences that communicate the meaning of the words they are using. **Approaching** **Graphic Organizer.** To support students in comparing their predictions with the correct meanings, have them complete the graphic organizer on the Access 4 handout to record the vocabulary words, their initial analysis, and the definitions. Then have them write sentences using the words.
Review. Have students complete the fill in the blank vocabulary worksheet for this selection. Answers for the worksheet are listed at the end of the lesson plan online.	
	Extend **Write Together.** Have groups of students compose paragraphs of linked sentences for the vocabulary words. The first student writes the opening sentence using one of the vocabulary words; the next writes the second sentence using any of the remaining words; and so on, until all words are used, one per sentence. Invite groups to share their paragraphs with the class, and see what different imaginative topics, setting, and actions they have described. Have students from other groups confirm each group's use of the five words. Correct them when necessary.

Core Path	Access Path
	Extend **Tech Infusion** **Collage.** Invite students to create collages showing the lives of migrant farm workers past and present, using graphics software such as Glogster (http://tinyurl.com/ydeyklq) or Google Drawing. Recommend that when applicable, students should annotate the images in their collages with brief quotations from "The Circuit." For example, if they find a photo of workers in the approximate period when the story takes place, they could annotate it with a sentence from the story that describes Francisco's family picking crops. Select volunteers to present their collages to the class.

2. READ

Core Path	Access Path
Model Close Reading. Project the text onto the board and model a close reading of the first few paragraphs using the annotation strategies mentioned below and on the following page. While modeling annotation strategies, make notes that tie the text to the focus skill and demonstrate what students are looking for as they read. Here is some guidance for you as you annotate for your students: • As the Skills lesson that precedes this text makes clear, identifying a story's point of view is the first step toward analyzing its impact on the storytelling and our understanding of the characters and plot events.	

Core Path	Access Path
• Based on the First Read, we remember that the narrator of "The Circuit" is Francisco. We begin to read, looking for the personal pronouns that signal first-person point of view: *I, me, we, us*, and so on. If this were the first time we were reading the story, we might be fooled into thinking the narrative is third person, because the opening paragraph doesn't use any signal words. But in the second paragraph, we see the first *I*. The use of first-person pronouns is consistent from that point. • Point of view is part of the author's toolkit for presenting information about a character's thoughts and feelings. As we read, we can look for *I* passages in which Francisco communicates what he's thinking. Here's an example about his co-worker Ito in paragraph 2: "I liked him." • At other times, Francisco doesn't state his feelings directly, but we can tell what they are by thinking about what he does say. When he says about Ito, "That Sunday was the last time I saw him" we can guess, or infer, that Francisco misses Ito. • We also think about how Francisco's point of view affects events in the plot. For example, Francisco doesn't report any scenes that involve only the adults. That's because he didn't witness those scenes. He doesn't see adults making decisions about what to do at the end of the strawberry picking season. He only sees the results and follows along. Many events and conversations concerning this situation must be occurring in the camp, but we only see the ones that Francisco takes part in or observes.	
Read and Annotate. Read the Skills Focus questions as a class, so your students know what they should pay close attention to as they read. Then have students read and annotate the excerpt. Ask students to use the annotation tool as they read to: 1. respond to the Skills Focus section 2. ask questions	**Note:** While on–grade level students are reading and annotating, work one-on-one or in small groups with Beginning, Intermediate, Advanced, and Approaching students to support them as they read and annotate the text.

Please note that excerpts and passages in the StudySync® library, workbooks, and PDFs are intended as touchstones to generate interest in an author's work. The excerpts and passages do not substitute for the reading of entire texts, and StudySync® strongly recommends that teachers and students seek out and purchase the whole literary or informational work in order to experience it as the author intended. Links to online resellers are available in our digital library. In addition, complete works may be ordered through an authorized reseller by filling out and returning to StudySync® the order form enclosed in this workbook.

Teacher's Edition   **235**

Core Path	Access Path
3. make connections 4. identify key information, examples, characters, and themes 5. note unfamiliar vocabulary 6. capture their reaction to the ideas and examples in the text As they reread the text, remind students to use the comprehension strategy of Making, Confirming, and Revising Predictions that they learned in the First Read.	**Beginner & Intermediate** **Summarize and Analyze the Text.** Work with these students to complete the sentence frames on the Access 1 and 2 handouts (note: the sentence frames for Intermediate students on the Access 2 handout contain fewer scaffolds). They will then use the completed sentence frames to help them analyze and annotate the text by completing the Skills Focus questions. Refer to the sample Skills Focus answers to help them complete the sentence frames and annotate the text. **Advanced** **Work in Pairs.** Pair these students with more proficient English speakers to work together on analyzing and annotating the text to complete the Skills Focus questions. If these students need more support, have them use the sentence frames on the Access 3 handout as they work with their more proficient peers. **Approaching** **Summarize the Text.** Have these students discuss and complete the text summary on the Access 4 handout and use their summary to help them analyze and annotate the text by completing the Skills Focus questions. Correct answers for the summary are at the end of this lesson plan online. Also refer to the sample Skills Focus answers to aid students with their annotations.
Discuss. After students have read the text, use the sample responses to the Skills Focus questions at the end of this lesson plan online to discuss the reading and the process of analyzing point of view. Make sure that students have acquired and accurately use academic-specific words and phrases related to the skill, and demonstrate a command of formal English appropriate to the discussion.	**Extend** **Pair and Share.** In small, heterogeneous groups or pairs, ask students to share and discuss their annotations with a focus on the point of view presented in the selection.

Core Path	Access Path
	You can provide students with these questions to guide their discussion:
	1. How does Francisco describe his family? How does using a first-person narrative make the description more personal? Cite specific textual evidence to support your statements. (He tells a story of how Papá got their car; on their last day of work, he says that his father and brother, Roberto, are silent. He describes how much his mother loved her "special" pot. Using first-person narrative makes the descriptions personal and makes the readers feel as if they are right there with the narrator experiencing things.)
	2. How does Francisco feel about moving? Cite specific textual evidence to support your answer. (He says that he will be sad that he will not hear Ito call the end of the day. He also realizes it is the end of the season and he and his family have to move. The night before they have to move, he could not sleep. This makes me think moving is very difficult for him.)
	3. Francisco is happy at school with Mr. Lema, who helps him with English and encourages him to learn. How does the ending seem sad? Cite specific textual evidence to support your answer. (Francisco is excited about learning to play an instrument, but when he returns home he sees "everything we owned was neatly packed in cardboard boxes." This means the family is moving and he will not get to learn to play an instrument. This is sad because Francisco was happy and now again his future is uncertain.)
	Extend **Compare and Contrast.** Ask students to compare and contrast Francisco's point of view about moving with other characters' possible first-person points of view. Provide a Venn diagram (See Resources) to help students organize ideas before discussion and to help them take notes during and after discussion.

3. WRITE

Core Path	Access Path
Prewrite and Plan. Read the prompt as a class and ask students to talk together about the use of first-person point of view in "The Circuit," and how it provides readers with a look at the migrant experience. Have students brainstorm ways that changing the point of view in the story to the parents' perspective would change what readers know about events and characters. Students can brainstorm together either as a class or in small groups to begin planning their responses. Remind your students to look at the story and their annotations to find textual evidence such as quotations, examples, and details to support their ideas about the impact of point of view.	**Beginner & Intermediate** **Answer and Discuss.** Have students complete the prewriting questions on the Access 1 and 2 handouts and then explain their answers to a partner before they write. Explain to students that when they answer a question—such as *How are the children's experiences in both texts similar?*—they need to include a detail, example, or quote from the text that supports the statement. For example, students could include quotes about their school experiences. In *Children of the Dust Bowl: The True Story of the School at Weedpatch Camp*, Leo Hart works to help the Okie children by building a school just for them, while in "The Circuit," Mr. Lema helps Francisco learn English and wants to teach him to play an instrument. In both stories, an educator tries to make the children's lives better. **Approaching** **Answer Prewriting Questions.** Have students complete the prewriting questions on the Access 4 handout to summarize their thoughts before they write.
	Extend **Organize.** Encourage students to take notes before they draft. Suggest that they use separate columns or separate pages to take notes on the advantages and disadvantages of first-person and third-person points of view, along with textual evidence to support each advantage or disadvantage. Remind them to use their evidence as early in their response as possible and to organize their ideas in a logical way.

Copyright © BookheadEd Learning, LLC

Core Path	Access Path
	Extend **Tech Infusion** **Prepare to Critique.** Before students begin their critiques, hold a brief discussion in which they share ideas about what strategies they plan to use in this process, and what approaches and focal points have had the most positive results for them in writing critiques in the past. You may want to conduct their discussion via a backchannel medium such as TodaysMeet (http://tinyurl.com/nogqjow).

Discuss. Project these instructions for the peer review onto the board and review them with your class, so students they know what they are looking for when they begin to provide their classmates with feedback:

- How effectively does the essay explain the impact of point of view?

- How well has the writer identified aspects of the story that might be changed by changing the point of view?

- What sort of textual evidence, including quotations, details, and examples, does the writer use to support his or her writing and understanding of point of view?

- What specific suggestions can you make to help the writer improve the response?

- What thing(s) does this response do especially well?

- Be sure to tell the writer what he or she did well and what he or she needs to work on. Remember that your comments are most useful when they are constructive.

After you've looked at the peer review instructions, review the rubric with students before they begin writing. Allow time for students briefly to raise and discuss any questions they may have about the peer review instructions and the rubric. Tell students how many peer reviews they will need to complete once they submit their writing.

Please note that excerpts and passages in the StudySync® library, workbooks, and PDFs are intended as touchstones to generate interest in an author's work. The excerpts and passages do not substitute for the reading of entire texts, and StudySync® strongly recommends that teachers and students seek out and purchase the whole literary or informational work in order to experience it as the author intended. Links to online resellers are available in our digital library. In addition, complete works may be ordered through an authorized reseller by filling out and returning to StudySync® the order form enclosed in this workbook.

Teacher's Edition   239

Core Path	Access Path
Write. Ask students to complete the writing assignment using textual evidence to support their answers. Once they have completed their writing, they should click "Submit."	
Review. Once students complete their writing assignment, they should submit substantive feedback to two peers. Students should use their peers' feedback to improve their writing.	
Deliver a Presentation. Have students present their written response to the Close Read prompt as an oral presentation to the class. Before beginning the presentations, review Presentation Skills in the Speaking and Listening Handbook.	

BLAST:
Down with the King

OVERVIEW

To enhance understanding of *Les Misérables* and to add context, students will learn about the factors leading up to the French Revolution. Research links explore other aspects of the revolution, including the guillotine and the Broadway musical inspired by Victor Hugo's book.

OBJECTIVES

1. Explore background information about the French Revolution and how it began.
2. Research using the hyperlinks to learn more about other aspects of the revolution, including the guillotine and the Broadway musical adapted from Victor Hugo's book.
3. Participate effectively in a range of conversations and collaborations to express ideas and build upon the ideas of others.

   ELA Common Core Standards:
   Reading: Informational Text - RI.6.1
   Writing - W.6.1.A, W.6.1.B, W.6.5, W.6.6
   Speaking & Listening - SL.6.1.A, SL.6.1.B, SL.6.1.C, SL.6.1.D, SL.6.2

RESOURCES

Access 1 handout (Beginner)

Access 2 handout (Intermediate)

Access 4 handout (Approaching)

TITLE/DRIVING QUESTION

Core Path	Access Path
Discuss. As a class, read aloud the title and driving question for this Blast. Ask students what they already know about the French Revolution. Do they have any ideas about how people decide when a government needs to change? Remind students that they should not immediately reply to this question. They'll be returning to this question and responding after they've read the Background and some of the Research Links.	**English Learners All Levels** **Discuss a Visual.** Have students view paintings that depict the French Revolution, such as the ones below: http://tinyurl.com/lf6l5ax or http://tinyurl.com/qdsjcko. Ask students to think about the questions listed. • How do the paintings show what happened? • How would you describe the art? • How does the art make you feel? • How does the art change your perspective of the revolution? Have students discuss the paintings, using the questions as the guide for their discussion.
Draft. In their notebooks or on scrap paper, have students draft their initial responses to the driving question. This will provide them with a baseline response that they will be altering as they gain more information about the topic in the Background and Research Links sections of the assignment.	**Beginner & Intermediate** **Draft with Sentence Frame.** When drafting their initial response to the driving question, have students refer to this Blast sentence frame on their Access 1 and 2 handouts: • People know it's time for the government to change when _____. Point out these two key features of the sentence frame: 1. The introductory clause "People know it's time for the government to change" borrows language directly from the Blast driving question to provide a response. 2. Ask students to make special note of the word *when* that prompts students to complete the sentence with their own ideas.

BACKGROUND

Core Path	Access Path
Read. Have students read the Blast background to provide context for the driving question.	**Beginner & Intermediate** **Read with Support.** Have students read the Blast background to provide context for the driving question. When they encounter unfamiliar words or phrases, have students refer to the Blast Glossary on their Access 1 and 2 handouts. If there are unfamiliar words that are not included in their Blast Glossary, encourage students to check a dictionary or online reference tool, like http://tinyurl.com/6ytby. **Approaching** **Read and Summarize.** Have students read the Blast background to provide context for the driving question. As they read, ask students to complete the Read and Summarize activity provided on their Access 4 handout. When they encounter unfamiliar words or phrases, have students refer to the Blast Glossary on their Access 4 handout.
Discuss. Pair students and have them discuss the following questions. Make sure students follow the rules for collegial discussions. 1. Why was Louis XVI in debt? (He inherited debt from his predecessors, and he also gave money to America during the American Revolution.) 2. What did Louis XVI do about France's debt? (He tried to tax the rich, but they refused to pay, so he put together a council to try to find a solution.) 3. What was a major turning point during the French Revolution? (the storming of the Bastille) 4. What is a *catalyst*? (It's a factor that causes change.)	**Beginner** **Discuss.** Pair Beginning with Advanced (or Beyond) students and have them use the dialogue starter on their Access 1 handout to discuss the topic. Advise them to return to the dialogue and switch roles if they get stuck. **Intermediate** **Discuss.** Pair Intermediate with Advanced (or Beyond) students and have them use the dialogue starter on their Access 2 handout to discuss the topic. Advise them to return to the dialogue and switch roles if they get stuck. If their conversation is progressing smoothly, encourage them to continue the discussion beyond the dialogue starter sheet. They can expand their conversations to discuss other examples of when people knew it was time for a change in government.

Core Path	Access Path
Brainstorm. Remind students about the Driving Question for this Blast: How do people decide when it's time for the government to change? In their notebooks, ask students to think about the reasons for the American Revolution and compare it to the reasons behind the French Revolution. Have them make a Venn diagram with the heading "American Revolution" over one circle and "French Revolution" over the other and list ways the two revolutions were similar and different, or use a chart similar to the one below. Here's a short example of how this might look:	

American Revolution	Both	French Revolution
wanted to gain independence from Britain; instigated by colonists living across an ocean from Britain	wanted fair representation in government	wanted a new system of government; too wide a gap between classes; instigated by peasants

RESEARCH LINKS

Core Path	Access Path
Examine and Explore. Before asking students to explore the research links, use these activities and questions to guide their exploration: 1. Which link would you use to find out about another revolution that took place in a different country? ("The Russian Revolution")	

Core Path	Access Path
2. Why do you think information on the Russian Revolution is included? (so that we can see another example of a time when people decided the government needed to change—this might give us more information to help us answer the driving question) 3. What's the most important thing to look out for in any research link you click on? (examples of how people decide when it's time for the government to change)	

	Extend
	Research, Discuss and Present.
	
	1. Assign each group one link to explore in depth.
	2. Ask them to discuss the information:
	   a. What are the key points?
	   b. What inferences did you make as you read?
	   c. What did you learn about this "big idea" from reading this research?
	   d. How did this help you to better understand the topic?
	   e. What questions does your group have after exploring this link?
	3. Allow students time to informally present what they learned.

	Extend **Tech Infusion** **Share.** As students explore the links, encourage them to keep track of their thoughts using an online journal like Penzu (http://tinyurl.com/lwuy989). Students can share their thoughts with others.

Please note that excerpts and passages in the StudySync® library, workbooks, and PDFs are intended as touchstones to generate interest in an author's work. The excerpts and passages do not substitute for the reading of entire texts, and StudySync® strongly recommends that teachers and students seek out and purchase the whole literary or informational work in order to experience it as the author intended. Links to online resellers are available in our digital library. In addition, complete works may be ordered through an authorized reseller by filling out and returning to StudySync® the order form enclosed in this workbook.

Teacher's Edition   **245**

QUIKPOLL

Core Path	Access Path
Participate. Answer the poll question. Have students use information from the background and research links to explain their answers.	

NUMBER CRUNCH

Core Path	Access Path
Predict, Discuss, and Click. Before students click on the number, break them into pairs and have them make predictions about what they think the number is related to. After they've clicked the number, ask students if they are surprised by the revealed information.	

CREATE YOUR BLAST (140 CHARACTERS)

Core Path	Access Path
Blast. Ask students to write their Blast response in 140 characters or less.	**Beginner** **Blast with Support.** Have students refer back to the sentence frame on their Access 1 handout that they used to create their original Blast draft. Ask them to use this frame to write and enter their final Blast. **Intermediate** **Blast with Support.** Have students attempt to draft their Blast without the sentence frame on their Access 2 handout. If students struggle to compose their Blast draft without the sentence frame, remind them to reference it for support.

Core Path	Access Path
	Beyond **Write a Claim.** Ask students to use their answer to the poll question to write a strong claim that could be used as the foundation for a piece of argumentative writing. Once students have written their claims, ask them to read the claims to a small group of their peers. This activity will provide them practice writing claims, as well as expose them to claims written by their peers.
Review. After students have completed their own Blasts, ask them to review the Blasts of their peers and provide feedback.	**Extend** **Discuss.** As a whole class or in groups, identify a few strong blasts and discuss what made those responses so powerful. As a group, analyze and discuss what characteristics make a blast interesting or effective.
	Extend **Revise.** Resend a second version of this Blast assignment to your students and have them submit revised versions of their original Blasts. Do the same responses make the Top 10? How have the answers improved from the first submissions?

OVERVIEW

The novel *Les Misérables,* by Victor Hugo, examines how the character of Jean Valjean navigates the moral crossroads that political and social turmoil and poverty generate in his life. The First Read gives students the opportunity to experience the text with a limited context.

OBJECTIVES

1. Perform an initial reading of a text and demonstrate comprehension by responding to short analysis and inference questions with textual evidence.
2. Practice defining vocabulary words using context as well as Greek and Latin word roots and affixes.
3. Practice using concrete strategies for recognizing and correcting vague pronouns.
4. Participate effectively in a range of conversations and collaborations to express ideas and build upon the ideas of others.

ELA Common Core Standards:
Reading: Literature - RL.6.1, RL.6.3, RL.6.4, RL.6.10
Writing - W.6.4
Speaking & Listening - SL.6.1.A, SL.6.1.B, SL.6.1.C, SL.6.1.D, SL.6.2, SL.6.6
Language - L.6.1.D, L.6.4.A, L.6.4.B, L.6.4.D

RESOURCES

Grammar handout: Recognizing and Correcting Vague Pronouns

Access 1 handout (Beginner)

Access 2 handout (Intermediate)

Access 3 handout (Advanced)

Access 4 handout (Approaching)

ACCESS COMPLEX TEXT

In this excerpt from *Les Misérables,* Victor Hugo uses the Bishop's encounter with Valjean to explore the power of love and compassion to redeem a person. To help students uncover the theme and understand the story, use the following suggestions to provide scaffolded instruction for a close reading of the more complex features of this text:

- **Connection of Ideas** - Students are asked to determine the theme of the excerpt. Since the theme is not directly stated, students must look for clues, paying special attention to the setting and the characters. The deep psychological and social undertones of the selection may challenge students.

- **Prior Knowledge** - Victor Hugo was writing in the 1800s during the turbulent years in France following Napoleon's defeat. Students are unlikely to have sufficient background knowledge to understand Hugo's political and social motivations. This may make it more difficult for students to understand the actions and motivations of both Valjean and the Bishop.

- **Specific Vocabulary** - Some students may have difficulty with unfamiliar English and French words and with understanding the connotation of descriptive words in the narration and dialogue.

1. INTRODUCTION

Core Path	Access Path
Watch. As a class, watch the video preview of *Les Misérables*.	**English Learners All Levels** **Fill in the Blanks.** Ask students to use their Access 1, 2, and 3 handouts to fill in the blanks of the transcript for the preview's voiceover as they watch the preview along with their classmates. Answers are located at the end of this lesson plan online.
Read and Listen. Individually or as a class, read and listen to the Introduction for *Les Misérables*. The introduction provides context for the excerpts taken from Chapters v (5) and xii (12).	**English Learners All Levels & Approaching** **Read and Listen.** Ask students to read and listen to the introduction for *Les Misérables*. Have them refer to the vocabulary listing on their Access 1, 2, 3, and 4 handouts for definitions of key vocabulary terms. If there are unfamiliar words that are not included in their glossary, encourage students to check a dictionary or online reference tool, like http://tinyurl.com/6ytby.

Core Path	Access Path
	Extend **Make Predictions.** Since the reading comprehension strategy will be making predictions, have pairs of students collaborate to make predictions about the setting, characters, and events of the text based on the introduction.

Build Background. In order to understand Valjean's predicament and Hugo's social and political commentary, students will need to build background information regarding 19th century French politics and society. You may want to group students and assign each group a topic to research including:

- July Revolution and ascension of King Louis-Philippe, 1830

- June Rebellion and the death of Jean Maximilien Lamarque, 1832

- income gap and conditions of the working class, mid-19th century

- cholera epidemic, 1832

Students may record and present their findings using print or digital graphic organizers that feature the reporter's questions and answers: *Who, What, When, Where, Why,* and *How.* You may wish to have groups create a video recording of their presentations.

Beginner
Discuss a Visual. Pair Beginning and more proficient (Beyond) readers. Have them look at and discuss a painting of 19th century France such as "Workers unloading flour in Paris 1885" (http://tinyurl.com/npbx3qm/). Prompt the discussion by asking questions like:

- What do you think the lives of these workers are like?

- What are their families like?

- How is the life of upper class people similar or different?

Intermediate & Advanced
Discuss a Visual. Pair Intermediate and Advanced students. Have them look at and discuss a painting of 19th century France such as "Workers unloading flour in Paris 1885" (http://tinyurl.com/npbx3qm). Prompt the discussion by asking questions like:

- What do you think the lives of these workers are like?

- What are their families like?

- How is the life of upper class people similar or different?

Approaching
Graphic Organizer. Rather than researching a specific incident, have Approaching students research social life in 19th century France using a site like http://tinyurl.com/p5kljf5. Have students complete the graphic organizer on their Access 4 handouts to help them synthesize the information about the lives of upper, middle, and lower class people and share their results with the class.

Core Path	Access Path
	Extend **Discuss the Introduction.** Use the information gathered in the Introduction section to facilitate a prereading discussion to get students thinking about the events and themes in *Les Misérables*. 1. What are some examples of "moral challenges" or "facing a crossroads" you have heard of or read about? 2. How does a person's response to a moral challenge define or change his or her character?
	Extend **Analyze and Discuss a Quotation.** "It is by suffering that human beings become angels" (Victor Hugo). 1. What do you think this quotation means? 2. Do you agree with this quotation? Why or why not? 3. How would you define "suffering"? In what ways does the act of suffering have the power to transform an individual?

2. READ

Core Path	Access Path
Make Predictions about Vocabulary. There are five bold vocabulary words in the text. As students read the text, ask them to make predictions about what they think each bold vocabulary word means based on the context clues in the sentence. If you are in a low tech classroom and students are reading from printed copies or a projected text, ask students to record predictions in their notes, so they can be easily referenced in class. If your students have access to technology, they can use the annotation tool to make their predictions.	**Note:** This exercise, which extends vocabulary instruction, should be completed when the class shifts from whole group instruction to individual work during the "Read and Annotate" exercise. **Beginner, Intermediate & Approaching Pair Practice.** 1. Pair students with more proficient readers. 2. Give them an additional sentence that contains a new vocabulary word.

Please note that excerpts and passages in the StudySync® library, workbooks, and PDFs are intended as touchstones to generate interest in an author's work. The excerpts and passages do not substitute for the reading of entire texts, and StudySync® strongly recommends that teachers and students seek out and purchase the whole literary or informational work in order to experience it as the author intended. Links to online resellers are available in our digital library. In addition, complete works may be ordered through an authorized reseller by filling out and returning to StudySync® the order form enclosed in this workbook.

Teacher's Edition   251

Core Path	Access Path

Core Path

It might be helpful to model this practice for students before they begin reading. Either using the board or projecting the actual text, focus in on the sentence that uses the word "perdition":

- "Jean Valjean, my brother, you no longer belong to evil, but to good. It is your soul that I buy from you; I withdraw it from black thoughts and the spirit of perdition, and I give it to God."

Model for the class how to use the overall structure and meaning of the sentence and the sentences around it, the word's position, and other clues to define the unfamiliar vocabulary word. In this case, point out these context keys:

1. Look at the words and phrases from which the Bishop "withdraws," or pulls back, Valjean's soul: "evil," "black thoughts," and the "spirit of perdition." I can see that these words are all bad or negative, so I think that "perdition" is probably something negative.

2. I can also see that the Bishop brings Valjean toward "good" and "God," words that are pretty positive.

3. The Latin root *perdere* means "to destroy," and the suffix *-tion* often means "state of." This also suggests not only that the state of "perdition" is negative, but also that the "spirit of perdition" might be a particular destructive force.

4. The Bishop is a religious man, and there seems to be a religious theme to his words, so perdition probably has a religious meaning as well. If he's drawing Valjean toward God and away from perdition, I can conclude that perdition might have something to do with eternal punishment and the loss of salvation. Given the origin, it might also refer to the destruction of Valjean's soul.

5. Looking up the word in a dictionary, we can confirm that "perdition" means "the state of being eternally punished after death."

Access Path

3. Ask the students to complete a Think Aloud using the teacher-led Make Predictions about Vocabulary activity as a model, while the proficient student actively listens.

4. The student should use the context clues in the sentence to try to determine the meaning of the new vocabulary word.

5. After the student has completed the Think Aloud and made a prediction about the word's meaning, allow time for the proficient reader to add his/her own thoughts and clarify any points of confusion.

6. Once they've completed this Think Aloud, encourage them to use a dictionary to confirm the definition of the new vocabulary word. Have them refer to the vocabulary listing on their Access 1, 2, and 4 handouts for definitions of key vocabulary terms in the text. Encourage them to add any additional vocabulary words or idioms they find in the text and look up definitions for those words and idioms online or in a dictionary.

Beyond
Tech Infusion
Dramatize. Assign passages from the excerpt to small groups. Have group members use Blabberize (http://tinyurl.com/cyoqtl) to create a dramatic reading of their passage. Encourage students to be creative in the images they Blabberize by photographing themselves as the characters in the story or by creating a collage of characters using images from the Internet. Have groups share their readings with the class and discuss what their passages contribute to the central idea of the story.

Core Path	Access Path
Model Reading Comprehension Strategy. Before students begin reading, model the reading comprehension strategy of making, confirming, and revising predictions by using this Think Aloud that talks students through the first fifteen paragraphs of text. First explain to your students that making, confirming, and revising predictions is using text clues and prior knowledge to make logical guesses about coming events or information and then confirming or revising these guesses as new information becomes available.	**Note:** This exercise, which extends instruction around reading comprehension strategies, should be completed when the class shifts from whole group instruction to individual work during the "Read and Annotate" exercise.

Core Path

Model for students how making, confirming, and revising predictions will help them better comprehend the selection and help drive their discussions.

- When I read the opening scene, I notice the mention of silver candlesticks and silverware and the description of the layout of the quarters, particularly the proximity of the Bishop to all else.

- Then, I note the guest's "monstrous" laugh at the mention of assassination.

- At this point, I may use these clues to predict that the guest will steal from the Bishop and/or harm him.

- As I continue to read, I will use additional text information to confirm my predictions or revise them, if necessary. This practice helps me set a purpose for my reading as I make inferences and construct meaning from the text.

Access Path

Beginner, Intermediate & Approaching
Apply Reading Comprehension Strategy.

1. Have students listen to the audio version of the excerpt from *Les Misérables*. As they listen to the audio, pause the recording after paragraph 8. Instruct them to write one sentence predicting who the characters are and what will happen after the Bishop leaves.

2. Resume the audio, pausing periodically to allow students to write a new sentence underneath, refining their previous predictions. Offer guidance to help them notice clues in the events, descriptions, and dialogue.

3. Once they have finished listening to the audio, have them write one final sentence, summarizing the text.

4. Pair students with more proficient readers and ask them to discuss the differences between their initial predictions and their final summaries. Which predictions changed and which stayed the same? What clues were the most important? Encourage groups to share their findings with the class, and point out strategies that may have used without realizing it.

Core Path	Access Path
Read and Annotate. Have students independently read and annotate the excerpt. Ask students to use the annotation tool as they read to: 1. use context clues to analyze and determine the meaning of the bolded vocabulary terms 2. ask questions about passages of the text that may be unclear or unresolved 3. identify key information, events, characters, and connections between them 4. note unfamiliar vocabulary 5. capture reactions to characters and events	**Beginner** **Coach the Reading.** While other students read, annotate, and discuss the text independently, work with Beginning students, listening to the audio of the text and pausing periodically or when any student has a question. Coach students in articulating their questions for the group and in highlighting and annotating the text. Have students use the Annotation Guide in the Access 1 handout to support them as they highlight and annotate the text. For further support, ask questions about the text such as: • Is there anything about the story that you don't understand? • What do you think will happen in the story? • What do you think about the two main characters? Are they good or bad? **Intermediate & Advanced** **Paired Practice.** Have Intermediate students work with Advanced students. Ask student pairs to read and annotate the text. Have students use the Annotation Guide in the Access 2 and 3 handouts to support them as they highlight and annotate the text. **Approaching** **Use the Annotation Guide.** Have students use the Annotation Guide in the Access 4 handout to support them as they highlight and annotate the text. To help students understand the basic points of the text, ask them to work in pairs to answer the comprehension questions of the Access 1 handout.

Core Path

Discuss. In small groups or pairs, have students discuss the questions and inferences they made while reading. Make sure students follow the rules for collegial discussions: Refer to Collaborative Discussions in the Speaking & Listening Handbook.

1. What predictions do you make about the Bishop's motivation for allowing Valjean to see the silver as it is put away, along with the layout of the quarters? Support your response with textual evidence. (Answers will vary, but students may predict that Valjean's integrity and honesty are being tested.)

2. What predictions do you make about Valjean's stay? Will he "pass a good night" and "drink a cup of warm milk" before he departs the next morning? Support your response with textual evidence. (Answers will vary, but students may predict that Valjean may succumb to the temptation before him and steal the Bishop's silver, leaving before the Bishop and Madame Magliore discover the theft.)

3. The Bishop responds to Valjean's threat with, "That is the concern of the good God." What predictions do you make about power and control in the story? Support your response with textual evidence and prior knowledge. (Answers will vary.)

(G) **Grammar, Usage, and Mechanics.** Distribute the StudySync grammar handout on pronoun antecedents. Review with students the definition of an antecedent and the need to correct any vague or unclear pronouns in writing, as explained in the handout. Then, have students complete the practice exercise. (Answers for the practice exercise appear at the end of the lesson plan online.) Finally, encourage students to apply what they have learned by analyzing the relationships between pronouns and antecedents in *Les Misérables* :

Access Path

English Learners All Levels & Approaching
Use the extra time while on– and beyond–grade level students are discussing their first reads of the text to work individually and in small groups with Approaching readers and English Learners as outlined on the previous page. Should those students complete their first reads quickly, integrate them into the on and beyond grade level discussion groups. Otherwise English Learners and Approaching readers will be given an opportunity to participate in text discussions with their peers later in the lesson.

Beginner & Intermediate
Work with the Teacher. Remind these students that pronouns are words that can be used to represent other, more specific nouns. The noun to which a pronoun refers to is called the antecedent. For example, the pronoun *he* can stand in for a person with a proper name such as *Jim* or *Pablo*.

Pronoun antecedents are important because they make your writing clear and precise. For example, if there is no antecedent, a sentence like *He is very nice.* is vague and unclear.

Core Path	Access Path
1. Reread the first paragraph. What is the antecedent of the pronoun "him"? ("guest") How is this relationship made clear in the text? (Since Monseigneur Bienvenu is the one speaking, the "him" refers to the person to whom he is speaking—"his guest.") 2. Reread the first sentence of paragraph 9. Who does the pronoun "he" refer to? (the man) How are you able to determine this? (The "he" in the sentence is described as just having "pronounced these words," and the man was the last person to have spoken.) 3. Why might the pronoun/antecedent relationship in the first sentence of paragraph 9 be considered confusing? (The text says that "he" just spoke words "full of peace," but that seems to more closely describe the Bishop's words spoken earlier than it does the man's brief thanks.) How might the speaker's identity be clarified? ("The man" could be substituted for the first "he" in the sentence.)	Write the following sentence on the board: *The counselor and the student talked about his future.* Ask: *Who does the word* his *refer to? How can you revise the sentence to make it more clear?* **Advanced & Beyond** **Extend the Search.** Challenge these students to work in pairs or small groups to find sentences with pronouns and antecedents in the text. Ask: *How do the antecedents help you understand what is happening?* **Approaching** **Analyze an Example.** If students need more support identifying examples of pronoun antecedents, call their attention to these words in paragraph 53: *I gave you the candlesticks too, which are of silver like the rest, and for which you can certainly get two hundred francs. Why did you not carry them away with your forks and spoons?* Ask: *What does* them *refer to? What importance do the nouns in this sentence have?* Encourage students to recognize that the items show Valjean's desperate situation and his moral dilemma. Then have students complete the Recognizing and Correcting Vague Pronouns Handout.
	Extend **Identify and Define.** After reading the text, compile a list of additional vocabulary words. Ask students to reference their annotations and share any vocabulary words that were unfamiliar. 1. As a class, compile a list of unknown words on the board. 2. In small groups, ask students to make predictions about what they think these words mean based on how they are used in the sentence. 3. Each group should work together using dictionaries or devices to define the words and write the definitions in their notebooks.

3. SYNCTV

Core Path	Access Path
Watch. As a class, watch the SyncTV video on *Les Misérables*. Pause the video at these key moments to discuss the information with your students. Make sure students follow the rules for collegial discussions. Have students review and reflect on the ideas expressed, paraphrasing as necessary. 1. 0:14 – One of the students says, "I'm just arguing he's as much a psychologist as he is a bishop." In what ways does the Bishop behave like a psychologist? In what ways does he behave like a bishop? 2. 1:44 – The students discuss Valjean's "monstrous" behavior toward the Bishop. In what ways does Valjean behave like a monster? If Valjean is more monstrous than human, is he responsible for his actions? 3. 7:09 – One student mentions the idea of improvisation and suggests that Valjean and the Bishop conspire to improvise a new reality. In what ways do Valjean's actions define and redefine his character?	**Beginner & Intermediate** **Analyze the Discussion.** Have students use the "Analyze the Discussion" guide on the Access 1 and 2 handouts to identify key points in the discussion and the evidence the students use to determine those points. Sample answers are at the end of this lesson plan online. **Advanced** **A Trick or a Lesson?** Have students discuss and complete the chart on the Access 3 handout, referring back to the SyncTV video as needed to clarify their answers. Sample answers appear at the end of this lesson plan online. **Approaching** **Analyze the Discussion.** Have students complete the chart on the Access 4 handout by listing textual evidence cited by the students in the video. Sample answers are at the end of this lesson plan online.
	Extend **Tech Infusion** **Record.** Ask one student in each group to videotape the conversation. They can upload these videos to YouTube, share them via Google Drive or email them to you for review. They can also play the videos back and critique their own conversations to continually improve.

4. THINK

Core Path	Access Path
Answer and Discuss. Have students complete the Think questions and then use the peer review instructions and rubric to complete two peer reviews. Refer to the sample answers at the end of this lesson plan online to discuss responses with your students.	**Beginner & Intermediate** **Sentence Frames.** Have students use the Sentence Frames on the Access 1 and 2 handouts to support their responses to the Think questions. If necessary, distribute sentence frames to Advanced students as well. **Approaching** **Find the Evidence.** Have students use Find the Evidence on the Access 4 handout to help them identify the evidence needed to answer the questions.
SyncTV Style Discussion. Put students into heterogeneous small groups and give them a prompt to discuss. Remind them to model their discussions after the SyncTV episodes they have seen. Stress the importance of using academic language correctly and citing textual evidence in their conversations to support their ideas To help students prepare for, strategize, and evaluate their discussions, refer to the Collaborative Discussions section of the Speaking & Listening Handbook. Discussion prompts: 1. Who controls the outcome of the scene and how—the Bishop, "the good God," Valjean, or someone else? 2. Has Valjean made a promise, and if so, in what way? What are the the possible consequences of keeping or breaking this promise? Have students review the key ideas expressed, demonstrating an understanding of multiple perspectives through reflection and paraphrasing. You may wish to have students create a video or audio recording of their SyncTV-Style Discussion.	**Beginner & Intermediate** **Discussion Questions.** Have pairs of students discuss the questions on the Access handouts 1 and 2 to help them participate in the discussion. Remind these students to refer back to their answers to the Think questions to help them participate in the group discussion. **Approaching** **Use Think Questions.** Remind these students to refer back to their answers to the Think questions to help them participate in the group discussion.

Core Path	Access Path
	Extend **Analyze the Titles.** Form small student groups. Assign each group one of the following titles: *Les Misérables,* "Tranquility," or "The Bishop Works." Have students discuss the following questions as appropriate: 1. Which characters are miserable and why? Who or what is responsible for the misery? 2. In chapter v, who experiences "tranquility" and how? 3. In chapter xii, how does the Bishop work and for what purpose? Is he successful in his work? Why or why not? Have each group present its ideas to the class by discussing all comments related to their novel title. Have students cite textual evidence to support their ideas.

SKILL:
Theme

OVERVIEW

Determining the theme in a text is a key to understanding a work of literature. This lesson plan provides follow-up questions and useful enrichments to help teachers guide students toward a usable, repeatable method for uncovering theme.

OBJECTIVES

1. Learn the definition of theme.
2. Practice using concrete strategies for identifying and analyzing theme.
3. Participate effectively in a range of conversations and collaborations to express ideas and build upon the ideas of others.

   ELA Common Core Standards:
   Reading: Literature - RL.6.1, RL.6.2, RL.6.3
   Speaking & Listening - SL.6.1.A, SL.6.1.B, SL.6.1.C, SL.6.2

RESOURCES

Access 1 handout (Beginner)

Access 2 handout (Intermediate)

Access 3 handout (Advanced)

Access 4 handout (Approaching)

1. DEFINE

Core Path	Access Path
Watch. Watch the Concept Definition video on theme with your students. Ask students to write the definitions and the key evidence they can examine to determine theme in their notes. Pause the video at these key moments to discuss the information with your students:	**English Learners All Levels & Approaching** **Match.** Have students complete the matching exercise on the Access 1, 2, 3, and 4 handouts as they watch the video. Answers are located at the end of this lesson plan online.

1. 1:00 – Why would authors choose to have readers infer stories' themes? Why don't all authors just come out and state the theme like they do in fables?

2. 1:25 – What are some other real life examples of times when inference skills are important?

3. 2:37 – Can you think of any evidence that might help a reader identify theme that the students in the video don't mention? Are some pieces of evidence more important for determining theme?

Core Path	Access Path
Read and Discuss. After watching the Concept Definition video, have students read the definition of theme. Either in small groups or as a whole class, use these questions to engage students in a discussion about theme. Make sure students follow the rules for collegial discussions.	**Beginner & Approaching** **Finish the Sentences.** Have these students complete the sentences on the Access 1 and 4 handouts as they read the definition. Have them use the completed sentences to help them participate in the discussion. Answers for this exercise are located at the end of the lesson plan online.

1. What do good readers do when they try to find the theme of a story? (They make inferences about the characters, plot, and setting to find the author's underlying message or theme.)

2. How can characters' words and actions help readers figure out a story's theme? (The things that happen to the characters, how they react, and what they say about events can help to determine a story's theme.)

3. Can you think of a time when you figured out a story's theme? What did you do that made you successful?

Intermediate & Advanced
Discuss Prompts. To help these students participate in the discussion, prompt them with questions that can be answered with a few words, such as:

- What is the theme of a story? (the message that the story is about)

- Why is the theme of a story sometimes hard to identify? (because it isn't always stated)

- What are some examples of themes you can think of?

Please note that excerpts and passages in the StudySync® library, workbooks, and PDFs are intended as touchstones to generate interest in an author's work. The excerpts and passages do not substitute for the reading of entire texts, and StudySync® strongly recommends that teachers and students seek out and purchase the whole literary or informational work in order to experience it as the author intended. Links to online resellers are available in our digital library. In addition, complete works may be ordered through an authorized reseller by filling out and returning to StudySync® the order form enclosed in this workbook.

Teacher's Edition   261

Core Path	Access Path
	Beyond **Discuss.** Have students select a book they've read and describe its theme. Compile a list of examples. Have students discuss how the theme of each work is expressed through the characters and plot. Is it obvious from the title? Is it hard to discover?
	Extend **Map Common Themes.** Point out to students that the driving question of the unit suggests a common theme among the works: *How do people decide when to stand up for others and themselves?* Form small student groups and have them prepare print or digital concept maps to analyze this theme within the unit. Students may write the driving question in the center circle. In the radiating circles, students should write the central idea or lesson that each text they've read suggests about this theme. Ask volunteers to share selected entries with the class.

2. MODEL

Core Path	Access Path
Read and Annotate. Have students independently read the Model section. As they read, ask students to use the annotation tool to: • highlight key points • ask questions • identify places where the Model applies the strategies laid out in the Identification and Application section	**Note:** During this portion of the lesson, instruction shifts from whole group to individual work. Use this time to work one-on-one or in small groups with Beginning, Intermediate, Advanced, and Approaching students. **Beginner & Intermediate** **Coach the Reading.** Work with these students (either individually or in small groups) to fill out the guided reading questions on the Access 1 and 2 handouts. Have Beginning students refer to the glossary on the Access 1 handout to help them determine the meaning of difficult words. (note: Provide the Access 1 handout glossary to Intermediate students if necessary.) Let students know they'll use these answers to help participate in the discussion about the Model. Sample answers for this exercise are located at the end of the lesson plan online.

Core Path	Access Path
	Advanced **Identify Evidence.** Provide these students with the same instructions to read and annotate as on–grade level and Beyond students. In addition, ask Advanced students to complete the Identifying Evidence exercise on the Access 3 handout. Let students know that they'll use these answers to help participate in the discussion about the Model. **Approaching** **Guided Reading.** Have students complete the guided reading questions on the Access 4 handout as they read. Let them know that they'll use these answers to help participate in the discussion about the Model. Sample answers for this exercise are located at the end of the lesson plan online.
Discuss. After students read the Model text, use these questions to facilitate a whole group discussion that helps students understand how to determine the theme of the passage. 1. How does the Model approach finding the theme of the passage? (It says that readers must make inferences about story elements, including what characters think, say, and do, to figure out a story's theme.) 2. Why does the Model first establish Valjean's background? (The Model establishes his background because it is essential to understanding events in the excerpt and the theme of the story. He has been in prison and treated unjustly. On release, he is bitter and desperate.) 3. What story elements does the Model focus on as clues to the theme? (The Model takes a look at Jean Valjean's actions, the Bishop's actions, and the dialogue between them.) 4. How does the Bishop's response to the theft provide clues to the theme? (He does not react harshly. He says that the silver belonged to Valjean, a poor person, to begin with.)	

Core Path	Access Path
5. How do the interactions between the Bishop and Valjean reveal the true character of each man and, in turn, the story's theme? (Answers will vary, but show the need for creating a society that is just, compassionate, and fair. Valjean steals because of his situation in life. The Bishop realizing this, forgives Valjean, and works to better his situation.)	
	Extend **Tech Infusion** **Write.** Ask students to imagine that Valjean has a moment to gather his thoughts after the departure of the gendarmes. What might Valjean say to the Bishop? Have students write emails to the Bishop in the voice of Jean Valjean. Tell students to comment on what the Bishop has taught Valjean and how. Then, have Valjean address the promise that the Bishop claims Valjean has made. Ask volunteers to read aloud their emails to the class in an open-mike style reading.

3. YOUR TURN

Core Path	Access Path
Assess and Explain. Have students answer the comprehension questions to test for understanding. Share the explanations for Parts A and B (located online) with your students.	
	Extend **Freewrite.** Before students respond to the questions, have them use this sentence starter to freewrite about the Bishop's words and actions and the story's theme: • The Bishop does not accuse Valjean of theft because _____.

Copyright © BookheadEd Learning, LLC

Core Path	Access Path
	Extend **Tech Infusion** **Blog for the Bishop.** Have students post blog entries for the Bishop stating his position on a social and political system that allows the poor to go hungry. Remind them to cite evidence from the text.

Please note that excerpts and passages in the StudySync® library, workbooks, and PDFs are intended as touchstones to generate interest in an author's work. The excerpts and passages do not substitute for the reading of entire texts, and StudySync® strongly recommends that teachers and students seek out and purchase the whole literary or informational work in order to experience it as the author intended. Links to online resellers are available in our digital library. In addition, complete works may be ordered through an authorized reseller by filling out and returning to StudySync® the order form enclosed in this workbook.

Teacher's Edition   265

CLOSE READ:
Les Misérables

OVERVIEW

The novel *Les Misérables*, by Victor Hugo, examines how the character of Jean Valjean navigates the moral crossroads that political and social turmoil and poverty generate in his life. The Close Read gives students the opportunity to identify and analyze the development of theme.

OBJECTIVES

1. Complete a close reading of a passage of literature.
2. Practice and apply concrete strategies for identifying theme.
3. Participate effectively in a range of conversations and collaborations to express ideas and build upon the ideas of others.
4. Prewrite, plan, and produce clear and coherent writing in response to a prompt.

ELA Common Core Standards:
Reading: Literature - RL.6.1, RL.6.2, RL.6.3, RL.6.4, RL.6.5, RL.6.10
Writing - W.6.4, W.6.5, W.6.6, W.6.9.A, W.6.10
Speaking & Listening - SL.6.1.A, SL.6.1.B, SL.6.1.C, SL.6.1.D, SL.6.6
Language - L.6.4.A, L.6.4.C, L.6.4.D

RESOURCES

Les Misérables Vocabulary handout
Les Misérables Graphic organizer
Access 1 handout (Beginner)
Access 2 handout (Intermediate)
Access 3 handout (Advanced)
Access 4 handout (Approaching)

1. INTRODUCTION

Core Path	Access Path
Define and Compare. Project the vocabulary words and definitions onto the board or provide students with handouts so they can copy the vocabulary into their notebooks. Suggest that students consult general and specialized reference materials, both print and digital, to compare the precise meaning of a specific word with their initial vocabulary predictions from the First Read. Review words that students defined incorrectly to understand why they were unable to use context clues to develop usable definitions.	**Beginner & Intermediate** **Complete the Sentences.** Have students complete the sentence frames on the Access 1 and 2 handouts using the vocabulary words. Point out that some of the words are in the questions and some will be in the answers. Sample answers are located at the end of this lesson plan online. **Advanced & Beyond** **Write in Journals.** Have students write a journal entry using all of their vocabulary words. Remind them to write sentences that communicate the meaning of the words they are using. **Approaching** **Graphic Organizer.** To support students in comparing their vocabulary predictions with the correct meanings, have them complete the graphic organizer on the Access 4 handout. They should record the vocabulary words, their initial predictions, and the correct definitions. Then have them write sentences using the words.
Review. Have students complete the fill in the blank vocabulary worksheet for this selection. Answers for the worksheet are listed at the end of the lesson plan online.	
	Extend **Tech Infusion** **Create.** Have each student create artwork or a collage to visually represent one of the vocabulary words using an iPad or Android art app. Have students who choose the same word take turns posting and presenting their works.

Core Path	Access Path
	Extend **Tech Infusion** **Create.** Create online flashcards for the vocabulary using Quizlet (http://tinyurl.com/2vdfxf) or StudyBlue (http://tinyurl.com/ov6xbl). Have students quiz each other in small groups.

2. READ

Core Path	Access Path
Model Close Reading. Project the text onto the board and model a close reading of the first few paragraphs using the annotation strategies mentioned below. While modeling annotation strategies, make notes that tie the text to the focus skill and demonstrate what students are looking for as they read. Here is some guidance for you as you annotate for your students: • As the Skills lesson that precedes this text makes clear, authors use character, setting, and plot to create theme. • In paragraph 9 of chapter V, the author begins with a reference to Valjean's "words of peace," but then he quickly shifts to a series of contrasting words: *strange, horror, warning, menace,* and *savage.* • So, we know that Valjean tries, and perhaps even wants to be a man of peace, but he is not such a man. We also know that Valjean's menacing behavior overtakes him as a kind of "instinctive impulse," whether he desires it or not. • We also know that conflict is an element of plot. In this case, the conflict appears to be an internal one—Valjean struggles between the man he wants to be and the man he is. The outcome of this conflict will likely shed light on the story's theme.	

Core Path	Access Path
Read and Annotate. Read the Skills Focus questions as a class, so your students know what they should pay close attention to as they read. Then have students read and annotate the excerpt. Ask students to use the annotation tool as they read to 1. respond to the Skills Focus section 2. ask questions 3. make connections 4. identify key information, examples, and themes 5. note unfamiliar vocabulary 6. capture their reaction to the ideas and examples in the text As they reread the text, remind students to use the comprehension strategy of Making, Confirming, and Revising Predictions that they learned in the First Read.	**Note:** While on–grade level students are reading and annotating, work one-on-one or in small groups with Beginning, Intermediate, Advanced, and Approaching students to support them as they read and annotate the text. **Beginner & Intermediate** **Summarize and Analyze the Text.** Work with these students to complete the sentence frames on the Access 1 and 2 handouts (note: the sentence frames for Intermediate students on the Access 2 handout contain fewer scaffolds). They will then use the completed sentence frames to help them analyze and annotate the text by completing the Skills Focus questions. Refer to the sample Skills Focus answers to help them complete the sentence frames and annotate the text. **Advanced** **Work in Pairs.** Pair these students with more proficient English speakers to work together on analyzing and annotating the text to complete the Skills Focus questions. If these students need more support, have them use the sentence frames on the Access 3 handout as they work with their more proficient peers. **Approaching** **Summarize the Text.** Have these students discuss and complete the text summary on the Access 4 handout. Have students then use their summary to help them analyze and annotate the text by completing the Skills Focus questions. Correct answers for the summary are at the end of this lesson plan online. Also refer to the sample Skills Focus answers to aid students with their annotations.
Discuss. After students have read the text, use the sample responses to the Skills Focus questions at the bottom of this lesson plan online to discuss the reading and the process of identifying and analyzing theme.	**Extend** **Pair and Share.** In small, heterogeneous groups or pairs, ask students to share and discuss their annotations with a focus on the theme presented in the selection.

Teacher's Edition

Core Path	Access Path
Make sure that students have acquired and accurately use academic-specific words and phrases related to the skill, and demonstrate a command of formal English appropriate to the discussion.	You can provide students with these questions to guide their discussion: 1. Why does Valjean's behavior change so suddenly? Cite specific textual evidence to support your statements. (He is not used to being trusted by others because he is a criminal. He is angry about the role that society has forced him to play.) 2. What does the Bishop say he will eat with after the silverware is gone? Cite specific textual evidence to support your answer. (He will eat with wooden forks and spoons. He does not seem concerned about eating with less fancy utensils, but he lives humbly and is a man of God.) 3. How does the Bishop act when Valjean returns? What does it tell you about his character? (He is happy to see Valjean, does not turn him into the police and gives him more valuables. He shows his trust in Valjean and his general belief in the goodness of people.)
	Extend **Mind Share.** In pairs, ask students to create print or digital open mind diagrams for Jean Valjean. Have students add words, phrases, and images that illustrate the external and internal forces at work in Valjean's life. Ask them to whether the forces are positive or negative, strong or weak. Ask volunteers to share their diagrams and lead students to discuss and draw conclusions regarding Jean Valjean's mental and emotional states (See Resources).
	Extend **Tech Infusion** **Connect.** Ask students to define "tranquility" in their own words and to give real-world examples. Have students post the definitions and examples on a Padlet Wall. Discuss the Padlet Wall as a class. 1. How are the definitions similar and/or different?

Core Path	Access Path
	2. Are you surprised by the variety of examples shared?
	3. Do the examples share any commonalities?
	Share the following quotation with students: "Only the development of compassion and understanding for others can bring us the tranquility and happiness we all seek" (Dalai Lama XIV). Lead students to discuss how the quotation applies to the text.

3. WRITE

Core Path	Access Path
Prewrite and Plan. Read the prompt as a class and ask students to brainstorm about the Bishop's treatment of Valjean, and how this behavior reveals the text's theme. Students can brainstorm together either as a class or in small groups to begin planning their responses. Remind your students to look at the excerpt and their annotations to find strong, relevant textual evidence to support their ideas.	**Beginner & Intermediate** **Answer and Discuss.** Have students complete the prewriting questions on the Access 1 and 2 handouts and then explain their answers to a partner before they write. Explain to students that when they answer a question—such *as How do the characters' actions help you identify the theme of a story?*—they need to include a detail, example or quote from the text that supports the statement. For example, students could include the line, "The Bishop sees goodness in Valjean and wants him to lead an honest life." This piece of textual evidence reveals the Bishop is a kind and forgiving person.
	Approaching **Answer Prewriting Questions.** Have students complete the prewriting questions on the Access 4 handout to summarize their thoughts before they write.

Please note that excerpts and passages in the StudySync® library, workbooks, and PDFs are intended as touchstones to generate interest in an author's work. The excerpts and passages do not substitute for the reading of entire texts, and StudySync® strongly recommends that teachers and students seek out and purchase the whole literary or informational work in order to experience it as the author intended. Links to online resellers are available in our digital library. In addition, complete works may be ordered through an authorized reseller by filling out and returning to StudySync® the order form enclosed in this workbook.

Teacher's Edition   271

Core Path	Access Path
	Extend **Tech Infusion** **Organize.** Encourage students to complete graphic organizers to organize their ideas before they draft their responses. Students can create concept maps, brainstorming and organizing either on paper or online using http://tinyurl.com/yceu2jg. Google drawing can also be used to design concept maps.
	Extend **Reflect.** After students have had an opportunity to evaluate peer samples, invite them to discuss their experiences of the review process. Ask them to consider the following points: • What did they learn about writing? • What did they learn about reviewing other writers' work? • What did they learn about having their own work read by their peers? Encourage students to share particular pieces of feedback that they found helpful or unhelpful.
Discuss. Project these instructions for the peer review onto the board and review them with your class, so they know what they are looking for when they begin to provide their classmates with feedback: • How does the writing help you understand the Bishop's view of Valjean? • How does the writer justify what the Bishop tells the gendarmes? • What theme does the writer identify? • What textual evidence does the writer cite to support this theme? • What specific suggestions will help the writer improve the response? • Which elements of this response are done especially well?	

Core Path	Access Path
• Be sure to tell the writer what he or she does well and what he or she needs to work on. Remember that your comments are most useful when they are specific and constructive. After you've looked at the peer review instructions, review the rubric with students before they begin writing. Allow time for students briefly to pose and discuss any questions they may have about the peer review instructions and the rubric. Tell students how many peer reviews they will need to complete once they submit their writing.	
Write. Ask students to complete the writing assignment using textual evidence to support their responses. Once they have completed their writing, they should click "Submit."	
Review. Once students complete their writing assignments, they should submit substantive feedback to two peers. Students should use their peers' feedback to improve their writing.	

Please note that excerpts and passages in the StudySync® library, workbooks, and PDFs are intended as touchstones to generate interest in an author's work. The excerpts and passages do not substitute for the reading of entire texts, and StudySync® strongly recommends that teachers and students seek out and purchase the whole literary or informational work in order to experience it as the author intended. Links to online resellers are available in our digital library. In addition, complete works may be ordered through an authorized reseller by filling out and returning to StudySync® the order form enclosed in this workbook.

Teacher's Edition 273

BLAST:
Wage Rage

OVERVIEW

Students will learn about the minimum wage worker strikes that took place in 2013, which led several states to raise their minimum wages. They will study an infographic to learn more about the subject.

OBJECTIVES

1. Explore background information about infographics in popular media, using the example of an infographic on minimum wage.
2. Research using the hyperlink to learn more about how an infographic can convey information.
3. Participate effectively in a range of conversations and collaborations to express ideas and build upon the ideas of others.

   ELA Common Core Standards:
   Reading: Informational Text - RI.6.1, RI.6.5
   Writing - W.6.1.A, W.6.1.B, W.6.5, W.6.6
   Speaking & Listening - SL.6.1.A, SL.6.1.B, SL.6.1.C, SL.6.1.D, SL.6.2

RESOURCES

Access 1 handout (Beginner)

Access 2 handout (Intermediate)

Access 4 handout (Approaching)

TITLE/DRIVING QUESTION

Core Path	Access Path
Discuss. As a class, read aloud the title and driving question for this Blast. Ask students what they already know about the minimum wage. Do they have any ideas about how infographics can help us understand new information? Remind students that they should not immediately reply to this question. They'll be returning to this question and responding after they've read the Background and Research Link.	**English Learners All Levels & Approaching** **Discuss a Visual.** Have students view an infographic of the average spending for an average American household, such as one at USA.gov's web portal: http://tinyurl.com/pzuszyh. Discuss what is being shown in the image, the information being conveyed, prompting students with questions such as: • What is the purpose of this infographic? • What does it tell you about the kinds of things the average American household buys? • Is this information easily understood? • Where does the information come from? Where on the graphic can you find this?
Draft. In their notebooks or on scrap paper, have students draft their initial responses to the driving question. This will provide them with a baseline response that they will be altering as they gain more information about the topic in the Background and Research Link sections of the assignment.	**Beginner & Intermediate** **Draft with Sentence Frame.** When drafting their initial response to the driving question, have students refer to this Blast sentence frame on their Access 1 and 2 handouts: • Infographics help us to understand new information by _____. Point out these two key features of the sentence frame: 1. The introductory clause "Infographics help us to understand new information" borrows language directly from the Blast driving question to provide a response. 2. Ask students to make special note of the preposition "by", which indicates that students must support their response with reasons and relevant evidence.

BACKGROUND

Core Path	Access Path
Read. Have students read the Blast background to provide context for the driving question.	**Beginner & Intermediate** **Read with Support.** Have students read the Blast background to provide context for the driving question. When they encounter unfamiliar words or phrases, have students refer to the Blast Glossary on their Access 1 and 2 handouts. If there are unfamiliar words that are not included in their Blast Glossary, encourage students to check a dictionary or online reference tool, like http://dictionary.reference.com. **Approaching** **Read and Summarize.** Have students read the Blast background to provide context for the driving question. As they read, ask students to complete the fill in the blank summary of the background provided on their Access 4 handout. When they encounter unfamiliar words or phrases, have students refer to the glossary on their Access 4 handout.
Discuss. Pair students and have them discuss the following questions. Make sure students follow the rules for collegial discussions. 1. **What is an infographic?** (a specific type of text feature—a visual aid— that conveys information and in itself includes other text features.) 2. **Why might writers want to use a feature such as an infographic?** (to present and explain a lot of complex information about a topic in a clear and concise way that is easy for people to understand) 3. **What does the term** *minimum wage* **refer to?** (the minimum amount per hour that an employer can legally pay their employees)	**Beginner** **Discuss.** Pair Beginning with Advanced (or Beyond) students and have them use the dialogue starter on their Access 1 handout to discuss the topic of infographics. Advise them to return to the dialogue and switch roles if they get stuck. **Intermediate** **Discuss.** Pair Intermediate with Advanced (or Beyond) students and have them use the dialogue starter on their Access 2 handout to discuss the topic. Advise them to return to the dialogue and switch roles if they get stuck. If their conversation is progressing smoothly, encourage them to continue the discussion beyond the dialogue starter sheet. They can expand their conversations to discuss other examples of how infographics help readers understand new information.

Core Path	Access Path
4. Why did many minimum wage workers go on strike in 2013? (because they felt that the minimum wage was too low for them to earn a decent living) 5. What three things does the infographic in the link show? (which states planned to raise their minimum wage in 2014; which states have a minimum wage that is higher than, lower than, or equal to the federal minimum; and how many workers earned minimum wage in 2007, 2008, 2009, 2010, 2011, and 2012)	
Brainstorm. Remind students about the Driving Question for this Blast: How can infographics help us understand new information? In their notebooks, ask students to make a Venn diagram with "infographics" on one side and "text" on the other. Have them compare and contrast these two things. Here's a short example of how this might look: 	infographics	both	text
---	---	---
include text and an image; can be a map, graph, or other	convey information in interesting ways	may contain more textual detail; no images		

RESEARCH LINKS

Core Path	Access Path
Examine and Explore. Before asking students to explore the research links, use these activities and questions to guide their exploration: 1. What text features do you notice in this article, aside from the infographic? (photographs, bullet points, a table, boldface type)	

Core Path	Access Path
2. Why do you think a list of story highlights is included? (to present the information in the article quickly, in case people don't have time to read it, or to pique people's interest in the story)	
3. How could you summarize the central idea of the article included with the infographic? (An increase in low-wage jobs has led to protests and efforts to raise the minimum wage.)	
4. Which paragraphs best help to develop the idea that a rise in the number of low-wage jobs is behind the protests? (paragraphs 3, 5, 9, and 14)	
5. Why do you think hyperlinks to other stories are included? (if you're interested in this story, you may also be interested in those other stories, or the other stories can give you more context for this one)	
6. What does the table at the end of the article show? (It shows which states are raising their minimum wages, and what their new minimum wages will be in 2014.)	

Research, Discuss, and Present.

1. Assign each group one link to explore in depth.

2. Ask them to discuss the information:

    a. What are the key points?

    b. What inferences did you make as you read?

    c. What did you learn about this "big idea" from reading this research?

    d. How did this help you to better understand the topic?

    e. What questions does your group have after exploring this link?

3. Allow students time to informally present what they learned.

Core Path	Access Path
	Extend **Tech Infusion** **Share.** As students explore the links, encourage them to keep track of their thoughts using an online journal like Penzu (www.penzu.com). Students can share their thoughts with others.

QUIKPOLL

Core Path	Access Path
Participate. Answer the poll question. Have students use information from the background and research links to explain their answers.	

NUMBER CRUNCH

Core Path	Access Path
Predict, Discuss, and Click. Before students click on the number, break them into pairs and have them make predictions about what they think the number is related to. After they've clicked the number, ask students if they are surprised by the revealed information.	

CREATE YOUR BLAST (140 CHARACTERS)

Core Path	Access Path
Blast. Ask students to write their Blast response in 140 characters or less.	**Beginner** **Blast with Support.** Have students refer back to the sentence frame on their Access 1 handout that they used to create their original Blast draft. Ask them to use this frame to write and enter their final Blast.

Please note that excerpts and passages in the StudySync® library, workbooks, and PDFs are intended as touchstones to generate interest in an author's work. The excerpts and passages do not substitute for the reading of entire texts, and StudySync® strongly recommends that teachers and students seek out and purchase the whole literary or informational work in order to experience it as the author intended. Links to online resellers are available in our digital library. In addition, complete works may be ordered through an authorized reseller by filling out and returning to StudySync® the order form enclosed in this workbook.

Teacher's Edition   **279**

Core Path	Access Path
	Intermediate **Blast with Support.** Have students attempt to draft their Blast without the sentence frame on their Access 2 handout. If students struggle to compose their Blast draft without the sentence frame, remind them to reference it for support. **Beyond** **Write a Claim.** Ask students to use their answer to the poll question to write a strong claim that could be used as the foundation for a piece of argumentative writing. Once students have written their claims, ask them to read the claims to a small group of their peers. This activity will provide them practice writing claims, as well as expose them to claims written by their peers.
Review. After students have completed their own Blasts, ask them to review the Blasts of their peers and provide feedback.	**Extend** **Discuss.** As a whole class or in groups, identify a few strong blasts and discuss what made those responses so powerful. As a group, analyze and discuss what characteristics make a blast interesting or effective.
	Extend **Revise.** Resend a second version of this Blast assignment to your students and have them submit revised versions of their original Blasts. Do the same responses make the Top 10? How have the answers improved from the first submissions?

FIRST READ:
"Jabberwocky"

OVERVIEW

Lewis Carroll's poem "Jabberwocky" is a nonsense verse that has delighted readers of all ages for more than a century. The First Read gives students the opportunity to experience the text with a limited context.

OBJECTIVES

1. Perform an initial reading of a text and demonstrate comprehension by responding to short analysis and inference questions with textual evidence.
2. Practice defining vocabulary words using context, and using dictionaries or other resources to determine the precise meanings and pronunciations of words.
3. Practice acquiring and using academic vocabulary accurately.
4. Participate effectively in a range of conversations and collaborations to express ideas and build upon the ideas of others.

   ELA Common Core Standards:
   Reading: Literature - RL.6.1, RL.6.2, RL.6.4, RL.6.10
   Speaking & Listening - SL.6.1.A, SL.6.1.B, SL.6.1.C, SL.6.1.D, SL.6.2, SL.6.6
   Language - L.6.4.A, L.6.4.C, L.6.6

RESOURCES

Access 1 handout (Beginner)

Access 2 handout (Intermediate)

Access 3 handout (Advanced)

Access 4 handout (Approaching)

Please note that excerpts and passages in the StudySync® library, workbooks, and PDFs are intended as touchstones to generate interest in an author's work. The excerpts and passages do not substitute for the reading of entire texts, and StudySync® strongly recommends that teachers and students seek out and purchase the whole literary or informational work in order to experience it as the author intended. Links to online resellers are available in our digital library. In addition, complete works may be ordered through an authorized reseller by filling out and returning to StudySync® the order form enclosed in this workbook.

Teacher's Edition   281

ACCESS COMPLEX TEXT

"Jabberwocky" by Lewis Carroll is a nonsensical poem about a brave boy's heroic quest. Throughout the poem, Carroll's use of invented language, rhyme, repetition of sounds, and punctuation help establish and maintain a fanciful tone. Use the following suggestions to provide scaffolded instruction for a close reading of the more complex features of this text:

- **Specific Vocabulary** - The invented language may challenge students. To understand and appreciate the poem, Carroll relies on the reader to use context to determine connotative meaning from the imaginative words.

- **Sentence Structure** - Given the nonsensical nature of the words, students need to consider how the words fit into the sentence structure. Students may need help seeing how they can pick out the nouns, adjectives, and verbs from their positions in the stanza and use these structural clues to create a mental picture of the creatures and what they are doing.

- **Genre** - Students are asked to analyze the tone of the poem. Carroll's use of imagery contributes to the poem's fantastical quality by helping the reader visualize a land full of strange and ominous beings. The whimsical rhyme and the strong, fast rhythm of meter also help create the tone. Students may need help isolating these elements.

1. INTRODUCTION

Core Path	Access Path
Watch. As a class, watch the video preview of *Jabberwocky*. Discuss with students how the graphics and audio features, including music, provide context for the selection they are about to read and contribute to the mood and tone.	**English Learners All Levels & Approaching Fill in the Blanks.** Ask students to use their Access 1, 2, 3, and 4 handouts to fill in the blanks of the transcript for the preview's voiceover as they watch the preview along with their classmates. Correct answers are located at the end of this lesson plan online.

Core Path	Access Path
Read and Listen. Individually or as a class, read and listen to the introduction for "Jabberwocky." The introduction provides context for the poem.	**English Learners All Levels & Approaching** **Read and Listen.** Ask students to read and listen to the introduction for *Jabberwocky*. Have them refer to the vocabulary listing on their Access 1, 2, 3, and 4 handouts for definitions of key vocabulary terms. If there are unfamiliar words that are not included in their glossary, encourage students to check a dictionary or online reference tool, like http://tinyurl.com/6ytby.
Access Prior Knowledge. Find out whether some of your students have already read or heard "Jabberwocky." If they have read Lewis Carroll's *Through the Looking Glass*, which is the sequel to his novel *Alice's Adventures in Wonderland*, they have experienced this poem, which is in Chapter 1. Invite students to share what they may know about the wonderful imaginary creatures and worlds featured in the *Alice* books. Students may either have read adaptations of the books or the books themselves, or they may have seen versions of the stories in the movies or on television. If they have previously heard or read "Jabberwocky," ask them to share when and where they were first introduced to it. As time allows, you might also invite students to share what they know about any other poems containing nonsense words.	**Beginner** **Complete and Discuss the Chart.** Pair Beginning and more proficient (Beyond) readers. Rather than discussing the sequel to *Alice's Adventures in Wonderland*, have these groups complete the "Imagine" exercise on the Access 1 handout that asks students to consider what their own responses would be upon seeing a terrifying creature. Have the pairs generate ideas, discuss the chart, and complete it together. **Intermediate & Advanced** **Complete and Discuss the Chart.** Pair Intermediate and Advanced students, and rather than discussing the sequel to *Alice's Adventures in Wonderland*, have these groups complete the "Imagine" exercise on the Access 2 and 3 handouts that asks students to consider what their own responses would be upon seeing a terrifying creature. Have the pairs generate ideas, discuss the chart, and complete it together. **Approaching** **Draw Responses.** 1. First, ask students to imagine that they have stumbled upon a scary creature in the woods. Allow students to work in pairs if they wish.

Please note that excerpts and passages in the StudySync® library, workbooks, and PDFs are intended as touchstones to generate interest in an author's work. The excerpts and passages do not substitute for the reading of entire texts, and StudySync® strongly recommends that teachers and students seek out and purchase the whole literary or informational work in order to experience it as the author intended. Links to online resellers are available in our digital library. In addition, complete works may be ordered through an authorized reseller by filling out and returning to StudySync® the order form enclosed in this workbook.

Teacher's Edition   283

Core Path	Access Path
	2. Have students create a comic strip of three or four frames showing themselves and their actions in such a situation. 3. After they've completed their comic strips, have students complete the "Imagine" exercise on the Access 4 handout.
	Extend **Analyze and Discuss a Quote.** "If you want sense you'll have to make it yourself" (Norton Juster, *The Phantom Tollbooth*). • What do you think this quote means? • Do you agree with this quote? Why or why not? • How would you define nonsense? How would you define sense?

2. READ

Core Path	Access Path
Make Predictions about Vocabulary. There are five bold vocabulary words in the text. As students read the poem, ask them to make predictions about what they think each vocabulary word means based on the context clues. If you are in a low-tech classroom and students are reading from printed copies or a projected text, ask students to record predictions in their notes, for ready reference in class. If your students have access to technology, they can use the annotation tool to make their predictions. It might be helpful to model this for students before they begin reading. Either using the board or projecting the actual text, focus in on the stanza that uses the word "chortled": • "And hast thou slain the Jabberwock? Come to my arms, my beamish boy! O frabjous day! Callooh! Callay!" He chortled in his joy.	**Note** This exercise, which extends vocabulary instruction, should be completed when the class shifts from whole group instruction to individual work during the "Read and Annotate" exercise. **Beginner, Intermediate & Approaching Pair Practice.** 1. Pair students with more proficient readers. 2. Give them an additional sentence that contains a new vocabulary word. 3. Ask the students to complete a Think Aloud using the teacher-led Make Predictions about Vocabulary activity as a model, while the proficient student actively listens. 4. The student should use the context clues in the sentence to try to determine the meaning of the new vocabulary word.

Core Path	Access Path
Model for the class how to use the overall structure and meaning of the stanza, the word's position, and other clues to define the unfamiliar vocabulary word. In this case, point out these context keys: 1. Look at the structure of the sentence. "He chortled" comes after a bit of dialogue. It is a speech tag, in the same position as "said" or "asked." So "chortled" must be the past tense of a verb that describes how someone says something. 2. We can read the dialogue to get a feeling for how the speaker is speaking. Even though some of the words are nonsense, we can tell the speaker is very happy: "O frabjous day! Callooh! Callay!" We can tell this from the word "joy" and from the context of the situation: celebrating killing a monster. 3. We can visualize ourselves in this situation. How would we feel and sound if we were saying this dialogue? Probably, we'd feel and sound happy. We might be laughing and smiling. 4. A dictionary and thesaurus would give us the definition of "chortled," plus other words with close meanings. Additionally, because the letter combination "ch" is sometimes pronounced in different ways, we can use the dictionary to determine its correct pronunciation.	5. After the student has completed the Think Aloud and made a prediction about the word's meaning, allow time for the proficient reader to add his/her own thoughts and clarify any points of confusion. 6. Once they've completed this Think Aloud, encourage them to use a dictionary to confirm the definition of the new vocabulary word. Have them refer to the vocabulary listing on their Access 1, 2, and 4 handouts for definitions of key vocabulary terms in the text. Encourage them to add any additional vocabulary words or idioms they find in the text and look up definitions for those words and idioms online or in a dictionary.
Model Reading Comprehension Strategy. Before students begin reading, model the reading comprehension strategy of visualizing by using this Think Aloud that talks students through the first stanza. First explain to your students that visualizing is forming a mental picture of something as you read, and using new details from the text to add to or change the mental images you have created.	**Note** This exercise, which extends vocabulary instruction, should be completed when the class shifts from whole group instruction to individual work during the "Read and Annotate" exercise.

Please note that excerpts and passages in the StudySync® library, workbooks, and PDFs are intended as touchstones to generate interest in an author's work. The excerpts and passages do not substitute for the reading of entire texts, and StudySync® strongly recommends that teachers and students seek out and purchase the whole literary or informational work in order to experience it as the author intended. Links to online resellers are available in our digital library. In addition, complete works may be ordered through an authorized reseller by filling out and returning to StudySync® the order form enclosed in this workbook.

Teacher's Edition   **285**

Core Path	Access Path
Model for students how visualizing will help them better comprehend the selection and help drive their discussions.	**Beginner, Intermediate & Approaching Apply Reading Comprehension Strategy.**

Core Path

Model for students how visualizing will help them better comprehend the selection and help drive their discussions.

- Visualizing the scene in this poem might be hard, because of the nonsense words. But if we can guess the meanings of some of the nonsense words, that will help us visualize the action and setting, and in turn, will help us guess at the meaning of more nonsense words.

- The first stanza is more than half nonsense words. But we can try to get a general feeling for what the subject is. It sounds to me like a description of a place. "Twas brillig" sounds like it refers to a time of day, or maybe a kind of weather. "The slithy toves did gyre and gimble in the wabe," sounds like a description of creatures moving about in a specific kind of place. To me, it sounds like some kind of water creatures, maybe frogs in a pond. They're not *exactly* frogs in a pond, because they're nonsense creatures. But by visualizing little creatures in a pond, I can sort of get an idea of the scene.

- Because the words are nonsense, I don't think there's one right way to visualize this scene. Part of the fun of it might be that different readers visualize different things. But there might be interesting ways in which the things they visualize are alike, too.

Access Path

Beginner, Intermediate & Approaching Apply Reading Comprehension Strategy.

1. Have Beginning and Intermediate students listen to the audio version of "Jabberwocky." As they listen to the audio recording, ask them to draw or sketch a picture of what they see in their minds as they visualize the poem. Encourage them to include as much detail as possible in the time allowed.

2. Once they have listened to the audio version and created a picture or series of pictures based on what they heard, pair Beginning and Intermediate students with more proficient readers and ask them to describe what they drew and why. Why did they include particular images and/or colors?

3. Allow pairs time to discuss the pictures. Were there any details from the text that were not included in the picture? If so, encourage them to add details to the drawing based on their conversations.

Read and Annotate. Direct students to independently read and annotate the excerpt. Before they begin, have them read the text aloud or play the voiceover (using either the Audio or the Audio Text Highlight tool). Ask students to use the annotation tool as they read to:

1. use context clues to analyze and determine the meaning of the bolded vocabulary terms

2. decipher nonsense words

Beginner
Coach the Reading. While other students read, annotate, and discuss the text independently, work with Beginning students, listening to the audio of the text and pausing periodically or when any student has a question. Coach students in articulating their questions for the group and in highlighting and annotating the text. Have students use the Annotation Guide on the Access 1 handout to support them as they highlight and annotate the text.

Core Path	Access Path
3. ask questions about passages of the text that may be unclear 4. visualize 5. identify key events, characters, and connections between them 6. capture their reactions to the text	For further support, ask questions about the text such as: • Is there anything about the poem that you don't understand? • What do you think was going through the main character's mind when he faced the Jabberwock? • What impression of the Jabberwock do you have after reading the poem? **Intermediate** **Listen to the Audio.** Have these students listen to the audio of the text and use the definitions on the Access 2 handout to help them with words or idioms that may be unfamiliar. If students need help with annotating the text, have them use the Annotation Guide on the Access 2 handout. After working with the Beginning students, you may wish to check this group's progress and provide support as needed. **Advanced** **Pair with Proficient Peers.** Have Advanced students work with English proficient peers to read, annotate, and discuss the text. Have students use the Annotation Guide on the Access 3 handout to support them as they highlight and annotate the text. Encourage them to listen to the audio of the text if needed. **Approaching** **Use the Annotation Guide.** Have students use the Annotation Guide on the Access 4 handout to support them as they highlight and annotate the text.

Please note that excerpts and passages in the StudySync® library, workbooks, and PDFs are intended as touchstones to generate interest in an author's work. The excerpts and passages do not substitute for the reading of entire texts, and StudySync® strongly recommends that teachers and students seek out and purchase the whole literary or informational work in order to experience it as the author intended. Links to online resellers are available in our digital library. In addition, complete works may be ordered through an authorized reseller by filling out and returning to StudySync® the order form enclosed in this workbook.

Teacher's Edition   **287**

Core Path	Access Path
Discuss In small groups or pairs, have students discuss the questions and inferences they made while reading. Make sure students follow the rules for collegial discussions: Refer to Collaborative Discussions in the Speaking & Listening Handbook.	**English Learners All Levels & Approaching** Use the extra time while on– and beyond–grade level students are discussing their first reads of the text to work individually and in small groups with Approaching readers and English Learners as outlined on the previous page. Should those students complete their first reads quickly, integrate them into the on– and beyond–grade-level discussion groups. Otherwise, Approaching readers and English Learners will be given an opportunity to participate in text discussions with their peers later in the lesson.

Core Path

1. What is the setting of the poem? (A fantastical land of interesting and unusual creatures.) How did visualizing help you understand the setting? (Answers will vary.)

2. What do you visualize when you read "all mimsy were the borogoves?" (Answers will vary.)

3. Which unfamiliar vocabulary turned out to be nonsense words? Which turned out to be real words? (Answers will vary.)

4. What actions does the son perform in the poem? (He killed the monstrous creature known as the Jabberwock.) How do nonsense words help you visualize it? How do real words help you visualize it? (Answers will vary.)

5. In what other ways does visualizing help you understand the action in the poem? (Answers will vary.)

Access Path

Extend

Synonyms. After students read the text, have small groups rewrite the sentences or stanzas in which the vocabulary words appear, using synonyms for the vocabulary words. (The synonyms will probably not fit into the rhyme and meter of the verse.)

1. Challenge students to think of synonyms on their own first; then, have them use the dictionary and, especially, the thesaurus, to find synonyms. Discuss how knowing synonyms helps them understand the vocabulary words more precisely.

2. You may also want to have students discuss the connotations that make the words in the text preferable to their synonyms.

3. SYNCTV

Core Path	Access Path
Watch. As a class, watch the SyncTV video on "Jabberwocky." Remind students to listen for the way the students use academic vocabulary during their discussion. Pause the video at these key moments to discuss the information with your students. Make sure students follow the rules for collegial discussions. Have students review and reflect on the ideas expressed, paraphrasing as necessary.	**Beginner, Intermediate & Advanced** **Analyze the Discussion.** Have students use the "Analyze the Discussion" guide on the Access 1, 2, and 3 handouts to identify key points in the discussion and the evidence the students use to determine those points. Sample answers are at the end of this lesson plan online.

Core Path (continued):

1. 1:52 – One of the students says, "Lots of animals in this poem." Aside from the Jabberwock, what animals are there? What do you know about them? How do they increase the poem's effectiveness?

2. 2:18 – One of the students says, "Our teacher called it a ballad stanza. She said a lot of folk songs used it." Why was using ballad stanza form a good choice for this poem?

3. 4:23 – One student says, "The silly made-up language may sound like, 'Hey you can be silly *and* defeat monsters.'" How could being silly and defeating monsters go together?

Access Path (continued):

Approaching
Analyze the Discussion. Have students complete the chart on the Access 4 handout by listing textual evidence cited by the students in the video. Sample answers are at the end of this lesson plan online.

Extend
Tech Infusion
Record. Ask one student in each group to videotape their conversation. They can upload their videos to YouTube, share them via Google Drive, or email them to you for review. They can also play the video back and critique their own conversations to continually improve.

Please note that excerpts and passages in the StudySync® library, workbooks, and PDFs are intended as touchstones to generate interest in an author's work. The excerpts and passages do not substitute for the reading of entire texts, and StudySync® strongly recommends that teachers and students seek out and purchase the whole literary or informational work in order to experience it as the author intended. Links to online resellers are available in our digital library. In addition, complete works may be ordered through an authorized reseller by filling out and returning to StudySync® the order form enclosed in this workbook.

Teacher's Edition   289

4. THINK

Core Path	Access Path
Have students complete the Think questions and then use the peer review instructions and rubric to complete two peer reviews. Refer to the sample answers at the end of this lesson plan online to discuss responses with your students.	**Beginner & Intermediate** **Sentence Frames.** Have students use the Sentence Frames on the Access 1 and 2 handouts to support their responses to the Think questions. If necessary, distribute sentence frames to Advanced students as well (located in Access 3). **Approaching** **Find the Evidence.** Have students use Find the Evidence on the Access 4 handout to help them identify the evidence needed to answer the questions.
SyncTV Style Discussion Put students into heterogeneous small groups and give them a prompt to discuss. Remind them to model their discussions after the SyncTV episodes they have seen, being sure to use language appropriate to this task. Stress the importance of citing textual evidence in their conversations to support their ideas To help students prepare for, strategize, and evaluate their discussions, refer to the Collaborative Discussions section of the Speaking & Listening Handbook. Discussion prompt: 1. The students in the video discuss the possibility that the poem is about a battle between good and evil. Do you agree? Why or why not? Who is good and who is evil in this poem, and how can you tell? 2. Lewis Carroll invented his own nonsense words called *portmanteau words*. Make up some of your own portmanteau words to replace some of the nonsense words in "Jabberwocky." Discuss what the intended meaning is for each word you replaced.	

Core Path	Access Path
Have students review the key ideas expressed, demonstrating an understanding of multiple perspectives through reflection and paraphrasing. You may wish to have students create a video or audio recording of their SyncTV-Style Discussion.	
	Extend **Tech Infusion** **Create.** Invite pairs or small groups of students to create posters for "Jabberwocky" using Glogster (http://tinyurl.com/ydeyklq) or Google Drawing. Their posters should, of course, include their personal visualizations of the Jabberwock, the two human characters, and the setting. Students may also enjoy creating the visual appearances of the other creatures mentioned in the poem, such as mome raths and borogroves. Groups may use a collage style so that more than one visualization of the scene, representing different group members' imaginations, can be presented on a poster. Encourage students to use their creativity in novel ways, such as to write parts of the text in calligraphy, to add clip art of professional illustrations of the poem, and to add brief text passages such as labels, vocabulary word callouts, and dialogue of their own invention.

OVERVIEW

Tone may be a subtler concept than plot or character, but it can be equally important in gaining readers' understanding and appreciation of a text. In "Jabberwocky," the impact of the poem depends largely on the reader's recognition of the fanciful tone. This lesson plan provides follow-up questions and useful enrichments to help teachers guide students toward a usable, repeatable method for identifying the tone of a piece of literature.

OBJECTIVES

1. Learn the definition of tone.
2. Practice using concrete strategies for identifying and analyzing tone.
3. Participate effectively in a range of conversations and collaborations to express ideas and build upon the ideas of others.

   ELA Common Core Standards:
   Reading: Literature - RL.6.1, RL.6.4
   Speaking & Listening - SL.6.1.A, SL.6.1.B, SL.6.1.C, SL.6.2

RESOURCES

Access 1 handout (Beginner)

Access 2 handout (Intermediate)

Access 3 handout (Advanced)

Access 4 handout (Approaching)

1. DEFINE

Core Path	Access Path
Watch. Watch the Concept Definition video on tone with your students. Make sure students understand the basic definition of tone and the different tones the students in the video mention. Pause the video at these key moments to discuss the information with your students:	**English Learners All Levels & Approaching** **Match.** Have students complete the matching exercise on the Access 1, 2, 3, and 4 handouts as they watch the video. Answers are located at the end of this lesson plan online.

1. 0:07 – The students say that tone is attitude. Think of one or more things you have a strong attitude about. What tone do you use when you speak or write about them?

2. 0:38 – As one student names different tones, what tone is she using? Is it the same as the tones she names? How can you tell?

3. 0:58 – One student says that tone is sometimes "at odds with the subject matter." What does she mean? Give an example in addition to the two that she provides.

Read and Discuss. After watching the Concept Definition video, have students read the definition of tone. Either in small groups or as a whole class, use these questions to engage students in a discussion about the use of tone in literature. Make sure students follow the rules for collegial discussions.	**Beginner & Approaching** **Complete a Chart.** To prepare students to participate in the discussion, have them work in groups to complete the chart on the Access 1 and 4 handouts as they read the definition. The correct answers are located at the end of this lesson plan online.

1. Can you think of poems or stories that you have read in this class or elsewhere that have a memorable tone? If so, what were the works and what kind of tone did they have?

2. Can a piece of literature have more than one tone? Why or why not?

3. What clues in a poem or story can help a reader identify the tone?

Intermediate & Advanced
Discuss Prompts. To help these students participate in the discussion, prompt them with questions that can be answered with a few words, such as:

- What can tone express? (the attitude of an author toward a subject, character, or audience)

- What is it called when a speaker stresses certain words or phrases? (tone of voice)

- How do authors convey tone? (through elements such as word choice, sentence structure, and figures of speech)

- What is connotation? (an idea or feeling associated with certain words that is different from their definition)

Core Path	Access Path
	Beyond **Discuss.** Have students select a book they've read and describe its tone. Compile a list of examples. Have students discuss how the tone of each work affects what the reader learns about the characters and plot. How might a switch in tone affect not only what the reader learns, but how much he or she enjoys the story?
	Extend **Tech Infusion** **Blast.** Create a Blast and ask students to "blast out" the definition of tone in their own words and/or provide examples of tone from "Jabberwocky." Have students quote the relevant line(s) of the poem and name the tone. Use the poll question to ask students whether they usually prefer a serious tone or a comic tone in stories and poems.

2. MODEL

Core Path	Access Path
Watch. Ask students to take notes on the SkillsTV video on tone in "Jabberwocky" as you watch together. Pause the video at these key moments to discuss the information with your students: 1. 0:52 – What is the first strategy the students use to try to figure out the tone of the poem? 2. 1:55 – Why does Monica find the tone of the poem scary or "spooky"? Why do Alex and Josh disagree? 3. 2:28 – What elements do the students decide help to create tone, and what agreement does the group reach, if any, about the tone of "Jabberwocky"?	**Beginner, Intermediate, & Approaching** **Analyze the Discussion.** Have students watch the video again and complete the chart on the Access 1, 2, and 4 handouts as they watch the video. Sample answers for this exercise are located at the end of the lesson plan online. **Advanced** **Journals.** Have students note in their journals the strategies the students in the SkillsTV video use to determine tone.

Core Path

Read and Annotate. Have students independently read the Model section. As they read, ask students to use the annotation tool to:

- highlight important ideas and details
- ask questions
- clarify their understanding of tone
- identify places where the Model applies the strategies in the Identification and Application section

Access Path

Note: During this portion of the lesson, instruction shifts from whole group to individual work. Use this time to work one-on-one or in small groups with Beginning, Intermediate, Advanced, and Approaching students.

Beginner & Intermediate
Coach the Reading. Work with these students (either individually or in small groups) to fill out the guided reading questions on the Access 1 and 2 handouts. Have students refer to the glossary on their Access 1 and 2 handouts to help them determine the meaning of difficult words. Let students know they'll use these answers to help participate in the discussion about the Model. Sample answers for this exercise are located at the end of the lesson plan online.

Advanced
Identify Evidence. Provide these students with the same instructions to read and annotate as on–grade level and Beyond students. In addition, ask Advanced students to complete the Identifying Evidence exercise on the Access 3 handout. Let students know that they'll use these answers to help participate in the discussion about the Model. Sample answers for this exercise are located at the end of the lesson plan online.

Approaching
Guided Reading. Have students complete the guided reading questions on the Access 4 handout as they read. Students can refer to the glossary on their Access 4 handout to help them determine the meaning of difficult words. Let them know that they'll use these answers to help participate in the discussion about the Model. Sample answers for this exercise are located at the end of the lesson plan online.

Core Path	Access Path
Discuss. After students read the Model text, use these questions to facilitate a whole group discussion that helps students understand how to determine the tone of the passage:	

1. What adjective does the first paragraph of the Model use to describe the tone of "Jabberwocky"? What does the word mean? ("fanciful"; it means "imaginative, whimsical")

2. How does the Model discover the tone in the first stanza of the poem? (The model closely examines the words of the stanza. They suggest that this is no ordinary world, it is one filled with unknown creatures.)

3. The second paragraph of the Model discusses how readers can guess the meanings of nonsense words in "Jabberwocky." What methods does the Model suggest? (using the positions of the words in sentences to find their parts of speech; using personal word associations; reading the poem aloud and listening to the sounds; using onomatopoeia to imagine how the imaginary creatures look)

4. According to the Model, what are some specific words that contribute to the poem's tone in the second stanza? How is the tone of the second stanza different from that of the first? How is it similar? (The poet's choice of specific words such as "beware" and "shun," along with "jaws" and "claws," create a somewhat ominous and sinister tone. Although the second stanza, with its references to imaginary creatures such as the Jubjub bird, is similar to the first in maintaining a fanciful tone, the tone in the second stanza has definitely been tinged with a sense of danger.)

5. According to the Model, how can a reader understand the tone of a passage when many of the words are made up by the author? (The reader can infer the tone from the context, the images, the sounds, and other clues including punctuation and poetic elements such as rhyme and meter.)

Core Path	Access Path
	Extend **Talk Together.** Have pairs of students talk together about what "Jabberwocky" might have been like if it had had a serious tone rather than a comic one. Would the poet's use of invented words (including the title) be the same? Would the rhyme and meter remain unchanged? Would the characters, actions, and dialogue be as they are now? What are some words and phrases the poet might use instead of the ones in the text? What about the mood, or feeling, of the poem, and the meaning readers would find in it? Consider having students create screencasts of the talks using Educreations (http://tinyurl.com/cwz6aq8).

3. YOUR TURN

Core Path	Access Path
Assess and Explain. Have students answer the comprehension questions to test for understanding. Share the explanations for Parts A and B (located online) with your students.	
	Extend **Share and Discuss.** Have students complete the Your Turn section in class. Poll students about their responses and as a class discuss the different strategies they used to determine the correct answers. Ask students which aspects of the questions they found hard, and how they solved the difficulty. Conduct your poll by asking your students to complete a handout with questions or using Poll Everywhere (http://tinyurl.com/3zyw33) or Socrative (http://tinyurl.com/3bxbjpt).

Core Path	Access Path
	Extend **Tech Infusion** **Rewrite the Poem.** Assign one stanza of "Jabberwocky" apiece to pairs or small groups, and have them rewrite the stanza by changing only the invented words. For each invented word, the students will substitute a real English word that makes sense in the context. Have students collaborate using Google Docs (http://tinyurl.com/u7u9k) or TitanPad (http://tinyurl.com/kla4kmd). After they have completed their versions, have them share with the class. As a concluding step, you may want to have the class create a whole-class poem by choosing one revised version of each stanza and assembling them. (Or, if convenient, have them assemble one serious version and one comic version, and post both.) Have students discuss the tones of the revisions and how the connotations of the new words affected the tone.

OVERVIEW

The classic nonsense poem "Jabberwocky," by Lewis Carroll, plunges the reader into a world of flame-eyed creatures, "vorpal" swords, "borogoves," and many more outlandish creations. The Close Read gives students the opportunity to penetrate the mysteries of Carroll's world by analyzing his words, including the many words Carroll made up, as well as their impact on tone and meaning.

OBJECTIVES

1. Complete a close reading of a poem.
2. Practice and apply concrete strategies for identifying tone and connotations.
3. Participate effectively in a range of conversations and collaborations to express ideas and build upon the ideas of others.
4. Prewrite, plan, and produce clear and coherent writing in response to a prompt.

    ELA Common Core Standards:
    Reading: Literature - RL.6.1, RL.6.2, RL.6.3, RL.6.4, RL.6.10
    Writing - W.6.4, W.6.5, W.6.6, W.6.9.A, W.6.10
    Speaking & Listening - SL.6.1.A, SL.6.1.B, SL.6.1.C, SL.6.1.D, SL.6.6
    Language - L.6.4.A, L.6.4.C, L.6.4.D

RESOURCES

"Jabberwocky" Vocabulary handout

"Jabberwocky" Graphic organizer

Access 1 handout (Beginner)

Access 2 handout (Intermediate)

Access 3 handout (Advanced)

Access 4 handout (Approaching)

1. INTRODUCTION

Core Path	Access Path
Define and Compare. Project the vocabulary words and definitions onto the board or provide students with handouts so they can copy the vocabulary into their notebooks. Suggest that students consult general and specialized reference materials, both print and digital, to compare the precise meaning of a specific word with their initial vocabulary predictions from the First Read. Review words that students defined incorrectly to understand why they were unable to use context clues to develop usable definitions.	**Beginner & Intermediate** **Complete the Sentences.** Have students work in groups to complete the sentence frames on the Access 1 and 2 handouts using the vocabulary words. Point out that some of the words are in the questions and some will be in the answers. Correct answers are located at the end of this lesson plan online. **Advanced & Beyond** **Write in Journals.** Have students write a journal entry using all of their vocabulary words. Remind them to write sentences that communicate the meaning of the words they are using. When students are done, have them exchange their journal entry with a partner so that they can see additional examples of the words in context and give each other feedback. **Approaching** **Graphic Organizer.** To support students in comparing their vocabulary predictions with the correct meanings, have them complete the graphic organizer on the Access 4 handout to record the vocabulary words, their initial analysis, and the definitions. Then have them use the space provided on the Access 4 handout to write sentences using the words. Remind them to write sentences that communicate the meaning of the words they are using. Once students have completed this activity, have them exchange their sentences with a partner so they can see more examples of the words in context and give each other feedback.
Review. Have students complete the fill in the blank vocabulary worksheet for this selection. Answers for the worksheet are listed at the end of the lesson plan online.	

Copyright © BookheadEd Learning, LLC

Core Path	Access Path
	Extend **Tech Infusion** **Act and Record.** Break students into small groups, assign each group a vocabulary word, and ask them to design a short skit to act out the meanings of the words for their peers. Encourage students to use what they think is the setting of "Jabberwocky." If possible, record skits and post them to your class YouTube Channel, so that students can watch them.
	Extend **Tech Infusion** **Write.** Challenge small groups of students to collaborate in writing a paragraph that uses all five vocabulary words. The paragraph may be based on "Jabberwocky," but students may instead use their imaginations to write about a different topic entirely. In that case, the result might be a nonsense paragraph in the tradition of Lewis Carroll, but about material of the students' choice. Have students briefly revise their draft paragraphs into a version they all agree on, and upload it for the class to read and share, using Google Docs (http://tinyurl.com/u7u9k), TitanPad (http://tinyurl.com/lfombhw), or a class blog.

2. READ

Core Path	Access Path
Model Close Reading. Project the text onto the board and model a close reading of the first few stanzas using the annotation strategies mentioned on the following page. While modeling annotation strategies, make notes that tie the text to the focus skill and demonstrate what students are looking for as they read. Here is some guidance for you as you annotate for your students:	

Core Path	Access Path
• As the Skills lesson that comes before this lesson makes clear, words and phrases help create a tone. In the first stanza, the many nonsense words may cause different readers to interpret the tone differently. When I read the stanza closely, I try to hear the sound of the words in my mind. Words like "brillig" and "mimsy" have a funny, nonsensical sound. They remind me of the sounds I might hear in a tongue twister or nursery rhyme. They're playful.	
• Another aspect of the first stanza to consider is how the words and sentence structure fit together to create the tone. The first sentence seems to be about things called "slithy toves" that do something called "gyre and gimble." Whatever "borogoves" may be, I know that they are "all mimsy." It feels to me as if there's a lot of activity going on. Whatever place this is, it's lively. Again, the tone is fanciful and playful.	
• Especially in a poem, rhyme and meter help create the tone. In this poem, the meter has a strong, fast rhythm, again contributing to a lively, upbeat feeling. Also, because so many words are invented, the rhymes in this poem are delightfully silly. It sounds almost as if the words were made up for the sake of rhyming, such as "wabe" and "outgrabe." These factors add to the lighthearted tone of the stanza.	
• Of course, as soon as I read the first line of the second stanza, I experience a shift in tone. The first word, "Beware," lets me know that there's something dangerous or ominous in this fanciful world—the Jabberwock! While the silliness persists, the reader is also reminded of scary things like "jaws that bite." The tone becomes a little more complex—still light but with a few shadows.	

Core Path	Access Path
Read and Annotate. Read the Skills Focus questions as a class, so your students know what they should pay close attention to as they read. Then have students read and annotate the excerpt. Ask students to use the annotation tool as they read to:	**Note:** While on–grade level students are reading and annotating, work one-on-one or in small groups with Beginning, Intermediate, Advanced, and Approaching students to support them as they read and annotate the text.

Core Path

Read and Annotate. Read the Skills Focus questions as a class, so your students know what they should pay close attention to as they read. Then have students read and annotate the excerpt. Ask students to use the annotation tool as they read to:

1. respond to the Skills Focus section
2. ask questions
3. make connections
4. identify key themes, events, characters, and details
5. note unfamiliar vocabulary
6. capture their reaction to the ideas and examples in the text

As they reread the text, remind students to use the comprehension strategy of Visualizing that they learned in the First Read.

Access Path

Note: While on–grade level students are reading and annotating, work one-on-one or in small groups with Beginning, Intermediate, Advanced, and Approaching students to support them as they read and annotate the text.

Beginner & Intermediate
Summarize and Analyze the Text. Work with these students to complete the Summarize and Analyze the Text on the Access 1 and 2 handouts. They will then use the completed sentence frames to help them analyze and annotate the text by completing the Skills Focus questions. Refer to the sample Skills Focus answers to help them complete the sentence frames and annotate the text.

Advanced
Work in Pairs. Pair these students with more proficient English speakers to work together on analyzing and annotating the text to complete the Skills Focus questions. If these students need more support, have them use the Sentence Frames on the Access 3 handout as they work with their more proficient peers.

Approaching
Summarize the Text. Have these students discuss and complete the text summary on the Access 4 handout and use their summary to help them analyze and annotate the text by completing the Skills Focus questions. Correct answers for the summary are at the end of this lesson plan online. Also refer to the sample Skills Focus answers to aid students with their annotations.

Please note that excerpts and passages in the StudySync® library, workbooks, and PDFs are intended as touchstones to generate interest in an author's work. The excerpts and passages do not substitute for the reading of entire texts, and StudySync® strongly recommends that teachers and students seek out and purchase the whole literary or informational work in order to experience it as the author intended. Links to online resellers are available in our digital library. In addition, complete works may be ordered through an authorized reseller by filling out and returning to StudySync® the order form enclosed in this workbook.

Teacher's Edition   303

Core Path	Access Path
Discuss. After students have read the text, use the sample responses to the Skills Focus questions at the end of this lesson plan online to discuss the reading and the process of searching for the ways to figure out the tone of the poem. Make sure that students have acquired and accurately use academic-specific words and phrases related to the skill, and demonstrate a command of formal English appropriate to the discussion.	**Extend** **Pair and Share.** In small groups or pairs, ask students to share and discuss their annotations with a focus on tone, word choice, and connotations. You can provide students with questions to guide their discussion: 1. Which words, scenes, and actions did you find easiest to understand and visualize? (Student responses will vary but may include: "'Twas brillig, and the slithy toves / Did gyre and gimble in the wabe"; or "The jaws that bite, the claws that catch!") 2. Which did you find most difficult? (Student responses will vary, but may include: "All mimsy were the borogoves, /And the mome raths outgrabe"; because these are all made-up words and I am not sure what they mean.) 3. Because Lewis Carroll was inventing his own words, he could have used any combinations of sounds he wanted. What makes the specific words he invented, such as "mimsy," feel so right? (Student responses will vary but may include: Words like "mimsy" and "snicker-snack" are fun to say and add to the silly, fantastical tone of the poem.) 4. Discuss other examples of such words in the poem. Talk about the connotations the nonsense words develop in your mind, and why they do. (Student responses will vary but may include: The nonsense words in the first stanza help me visualize a forest with strange creatures moving and dancing around, which makes the poem seem silly and fun, but also a little eerie and ominous; because I don't know exactly what these creatures are.)

Core Path	Access Path
	Extend **Tech Infusion** **Create a Glossary.** Have pairs of students create a glossary defining all the nonsense words in "Jabberwocky." To begin, ask the class what their first step should be. (List the words in alphabetical order.) Then tell the pairs to begin discussing the clues, including concept, sound, and sentence structure, that guide them toward possible meanings. Tell students to include as many of the following elements as they can in each entry: • definition • pronunciation • origin: real English word(s) that the nonsense word seems related to • example sentence of their own Encourage students to make their glossary look attractive, like glossaries they have encountered in their reading. They may want to turn their glossary into a poster using Glogster (http://tinyurl.com/ydeyklq). Optionally, they may create thumbnail illustrations for one or more words. Consider gathering the class's glossaries in the classroom or online so that all can share and compare.

Please note that excerpts and passages in the StudySync® library, workbooks, and PDFs are intended as touchstones to generate interest in an author's work. The excerpts and passages do not substitute for the reading of entire texts, and StudySync® strongly recommends that teachers and students seek out and purchase the whole literary or informational work in order to experience it as the author intended. Links to online resellers are available in our digital library. In addition, complete works may be ordered through an authorized reseller by filling out and returning to StudySync® the order form enclosed in this workbook.

Teacher's Edition   305

3. WRITE

Core Path	Access Path
Prewrite and Plan. Read the prompt as a class and ask students to brainstorm about funny and serious aspects of "Jabberwocky." Tell them to consider tone, word choice, and connotations as they think about what serious point the poem may be making. Students can brainstorm together either as a class or in small groups to begin planning their responses. Remind them to look at the poem and their annotations to find textual evidence to support their ideas.	**Beginner & Intermediate** **Answer and Discuss.** Have students complete the prewriting questions on the Access 1 and 2 handouts and then explain their answers to a partner before they write. Explain to students that when they answer a question—such as *What is the tone in "Jabberwocky"?* —they need to include a detail, example, or quote from the text that supports the statement. For example, students could include the first line, "Beware the Jabberwock my son!," which reveals that the story is written in the third-person point of view. **Approaching** **Answer Prewriting Questions.** Have students complete the prewriting questions on the Access 4 handout to summarize their thoughts before they write.
	Extend **Organize.** Encourage students to use a Venn diagram, comparing aspects of the poem that are not serious, parts that are (or could be) serious, and parts that may be taken as serious or comedic, depending on one's interpretation, to organize their ideas before they input or write their responses (See Resources).
	Extend **Post-Critique.** After students have read their peers' critiques of their papers, invite the class to discuss how to improve their reviewing skills. Lead the discussion with questions such as: • What piece of advice from a peer reviewer has helped you most? • What do you think peer reviewers should do more of?

Copyright © Bookheaded Learning, LLC

Core Path	Access Path
	• What do you think peer reviewers should do less of?
	• What have you learned about improving your own reviewing skills?
Discuss. Project these instructions for the peer review onto the board and review them with your class, so they know what they are looking for when they begin to provide their classmates with feedback: • How has this writer helped you understand the tone and the use of words in "Jabberwocky"? • Did the writer clearly express an opinion on the question that was asked? Was the writer's opinion supported convincingly with textual evidence? • What textual evidence did the writer use to support his or her claim? • What thing(s) does this response do especially well? • Be sure to tell the writer what he or she did well and what he or she needs to work on. Remember that your comments are most useful when they are constructive. After you've looked at the peer review instructions, review the rubric with students before they begin writing. Allow time for students briefly to raise and discuss any questions they may have about the peer review instructions and the rubric. Tell students how many peer reviews they will need to complete once they submit their writing.	
Write. Ask students to complete the writing assignment using textual evidence to support their answers. Once they have completed their writing, they should click "Submit."	

Core Path	Access Path
Review. Once students complete their writing assignment, they should submit substantive feedback to two peers. Students should use their peers' feedback to improve their writing.	

OVERVIEW

The "Point" and "Counterpoint" arguments in "Bullying in Schools" examine two points of view with regard to a controversial issue. The First Read gives students the opportunity to experience the text with a limited context.

OBJECTIVES

1. Perform an initial reading of a text and demonstrate comprehension by responding to short analysis and inference questions with textual evidence.
2. Practice defining vocabulary words using context.
3. Participate effectively in a range of conversations and collaborations to express ideas and build upon the ideas of others.

ELA Common Core Standards:

Reading: Informational Text - RI.6.1, RI.6.4, RI.6.6, RI.6.8, RI.6.10
Writing - W.6.10
Speaking & Listening - SL.6.1.A, SL.6.1.B, SL.6.1.C, SL.6.1.D
Language - L.6.4.A, L.6.4.B, L.6.4.D

RESOURCES

Access 1 handout (Beginner)

Access 2 handout (Intermediate)

Access 3 handout (Advanced)

Access 4 handout (Approaching)

Please note that excerpts and passages in the StudySync® library, workbooks, and PDFs are intended as touchstones to generate interest in an author's work. The excerpts and passages do not substitute for the reading of entire texts, and StudySync® strongly recommends that teachers and students seek out and purchase the whole literary or informational work in order to experience it as the author intended. Links to online resellers are available in our digital library. In addition, complete works may be ordered through an authorized reseller by filling out and returning to StudySync® the order form enclosed in this workbook.

Teacher's Edition   309

ACCESS COMPLEX TEXT

"Bullying in Schools" examines two points of view on how schools are handling the issue of bullying. Each author presents evidence with the goal of persuading readers to support his or her point of view. To evaluate the arguments, students must consider the effectiveness of each writer's evidence and logic. To help students identify claims and evaluate each author's argument, use the following suggestions to provide scaffolded instruction for the more complex features of this text:

- **Purpose** - Each author writes for the purpose of persuading readers to agree with one side of the argument. Consequently, students need to identify the claims each author makes and evaluate the strength of the reasons and evidence used in support.

- **Organization** - The article devotes one section to each of the opposing points of view. Within each section, the author organizes the text by first presenting a claim about the topic and then supporting that claim with reasons and evidence. Students must draw evidence from both sections and compare the effectiveness of the arguments in order to decide with which point of view they agree.

- **Connection of Ideas** - In order to identify and evaluate each argument, students must first determine the central ideas in the author's claims. Since the article contains two opposing arguments and points of view, students must identify and examine the claims made in each argument and determine how well each author has supported his or her position with evidence.

1. INTRODUCTION

Core Path	Access Path
Read and Discuss. As a class, read and discuss the introduction for "Bullying in Schools."	**English Learners All Levels & Approaching Read and Discuss.** Ask students to read the introduction for "Bullying in Schools." Have them refer to the Introduction Glossary on their Access 1, 2, 3, and 4 handouts for definitions of key vocabulary terms. If there are unfamiliar words that are not included in their glossary, encourage students to check a dictionary or online reference tool, like http://tinyurl.com/3qe7. Then, have students discuss the introduction in small groups. Check each group's understanding by asking questions to encourage discussion.

Core Path	Access Path
Access Prior Knowledge. Find out what your students already know about bullying by asking them to do focused freewrites on one, some, or all of the following questions: 1. What is bullying? 2. What are the different kinds of bullying? 3. What responsibilities does the school have in stopping bullying? What responsibilities do students and parents have in stopping bullying? 4. What is the school policy regarding bullying? Is the policy effective or ineffective and why? 5. What are the best ways to hold bullies accountable for their actions? 6. Is our school doing a good job of preventing bullying? Why or why not? 7. Have you or someone you know ever experienced bullying? What were the causes and effects of the situation? Ask volunteers to read aloud their entries to the class. Help students identify and discuss commonalities and differences among entries. Have students review and reflect on the key ideas expressed, paraphrasing to demonstrate understanding.	**English Learners All Levels & Approaching Access Prior Knowledge.** Find out what your students already know about bullying. In pairs, have students answer these questions: • What is bullying? • Should schools help to stop bullying? • Should parents help to stop bullying? Have pairs create a digital or print word wall that represents bullying. Pairs may choose to represent why bullying is problematic or may choose to represent how bullying can be resolved. If time allows, ask pairs to present their word walls to the class.

Please note that excerpts and passages in the StudySync® library, workbooks, and PDFs are intended as touchstones to generate interest in an author's work. The excerpts and passages do not substitute for the reading of entire texts, and StudySync® strongly recommends that teachers and students seek out and purchase the whole literary or informational work in order to experience it as the author intended. Links to online resellers are available in our digital library. In addition, complete works may be ordered through an authorized reseller by filling out and returning to StudySync® the order form enclosed in this workbook.

Teacher's Edition   311

2. READ

Core Path	Access Path

Core Path

Make Predictions about Vocabulary. There are five bold vocabulary words in the text. As students read the text, ask them to make predictions about what they think each bold vocabulary word means based on the context clues in the sentence. If you are in a low-tech classroom and students are reading from printed copies or a projected text, ask students to record predictions in their notes, so they can be easily referenced in class. If your students have access to technology, they can use the annotation tool to make their predictions.

It might be helpful to model this practice for students before they begin reading. Either using the board or projecting the actual text, focus in on the sentence that uses the word "repercussions":

- But we know now that the repercussions of bullying can be lasting and severe.

Model for the class how to use the overall structure and meaning of the sentence and the sentences around it, the word's position, and other clues to define the unfamiliar vocabulary word. In this case, point out these context clues:

1. The sentence says that the "repercussions of bullying can be lasting and severe." Something that is lasting goes on for a long time. "Severe" is a word with negative connotations, particularly when coupled with the use of the word "tragedy" in the next sentence.

2. The next sentence also includes the word "end," so repercussions come after bullying occurs.

3. I know that the suffix "-ion" often forms a noun. I think that "repercussions" may be "the negative effects or consequences" of bullying.

4. Looking up this word in a dictionary, to check my inferred meaning, I see that it does mean "something bad or unpleasant that happens as a result of an action or statement." That's pretty close to "negative effects or consequences."

Access Path

Note: This exercise, which extends vocabulary instruction, should be completed when the class shifts from whole group instruction to individual work during the "Read and Annotate" exercise.

Beginner, Intermediate & Approaching Pair Practice.

1. Pair students with more proficient readers.

2. Give them an additional sentence that contains a new vocabulary word.

3. Ask the students to complete a Think Aloud using the teacher-led Make Predictions about Vocabulary activity as a model, while the proficient student actively listens.

4. The student should use the context clues in the sentence to try to determine the meaning of the new vocabulary word.

5. After the student has completed the Think Aloud and made a prediction about the word's meaning, allow time for the proficient reader to add his/her own thoughts and clarify any points of confusion.

6. Once they've completed this Think Aloud, encourage them to use a dictionary to confirm the definition of the new vocabulary word. Have them refer to the vocabulary listing on their Access 1, 2, and 4 handouts for definitions of key vocabulary terms in the text. Encourage them to add any additional vocabulary words or idioms they find in the text and look up definitions for those words and idioms online or in a dictionary.

Core Path	Access Path
5. The dictionary definition also mentions that these effects or consequences "last a long time"--a meaning that is also supported by the rest of the sentence in the text!	

Model Reading Comprehension Strategy. Before students begin reading, model the reading comprehension strategy of Rereading by using this Think Aloud that talks students through the first few paragraphs of text. First explain to your students that rereading is reading the passage again to make sense of complex ideas, to answer questions, or to locate missed information.

Model for students how rereading will help them better comprehend the selection and help drive their discussions.

- When I read an argument to trace and evaluate its claims, reasons, and evidence, I may need to reread it several times to identify the structure of the argument and evaluate its content.

- For example, I know that the "Point" author's claim is that the schools are not doing enough to prevent bullying.

- If I read paragraph 4 again, I find one reason the writer gives to support his or her claim: cyber-bullying is extremely hard to track. This reason seems valid at first read.

- However, by rereading, I give myself the opportunity to evaluate the evidence. The author explains why cyber-bullying is hard to track and then claims that there are not enough programs to address the issue. This evidence leaves me with some questions: *Are there any programs? Where? How effective are they? What kind of training is missing from these programs?* My unanswered questions point to some gaps in the writer's logic, which weaken the effectiveness of the argument.

Beginner, Intermediate & Approaching Apply Reading Comprehension Strategy.

1. In small groups, have students read the text. Ask students to complete the first column in the First Read and Second Read Chart located on the Access 1, 2, and 4 handouts.

2. Then, have groups reread the text in order to complete the second column in the First Read and Second Read Chart.

3. Call on groups to discuss their initial answers and their answers after having reread the text.

Core Path	Access Path
Read and Annotate. Read and annotate the excerpt. Ask students to use the annotation tool as they read to:	**Beginner** **Coach the Reading.** While other students read, annotate, and discuss the text independently, work with Beginning students, reading the text and pausing periodically or when any student has a question. Coach students in articulating their questions for the group and in highlighting and annotating the text. Have students use the Annotation Guide in the Access 1 handout to support them as they highlight and annotate the text.

Read and Annotate. Read and annotate the excerpt. Ask students to use the annotation tool as they read to:

1. ask questions
2. make connections
3. identify purposes and points of view
4. evaluate claims, reasons, and evidence
5. note unfamiliar vocabulary
6. capture reactions to ideas in the text

Beginner

Coach the Reading. While other students read, annotate, and discuss the text independently, work with Beginning students, reading the text and pausing periodically or when any student has a question. Coach students in articulating their questions for the group and in highlighting and annotating the text. Have students use the Annotation Guide in the Access 1 handout to support them as they highlight and annotate the text.

For further support, ask questions about the text such as:

- Where can bullying happen?
- What are the effects of bullying?
- What are "zero-tolerance" policies?

Intermediate

Read and Discuss. Have these students take turns reading the text in small groups. Encourage students to use the definitions on the Access 2 handout to help them with words or idioms that may be unfamiliar. If students need help with annotating the text, have them use the Annotation Guide on the Access 2 handout.

Advanced

Pair with Proficient Peers. Have Advanced students work with English proficient peers to read, annotate, and discuss the text. Have students use the Annotation Guide on the Access 3 handout to support them as they highlight and annotate the text.

Approaching

Use the Annotation Guide. Have students use the Annotation Guide on the Access 4 handout to support them as they highlight and annotate the text.

Core Path	Access Path
Discuss. In small groups or pairs, have students discuss the questions and inferences they made while reading. Make sure students follow the rules for collegial discussions: Refer to the Collaborative Discussions in the Speaking & Listening Handbook.	**English Learners All Levels & Approaching** Use the extra time while on– and beyond–grade level students are discussing their first reads of the text to work individually and in small groups with Approaching readers and English Learners as outlined on the previous page. Should those students complete their first reads quickly, integrate them into the on– and beyond–grade level discussion groups. Otherwise, Approaching readers and English Learners will be given an opportunity to participate in text discussions with their peers later in the lesson.

Core Path

1. Reread to identify the "Point" author's argument. What is his or her claim? (Many schools are still not doing enough to prevent bullying.) What are some reasons why schools should be very concerned about bullying? (It is a serious problem that can cause students to do poorly in school, and it can create lasting scars.)

2. How does the "Point" author conclude his or her argument? (The author ends the argument by stating that schools need more policies and programs that educate students and staff on bullying, and they "need to show how to end bullying, and, most importantly, what *causes* it." The author believes that the only way to solve the problem of bullying is getting to the root of what causes it.)

3. Reread to identify the "Counterpoint" writer's argument. What is his or her claim? (Schools are doing a tremendous amount to curb bullying.) How do school programs to prevent bullying generally work? (there is no one single profile, but the federal government's website makes recommendations)

4. How does the "Counterpoint" author conclude his or her argument? (The author indicates that even the best programs will take time to bring about change and create an anti-bullying culture.)

Access Path

Extend
Tech Infusion
Brainstorm. Pair students and ask them to brainstorm ways in which schools could prevent bullying or make it less harmful. Encourage them to explore the Internet for sites on preventing bullying, including Stop Bullying.com.

3. THINK

Core Path	Access Path
Answer and Discuss. Have students complete the Think questions and then use the peer review instructions and rubric to complete two peer reviews. Refer to the sample answers at the end of this lesson plan online to discuss responses with your students.	**Beginner & Intermediate** **Use Sentence Frames.** Have these students use the sentence frames on the Access 1 and 2 handouts to help them participate in the discussion. Encourage students to use the sentence frames to answer the Think Questions. **Approaching** **Find the Evidence.** Have these students use the Find the Evidence exercise on the Access 4 handout to help them participate in the discussion. Remind these students to refer back to their answers to help them participate in the group discussion.
	Extend **Debate.** In addition to bullying, ask students to brainstorm a list of other issues that need to be addressed by the schools. Record students' ideas. Point out that the "Counterpoint" (second) author states that each school district in New Jersey, for example, is spending $30,000 per year on anti-bullying measures and that any more time or money would be at the expense of core subjects such as math and language arts. Lead students to debate whether the subject of bullying warrants this kind of time and money in relation to the other subjects on their list. Which listed subject is most important and why?

SKILL:
Arguments and Claims

OVERVIEW

Tracing and evaluating arguments and claims is key to determining whether an author's opinions are valid and logical. This lesson plan provides follow-up questions and useful enrichments to help teachers guide students toward a usable, repeatable method for tracing and evaluating arguments and claims.

OBJECTIVES

1. Learn the definitions of arguments and claims.
2. Practice using concrete strategies for tracing and evaluating arguments and claims.
3. Participate effectively in a range of conversations and collaborations to express ideas and build upon the ideas of others.

ELA Common Core Standards:
Reading: Informational Text - RI.6.1, RI.6.6, RI.6.8
Speaking & Listening - SL.6.1.A, SL.6.1.B, SL.6.1.C, SL.6.2, SL.6.3

RESOURCES

Access 1 handout (Beginner)

Access 2 handout (Intermediate)

Access 3 handout (Advanced)

Access 4 handout (Approaching)

1. DEFINE

Core Path	Access Path
Watch. Watch the Concept Definition video on arguments and claims with your students. Make sure students write the definitions of argument and claim—as well as the functions of reasons and evidence—in their notes. Pause the video at these key moments to discuss the information with your students: 1. 0:26 – What are some other frequently debated topics similar to the one shared in the video? Is there ever a "right" or "wrong" side to these kinds of debates? Why or why not? 2. 1:11 – List the different types of reasons and evidence (e.g., facts, data, etc.) an author can use to support his or her argument. How do we determine if reasons and evidence are strong enough? 3. 1:31 – What are some things you might do if you're having difficulty disproving a counterargument to your claim?	**English Learners All Levels & Approaching** **Match.** Have students complete the matching exercise on the Access 1, 2, 3, and 4 handouts as they watch the video. Correct answers are located at the end of this lesson plan online.
Read and Discuss. After watching the Concept Definition video, have students read the definitions of argument and claim. Either in small groups or as a whole class, use these questions to engage students in a discussion about argument and claim. Make sure students follow the rules for collegial discussions. • What are the three parts of an argument? (claim, reasons, and evidence) • What is the purpose of an argument? (to persuade someone to share a point of view) • What kinds of evidence might a writer include to support his or her claim or reasons? (facts, details, examples)	**Beginner & Approaching** **Finish the Sentences.** To prepare students to participate in the discussion, have students complete the chart on the Access 1 and 4 handouts as they read the definitions. The correct answers are located at the end of this lesson plan online. **Intermediate & Advanced** **Discuss Prompts.** To help these students participate in the discussion, prompt them with questions that can be answered with a few words, such as: • What is a claim? (the main idea or thesis of an argument) • What is the author's claim in the "Point" portion of this essay? (Schools are not doing enough to prevent bullying.)

Copyright © BookheadEd Learning, LLC

Core Path	Access Path
	• What is the author's claim in the "Counterpoint" portion of this essay? (Current practices are preventing bullying and are very expensive to implement.) • What are some of the elements that both authors have used? (details, examples, logical ideas, and facts)
	Extend **Write Collaboratively.** Form student groups of three. Tell the first student to write a claim or an opinion about a controversial issue in popular culture, such as whether violence in media creates violent behavior in teenagers or whether too much time spent using media affects students' attention spans. Then have the student pass the paper to the second student, who should write one reason to support the claim. Finally, have the student pass the paper to the third student, who will write one piece of evidence to support the reason and thereby the claim. If necessary, you may provide students with sentence starters. Ask volunteers to read their arguments aloud to the class. Have the class evaluate the effectiveness of each mini-argument.

2. MODEL

Core Path	Access Path
Read and Annotate. Have students independently read the Model section. As they read, ask students to use the annotation tool to: • identify purposes and points of view • trace and evaluate arguments • highlight key points • ask questions • identify places where the Model applies the strategies laid out in the Identification and Application section	**Note:** During this portion of the lesson, instruction shifts from whole group to individual work. Use this time to work one-on-one or in small groups with Beginning, Intermediate, Advanced, and Approaching students.

Core Path	Access Path
	Beginner & Intermediate
	Coach the Reading. Work with these students (either individually or in small groups) to fill out the Guided Reading questions on the Access 1 and 2 handouts. Have Beginning students refer to the Model Glossary on the Access 1 handout to help them determine the meaning of difficult words. (note: Provide the Access 1 handout Model Glossary to Intermediate students if necessary.) Let students know they'll use these answers to help participate in the discussion about the Model. Sample answers for this exercise are located at the end of the lesson plan online.
	Advanced
	Identify Evidence. Students will participate in the same activity as on–grade and Beyond students, using the annotation tool to identify evidence that supports the points in both arguments. Advanced students should also complete the Identifying Evidence exercise on the Access 3 handout. Let students know that they'll use these answers to guide their discussion about the Model.
	Approaching
	Guided Reading. Have students complete the guided reading questions on the Access 4 handout as they read. Let them know that they'll use these answers to help participate in the discussion about the Model. Sample answers for this exercise are located at the end of the lesson plan online.
Discuss. After students read the Model text, use these questions to facilitate a whole group discussion that helps students understand how to trace and evaluate argument and claim: 1. How does the Model begin to trace the "Point" author's argument? (It identifies the central idea and the claim.) 2. How does the Model continue to trace the argument? (The Model identifies a supporting reason.)	

Core Path	Access Path
3. How does the Model begin to evaluate the argument? (The Model notes that the supporting reason is not supported by solid evidence. Therefore, it lacks logic.) 4. Why is it important to trace and evaluate arguments? (This skill helps one form his or her own opinions based on an evaluation of the reasons and evidence provided. If a speaker's or writer's claims are not supported by strong reasons and logical evidence their argument may be faulty.)	
	Extend **Provide Evidence.** Form small student groups. Ask students to create evidence for the following reasons in support of the claim that schools are not doing enough to prevent bullying: • one in three students is bullied • supervision of students while they are on campus is inadequate • cyber-bullying is difficult to track • school procedures and policies regarding bullying are inadequate Ask each group to share selected evidence with the class.

3. YOUR TURN

Core Path	Access Path
Assess and Explain. Have students answer the comprehension questions to test for understanding. Share the explanations for Parts A and B (located online) with your students.	

Core Path	Access Path
	Extend **Tech Infusion** **Use a Graphic Organizer.** Before responding to the questions, you may have students use graphic organizers using Creately (http://tinyurl.com/dk8xvq) to identify the claim, reason, and supporting evidence in the passage.
	Extend **Tech Infusion** **Blog about Bullying.** Have students post blog entries in response to one of the two articles based on personal observations and experiences within school. Which claim does this personal evidence best support and why?

OVERVIEW

The "Point" and "Counterpoint" arguments in "Bullying in Schools" examine two points of view with regard to a controversial issue. The Close Read gives students the opportunity to trace and evaluate the arguments.

OBJECTIVES

1. Complete a close reading of a passage of informational text.
2. Practice and apply concrete strategies for tracing and evaluating arguments and claims.
3. Participate effectively in a range of conversations and collaborations to express ideas and build upon the ideas of others.
4. Prewrite, plan, and produce clear and coherent writing in response to a prompt.

   ELA Common Core Standards:
   Reading: Informational Text - RI.6.1, RI.6.2, RI.6.4, RI.6.6, RI.6.8, RI.6.10
   Writing - W.6.1.A, W.6.1.B, W.6.4, W.6.5, W.6.6, W.6.8, W.6.9.B, W.6.10
   Speaking & Listening - SL.6.1.A, SL.6.1.B, SL.6.1.C, SL.6.1.D, SL.6.2, SL.6.3, SL.6.6
   Language - L.6.4.A, L.6.4.C, L.6.4.D

RESOURCES

"Bullying in Schools" Vocabulary handout

"Bullying in Schools" Graphic organizer

Access 1 handout (Beginner)

Access 2 handout (Intermediate)

Access 3 handout (Advanced)

Access 4 handout (Approaching)

1. INTRODUCTION

Core Path	Access Path
Define and Compare. Project the vocabulary words and definitions onto the board or provide students with handouts so they can copy the vocabulary into their notebooks. Suggest that students consult general and specialized reference materials, both print and digital, to compare the precise meaning of a specific word with their initial vocabulary predictions from the First Read. Review words that students defined incorrectly to understand why they were unable to use context clues to develop usable definitions.	**Beginner & Intermediate** **Complete the Sentences.** Have students use the Complete the Sentences exercise on the Access 1 and 2 handouts to review vocabulary. Point out that some of the words are in the questions and some will be in the answers. Correct answers are located at the end of this lesson plan online. **Advanced & Beyond** **Write in Journals.** Have students write a journal entry using all of their vocabulary words. Remind them to write sentences that communicate the meaning of the words they are using. **Approaching** **Graphic Organizer.** To support students in comparing their vocabulary predictions with the correct meanings, have them complete the graphic organizer on the Access 4 handout to record the vocabulary words, their initial analysis, and the definitions. Then have them write sentences using the words.
Review. Have students complete the fill in the blank vocabulary worksheet for this selection. Answers for the worksheet are listed at the end of the lesson plan online.	
	Extend **Tech Infusion** **Act and Record.** Form small student groups. Have students prepare two skits to perform side-by-side. In one skit, a "perpetrator" should commit a negative act within a particular "venue" and suffer the "repercussions." In the second skit, two individuals who are quarreling about something should attempt to resolve their differences with "civility" and "tolerance." Record students' performances and post them to the class YouTube channel.

Core Path	Access Path
	Extend **Create.** Divide students into small groups and ask them to create a campaign against bullying. Give each small group one of the vocabulary words and ask them to create a slogan against bullying using that word. Then ask them to create a poster using their slogans.

2. READ

Core Path	Access Path
Model Close Reading. Project the text onto the board and model a close reading of the first few paragraphs of each argument using the annotation strategies mentioned below. While modeling annotation strategies, make notes that tie the text to the focus skill and demonstrate what students are looking for as they read. Here is some guidance for you as you annotate for your students: • As the Skills lesson that precedes this text makes clear, writers construct arguments by making claims that are supported by reasons and evidence. To evaluate these arguments, readers must consider the writer's evidence and logic. • While the author of the "Point" article gives several reasons to support his or her claim, the author doesn't offer credible supporting evidence. For example, the author gives the reason that "most schools also do not have a clear procedure or policy for investigating bullying." However, readers may be unconvinced by this reason due to the lack of credible evidence, such as statistics or quotations. • The author of the "Counterpoint" article essentially offers one main reason to support his or her claim: an increasing amount of attention is being devoted to the issue and is making its mark. Then the author offers multiple pieces of evidence to support this reason, including facts and statistics.	

Copyright © BookheadEd Learning, LLC

Core Path	Access Path
Delineate a Speaker's Argument and Claim. Listen to the audio of "Bullying in Schools." Have students use the Critical Listening Handout in the Speaking & Listening Handbook to help them evaluate the Point and Counterpoint arguments, claims, and supporting evidence.	
Read and Annotate. Read the Skills Focus questions as a class, so your students know what they should pay close attention to as they read. Then have students read and annotate the articles. Ask students to use the annotation tool as they read to: 1. respond to the Skills Focus section 2. ask questions 3. make connections 4. identify key information, examples, and ideas 5. note unfamiliar vocabulary 6. capture their reaction to the ideas and examples in the text As they reread the text, remind students to use the comprehension strategy of Rereading that they learned in the First Read.	**Note:** While on–grade level students are reading and annotating, work one-on-one or in small groups with Beginning, Intermediate, Advanced, and Approaching students to support them as they read and annotate the text. **Beginner & Intermediate** **Summarize and Analyze the Text.** Work with these students on the Summarize and Analyze the Text exercise on the Access 1 and 2 handouts. They will then use the completed sentence frames to help them analyze and annotate the text. Encourage students to use the completed sentence frames to answer the Skills Focus questions. Refer to the sample Skills Focus answers to help them complete the sentence frames and annotate the text. **Advanced** **Work in Pairs.** Pair these students with more proficient English speakers to work together on analyzing and annotating the text to complete the Skills Focus questions. If these students need more support, have them use the Summarize and Analyze the Text exercise on the Access 3 handout as they work with their more proficient peers. **Approaching** **Summarize the Text.** Have these students discuss and complete the Summarize the Text exercise on the Access 4 handout. Have students use their summary to help them analyze and annotate the text by completing the Skills Focus questions. Correct answers are at the end of this lesson plan online. Also refer to the sample Skills Focus answers to aid students with their annotations.

Core Path	Access Path
Discuss. After students have read the text, use the sample responses to the Skills Focus questions at the end of this lesson plan online to discuss the reading and the process of tracing and evaluating arguments and claims. Make sure that students have acquired and accurately use academic-specific words and phrases related to the skill, and demonstrate a command of formal English appropriate to the discussion.	**Extend** **Pair and Share.** In small, heterogeneous groups or pairs, ask students to share and discuss their annotations with a focus on the reading and the process of tracing and evaluating arguments and claims. You can provide students with these questions to guide their discussion: 1. Why does the "Point" author claim that bullying is a bigger problem than most people realize? (Statistics demonstrate the large number of students who are affected by bullying.) 2. According to the "Point" author, why is cyber-bullying so hard to control? (Cyber-bullying is hard to trace because comments can be deleted before they are discovered.) 3. According to the "Counterpoint" author, what are some steps communities are taking to stop bullying? (Many states have laws against bullying. Many communities require that schools have anti-bullying programs in place.)
	Extend **Tech Infusion** **Research.** Form small student groups. Draw students' attention to the final paragraph of the "Point" author's text. He or she says that anti-bullying programs need to contain the following elements: • definition of bullying • causes of bullying • signs of bullying • strategies for ending bullying Point out that the "Counterpoint" author argues for the effectiveness of the following strategies: • laws that protect students, require education programs, and dictate mandatory action from school personnel • anti-bullying coordinators • funding for anti-bullying education

Please note that excerpts and passages in the StudySync® library, workbooks, and PDFs are intended as touchstones to generate interest in an author's work. The excerpts and passages do not substitute for the reading of entire texts, and StudySync® strongly recommends that teachers and students seek out and purchase the whole literary or informational work in order to experience it as the author intended. Links to online resellers are available in our digital library. In addition, complete works may be ordered through an authorized reseller by filling out and returning to StudySync® the order form enclosed in this workbook.

Teacher's Edition  327

Core Path	Access Path
	• involvement from educational organizations • special programs such as Challenge Day • parent involvement Ask students to utilize these ideas as well as ideas from print and digital research to create plans for effective anti-bullying programs. Ask each group to present selected elements from its plan to the class. Lead the class to discuss similarities and differences among the plans.

3. WRITE

Core Path	Access Path
Prewrite and Plan. Read the prompt as a class and ask students to brainstorm about the effectiveness of the claim, reasons, and evidence presented in each of the two arguments. Students can brainstorm together either as a class or in small groups to begin planning their responses. Remind your students to look at the arguments and their annotations to find relevant textual evidence to support their evaluations.	**Beginner & Intermediate** **Answer and Discuss.** Have students complete the prewriting questions on the Access 1 and 2 handouts and then explain their answers to a partner before they write. Explain to students that when they answer a question—such as *Why is it so hard to control bullying?* —they need to include a detail, example, or quote from the text that supports the statement. For example, students could include the quote, "Bullying usually happens in unsupervised areas like bathrooms, cafeterias, and school buses," which is supporting evidence for the question. **Approaching** **Answer Prewriting Questions.** Have students complete the prewriting questions on the Access 4 handout to summarize their thoughts before they write.

Core Path	Access Path
	Extend **Organize.** Encourage groups of students to complete three-column charts to identify the claims of both authors and the reasons and evidence that support their claims in the point/counterpoint texts "Bullying in Schools." Assign groups of students either the "Point" or "Counterpoint" text. Have each group record the author's claim and then list reasons and evidence the author provides to support the claim. Have groups share their graphic organizers in a class discussion.
	Extend **Critique.** Have students exchange papers with partners and complete the following tasks: • circle all comparison-and-contrast transition words and phrases • underline all similarities between the two articles • place boxes around all differences between the two articles • in writing, state whether or not the writer convinces you of his or her claim and why
Discuss. Project these instructions for the peer review onto the board and review them with your class, so they know what they are looking for when they begin to provide their classmates with feedback: • How well does this essay evaluate the effectiveness of each argument? • How well does this essay demonstrate that one author's claim, reasons, and evidence are better or more convincing than the other author's? • What relevant textual evidence does the essay present in support of the writer's opinion about the two arguments? • How well does the writer connect the evidence to his or her reasons and claim?	

Core Path	Access Path
• What elements does this response do especially well? • Be sure to tell the writer what he or she does well and what he or she needs to improve. Remember that your comments are most useful when they are specific and constructive. After you've looked at the peer review instructions, review the rubric with students before they begin writing. Allow time for students briefly to raise and discuss any questions they may have about the peer review instructions and the rubric. Tell students how many peer reviews they will need to complete once they submit their writing.	
Write. Ask students to complete the writing assignment using textual evidence to support their responses. Once they have completed their writing, they should click "Submit."	
Review. Once students complete their writing assignment, they should submit substantive feedback to two peers. Students should use their peers' feedback to improve their writing.	

OVERVIEW

To provide closure for this unit, students will learn about Dr. Martin Luther King, Jr. and Elizabeth Cady Stanton as examples of people who stood up for what they believed in, but didn't see the complete fruition of their efforts. Research links explore more about the civil rights movement, the women's rights movement, and other examples of people showing courage.

OBJECTIVES

1. Explore background information about how it can take a long time to see the effects of someone standing up for themselves or others, using Dr. Martin Luther King, Jr. and Elizabeth Cady Stanton as examples.
2. Research using the hyperlinks to learn more about the civil rights movement, the women's rights movement, and other examples of people showing courage.
3. Participate effectively in a range of conversations and collaborations to express ideas and build upon the ideas of others.

ELA Common Core Standards:
Reading: Informational Text - RI.6.1
Writing - W.6.1.A, W.6.1.B, W.6.5, W.6.6
Speaking & Listening - SL.6.1.A, SL.6.1.B, SL.6.1.C, SL.6.1.D

RESOURCES

Access 1 handout (Beginner)

Access 2 handout (Intermediate)

Access 4 handout (Approaching)

Please note that excerpts and passages in the StudySync® library, workbooks, and PDFs are intended as touchstones to generate interest in an author's work. The excerpts and passages do not substitute for the reading of entire texts, and StudySync® strongly recommends that teachers and students seek out and purchase the whole literary or informational work in order to experience it as the author intended. Links to online resellers are available in our digital library. In addition, complete works may be ordered through an authorized reseller by filling out and returning to StudySync® the order form enclosed in this workbook.

Teacher's Edition   331

TITLE/DRIVING QUESTION

Core Path	Access Path
Discuss. As a class, read aloud the title and driving question for this Blast. Ask students what they already know about what happens after you stand up for yourself or what you believe in. Do they have a sense of how standing up against injustice can cause change? Remind students that they should not immediately reply to this question. They'll be returning to this question and responding after they've read the Background and some of the Research Links.	**English Learners All Levels & Approaching** **Discuss a Visual.** Have students view photographs of women voting in 1920 and African Americans voting in the 1960s, such as the ones below: http://tinyurl.com/mk57vn2 http://tinyurl.com/lzn5rd3. Discuss how the pictures show an important right fought for by Dr. Martin Luther King, Jr. and Elizabeth Cady Stanton, prompting students with questions such as: • What is happening in the photos? • Why is voting such an important right? • How do you think these people feel about voting? • How can being able to vote change a person's life?
Draft. In their notebooks or on scrap paper, have students draft their initial responses to the driving question. This will provide them with a baseline response that they will alter as they gain more information about the topic in the Background and Research Links sections of the assignment.	**Beginner & Intermediate** **Draft with Sentence Frame.** When drafting their initial response to the driving question, have students refer to this Blast sentence frame on their Access 1 and 2 handouts: • When people stand up for others, things can change because _____. Point out these two key features of the sentence frame: 1. The introductory clause "When people stand up for others," borrows language directly from the Blast driving question to provide a response. 2. Ask students to make special note of the comma that separates the introductory clause from the subject and predicate ("things can change"). Have students think about what and how things can change.

Copyright © BookheadEd Learning, LLC

BACKGROUND:

Core Path	Access Path
Read. Have students read the Blast background to provide context for the driving question.	**Beginner & Intermediate** **Read with Support.** Have students read the Blast background to provide context for the driving question. When they encounter unfamiliar words or phrases, have students refer to the glossary on their Access 1 and 2 handouts. If there are unfamiliar words that are not included in their glossary, encourage students to check a dictionary or online reference tool, like http://tinyurl.com/3qe7. **Approaching** **Read and Summarize.** Have students read the Blast background to provide context for the driving question. As they read, ask students to complete the fill-in-the-blank summary of the background provided on their Access 4 handout. When they encounter unfamiliar words or phrases, have students refer to the glossary on their Access 4 handout.
Discuss. Pair students and have them discuss the following questions. Make sure students follow the rules for collegial discussions. 1. What happened shortly after Dr. King was assassinated? (President Johnson signed the Civil Rights Act of 1968.) 2. What happened in 1991? (President Bush signed another Civil Rights Act, which strengthened anti-discrimination laws.) 3. Who was Elizabeth Cady Stanton? (Stanton was a women's rights activist who helped put together the Seneca Falls conference, where the Declaration of Sentiments was written and signed.) 4. What do the two examples, the women's rights movement and the civil rights movement, have in common? (Both took a lot of courage on the part of the people who participated; they each took many years to change the way things were done.)	**Beginner** **Discuss.** Pair Beginning with Advanced (or Beyond) students and have them use the dialogue starter on their Access 1 handout to discuss the topic. Advise them to return to the dialogue and switch roles if they get stuck. **Intermediate** **Discuss.** Pair Intermediate with Advanced (or Beyond) students and have them use the dialogue starter on their Access 2 handout to discuss the topic. Advise them to return to the dialogue and switch roles if they get stuck. If their conversation is progressing smoothly, encourage them to continue the discussion beyond the dialogue starter sheet. They can expand their conversations to discuss other examples of movements and leaders who have stood up for others and made a difference in the lives of many.

Core Path	Access Path
Brainstorm. Remind students about the Driving Question for this Blast and the driving question for this unit: What happens when people stand up for others and themselves? In their notebooks, ask students to make a Venn diagram in which they compare Dr. Martin Luther King, Jr. and Elizabeth Cady Stanton, using information from the Background. Here's a short example of how this might look:	

Elizabeth C. Stanton	both	Dr. King
wanted equal rights for women; lived during the last half of the 19th century	important leaders; saw much progress during their lifetimes but died before their goals were met; efforts were carried on by others	wanted equal rights for African Americans; lived during the first part of the 20th century

RESEARCH LINKS

Core Path	Access Path
Examine and Explore. Before asking students to explore the research links, use these activities and questions to guide their exploration: 1. What's the most important thing to look for in any research link you click on? (examples of what happens when you stand up for yourself or others) 2. Why do you think a link called "Examples of Courage" is included? (maybe because it takes a lot of courage to stand up for yourself and others—maybe it will have more stories and examples of people who have done that)	

Core Path	Access Path
3. Ask students to look at "How (and How Not) to Stand Up For Yourself." What useful advice did you get from this article? (how to stand up for ourselves without hurting others' feelings or being aggressive, etc.) 4. As a class, scan through "Examples of Courage" to see examples of people who have stood up for what they believe in on a large scale. Ask students which historical figures they think are the best examples of courageous people, and why.	
	Extend **Research, Discuss and Present.** 1. Assign each group one link to explore in depth. 2. Ask them to discuss the information: a. What are the key points? b. What inferences did you make as you read? c. What did you learn about this "big idea" from reading this research? d. How did this help you to better understand the topic? e. What questions does your group have after exploring this link? 3. Allow students time to informally present what they learned.

Core Path	Access Path
	Extend **Tech Infusion** **Share.** As students explore the links, allow them to compile their findings with an online post-it note canvas like Lino.it (http://tinyurl.com/ylewks3).

QUIKPOLL

Core Path	Access Path
Participate. Answer the poll question. Have students discuss their reasons for their answers. Students should refer to evidence from the Background and Research Links to defend their answer.	

NUMBER CRUNCH

Core Path	Access Path
Predict, Discuss, and Click. Before students click on the number, break them into pairs and have them make predictions about what they think the number is related to. After they've clicked the number, ask students if they are surprised by the revealed information.	

CREATE YOUR BLAST (140 CHARACTERS)

Core Path	Access Path
Blast. Ask students to write their Blast response in 140 characters or less.	**Beginner** **Blast with Support.** Have students refer back to the sentence frame on their Access 1 handout that they used to create their original Blast draft. Ask them to use this frame to write and enter their final Blast. **Intermediate** **Blast with Support.** Have students attempt to draft their Blast without the sentence frame on their Access 2 handout. If students struggle to compose their Blast draft without the sentence frame, remind them to reference it for support. **Beyond** **Write a Claim.** Ask students to use their answer to the poll question to write a strong claim that could be used as the foundation for a piece of argumentative writing. Once students have written their claims, ask them to read the claims to a small group of their peers. This activity will provide them practice writing claims, as well as expose them to claims written by their peers.
Review. After students have completed their own Blasts, ask them to review the Blasts of their peers and provide feedback.	**Extend** **Discuss.** As a whole class or in groups, identify a few strong Blasts and discuss what made those responses so powerful. As a group, analyze and discuss what characteristics make a Blast interesting or effective.
	Extend **Revise.** Resend a second version of this Blast assignment to your students and have them submit revised versions of their original Blasts. Do the same responses make the Top 10? How have the answers improved from the first submissions?

Extended Writing Project

Facing Challenges

EXTENDED WRITING PROJECT:
Narrative Writing

OVERVIEW

For this unit's Extended Writing Project, students will be writing a fictional narrative. This lesson provides students with a definition of narrative writing and its major features, as well as a sample student narrative.

OBJECTIVES

1. Demonstrate an understanding of the features of narrative writing.
2. Practice and apply concrete strategies for identifying the features of narrative writing.
3. Participate effectively in a range of conversations and collaborations to express ideas and build upon the ideas of others.

ELA Common Core Standards:
Reading: Literature - RL.6.1, RL.6.2, RL.6.3, RL.6.4
Reading: Informational Text - RI.6.1, RI.6.2
Writing - W.6.3.A, W.6.3.B, W.6.3.C, W.6.3.D, W.6.3.E, W.6.5, W.6.10
Speaking & Listening - SL.6.1.A, SL.6.1.B, SL.6.1.C, SL.6.1.D

RESOURCES

Access 1 handout (Beginner)

Access 2 handout (Intermediate)

Access 3 handout (Advanced)

Access 4 handout (Approaching)

Please note that excerpts and passages in the StudySync® library, workbooks, and PDFs are intended as touchstones to generate interest in an author's work. The excerpts and passages do not substitute for the reading of entire texts, and StudySync® strongly recommends that teachers and students seek out and purchase the whole literary or informational work in order to experience it as the author intended. Links to online resellers are available in our digital library. In addition, complete works may be ordered through an authorized reseller by filling out and returning to StudySync® the order form enclosed in this workbook.

Teacher's Edition   341

1. INTRODUCTION

Core Path	Access Path
Read and Discuss. Have students read the prompt for the Extended Writing Project on narrative writing. Ask them to look at the various parts of the prompt and respond to the following questions in pairs or small groups: • What is the prompt asking you to do? • What specific requirements does the prompt lay out? • What does the prompt specifically ask you to think about? • How might the questions in the prompt guide you in writing your own fictional narrative? Explain to students that they will be developing their writing in stages, with time to reflect on the assignment, revise their work, and benefit from peer review. Give students an opportunity to ask any questions they may have about the prompt.	**Beginner & Intermediate** **Paraphrase.** Have students follow along with the text as they listen to the audio recording of the prompt. After they've heard the audio recording, have them fill in the blanks on their Access 1 and 2 handouts to create their own paraphrased version of the prompt. After they've completed their prompt paraphrase, have students participate in the whole class discussion of the prompt using the questions provided in the Core Path. A sample paraphrase is located in the answer key at the end of the lesson plan online. **Approaching** **Listen and Discuss.** Have students follow along with the text as they listen to the audio recording of the prompt. Then, have them participate in the whole class discussion of the prompt using the questions provided in the Core Path.
Read and Annotate. Individually or as a class, read the Introduction to Narrative Writing. The introduction defines narrative writing and explains its six main features. If you are reading the introduction as a class, encourage students to take Cornell notes defining narrative writing, identifying the purpose of narrative writing and putting the six features of narrative writing into their own words. If students are reading independently online, ask them to use the StudySync annotation tool to make notes about the features of narrative writing. Point out that students will learn more about each of these features and about how to incorporate them into their own writing as they craft a fictional narrative in response to the Extended Writing Project prompt.	**Beginner & Intermediate** **Fill in the Blanks.** As they read and listen to the introduction, have Beginning and Intermediate students work together to fill in the blanks on the Access 1 and 2 handouts. They can also refer to the introduction glossary provided on those handouts. Provide assistance and clarification as needed. Sample answers are located at the end of the lesson plan online. **Approaching & Advanced** **Identify Features of Narrative Writing.** After reading the introduction, have students list the four features of narrative writing on their Access 3 and 4 handouts in their own words.

Core Path	Access Path
	Extend **Summarize.** Have students meet in pairs or small groups to discuss the writing prompt. Provide them with these questions to guide them as they discuss: 1. What kind of writing is the prompt asking me to write? 2. What kinds of ideas is the prompt telling me to think and write about? 3. What are the elements I need to include in my writing? After students discuss the prompt by using the questions, have them work together to summarize what the prompt is asking them to do. After bringing the class together, ask a volunteer from each pair or group to share its summary. As a class, compare the summaries. Do they all restate the most important parts of the prompt? Make sure students understand the focus of the prompt before discussing the Student Model.
	Extend **Tech Infusion** **Journaling.** Allow students time to use an online journaling app, such as Penzu (http://tinyurl.com/lwuy989) to write a brief journal entry about their past experiences writing narratives or writing stories in response to formal prompts. Encourage students to be honest about the process and to focus on the things they do well as well as those that challenge them when writing for school. Ask volunteers to share their thoughts. Or ask volunteers to allow you to present their ideas anonymously as you lead a discussion about the challenges and rewards of writing fictional narratives.

2. READ

Core Path	Access Path
Read and Label. Have students read the Student Model titled "Taking the Shot." Ask them to identify the six features of narrative writing in the Model and label them using the annotation tool. 1. Setting 2. Characters or Real Individuals 3. Plot 4. Point of View 5. Precise Language and Descriptive Details 6. Theme	**Beginner** **Coach the Reading.** While other students read, annotate, and discuss the text independently, work with Beginning students as they listen to the audio of the text and use the model glossary on the Access 1 handout. Coach students in articulating their questions for the group and in highlighting and annotating the text using the Annotation Guide on the Access 1 handout. **Intermediate** **Listen to the Audio.** Have Intermediate students listen to the audio of the text and use the model glossary on the Access 2 handout to help them with words or idioms that may be unfamiliar. If students need help with annotating the text, have them use the Annotation Guide on the Access 2 handout. After working with the Beginning students, you may wish to check this group's progress and provide support as needed. **Advanced** **Pair with Proficient Peers.** Have Advanced students work with English proficient peers to read, annotate, and discuss the text. You can also provide them with the model glossary from the Access 3 handout if necessary. Have these student pairs use the Annotation Guide on the Access 3 handout to support them as they highlight and annotate the text. Encourage them to listen to the audio of the text if needed. **Approaching** **Use the Annotation Guide.** Have students use the Annotation Guide on the Access 4 handout to support them as they highlight and annotate the text.

Core Path	Access Path
Discuss. In small groups or pairs, have students discuss the observations and annotations they made while reading. Have them examine the "Constructed Response — Narrative" grading rubric this Student Model was written to satisfy. Inform students that this is the same rubric that will be used to evaluate their completed Narrative Extended Writing Project. They should consider how understanding the Student Model can help them as they begin to craft their own fictional narrative in response to the prompt.	**English Learners All Levels & Approaching** Use the extra time while on- and beyond-grade-level students are discussing their first reads of the text to work individually and in small groups with Approaching readers and English Learners as outlined above. Should those students complete their first reads quickly, integrate them into the on- and beyond-grade-level discussion groups. Otherwise Approaching readers and English Learners will be given an opportunity to participate in text discussions with their peers in future Extended Writing Project lessons.
	Extend **Feature Focus.** Place students in groups of four. Have students gather to analyze the Student Model for each of the four features of narrative writing. After students have discussed the Student Model, assign each student in each group a number from 1 to 4. Have all the 1s meet to discuss the story's setting. Have all the 2s meet to discuss the characters and narrator, and so on. Finally, lead the whole class in a discussion of the features of the model narrative. Ask students to comment on the student writer's strengths and weaknesses and to identify the feature or features that could have been stronger in the Student Model.

3. THINK

Core Path	Access Path
Answer and Discuss. Have students complete the Think questions. Collect papers or discuss answers as a class. Refer to the sample answers at the end of the lesson plan online.	

Core Path	Access Path
	Beginner **Answer Questions with Support.** Review all of the Think questions with students to clarify vocabulary and comprehension. Read question 1 aloud. Then, ask students to look at the first few paragraphs of the story and identify the setting (at school gym class). Once you've completed this instruction with students, have them complete the remaining Think questions using the sentence frames on their Access 1 handout. **Intermediate** **Support.** Have partners review the Think questions and help one another with any terms or concepts that need to be clarified. Tell them that they may ask you about any vocabulary or concepts they cannot clarify for themselves, and then have them use the sentence frames on their Access 2 handout to assist them in writing the answers to the questions. **Advanced** **Discuss.** Have students read and answer the Think questions independently. Then have them discuss their answers to questions with an English-proficient partner. Have them share the ideas they want to develop into their own writing, and the reasons why these ideas are interesting to them. They can take notes on their discussion and save them for their prewrite. **Approaching** **Rewrite the Think Questions.** Preview the Think questions and ask students to rewrite each question in their own words on the Access 4 handout. Have students use their paraphrased versions of the Think questions to help them respond. Sample answers to the Think questions are located at the end of the lesson plan online.

Core Path	Access Path
	Extend **Identify.** Show students a short episode of a children's cartoon or another appropriate short narrative. Before students watch the episode, have them write down the elements of a fictional narrative. Remind them to look for those elements as they watch the episode. After students view the episode, adapt and ask students the first three Think questions: 1. What is the setting? 2. Who is the story's narrator? Who are the characters? What do you know about them? 3. What happens in the story? Lead students in a class discussion of these questions. Whenever possible, point out the similarities between the elements of the Student Model and the episode students watched. If time allows, challenge students to look for deeper connections between the Student Model and the episode they viewed; for example, ask for their thoughts about similarities in the narratives' themes.

Please note that excerpts and passages in the StudySync® library, workbooks, and PDFs are intended as touchstones to generate interest in an author's work. The excerpts and passages do not substitute for the reading of entire texts, and StudySync® strongly recommends that teachers and students seek out and purchase the whole literary or informational work in order to experience it as the author intended. Links to online resellers are available in our digital library. In addition, complete works may be ordered through an authorized reseller by filling out and returning to StudySync® the order form enclosed in this workbook.

Teacher's Edition   **347**

EXTENDED WRITING PROJECT:
Prewrite

OVERVIEW

This lesson first asks students to consider the texts they have read in this unit about characters or real individuals who must decide whether to take a risk by standing up for themselves or others. Students will consider how the characters or individuals in the selections respond to their situations, and they will look for commonalities and patterns that they can use as inspiration for their own stories. The lesson then asks students to complete a prewriting brainstorm activity to generate ideas for their own stories about characters who decide to stand up for themselves or others.

OBJECTIVES

1. Demonstrate understanding of the features of fictional narrative writing.
2. Analyze the prompt and generate ideas for a fictional narrative.
3. Participate effectively in a range of conversations and collaborations to express ideas and build upon the ideas of others.

ELA Common Core Standards:
Reading: Literature - RL.6.1, RL.6.2
Reading: Informational Text - RI.6.1, RI.6.2
Writing - W.6.3.A, W.6.5, W.6.6
Speaking & Listening - SL.6.A, SL.6.1.B, SL.6.1.C, SL.6.1.D

RESOURCES

Access 1 handout (Beginner)

Access 2 handout (Intermediate)

1. WRITE

Core Path	Access Path
Define and Compare. Before students begin a prewriting brainstorm activity to generate ideas for their own fictional narratives, ask them to work in groups of three to complete a "mind map" analyzing some of the selections they have read in the unit. Encourage students to draw three circles. In each circle, they should write the title of a unit selection they have read that featured a character or an individual who acted to defend himself or herself or who tried to protect someone else.	**Beginner & Intermediate** **Support the Prewrite.**
1. From this circle, students can draw lines connected to other circles where they should jot down notes about the characters or individuals and their situations and choices. Students are welcome to add drawings, sketches or symbols to help them conceptualize their ideas.	1. Group students in mixed-proficiency pairs or small groups.
2. After students have compiled their notes, tell them to use a highlighter or colored marker to illuminate the story elements or ideas that the three selections have in common.	2. Assign each group a single unit selection, and have them complete a mind map for that selection. Each group should focus on a different selection.
3. Invite students to discuss similarities among the selections, as well as ways the selections might serve as models or as inspiration as students craft their own stories.	3. Then have all groups display their mind maps so that all students can then draw from the complete collection of information for their essays.
	Advanced **Share and Discuss.** Have students complete their mind maps with a group that includes at least one English-proficient student. Have them discuss the connections they found between the selections and what they found most inspiring about them before they move on to do their prewrite.

Prewrite and Plan. Review with the class the writing prompt/directions. Have a volunteer read them aloud. Ask whether students have any questions either about the prompt or the directions. Then discuss with students the questions they will answer as they complete their prewriting brainstorm activity to generate ideas for their own fictional narratives:	**Beginner & Intermediate** **Organize the Prewrite.** Have Beginning and Intermediate students use Access 1 and 2 handouts to answer the questions. With partners or small groups, have them discuss their answers orally before writing them. Provide writing assistance as needed.
• Who are your characters?	
• Who is telling the story?	
• In what situation do your characters find themselves?	
• What risks do your characters face if they stand up for themselves—and if they don't?	

Copyright © BookheadEd Learning, LLC

Core Path	Access Path
• What choices do your characters make? • How will you organize your story's events? • How does your story end? Encourage students to keep readers in mind when brainstorming for their narratives. The events and characters in their stories should interest and engage readers.	
Review. Once students complete their prewriting brainstorm, they should submit substantive feedback to three peers. Review the prewriting rubric and peer review instructions with students to ensure that they know what elements of their peers' prewriting brainstorm activity they will be evaluating. The peer review instructions ask students to consider these questions: • How well does the writer answer the questions presented in the prewriting activity? • Who will be the narrator of the writer's story? • Does the end of the story seem to make sense? • Does the writer provide enough details to help you understand what the story will be about? Remind students that they are in the early stages of the writing process and to be kind and supportive when they make their comments. Students will use their peers' feedback to develop their writing in different stages of the writing process.	

Core Path	Access Path
	Extend **Tech Infusion** **Quick Polling.** Before students meet in their groups to create a mind map, get them thinking about the unit's selections by engaging in a quick poll. Use a polling app, such as Socrative (http://tinyurl.com/3bxbjpt) or Poll Everywhere (http://tinyurl.com/3zyw33) to pose the question: *Which situation faced by the characters or individuals in the unit selections struck you as the most serious?* Then poll students about the characters or individuals in the top three selections they identified for the first question: *Which character or individual acted most bravely? Which character or individual did you most admire? Which character or individual did you like least?* Tell students to keep their responses to these questions in mind as they meet in groups to create mind maps for their own stories.
	Extend **Tech Infusion** **Drawing Tools.** Suggest that students use Google Drawing or another online drawing app as they work together to create their mind maps. Students can use the line drawing, text box, highlighting, and spelling tools to create and then save their maps for future reference. You can have students submit their maps to you. Choose one map to use as a teaching tool to show students the process of creating a mind map.
	Extend **Discuss.** Ask the class to share some favorite stories they have read in the past and to analyze them using the list of prewriting questions. Who were the characters? What did students admire about the characters? What was the situation? What made it exciting or intriguing? What message was the author communicating? Students should consider the features that made these favorite stories memorable as they complete the prewriting activity. How can their favorite stories be used as inspiration as they think about creating their own narratives?

OVERVIEW

Students will learn why it is important to consider both audience and purpose when writing a fictional narrative.

OBJECTIVES

1. Learn the definition of audience and purpose for writing a fictional narrative.
2. Practice identifying audience and purpose for a narrative text.
3. Participate effectively in a range of conversations and collaborations to express ideas and build upon the ideas of others.

   ### ELA Common Core Standards:
   Writing - W.6.3.A, W.6.3.B, W.6.4, W.6.5, W.6.6, W.6.10
   Speaking & Listening - SL.6.1.A, SL.6.1.C, SL.6.1.D

RESOURCES

Access 1 handout (Beginner)

Access 2 handout (Intermediate)

Access 4 handout (Approaching)

TITLE/DRIVING QUESTION

Core Path	Access Path
Discuss. As a class, read aloud the title and Driving Question for this Blast: "Who is your audience and what is your purpose for writing your fictional narrative?" Ask students why it might be important for an author to think about his or her audience, or who will be reading the text. Then discuss what students know about the purpose of narrative writing. How might elements such as character, plot, and setting change according to a narrative's audience and purpose? Remind students that they should not immediately reply to the Driving Question. They'll be returning to this question and responding after they've read the Background.	**English Learners All Levels & Approaching** **Share.** Have students backchannel using TodaysMeet (http://tinyurl.com/psef72j) to add their ideas about why audience and purpose might be important. Have students revisit their notes after they have read the Background section of the lesson. Then have them compare their notes with what they have learned.
Draft. In their notebooks or on scrap paper, have students draft their initial responses to the driving question. This will provide them with a baseline response that they will be developing as they gain more information about the topic in the Background section of the assignment. (*Note: you will need to create a write assignment if they are going to submit their responses online.*) Ask students to think about how certain narrative techniques, such as the dialogue used to develop character, the pacing required to propel events forward, and the description used to enhance the overall story, can be tailored to suit a specific audience and purpose.	**Beginner & Intermediate** **Draft with Sentence Frame.** When drafting their initial response to the driving question, have students refer to this Blast sentence frame on their Access 1 and 2 handouts: • The audience for my narrative is people who _____. Point out these two key features of the sentence frame: 1. The beginning of the prompt borrows language directly from the Blast driving question to provide a response. 2. Ask students to make special note of the phrase "is people who" which prompts students to specify who their audience might be. Caution students that the driving question asks students to name both an audience *and* a purpose.

Core Path	Access Path
	Extend **Tech Infusion** **Initial Response.** Invite students to use a journaling app, such as Penzu (http://tinyurl.com/ycyxmc2), or a vocal recording app, such as Vocaroo (http://tinyurl.com/lhoqe8), to record their initial responses to the driving question. This will provide them with a baseline response that they can revise as they learn more about the topic in the Background section of the assignment.

BACKGROUND

Core Path	Access Path
Read. Have students read the Blast background to provide context for the driving question and to consider the audience and purpose for their fictional narrative.	**Beginner & Intermediate** **Read with Support.** Have students read the Blast Background to provide context for the driving question. When they encounter unfamiliar words or phrases, have students refer to the glossary on their Access 1 and 2 handouts. If there are unfamiliar words that are not included in their glossary, encourage students to check a dictionary or online reference tool, like http://tinyurl.com/6ytby. **Approaching** **Read and Summarize.** Have students read the Blast Background to explain the driving question. As they read, ask students to complete the fill in the blank summary of the background provided on their Access 4 handout. When they encounter unfamiliar words or phrases, have students refer to the glossary on their Access 4 handout.
	Beginner & Intermediate **Q & A.** Pair Beginning and Intermediate with Advanced (or Beyond) students and have them take turns asking and answering questions about the audience and purpose of writing. Have students use the charts on the Access 1 and 2 handouts to record their answers.

Core Path	Access Path
Discuss. Pair students and have them discuss the following questions:	**Beginner**

Core Path

Discuss. Pair students and have them discuss the following questions:

1. Why do effective writers aim for specific audiences? (Effective writers aim for specific audiences so that they can appeal to readers who will want to read the story. Also, if you start out writing for a general audience, your material may be so general that it's uninteresting. However, the more specific your narrative is, with intriguing characters and details and action, the more likely it is that you'll attract an even broader audience than you originally intended.)

2. What is your purpose for writing a fictional narrative? (My purpose is to entertain my readers and also to suggest an important idea about life.)

3. Who is the audience for your narrative, and how can you appeal to these readers? (My audience is readers who enjoy reading stories. My audience might also include my teacher, my classmates, my family, and my friends. Three ways I can appeal to them is with vivid description, good dialogue between characters, and an interesting theme or message.)

4. Will you directly reveal your purpose to your readers? Why or why not? (Because I am writing a fictional narrative, readers will have to figure out my purpose on their own. In a story, you don't often state your purpose directly.)

5. How will you get your readers to consider your theme, or your important message about life? (I will work my theme into my story, so that when my readers finish reading, they will have something to think about.)

Access Path

Beginner
Discuss. Pair Beginning with Advanced (or Beyond) students and have them use the dialogue starter on their Access 1 handout to discuss the topic. Advise them to return to the dialogue and switch roles if they get stuck.

Intermediate
Discuss. Pair Intermediate with Advanced (or Beyond) students and have them use the dialogue starter on their Access 2 handout to discuss the topic. Advise them to return to the dialogue and switch roles if they get stuck. If their conversation is progressing smoothly, encourage them to continue the discussion beyond the dialogue starter sheet. They can expand their conversations to discuss other examples of when audience and purpose must be considered for writing.

Please note that excerpts and passages in the StudySync® library, workbooks, and PDFs are intended as touchstones to generate interest in an author's work. The excerpts and passages do not substitute for the reading of entire texts, and StudySync® strongly recommends that teachers and students seek out and purchase the whole literary or informational work in order to experience it as the author intended. Links to online resellers are available in our digital library. In addition, complete works may be ordered through an authorized reseller by filling out and returning to StudySync® the order form enclosed in this workbook.

Teacher's Edition **355**

Core Path	Access Path
Brainstorm. Remind students about the Driving Question for this Blast: "Who is your audience and what is your purpose for writing your fictional narrative?"	

Ask students to think about how they will appeal to their audience by answering the following questions:

- Who will be reading my story?
- How do I think the audience will respond to my story's narrator and characters, and their conflict, or problem?
- How can I present my events and characters so that my audience will find them interesting?
- How familiar is the audience with the kind of story I am telling?
- Why am I trying to reach this audience?
- What theme (or message) about life do I want my audience to understand from reading my story?
- Who will be interested in my theme (or message)?

Ask students to create a two-column chart that looks like the one on the following pages. Have them write or find an example for each way to achieve their purpose in a narrative. The example can be from students' own writing or from the Student Model, "Taking the Shot," or another selection in the unit. Before they complete the chart, have students write information about their theme at the top of their chart.

Core Path	Access Path

Core Path

My purpose: To entertain readers and get them to think about my theme, which is _____ _____.

I can entertain readers and express my theme through:	Example
Vivid Descriptions	I snatched the ball away from him and started dribbling. "No," I snapped. I was getting pretty angry myself. "Why would I be afraid of those guys?"
Interesting Dialogue	I said, "Why don't you let me teach you how to do a free throw, so those guys will leave you alone?" He said, "Celia, those guys don't bother me. Why do they bother you?"
Conflict	The minute the coach turned his back, the trio of mean boys would start laughing and talking trash. They'd say stuff like "Take cover, guys; Kyle is chucking the ball again. Your height is totally wasted on you, man. Your twin sister Celia has got all the athletic talent in your family, dude."

Core Path		Access Path
Characters' Thoughts and Actions	Stunned, I tossed the ball and blew the shot. The ball bounced off the edge of the hoop with a metallic bang and into the garage. I knew that Mac was right. I was wrong. It was time to fix things. "All right," I said. "But I'll need your help."	
Narrator's Thoughts	I made a plan and took a risk and it paid off. Phew! Now I could get back to the really important things in life—winning at basketball.	

QUIKPOLL (UP TO 5 ANSWERS)

Core Path	Access Path
Participate. Answer the poll question. Have students discuss their reasons for their answers. Students should refer to evidence from the Background to defend their answer.	

NUMBER CRUNCH

Core Path	Access Path
Predict, Discuss, and Click. Before students click on the number, break them into pairs and have them make predictions about what they think the number is related to. After they've clicked the number, ask students if they are surprised by the revealed information.	

CREATE YOUR BLAST (140 CHARACTERS)

Core Path	Access Path
Blast. Ask students to write their Blast response in 140 characters or less. Students should consider whether their fictional narrative will appeal to the audience they hope to target and fulfill the purpose they plan to achieve.	**Beginner** **Blast with Support.** Have students refer back to the sentence frame on their Access 1 handout that they used to create their original Blast draft. Ask them to use this frame to write and enter their final Blast. **Intermediate** **Blast with Support.** Have students attempt to draft their Blast without the sentence frame on their Access 2 handout. If students struggle to compose their Blast draft without the sentence frame, remind them to reference it for support. **Beyond** **Write a Claim.** Ask students to use their answer to the poll question to write a strong claim that could be used as the foundation for a piece of argumentative writing. Once students have written their claims, ask them to read the claims to a small group of their peers. This activity will provide them practice writing claims, as well as expose them to claims written by their peers.
Review. After students have completed their own Blasts, ask them to review the Blasts of their peers and provide feedback.	**Extend** **Discuss.** As a whole class or in groups, identify a few strong blasts and discuss what made those responses so powerful. As a group, analyze and discuss what characteristics make a blast interesting or effective.

OVERVIEW

As students move toward the planning stage of their Extended Writing Project, they'll need to think about the text structure (or organizational pattern) of their story. This lesson defines story structure and explains how students can determine the overall text structure of their fictional narrative and develop an event sequence that unfolds naturally and logically.

OBJECTIVES

1. Demonstrate an understanding of story structure in narrative writing.
2. Practice using concrete strategies for identifying and developing story structure in narrative text.
3. Participate effectively in a range of conversations and collaborations to express ideas and build upon the ideas of others.

ELA Common Core Standards:
Reading: Literature - RL.6.1, RL.6.3
Writing - W.6.3.A, W.6.3.C, W.6.5
Speaking & Listening - SL.6.1.A, SL.6.1.C

RESOURCES

Organize Narrative Writing Graphic organizer

Access 1 handout (Beginner)

Access 2 handout (Intermediate)

Access 3 handout (Advanced)

Access 4 handout (Approaching)

1. DEFINE

Core Path	Access Path

Core Path

Read and Discuss. Either individually or as a class, read the Define section of the lesson. In small groups or as a class, use these questions to engage students in a discussion about the text structure (or organizational pattern) of fictional narrative texts:

1. The definition explains that most writers use chronological (or sequential) order to tell a story. What is chronological order? Why is it an effective way to tell a story? (Chronological order is time order or the sequence in which the events in a story take place, from beginning to end. It's a good way to tell a story because it's logical, and it covers all the events in a story in a way that makes sense and is easy to follow.)

2. According to the definition of *narrative text structure,* what other kinds of organizational structure might a writer use to organize a fictional narrative? Why? (A writer might use cause-effect text structure to show the consequences of a character's words or actions. He or she might also decide to use comparison-contrast to show the different ways characters react to an event in the story.)

3. The definition points out that writers can place story events in any order they wish. For example, they can use flashbacks or start in the middle or at the end. Why might a writer want to structure his or her story in non-chronological order? Think of a story—or movie or comic—that does this. (Starting a story in the middle or at the end can make it more mysterious and can build suspense. Answers will vary for examples.)

4. How does word choice relate to organizational structure? (Clue words can signal the organizational structure of the narrative.)

Access Path

Beginner
In Your Own Words. Have students read the definition and then use their Access 1 handouts to pause after each bullet point to rewrite the components of narrative text structure in their own words. Once students have completed this activity, ask them to complete the fill-in-the-blanks activity on the Access 1 handout.

Intermediate
In Your Own Words. Have students read the definition of narrative text structure and then use their Access 2 handout to pause after each bullet point to rewrite it in their own words. After they've rewritten each of the bullet points in their own words, work with students to develop their own definitions of the term.

Advanced
In Your Own Words. Have Advanced students read and then discuss what they have learned about narrative text structure with an English-proficient partner or in mixed-proficiency groups. After their conversation, have Advanced students write the definition of narrative text structure on the Access 3 handout.

Approaching
Restate the Definition. Have students read the Define section and then use their Access 4 handouts to restate the most important points in their own words. Clarify questions to aid students' comprehension as needed. Then have students participate in mixed-level groups with the class to discuss the purpose of narrative text structure in a narrative.

Please note that excerpts and passages in the StudySync® library, workbooks, and PDFs are intended as touchstones to generate interest in an author's work. The excerpts and passages do not substitute for the reading of entire texts, and StudySync® strongly recommends that teachers and students seek out and purchase the whole literary or informational work in order to experience it as the author intended. Links to online resellers are available in our digital library. In addition, complete works may be ordered through an authorized reseller by filling out and returning to StudySync® the order form enclosed in this workbook.

Teacher's Edition   **361**

Core Path	Access Path
	Beyond **Identify and Analyze Organizational Text Structure.** Organize students into small groups. Assign to each group a narrative text from the unit, such as the excerpt from *A Wrinkle in Time*. Have each group identify the excerpt's overall organizational structure and discuss how that text structure is conveyed. Ask students to complete a timeline or another graphic organizer, such as a sequence-of-events chart, to illustrate the structure and share it with the class. Have them discuss how the story would be different if other text structures were used.
	Extend **Tech Infusion** **Poster-Making Software.** Invite students to use an online poster-making app such as Google Drawing or Glogster (http://tinyurl.com/ydeyklq) to create a graphic that illustrates the organizational structure of the unit text they are analyzing. Students can create a timeline, flowchart, sequence-of-events chart or another graphic organizer to show the order of the events in the story. Then have students write a brief summary of what their organizer shows.

2. MODEL

Core Path	Access Path
Read and Discuss. As students read the Model text, use these questions to help them understand how the timeline graphic organizer helped the writer clarify the organization of events in the narrative:	**Beginner, Intermediate & Approaching** **Focus on Verb Tenses.** Have students listen to the Model section of the student lesson and discussion questions and answers. Then take time to focus more on verb tenses in the Student Model using the Access 1 and 2 handouts. Walk students through the instruction on the handout.

1. The Model includes an Organize Narrative Writing Timeline. How does this graphic organizer help the writer organize the events in the story? (It visually maps out the order of the events. It shows how the writer wants to tell about the events in the story. It makes the event sequence really clear. It also shows the relationship between events and setting, indicating when a time shift is accompanied by a change in place.)

2. The graphic organizer shows you that the writer is thinking of presenting events in the order they occurred. Why not tell events in a different order, such as starting at the end or in the middle? (The writer might want to tell the story from the first event to the last because he or she thinks it is important for the readers to follow the sister through the process of figuring out why she is afraid to stand up for her brother. If the order of the events were less straightforward, then the sister's decision to take a stand might not be the high point of the story.)

3. The Model explains that the writer's use of time-order words and phrases helps readers follow the shifts of time and place in the story. Why is this important? How would the lack of time-order words and phrases affect the story? (The time-order words and phrases let readers know how the events connect—they are moving forward in time and they take place in different settings. Without the words or phrases, readers might have to guess when an event happened or where it took place.)

Have them orally answer questions such as the following:

- What kind of action does the verb phrase "would be going" show? (ongoing action)

- If a teacher "handed out your homework," did you get your homework right now or in the past? (in the past)

- If something happens "every time," does it happen just once, or does it repeat more than once? (more than once)

Then have them complete the handout in mixed-proficiency pairs. Have the group come back together to discuss and clarify their answers.

Advanced
Read and Discuss. Have students read the Model section independently and then discuss the questions with an English proficient partner or group.

Core Path	Access Path
Practice. Have students organize the information they gathered in the Prewrite stage by filling in a StudySync Organize Narrative Writing Graphic Organizer as used in the Model. Students can complete this organizer on paper, or you can create a write assignment on StudySync, and they can submit their organizers online for anonymous peer review. Comments should focus on how clearly events are organized, and how well transitions are used to signal time order and change in setting.	**Beginner** **Write with Support.** 1. Prior to completing their Organize Narrative Writing Graphic Organizer, ask students to complete the sentence frames on the Access 1 handout. 2. After students have answered the questions, ask them to discuss with a partner what they plan to write about, clarifying any language as needed before completing their graphic organizer. 3. Then students should complete their own graphic organizers using the direction from the writing prompt to guide their work. Encourage them to refer back to the writing prompt and to the Prewrite Worksheet they completed. 4. Have them use the sentence frames on the Access 1 handout to help them complete their graphic organizers. **Intermediate** **Finish Sentences.** Have students fill in the sentence frames on the Access 2 handout. Review their answers with them, and after making any clarifications needed, allow them to use their answers to complete their Organize Narrative Writing Graphic Organizer. Then allow them to join Advanced students to discuss and edit graphic organizers. **Advanced** **Write and Evaluate.** After students fill in the StudySync Organize Narrative Writing Timeline using their prewrite information, have them share their chart with an Advanced or English-proficient partner and evaluate whether they have placed their events in the correct sequence. Then have them see if they can find one section of their outline where they might use compare-and-contrast or a flashback, and make a note of it on the outline.

Core Path	Access Path
	Approaching **Finish the Sentences & Complete the Graphic Organizer** 1. Prior to completing their Organize Narrative Writing Graphic Organizers, ask students to complete the sentence frames on the Access 4 handout. 2. Once they have completed the statements with the information they plan to write about, instruct them to complete the Organize Narrative Writing Graphic Organizer using the information they filled in the sentence frames. Remind students to complete the graphic organizer with information they plan to write about in their own narratives.
	Extend **Tech Infusion** **Create Flashcards.** 1. Pair or group students and have them choose another short story or a film with which they're familiar. 2. Have students use a flashcard app, such as StudyBlue (http://tinyurl.com/ov6xbl) or Quizlet (http://tinyurl.com/4gj6tz) to create a series of flashcards for each of the events in their chosen story. Students should write a brief description of a story event on one side of the flashcard. On the reverse side, they should number the event (to indicate when it takes place in the story sequence, and, if events are told out of order, when it is presented in the story). Encourage students also to use images on their flashcards as appropriate. 3. Once students have finished, ask each pair or group to present their flashcards to the class. Students should be able to comment thoughtfully about the organizational structure of the original text or film. For example, they should be able to describe it as straightforwardly chronological or as using flashbacks. If the timeline of events was not strictly chronological, have students talk about how changing the order of the events might affect the story.

Please note that excerpts and passages in the StudySync® library, workbooks, and PDFs are intended as touchstones to generate interest in an author's work. The excerpts and passages do not substitute for the reading of entire texts, and StudySync® strongly recommends that teachers and students seek out and purchase the whole literary or informational work in order to experience it as the author intended. Links to online resellers are available in our digital library. In addition, complete works may be ordered through an authorized reseller by filling out and returning to StudySync® the order form enclosed in this workbook.

Teacher's Edition   365

Core Path	Access Path
	Extend **Record.** Allow students to record themselves as they present their flashcards, by using Aurasma (http://tinyurl.com/o25s8kn) or Vocaroo (http://tinyurl.com/lhoqe8).

3. YOUR TURN

Core Path	Access Path
Assess and Explain. Have students answer the comprehension questions to test for understanding. Share the explanations for Part A and B (located online) with your students.	
	Extend **Analyze.** Have students work individually or in pairs to analyze the text structure of a different section of "Taking the Shot" or of another selection in the unit. Students should scan the section for clue words that indicate a cause-effect, comparison-contrast, or order of importance text structure. Have students identify the sentence (or sentences) that best illustrates the organizational structure they identified. Ask volunteers to share their findings with the class.
	Extend **Tech Infusion** **Quiz.** Collect the sections of text students analyzed during the Analyze activity above. Use a quiz-making app, such as Socrative (http://tinyurl.com/3bxbjpt) to generate a quiz in which students must analyze paragraphs or sections from unit narratives to identify their secondary organizational structure. Have the class take the quiz. Use the results to determine which concepts need reteaching or reinforcement.

Descriptive Details

OVERVIEW

As students move toward the planning stage of their Extended Writing Project, they will need to consider the ways in which they will incorporate details that describe the characters, settings, and events that bring their story to life. This lesson discusses how to identify and develop relevant, descriptive details that will help make a fictional narrative more interesting to read.

OBJECTIVES

1. Demonstrate understanding of the role of description and descriptive details in fictional narratives.
2. Practice identifying and developing description and descriptive details in a fictional narrative.
3. Participate effectively in a range of conversations and collaborations to express ideas and build upon the ideas of others.

ELA Common Core Standards:
Reading: Literature - RL.6.1, RL.6.5
Writing - W.6.3.A, W.6.3.B, W.6.3.D
Speaking & Listening - SL.6.1.A, SL.6.1.C

RESOURCES

Descriptive Details Graphic organizer

Access 1 handout (Beginner)

Access 2 handout (Intermediate)

Access 3 handout (Advanced)

Access 4 handout (Approaching)

Please note that excerpts and passages in the StudySync® library, workbooks, and PDFs are intended as touchstones to generate interest in an author's work. The excerpts and passages do not substitute for the reading of entire texts, and StudySync® strongly recommends that teachers and students seek out and purchase the whole literary or informational work in order to experience it as the author intended. Links to online resellers are available in our digital library. In addition, complete works may be ordered through an authorized reseller by filling out and returning to StudySync® the order form enclosed in this workbook.

Teacher's Edition   367

1. DEFINE

Core Path	Access Path
Read and Discuss. Either individually or as a class, read the Define section of the lesson. In small groups or as a class, use these questions to spur discussion among your students about descriptive details: 1. The definition explains that writers develop their stories in part by using description and descriptive details. Why are details important in a narrative? What would a story be like without them? (Descriptive details help readers understand the characters' experiences. They use specific language that helps readers "see" what is happening in the story. Some details appeal to one of the five senses. Without description and descriptive details, the story would probably be just a series of statements about what the characters did. Details help flesh out the characters and the world in which they live.) 2. The definition states clearly that it is important for the descriptive details to be relevant. It also says that it's possible to have too many details. Why is it important to include only relevant details? (Relevant details tell readers what they need to know about characters or events in a story. Irrelevant details are details that are distracting because they don't help readers "see" what is going on. By including only relevant details, writers help readers get through the story and not get bogged down by unnecessary details.)	**Beginner** **In Your Own Words.** Have students read the definition and then use their Access 1 handouts to pause after each bullet point to rewrite the components of descriptive details in their own words. Once students have completed this activity, ask them to complete the fill-in-the-blanks activity on the Access 1 handout. If students have any difficulty with the words in the definition, refer them to the Glossary on their Access 1 handout. **Intermediate** **In Your Own Words.** Have students read the definition of descriptive details and then use their Access 2 handout to pause after each bullet point to rewrite the components of descriptive details in their own words. After they've rewritten each of the bullet points in their own words, work with students to develop their own definitions of the term. If students have any difficulty with the words in the definition, refer them to the Glossary on their Access 2 handout. **Advanced** **In Your Own Words.** Have Advanced students read and then discuss what they have learned about descriptive details with an English-proficient partner or in mixed-proficiency groups. After their conversation, have Advanced students write the definition of descriptive details on the Access 3 handout.

Core Path	Access Path
3. Why do many stories include details that appeal to the senses? Give an example of a detail from the Student Model or another selection from the unit that appeals to the sense of hearing. Is the detail relevant? (*Sensory language makes readers think about how something looks, sounds, feels, smells, or tastes. As a result, the details draw readers more deeply into the story. An example from the Student Model is when Trey responds to Celia after she mentions Mr. Simon. "'Mr. Simon would never let you do that,' he snarled." The detail is relevant because it shows how angry Trey is.*)	**Approaching** **Restate the Definition.** Have students read the Define section and then use their Access 4 handouts to restate the most important points in their own words. Clarify questions to aid students' comprehension as needed. Then have students participate in mixed-level groups with the class to discuss the purpose of descriptive details in a narrative. If students have any difficulty with the words in the definition, refer them to the Glossary on their Access 4 handout. **Beyond** **Add and Analyze Details.** Have individuals rewrite the same section of the Student Model to add more sensory details. Then have them read and compare their rewritten sections with a partner. Have them discuss the following questions. • Are the added details relevant? Why or why not? • How do the added details change the feeling of the story? • Do you like the story better with the added details? Why or why not?
	Extend **Analyze and Revise.** Have students meet with partners or in small groups. Provide each group with a copy of the following paragraph from a fictional narrative (or story): *It was another school day. As Ted walked to school, he saw many interesting things. In his backpack, he carried the things he needed. As Ted entered the schoolyard, he noticed something surprising. The playground was full of machinery and people wearing hard hats.* Tell students to work together to analyze the details in the paragraph. They should discuss whether the details are relevant or irrelevant. Have them work together to consider ways to make the paragraph more interesting, such as by adding to or revising the descriptive details. Allow students time to add to and revise the descriptive details. Then ask volunteers to share their overall assessment of the paragraph and their suggested changes.

Core Path	Access Path
	Extend **Tech Infusion** **Digital Revising.** Distribute the paragraph for the previous activity as a digital document, such as a Google Doc, which will allow students to write comments and make revisions simultaneously. Ask students to share their revised paragraphs with their comments with the rest of the class.

2. MODEL

Core Path	Access Path
Read and Discuss. As students read the Model text, use these questions to help them understand how to recognize, analyze, and use descriptive details in a story:	**Beginner & Intermediate** **Focus on Active Verbs.** After listening to the Model section and discussion questions, use the instruction on the Access 1 and 2 handouts to give students additional instruction on how to add precise details to their writing. Display the following list of general verbs and other verbs you may choose to add.

Core Path (continued):

1. The Model includes a chart that spotlights several kinds of descriptive details from the Student Model. What do these details have in common? Are they all relevant to the story? How do you know? (They all help readers understand what is going on in the story. They are all relevant because they help readers imagine the story and the characters.)

2. Based on the questions below the Model chart, what are two criteria for determining whether a detail should be included in a story? (The detail needs to be interesting, but it should also help the reader understand something in the story, such as what a character is like or experiencing.)

3. The Model focuses the opening paragraph of the Student Model. How would this paragraph be different if it did not include any of the sensory details? (It would be short and pretty boring. It might just say something like, "Celia's brother Kyle was a poor basketball player. He was teased. The teasing upset her a lot.)

Access Path (continued):

- **walk** (wander, stroll, hike)
- **run** (dash, speed, rush, gallop)
- **said** (exclaim, shout, whisper)
- **saw** (spied, noticed, discovered)

Have the group brainstorm specific verbs that could be used in the place of the general verb. Display this list for them to refer to when they are writing.

Copyright © BookheadEd Learning, LLC

Core Path	Access Path
	Advanced **Fill in the Blanks.** Have students complete the fill-in-the-blanks activity on the Access 3 handout with a partner. Tell them to fill in the blanks in the Student Model excerpt with specific relevant details. Encourage them to think of more than one word that could work for each blank. **Approaching** **Answer Questions.** Have students read or listen to the Model section with a higher level partner. Then have them focus on the boldfaced words in each section of the Student Model graphic organizer and discuss the following questions. • What makes these words and phrases precise? (They are sports terms and active verbs.) • What makes these descriptive details relevant? (They give more information about the character.) • Why is this an example of sensory language? (It appeals to the sense of touch.)
Practice. Have students think of and list descriptive details for their stories by completing the Descriptive Details Graphic Organizer such as the one used in the Model. Students can complete this organizer on paper, or you can create a write assignment on StudySync, and they can submit their organizers online for anonymous peer review. Comments should focus on how relevant the details are to the story, how precise the writer's language is, and how vivid the descriptive or sensory words are.	**Beginner & Intermediate** **Support Writing.** Students may use the chart in the Practice section of the Access 1 and 2 handouts instead of or in addition to the Descriptive Details Graphic Organizer. **Advanced** **Review and Evaluate.** Have students share their completed Descriptive Details Graphic Organizer with a partner and help one another to review their added details using the questions on Access 3 handout. **Approaching** **Use Questions.** As students complete their Descriptive Details Graphic Organizer, remind them to use the questions listed on their Access 4 handout to help them decide what details to add.

Please note that excerpts and passages in the StudySync® library, workbooks, and PDFs are intended as touchstones to generate interest in an author's work. The excerpts and passages do not substitute for the reading of entire texts, and StudySync® strongly recommends that teachers and students seek out and purchase the whole literary or informational work in order to experience it as the author intended. Links to online resellers are available in our digital library. In addition, complete works may be ordered through an authorized reseller by filling out and returning to StudySync® the order form enclosed in this workbook.

Teacher's Edition   371

Core Path	Access Path
	Extend **Jigsaw.** 1. Have students count off from 1 to 3. Place students with the same number in groups. 2. Assign each group a type of descriptive detail. For example, assign the 1's precise words and phrases. 3. Then give each group a paragraph or section from the Student Model or another narrative from the unit. Allow students time to scan the text for their group's type of descriptive detail. Students should highlight the details or make a list of them. 4. Then have groups discuss the impact of the descriptive details they found in the text. They should consider how the text would be affected if the details had not been included. 5. Lead a class discussion in which a representative from each group gives a brief summary of the details in the text. After each group has presented, talk together about what students learned from the activity about the relevance or importance of descriptive details in fictional narratives.

3. YOUR TURN

Core Path	Access Path
Assess and Explain. Have students answer the comprehension questions to test for understanding. Share the explanations for Part A and B (located online) with your students.	

Core Path	Access Path
	Extend **Write.** Have students work in pairs to select a different paragraph or section from the Student Model or another selection in the unit as the basis for the same types of questions: • Which sentence from the section contains a descriptive detail that appeals to one of the five senses? • To which sense does the descriptive detail you identified in Part A appeal?

EXTENDED WRITING PROJECT:
Plan

OVERVIEW

This lesson asks students to plan the draft of their fictional narrative. Using their completed Organize Narrative Writing Graphic Organizer and their Descriptive Details Graphic Organizer, they will complete a Story Road Map to organize and develop the characters, setting, and events of their story.

OBJECTIVES

1. Demonstrate understanding of narrative writing skills: Plan Narrative Writing
2. Plan a fictional narrative by creating a Story Road Map for developing characters, setting, and story structure
3. Participate effectively in a range of conversations and collaborations to express ideas and build upon the ideas of others.

ELA Common Core Standards:
Writing - W.6.3.A, W.6.3.B, W.6.3.D, W.6.3.E, W.6.5, W.6.6
Speaking & Listening - SL.6.1.A, SL.6.1.C, SL.6.1.D

RESOURCES

Completed Organize Narrative Writing Graphic organizer
Completed Descriptive Details Graphic organizer
Story Road Map Graphic organizer
Access 1 handout (Beginner)
Access 2 handout (Intermediate)

1. WRITE

Core Path	Access Path
Discuss. As a class, review the concept of story structure, along with the characteristics of organizational patterns, as used in narrative writing. Remind students that most stories employ chronological order to tell events in the sequence in which they happen—from the beginning to the end. Explain that some writers start their stories in the middle or at the end in order to challenge readers or to make the stories more suspenseful. Students should consider which techniques, if any, to use to vary the time order of their story. For example, they can use a flashback or a flash forward to provide hints about the characters and the plot. In addition, writers also can vary the pacing of events, lingering on some sections and moving quickly through others to propel the story forward and hold readers' attention. If a writer wishes to describe events and characters in great detail in a specific section of a story, the pacing will be slower there than in other sections of the story.	**Beginner & Intermediate** **Use Sentence Frames.** Include Beginning and Intermediate students in the whole class discussion. Then work with a small group to have them discuss their own writing ideas using the sentence frames on the Access 1 and 2 handouts. Once they've had a chance to discuss their own ideas, ask them to complete the final sentence frame stating which organizational structure they think will work best for their narratives.

Read through the writing prompt's seven suggestions about what students' narratives should include. Then ask the class to consider the following questions:

- What conflict, or problem, do your characters face?

- How do your characters deal with the problem? Do they stand up for themselves or for someone else?

- How do your characters grow or change as the story moves forward?

- What are some specific details you will include to help readers understand the setting, characters, and events in your story? Which descriptive details are the most relevant to your story?

Core Path	Access Path
• What happens to your characters at the end of the story? Does the conclusion follow naturally and logically from events in the plot as well as from characters' actions? Solicit examples of answers from the class.	
Organize. Remind students that, as part of the planning process, they will use the Organize Narrative Writing Graphic Organizer and the Descriptive Details Graphic Organizer they have completed in previous skills lessons. Encourage students to make use of these organizers as they create their Story Road Map. Note that their Road Map assignment requires them to plan the beginning, middle, and end of their story. Point out that, as students plan the sequence of events in their story, they may wish to structure events in a different way from what they had originally decided, in order to build anticipation, mystery, or suspense. Remind them that, as they write their stories, they'll have the opportunity to fully develop the characters and events they've outlined on their Story Road Map by using the narrative techniques of dialogue, pacing, and description.	**Note:** As the on- and beyond-grade-level students begin the organization and writing stage of this lesson, support Beginning, Intermediate, and Approaching students to ensure they understand what type of information they need to include in their story road maps. **Beginner & Intermediate** **Preview Story Road Map.** Give students the Story Road Map Graphic Organizer and explain what kind of information they will write in each section. Have them review their previously completed assignments to identify and underline character names and details they can use in each section of their story road map. **Approaching** **Use Organizational Supports.** Make sure students have access to all of their previous assignments to draw upon. Then preview the Story Road Map Graphic Organizer to help them structure their organization. Go over each of the categories. Explain that they can use information from their previously completed assignments to help them complete their graphic organizer.

Core Path	Access Path
	Extend **Tech Infusion** **Explore Organizational Options and Features.** Suggest that students use a presentation app, such as Aurasma (http://tinyurl.com/o25s8kn) to record themselves as they work alone or with a partner to complete their Story Road Maps. Guide students to use their tablet devices to take a picture of their completed Organize Narrative Writing Timeline organizer. Then they can record videos of themselves as they talk and take notes about the process of determining the order of story events. Remind students to consider these textual and visual features, which can help them clarify the order of events: • Clear transition words and phrases • Scene or chapter titles that identify time or place • Scene or chapter numbers • Scene or chapter titles that tell who is narrating the scene or chapter If students are working with partners, the partners should ask questions about how changes to the order of story events or the addition of an event might affect the story's timeline or flow of events.
Write. Ask students to complete the writing assignment by inserting ideas and details about their story's setting and characters, as well as their story's beginning, middle, and end, onto a Story Road Map. Once they have completed their plan for their fictional narrative, they should click "Submit."	**Beginner** **Complete Story Road Map with Support.** Help students use the underlined sections of their previously completed materials to fill in the Story Road Map Graphic Organizer. Before writing, have them use their previously completed assignments to help them state orally what they want to write in each section to evaluate where they may need help with vocabulary, grammar, and sentence structure. You can work with Beginning students individually as needed or in a small group offering support to multiple students at one time. Then have them write, providing assistance as needed.

Core Path	Access Path
	Intermediate
	Write and Discuss. Remind students that they can use what they underlined in their previous assignments to complete their Story Road Map Graphic Organizer. Have partners or small groups ask one another questions about the content of their completed story road maps such as:
	• Did you include all your characters?
	• What is the setting of your story? Is there more than one setting? What is it?
	• What is the problem or conflict at the beginning of your story?
	• How do your characters try to solve the problem in the middle?
	• What is the solution at the end?
	Have them make any changes necessary before submitting their writing for further peer review.
	Advanced
	Clarify Organization. Have students share their completed Story Road Map Graphic Organizer with another Advanced or English-proficient partner. Have them work together to answer the following questions about their writing and make changes if necessary:
	• Did I fill out all the details I need for each section?
	• Do I have all the correct events in the beginning, middle, and end?
	• Are there any other story events or details I should add?
	Approaching
	Complete Story Road Map. Provide students with the following questions to help them complete and review their Story Road Map Graphic Organizer.
	• Did I include all my characters?
	• If there is more than one setting in my story, did I include them all?

Core Path	Access Path
	• Did I introduce a problem or conflict at the beginning? • Did I include how the characters try to solve the problem in the middle? • Did I provide a solution at the end?
Review. Once students have completed their writing assignment, they should submit substantive feedback to two peers. Students should use the feedback they receive to strengthen the content and organization of their Road Map.	

Please note that excerpts and passages in the StudySync® library, workbooks, and PDFs are intended as touchstones to generate interest in an author's work. The excerpts and passages do not substitute for the reading of entire texts, and StudySync® strongly recommends that teachers and students seek out and purchase the whole literary or informational work in order to experience it as the author intended. Links to online resellers are available in our digital library. In addition, complete works may be ordered through an authorized reseller by filling out and returning to StudySync® the order form enclosed in this workbook.

Teacher's Edition   379

SKILL:
Introduction

OVERVIEW

As students move toward the drafting stage of their Extended Writing Project, they will need to consider how to begin their story. This lesson explains the purpose and features of the introduction (or beginning) of a fictional narrative. It also helps students understand how to write a successful introduction to "hook" their readers from the beginning.

OBJECTIVES

1. Demonstrate an understanding of what makes a strong introduction (or beginning) in a fictional narrative.
2. Practice using concrete strategies for identifying and writing the beginning of a fictional narrative.
3. Participate effectively in a range of conversations and collaborations to express ideas and build upon the ideas of others.

ELA Common Core Standards:
Reading: Literature - RL.6.1, RL.6.5
Writing - W.6.3.A, W.6.5, W.6.10
Speaking & Listening - SL.6.1.A, SL.6.1.C, SL.6.1.D

RESOURCES

Access 1 handout (Beginner)

Access 2 handout (Intermediate)

Access 3 handout (Advanced)

Access 4 handout (Approaching)

1. DEFINE

Core Path	Access Path
Read and Discuss. Either individually or as a class, read the Define section of the lesson. Either in small groups or as a class, use these questions to engage students in a discussion about the purpose and function of the introduction in a fictional narrative:	**Beginner** **In Your Own Words.** Have students read the definition and then use their Access 1 handouts to pause after each bullet point to rewrite the components of an introduction in their own words. Once students have completed this activity, ask them to complete the fill-in-the-blanks activity on the Access 1 handout.

Read and Discuss. Either individually or as a class, read the Define section of the lesson. Either in small groups or as a class, use these questions to engage students in a discussion about the purpose and function of the introduction in a fictional narrative:

1. The definition says that the beginning of a story should provide readers with important details. What are those details and why do readers need them? (The details are about the story's setting, narrator and characters, plot, conflict, and theme. These details help set up the story. Without them, readers will not know what is going on.)

2. According to the definition, what does a strong introduction do? (It "captures readers' attention"; it makes them want to keep reading the rest of the story.)

3. The definition suggests that if the introduction isn't interesting and doesn't provide details, readers are not likely to keep reading. Do you agree? Why or why not? (Most readers start a story at the beginning. And most turn to stories for entertainment. If the beginning does not provide important details and make an effort to keep readers' interest, readers will likely go elsewhere to be entertained.)

Beginner

In Your Own Words. Have students read the definition and then use their Access 1 handouts to pause after each bullet point to rewrite the components of an introduction in their own words. Once students have completed this activity, ask them to complete the fill-in-the-blanks activity on the Access 1 handout.

Intermediate

In Your Own Words. Have students read the definition of an introduction and then use their Access 2 handout to pause after each bullet point to rewrite the components of an introduction in their own words. After they've rewritten each of the bullet points in their own words, work with students to develop their own definitions of the term.

Advanced

In Your Own Words. Have Advanced students read and then discuss what they have learned about introductions with an English-proficient partner or in mixed-proficiency groups. After their conversation, have Advanced students write the definition of an introduction on the Access 3 handout.

Approaching

Restate the Definition. Have students read the Define section and then use their Access 4 handouts to restate the most important points in their own words. Clarify questions to aid students' comprehension as needed. Then have students participate in mixed-level groups with the class to discuss the purpose of an introduction in a fictional narrative.

Core Path	Access Path
	Beyond **Make an Introduction.** Have students meet with partners to spend a few minutes asking questions and learning about each other. Suggest students ask their partners the following questions: *What is your full name? Where do you live? Where is your family from? What is the most interesting thing about you?* Students should take notes as their partners answer the questions. Then ask volunteers to introduce their partners to the rest of the class. Tell students that their goal is to convey information and also make the person sound as interesting as possible. After students have shared, draw connections to the writing of a story's introduction. Point out how identifying a character and sharing interesting details about him or her is the way many stories begin.
	Extend **Tech Infusion** **Online Sharing.** Use Padlet (http://tinyurl.com/n7l7cyy) or another sharing app to create a private wall for the classroom. Have students write brief versions of the introductions in the Beyond activity above and post them on the wall. Consider providing a limit on the number of words or characters of the introductions so that students learn to focus on the most important details.

2. MODEL

Core Path	Access Path
Read and Discuss. As students read the Identification and Application text and the Model text, use these questions to help them understand the function of the beginning of a story.	**Beginner, Intermediate, & Approaching Read with Support.** 1. Preview the vocabulary terms in the model glossary on the Access 1, 2, and 4 handouts with students before they read or listen to the text.

Core Path

1. What is exposition, and why do readers need it? (Exposition tells readers the important details of the story—who the characters are, what their conflict or problem is, and when and where the story is set. Without exposition, readers are likely to be confused.)

2. What is a hook and why should a narrative begin with one? (A hook is an exciting moment, a detailed description, or a surprising comment that grabs readers' attention right at the beginning of the story. It is important because it gets readers interested in the rest of the story.)

3. According to the model text, an effective story provides hints about the story's theme or big idea. How does that help readers? (By dropping hints about the theme in the introduction, the writer helps readers focus on the big idea or message the story is about.)

4. What are some elements shared by the beginnings of both fiction and nonfiction narratives? (Readers learn who the narrator is; both types include a hook and establish the context for the story, such as characters and real individuals who will be prominently featured, setting, structure, and what the story will be about.)

Access Path

2. Have them restate each term in their own words. Help them to clarify their understanding as necessary.

3. Have them listen to the Model or read it aloud with an English proficient or Advanced partner.

4. They can join with the whole class or mixed-level groups to discuss the questions.

Advanced

Read with Mixed-level Partners. Have Advanced students read the Model section with a Beginning or Intermediate partner. Have them provide language clarification for their partner as needed. Then have them join in mixed-level groups for the discussion.

Extend

Analyze. Show the class the opening scene of an appropriate classic film, such as *The Secret Garden*, *Babe*, or *E.T.* Then have students work with partners or in a small group to identify and discuss the elements of an effective introduction or story beginning. Provide students with these questions: *How did the opening of the film "hook" my interest? How well did it introduce the characters and the conflict? Did the film start at the beginning of the story or at another point? What big ideas about life did the opening of the film hint at?* Lead students in a discussion of their answers to these questions. Finally, remind them to apply the answers to their own story introductions.

Please note that excerpts and passages in the StudySync® library, workbooks, and PDFs are intended as touchstones to generate interest in an author's work. The excerpts and passages do not substitute for the reading of entire texts, and StudySync® strongly recommends that teachers and students seek out and purchase the whole literary or informational work in order to experience it as the author intended. Links to online resellers are available in our digital library. In addition, complete works may be ordered through an authorized reseller by filling out and returning to StudySync® the order form enclosed in this workbook.

Teacher's Edition   383

Core Path	Access Path
	Extend **Create.** For practice, have students write their own version of the opening scene of the film they viewed in the previous activity. Students should include the features of an effective introduction while at the same time accurately reflecting the characters and events in the film's opening scene. Remind students to use the opening sequence of the film you showed them as an inspiration for writing their own story introductions.
Practice. Have each student write a beginning for his or her story that includes a hook to "reel in" the reader. The introduction should introduce the narrator and establish context for the story, such as the setting and conflict or problem faced by the main character or characters. Once students have completed their rough draft introductions either on sheets of paper or online (*Note: you will need to create a write assignment if they are going to submit their introduction online), they will need to provide their peers with constructive feedback either on paper or online. Comments should focus on how effectively the writer introduces the context of the narrative, including the narrator and setting, and how successful the "hook" is in engaging the reader. Students should use the feedback they receive to strengthen the beginning of their story.	**Beginner** **Write with Support.** Work with students as they use the 'Write Introduction' exercise on Access 1 handout to support writing their introduction. Allow them to first state orally what they want to write, and then help them to clarify language as necessary. **Intermediate** **Write and Discuss.** Have students use the 'Write Introduction' exercise on Access 2 handout to support writing their introduction. Then have them partner with an Advanced or English-proficient partner to discuss their introduction. **Advanced** **Discuss and Edit.** Have students write their introductions independently, and then partner with an English-proficient student to give and receive feedback, editing language and concepts in their introductions as necessary. **Approaching** **Finish the Sentences & Complete the Fill in the Blank Introduction.** 1. Prior to writing their introductions, ask students to complete the sentence frames on the Access 4 handout.

Core Path	Access Path
	2. Once they have completed the statements with the information they plan to write about, allow students to use the fill-in-the-blank introduction provided on the Access 4 handout to construct their introductions. Remind students to include a hook, such as an exciting moment, a detailed description, or a surprising or thoughtful comment made by the narrator or main character. Additionally, you may want to remind students that the introduction usually introduces at least one character and may reveal the setting.
	Extend **Tech Infusion.** Ask students to share their revised introductions using a shared TodaysMeet backchannel. Project the backchannel onto the board and discuss the introductions as a class. • What do students notice about the introductions? Are there commonalities? • Which introductions are particularly effective? Why? What elements make them strong?

3. YOUR TURN

Core Path	Access Path
Assess and Explain. Have students answer the comprehension questions to test for understanding. Share the explanations for Part A and B (located online) with your students.	
	Extend **Write.** Before students check their answers to the Your Turn questions, have them work alone or with a partner to write their own rationales for the answer choices. Students should write one sentence for each answer choice, explaining why it is or is not correct. Then students can check their rationales against the real ones. If students disagree with the real rationales, lead a brief discussion of the question and its correct answer.

OVERVIEW

As students move toward the planning stage of their Extended Writing Project, they'll need to consider the manner in which they choose to tell their story. This lesson identifies the variety of tools that writers use to develop the plot and characters, explore the setting, and engage the reader.

OBJECTIVES

1. Demonstrate an understanding of narrative techniques and sequencing, including rising and falling action, in a fictional narrative.
2. Practice analyzing and using techniques, including description, pacing, and dialogue, to develop the characters, setting, and plot of a fictional narrative.
3. Participate effectively in a range of conversations and collaborations to express ideas and build upon the ideas of others.
4. Practice strategies for punctuating restrictive and nonrestrictive elements correctly.

ELA Common Core Standards:
Reading: Literature - RL.6.1, RL.6.3, RL.6.5
Writing - W.6.3.A, W.6.3.B, W.6.3.C, W.6.3.D, W.6.5, W.6.10
Speaking & Listening - SL.6.1.A, SL.6.1.C, SL.6.1.D
Language - L.6.2.A

RESOURCES

Grammar handout: Restrictive and Nonrestrictive Elements

Access 1 handout (Beginner)

Access 2 handout (Intermediate)

Access 3 handout (Advanced)

Access 4 handout (Approaching)

1. DEFINE

Core Path	Access Path
Read and Discuss. Either individually or as a class, read the Define section of the lesson. In small groups or as a class, use these questions to stimulate discussion among your students about a fictional narrative:	**Beginner** **In Your Own Words.** Have students read the definition of narrative techniques and sequencing and then use their Access 1 handouts to pause after each bullet point to rewrite the components of narrative techniques and sequencing in their own words. Once students have completed this activity, ask them to complete the fill in the blanks activity on the Access 1 handout.
1. What happens following the beginning part of a story? (The story develops the plot and tells how the characters try to solve the conflict, or problem, in the story.)	
2. The definition explains that writers manipulate the pacing of a narrative to slow down or speed up the action at certain parts of a story. What do you think this means? How do you think writers can manipulate a story's pacing? (An author can create suspense by pacing and drawing out a moment of uncertainty. Varying pacing is a way of adding interest to a story and holding readers' attention.)	**Intermediate** **In Your Own Words.** Have students read the definition of narrative techniques and sequencing and then use their Access 2 handouts to pause after each bullet point to rewrite the components of narrative techniques and sequencing in their own words. After they've rewritten each of the bullet points in their own words, work with students to develop their own definitions of the term.
3. The definition states that narrative sequencing follows a certain order: exposition, rising action, climax, falling action, resolution. What would happen to a story if the writer didn't follow that order? (Sample answer: Authors sometimes break these rules to create interesting or unexpected twists in their stories. For example, a writer might open with a flashback, without explaining who the characters are or what exactly is happening until the following chapter or section. This can create interest on the part of the reader, who keeps reading to find out what exactly is going on.) **Can you think of any stories that don't follow that order?** (Answers will vary.)	**Advanced** **In Your Own Words.** Have Advanced students read and then discuss what they have learned about narrative techniques and sequencing with an English-proficient partner or in mixed-proficiency groups. After their conversation, have Advanced students write the definition of narrative techniques and sequencing on the Access 3 handout. **Approaching** **Restate the Definition.** Have students read the Define section and then use their Access 4 handouts to restate the most important points in their own words. Clarify questions to aid students' comprehension as needed. Then have students participate in mixed-level groups with the class to discuss the purpose of narrative techniques and sequencing in a narrative.

Core Path	Access Path
	Beyond **Rewrite.** Have partners choose a substantial body paragraph from the Student Model and annotate it to point out what the author did well and what could be improved. Then have students rewrite the paragraph with their proposed improvements. Invite them to share and explain their rewrite to the class.
	Extend **Tech Infusion** **Analyze and Assess.** Find an appropriate fictional narrative and provide students with an excerpt of its middle section in a Google document. Have students work in small groups to analyze and assess the middle section by answering the following questions: • What plot events are taking place in these body paragraphs? • What do you notice about each character's words? • What transition words or phrases did the author use? What kinds of relationships did they suggest? • Are there places in the body paragraphs that you think would have been clearer if the writer had used a transition or, if there was one, a different transition? • How well does the writer balance dialogue and description in these body paragraphs? • What do you notice about the characters? How are they growing or changing? Students can use comments and editing and highlighting tools to annotate the document as they analyze and assess. Then lead a class discussion of how well the narrative's middle section used dialogue and transition words or phrases. Talk about how it moved the story forward and allowed the characters to grow and develop.

2. MODEL

Core Path	Access Path
Read and Discuss. As students read the Model text, use these questions to help them understand how to develop the characters and events of a story:	**Beginner & Intermediate** **Read and Answer.** Have Beginning and Intermediate students work in pairs. As they read the excerpt from the Student Model, have them refer to their Access 1 and 2 handouts. Have students follow the directions for identifying narrative techniques used in the text.

Core Path

1. According to the Model, what are some techniques that writers use to help develop events, experiences, and characters? (Description, including descriptive details, precise language, and sensory language; pacing; and dialogue.)

2. The Model explains that the paragraphs in the middle section of a story help develop the events. What events are covered in paragraphs 3–6 of the Student Model? (The paragraphs talk about how the narrator, Celia, feels about her brother getting teased. They also tell what the two characters say to each other.)

3. What is the relationship between paragraphs 4–5 to paragraph 3? (In paragraph 3, Celia describes what Kyle does well: cook. In paragraphs 4 and 5, she describes her reaction when her brother is teased for his poor athletic ability, and how she wants to help him.)

4. Why do some of these paragraphs include dialogue? (They reveal character information and vary pacing.)

5. What vivid descriptive detail does the Model cite to demonstrate how details develop character? (stirring a batch of vegetable soup)

Access Path

Approaching
Read and Answer. Have students join with the rest of the class for the general instruction. Then have them complete the Read and Answer activity on their Access 4 handouts independently or with a partner.

Core Path	Access Path

Core Path

⚙ Grammar, Usage, and Mechanics. Distribute the StudySync grammar handout on restrictive and nonrestrictive elements. Explain to students that writers of narratives find the use of nonrestrictive phrases and clauses particularly effective in first-person narration and in dialogue. This is because, in addition to adding meaning and varying pacing, they often make a character's speech or thoughts sound more realistic. Have students review the examples of restrictive and nonrestrictive elements on the handout before completing the practice exercise. (Answers for the practice exercise appear at the end of the lesson plan online.) After students have completed the exercise, point out these two passages from the Student Model and ask students to explain how the use of a nonrestrictive phrase or clause adds meaning.

1. Kyle even made ribs for the whole family last week—with just a little help from my dad. And Kyle's smart at a lot of things—especially science. (Although the nonrestrictive phrases "with just a little help from my dad" and "especially science" are not necessary information, they add meaning by making Kyle's description even more impressive. A reader might have assumed that Kyle had help with the ribs, and the nonrestrictive phrase makes it clear that he made the ribs mostly on his own. The phrase "especially" science" clarifies that Kyle is good at something many people would consider especially difficult.)

2. "Missed again," one of them—a boy named Trey—hissed just loud enough for Kyle to hear. (The phrase "a boy named Trey" is a nonrestrictive element in this sentence because knowing exactly who said the remark about Kyle is not as important as knowing that it's said at all. However, it also indicates that knowing the boy's name will perhaps be important to readers later.)

Access Path

Beginner & Intermediate
Teacher Support. Have Beginning and Intermediate students take part in the class instruction, then work with them separately to provide additional support. Explain the following:

*   **Restrictive** - A sentence *will not* make sense if the restrictive clause is removed. Don't use punctuation around a restrictive clause.

*   **Nonrestrictive -** A sentence *will* make sense if the restrictive clause is removed. Use punctuation such as commas, dashes, or parentheses around a restrictive clause.

Work with them to complete the practice items. Walk students through each item using the same modeling routine as is outlined above for Approaching students.

Advanced
Write Examples. Have students participate in the class instruction and complete the practice exercise with an Advanced partner. Then have them think of a sentence with a restrictive or nonrestrictive clause that they could write for their narrative. When they are done writing, have them share it with their partner. Have their partner identify the restrictive or nonrestrictive clause and check for correct punctuation.

Approaching
Model.

1. Have students join in the class instruction for restrictive and nonrestrictive elements.

2. Before they begin the practice items, model deciding whether the first item is restrictive or nonrestrictive. Read the sentence aloud. Then cover up the underlined phrase and read it again. Ask, *Does this sentence make sense without the underlined clause?* (Yes, it is nonrestrictive.) *Do we need to use punctuation around the nonrestrictive clause?* (Yes.) Have students decide whether to use commas, parentheses, or dashes, and rewrite the sentence.

Core Path	Access Path
Finally, tell students that, as they begin to draft their narratives, they should consider adding nonrestrictive elements to clarify ideas and make their writing sound more natural. Remind them to be sure to punctuate these elements correctly, using commas, dashes, or parentheses as needed.	3. Have them complete the remaining practice items with an on-level partner.

Practice. Ask students to complete a short writing assignment and apply the skills they have learned to write a draft of a paragraph that contributes to their story's rising action.

Once students have completed their rough draft paragraph either on sheets of paper or online (*Note: you will need to create a write assignment if they are going to submit their body paragraph online), they will need to provide their peers with constructive feedback either on paper or online. Comments should focus on how well the writer has developed an event that builds anticipation as the story moves toward a climax. Has the writer used sensory language, dialogue, or specific details effectively in his or her paragraph? How clear is the text structure, and are transitions used as needed to clarify any changes in time or setting, or to link ideas? Has the writer included nonrestrictive phrases or clauses and punctuated them correctly?

Remind students that a peer reviewer's comments are most useful when they are clear, constructive, and presented with a positive and supportive attitude. Make sure students understand your expectations for all aspects of the assignment before they begin their work. Students should use the comments they receive to improve their writing.

Beginner
Finish the Sentences. Read aloud the Writing Frame questions on Access 1 handout to help students organize and plan their paragraph. Allow them to answer orally before writing. Provide assistance with language as they write.

Intermediate
Finish the Sentences. Have students use the Writing Frame questions on the Access 2 handout to help them organize and plan their paragraph. Have them review their paragraph with an Advanced or English-proficient student.

Advanced
Use Language Elements. Remind students of the language elements they learned about in this lesson. Encourage them to use at least one sentence with a transition word and one sentence with a restrictive or nonrestrictive clause in their paragraph.

Approaching
Finish the Sentences. Have students use the Writing Frame questions on the Access 4 handout to help them organize and plan their paragraph.

Core Path	Access Path
	Extend **Scramble.** Split the class into four or five equal groups and give each group an envelope with slips of paper in it. In the envelope, they'll find slips with the terms *exposition, rising action, climax, falling action,* and *resolution* on them. Mixed in, they'll find slips of paper with details or events from a story in the unit (or a story that everyone in the class is familiar with). For example, you might write "When supper was ready, I eagerly grabbed the iron bell before Christopher-John or Little Man could claim it and ran onto the back porch to summon Papa, Mr. Morrison, and Stacey from the fields," as a piece of exposition from *Roll of Thunder, Hear My Cry*. You may choose to include several details for each part of the sequence of events, depending on the reading level of your students. Each group will need to put the sequence in order, and group the correct details from the story with the correct part of the sequence. You could turn it into a contest or race, giving the first group to get them all right a reward (or just bragging rights).
	Extend **Critique.** Project a body paragraph from the middle of an appropriate fictional narrative (or story) onto the board and ask the class to critique its use of transition words and phrases. Ask them which other elements of the writing they think are particularly strong and which are in need of improvement. Alternatively, you can put students in small groups and give them photocopies of a body paragraph to evaluate collaboratively. Then work as a class to generate strategies students can use as they complete their peer reviews to ensure that their critiques are substantive.

3. YOUR TURN

Core Path	Access Path
Assess and Explain. Have students answer the comprehension questions to test for understanding. Share the explanations for Parts A and B (located online) with your students.	
	Extend **Write.** Have students work in pairs to write a new and original two-part question about the excerpt from the Student Model. Challenge students to write a question that addresses the features of the middle section of a fictional narrative and that requires textual evidence in order to answer it. Students should also provide rationales that explain the answers to the questions. Compile students' questions and answers. Use the best ones as the basis for a quiz or assessment.

Please note that excerpts and passages in the StudySync® library, workbooks, and PDFs are intended as touchstones to generate interest in an author's work. The excerpts and passages do not substitute for the reading of entire texts, and StudySync® strongly recommends that teachers and students seek out and purchase the whole literary or informational work in order to experience it as the author intended. Links to online resellers are available in our digital library. In addition, complete works may be ordered through an authorized reseller by filling out and returning to StudySync® the order form enclosed in this workbook.

Teacher's Edition   393

OVERVIEW

As students move toward the drafting stage of their Extended Writing Project, they will need to consider how to end their stories. This lesson explains the features and purpose of a satisfying conclusion.

OBJECTIVES

1. Demonstrate an understanding of the features and purpose of the conclusion of a fictional narrative (or story).
2. Examine and practice strategies for concluding fictional narrative texts.
3. Participate effectively in a range of conversations and collaborations to express ideas and build upon the ideas of others.

   ELA Common Core Standards:
   Reading: Literature - RL.6.1, RL.6.2, RL.6.5
   Writing - W.6.3.E, W.6.5, W.6.10
   Speaking & Listening - SL.6.1.A, SL.6.1.C

RESOURCES

Access 1 handout (Beginner)

Access 2 handout (Intermediate)

Access 3 handout (Advanced)

Access 4 handout (Approaching)

1. DEFINE

Core Path	Access Path
Read and Discuss. Either individually or as a class, read the Define section of the lesson. In small groups or as a class, use these questions to spark discussion among your students about the purpose and function of the end of a fictional narrative:	**Beginner** **In Your Own Words.** Have students read the definition and then use their Access 1 handouts to pause after each bullet point to rewrite the components of a conclusion in their own words. Once students have completed this activity, ask them to complete the fill in the blanks activity on the Access 1 handout.
1. According to the definition, what is the purpose of a narrative's conclusion? (The point of the conclusion is to wrap up the story by telling readers what happens to the characters and how they solved their problems.)	**Intermediate** **In Your Own Words.** Have students read the definition of a conclusion and then use their Access 2 handout to pause after each bullet point to rewrite the components of a conclusion in their own words. After they've rewritten each of the bullet points in their own words, work with students to develop their own definitions of the term.
2. The definition explains that the ending of a fictional narrative (or story) is also called the resolution. What is a resolution? Why does it appear in the conclusion? (The resolution tells how the characters' problems are solved. It makes sense to appear in the conclusion, or end of the story, because that is where the story events are wrapped up.)	**Advanced** **In Your Own Words.** Have Advanced students read and then discuss what they have learned about conclusions with an English-proficient partner or in mixed-proficiency groups. After their conversation, have Advanced students write the definition of conclusion on the Access 3 handout.
3. Why would a narrative's writer want his or her readers to draw inferences about the story's theme? Why not just state it outright? (Some writers do state their themes outright, but it can be more interesting and engaging for readers if a writer reveals clues about the theme of his or her story that readers have to figure out on their own. Readers can often find more than one theme for a particular story.)	**Approaching** **Restate the Definition.** Have students read the Define section and then use their Access 4 handouts to restate the most important points in their own words. Clarify questions to aid students' comprehension as needed. Then have students participate in mixed-level groups with the class to discuss the purpose of a conclusion in a fictional narrative.

Core Path	Access Path
	Beyond **Rewrite.** Have partners annotate the conclusion from the Student Model to point out what the author did well and what could be improved. Then have students rewrite the conclusion with their proposed improvements. Invite them to share and explain their rewrite with the class.
	Extend **Tech Infusion** **Review.** Create a multimedia post-it note canvas using a website like Lino (http://tinyurl.com/n6nf78/) for students to weigh in on the conclusions to the unit's selections. Ask students to create a note that identifies the title of the selection with the conclusion they found most satisfying and also state one reason why it was satisfying. For example, it tied up all the loose ends, it had a surprise twist, it made students think or feel, or it inspired them to read other selections by the same author. As a class, discuss students' choices and reasons. If time allows, ask students to consider one of the selections whose conclusion they did not consider satisfying. Ask for ways the conclusion could have been improved.

2. MODEL

Core Path	Access Path
Read and Discuss. As students read the Model text, use these questions to help them understand the features and purpose of the conclusion: 1. According to the Model, the way a conclusion resolves a character's problem should be "logical." Why? What if a story does not resolve the problem logically? (The resolution should make sense. It should follow naturally from the rest of the story. If it does not, it might seem unrealistic or disconnected and therefore not very satisfying.)	**Beginner, Intermediate & Approaching** **Underline Key Words.** Have students look closely at the Model section on the Access 1, 2, and 4 handouts. Then ask them to find and underline words and phrases that reflect the following components of a conclusion: 1. Identify where the conflict of the excerpt is resolved. 2. Identify where the excerpt tells or shows how the character resolved the conflict.

Core Path	Access Path

Core Path

2. According to the Model, the conclusion might also include a memorable comment that helps readers understand the theme. Why is the conclusion a good place to do this? (The conclusion is the last thing a reader reads. That is the best place to include a statement or comment that hints at the message or theme of the selection—so readers can think about it even after they finish reading the story.)

3. What do the last few paragraphs of the Student Model do? (They resolve the conflict by having George and Kyle make gestures toward friendship, and by having Celia feel great relief at the way things have worked out. The last sentences end on an amusing note.)

Practice. Ask students to complete a short writing assignment and apply the skills they have learned for writing a satisfying conclusion to a story.

Once students have completed their rough draft conclusions either on sheets of paper or online (*Note: you will need to create a write assignment if they are going to submit their conclusions online), they will need to provide their peers with constructive feedback either on paper or online. Comments should focus on how well the characters' problems are resolved, and whether the conclusion follows from the events in the story. Students should use the feedback they receive to strengthen their conclusions.

Access Path

3. Identify, if available, where the author makes a memorable comment from the narrator or a character to help the reader understand the theme.

After students finish identifying these words and phrases, have them briefly explain their reasoning in small groups or in a class discussion.

Advanced
Identify the Parts. Have students read the Model excerpt and answer the questions on the Access 3 handout. Once they've completed the questions, pair Advanced students with more proficient students to allow them to share their answers.

Beginner
Write with Support. Read aloud the 'Write a Story Ending' questions on Access 1 handout to help students organize and plan their story ending. Allow them to answer orally before writing. Provide assistance with language as they write.

Intermediate
Write with Support. Have students use the 'Write a Story Ending' questions on Access 2 handout to help them organize and plan their story ending. After students have completed writing their story ending, have them share with an Advanced or English-proficient partner. Have students check for all elements of a successful conclusion.

Advanced
Write and Evaluate. After students have completed writing their story ending, have them share with a partner who is one proficiency level up or down. Have students check for all elements of a successful conclusion. Students should then offer suggestions for revisions.

Please note that excerpts and passages in the StudySync® library, workbooks, and PDFs are intended as touchstones to generate interest in an author's work. The excerpts and passages do not substitute for the reading of entire texts, and StudySync® strongly recommends that teachers and students seek out and purchase the whole literary or informational work in order to experience it as the author intended. Links to online resellers are available in our digital library. In addition, complete works may be ordered through an authorized reseller by filling out and returning to StudySync® the order form enclosed in this workbook.

Teacher's Edition   397

Core Path	Access Path
	Approaching **Write with Support.** Have students use the 'Write a Story Ending' questions on Access 4 handout to help them organize and plan the ending for their story.
	Extend **Tech Infusion.** **Compare and Contrast.** Have students use an online journaling app, such as Penzu (http://tinyurl.com/ycyxmc2) or a blogging tool, such as Pen.io (http://tinyurl.com/3edm9se) to write comparative reviews of the endings of the Student Model, "Taking the Shot," and another unit selection. Remind students to consider how well each story resolved the characters' problems, hinted at a theme, and gave the readers a satisfying experience. Have students post and exchange their reviews. Randomly select a review and discuss it with the class to get a sense of students' overall reactions to the Student Model and other selections in the unit.
	Extend **Write a New Ending.** Now that students have studied what makes a satisfying conclusion to a narrative, have them choose a selection from the unit and rewrite its ending. For example, students might have wanted a more definitive ending to the excerpt from *Red Scarf Girl*. Allow students time to plan and write a different ending. Remind them of the characteristics of a satisfying ending. Students can post their new endings to the class website or blog. Select a student's work at random and share it with the class. Discuss how and why the new ending is (or is not) more satisfying than the original.

3. YOUR TURN

Core Path	Access Path
Assess and Explain. Have students answer the comprehension questions to test for understanding. Share the explanations for Parts A and B (located online) with your students.	
	Extend **Tech Infusion.** **Analyze Questions.** Have students use a backchannel tool, such as TodaysMeet (http://tinyurl.com/psef72j) to tell you how they determined the answers to the Your Turn questions. Ask students to identify the steps they took to answer the questions—reading the question stem, considering the answer choices, selecting an answer, and then confirm or revise their choice after consulting the answer rationales. Then ask students to share how they might change or improve their approach to answering questions. For example, they might read more carefully and underline or highlight key terms.

Please note that excerpts and passages in the StudySync® library, workbooks, and PDFs are intended as touchstones to generate interest in an author's work. The excerpts and passages do not substitute for the reading of entire texts, and StudySync® strongly recommends that teachers and students seek out and purchase the whole literary or informational work in order to experience it as the author intended. Links to online resellers are available in our digital library. In addition, complete works may be ordered through an authorized reseller by filling out and returning to StudySync® the order form enclosed in this workbook.

Teacher's Edition   399

EXTENDED WRITING PROJECT:
Draft

OVERVIEW

This lesson asks students to write a draft of their fictional narrative. To do so, they will use relevant descriptive details to enrich the introduction, middle, and conclusion of their story. Students are instructed to use the ideas they brainstormed in the Prewrite lesson as well as the graphic organizers they created to help them structure the events of their story. As students write their drafts, they should focus on establishing their narrator, the logic and flow of their organizational structure, the relevance and precision of the descriptive details in creating and developing vivid characters and events, the usefulness of their transitions, and the effectiveness of their conclusion. Before they submit their drafts, students should check to be sure that they have fully addressed the writing prompt.

OBJECTIVES

1. Identify the features of fictional narrative writing: introduction of characters, context, and point of view; logical organization of events; descriptive details to develop characters, setting, and plot; body paragraphs including description, precise and sensory language, dialogue, and transitions; conclusion; and theme.
2. Draft a fictional narrative text in response to a prompt.
3. Participate effectively in a range of conversations and collaborations to express ideas and build upon the ideas of others.

   ELA Common Core Standards:
   Writing - W.6.3.A, W.6.3.B, W.6.3.C, W.6.3.D, W.6.3.E, W.6.4, W.6.5, W.6.6, W.6.10
   Speaking & Listening - SL.6.1.A, SL.6.1.C
   Language - L.6.2.A

RESOURCES

Completed Organize Narrative Writing Timeline

Completed Descriptive Details Graphic organizer

Completed Story Road Map Graphic organizer

Access 1 handout (Beginner)

Access 2 handout (Intermediate)

Access 3 handout (Advanced)

Access 4 handout (Approaching)

1. WRITE

Core Path	Access Path

Discuss. Before students begin to write, review with the class the writing prompt/directions. Have a volunteer read them aloud. Ask whether students have any questions either about the prompt or the directions. Respond to their questions, and explain the importance of addressing the prompt fully and completely. Then read aloud the peer review instructions that students will use to comment on one another's work. Point out that understanding the peer review instructions can help students focus their writing on important features of narrative texts. The peer review instructions ask students to consider the following questions:

- How well does the writer "grab" the readers' attention at the beginning? What suggestions can you make to improve the opening of the story?

- How well does the writer present the setting and introduce the conflict (or problem) that one or more characters will face?

- How has the writer organized the events of the plot? If the events do not flow logically or smoothly, what changes could you suggest?

- How successfully has the writer developed the characters' personalities and the narrator's point of view?

- Which transitions does the writer use? Could he or she use other transitions to make the events in the middle of the story clearer?

- How effectively has the writer used description, precise and sensory language, dialogue, and pacing to develop the story and appeal to readers?

- If the writer has used slang, idiomatic expressions, or dialect, is the language appropriate to the character, narrator, or situation?

English Learners All Levels & Approaching Review Writing Draft Guide. Read aloud the Drafting Guide on the Access 1, 2, 3, and 4 handouts with students. Encourage students to circle unfamiliar words and underline anything that is confusing or unclear. Then take a few minutes to clarify unknown vocabulary, answer questions, and provide examples for any items that students do not understand. Explain that they will need to include each of these items in their writing. For each checklist item, point out an example in the Student Model and read it aloud.

Advanced
Discuss. Have students use the Access 3 handout to review their drafts. Encourage partners to exchange their narratives and engage in peer review and discussion.

Approaching
Work with a Partner. Have pairs of students review the draft of their narrative, using the table on the Access 4 handout to examine and address specific aspects of their writing. Encourage partners to exchange their narratives and engage in peer review and discussion.

Beyond
Critique. If students have extra time, give small groups photocopies of a literature piece to collectively evaluate. Have them identify the elements of writing that are strong, as well as those that are weak or in need of improvement. Then ask them to generate strategies students can use when they complete their peer reviews to ensure their critiques are substantive. Have them make a list of their strategies to share with the class.

Please note that excerpts and passages in the StudySync® library, workbooks, and PDFs are intended as touchstones to generate interest in an author's work. The excerpts and passages do not substitute for the reading of entire texts, and StudySync® strongly recommends that teachers and students seek out and purchase the whole literary or informational work in order to experience it as the author intended. Links to online resellers are available in our digital library. In addition, complete works may be ordered through an authorized reseller by filling out and returning to StudySync® the order form enclosed in this workbook.

Teacher's Edition   401

Core Path	Access Path
• How interesting and effective is the conclusion? Does the writer need to add a concluding statement to sum up events and ideas? • How well does the writer resolve the conflict (or problem) of the plot? • What is the theme of the story? What suggestions might help the writer make the theme clearer and more easily understood? • Has the writer used nonrestrictive clauses effectively to vary the pacing of the writing, and have they been punctuated correctly? Remind students that a peer reviewer's comments are most useful when they are clear, constructive, and presented with a positive and supportive attitude. Make sure students understand your expectations for all aspects of the assignment before beginning their work.	
Organize. Remind students to refer to the following graphic organizers they have already completed before they begin writing to ensure that their draft fully addresses the prompt and includes all the main features of narrative writing: • Organize Narrative Writing Timeline • Descriptive Details Graphic Organizer • Story Road Map Graphic Organizer	**Beginner & Intermediate** **Add Transitional Words to Story Road Map.** Before students write their draft, have them talk through their completed Story Road Map. Have them read each paragraph or section aloud and help them identify places where they can use transition words and phrases such as *finally*, *at last*, *as a result*, and *similarly* to connect events and ideas. Have them write the transition words on their Story Road Map, and then reread each section aloud with the transition words in place.

Core Path	Access Path
	Extend **Discuss.** Talk with students about strategies they can use if they have trouble getting started on writing a draft of their story. Explain that writers of narratives often use the strategy of freewriting. Explain that a "freewrite" involves taking a few minutes to write absolutely freely and as fast as possible, without thinking about correct grammar or precise language, or even making sense. Have students try freewriting about a character or event in their story. Have them sit quietly and focus on an object, idea, or scene from their story. Then give them two or three minutes to write non-stop about it. Afterward, suggest they reread their freewrite to see if it has produced any images or phrases they might want to include in their first draft.
	Extend **Tech Infusion** **Storyboard.** An alternative to a freewrite is a storyboard. Tell students they can use Google drawing, or a presentation and creation app, such as ShowMe (www.showme.com), to find illustrations or to make sketches of the characters and events in their stories. Suggest that students work independently to locate online images or make sketches. Then have them meet with a trusted partner to "walk and talk" their way through the images.
	Extend **Tech Infusion** **Storyboard.** An alternative to a freewrite is for students to record themselves and they talk their way through the story. Have students use a digital voice recorder or an app such as Vocaroo (http://tinyurl.com/3a67tha) to record their retelling of the events in their completed Organize Narrative Writing Timelines. Students can then use the recording as a basis for their first draft.

Please note that excerpts and passages in the StudySync® library, workbooks, and PDFs are intended as touchstones to generate interest in an author's work. The excerpts and passages do not substitute for the reading of entire texts, and StudySync® strongly recommends that teachers and students seek out and purchase the whole literary or informational work in order to experience it as the author intended. Links to online resellers are available in our digital library. In addition, complete works may be ordered through an authorized reseller by filling out and returning to StudySync® the order form enclosed in this workbook.

Teacher's Edition   **403**

Core Path	Access Path
Write. Ask students to complete the writing assignment by using descriptive details and dialogue to create interesting scenes that move the plot forward. Remind students to keep in mind their purpose and audience as well. Once they have completed their writing, they should click "Submit."	**Beginner** **Write with Support.** Review the Drafting Guide on the Access 1 handout with students before they write. Then have students use their completed Story Road Map to complete their draft with teacher support as needed. Prior to writing each paragraph, ask students to state orally what they want to say in each paragraph. They can do this in small groups with support from the teacher or in pairs with an on-level partner who can provide quality feedback. Talking through their writing before they put pen to paper will help them clarify their language and use of transition words before they write. **Intermediate & Advanced** **Use Transition Words.** Have students use the Drafting Guide on the Access 2 and 3 handouts as they write. Remind them to focus on using transition words to smoothly connect ideas, sentences, and paragraphs. They may refer to the words listed in the student lesson. **Approaching** **Use the Story Road Map to Write a Draft.** Remind students to consult all the prewriting documents they have created — organize writing narrative timeline, descriptive details graphic organizer, and the story road map graphic organizer — to help them craft their narrative. It may be particularly useful for Approaching students to use their Story Road Map to structure their writing. Explain that they can follow the order of the outline they created, but in their draft they will need to add details and develop their writing. Have them use the Drafting Guide on the Access 4 handout to make sure they include a strong introduction with a hook strategy and smooth transitions, precise language, and a conclusion that provides a natural resolution to the conflict the characters face in the story.

Core Path	Access Path
Review. Once students have completed their writing assignment, they should submit substantive feedback to two peers. Students should use the feedback they receive to strengthen their narratives.	**Beginner** **Review the Drafting Guide.** Help students to go through the Drafting Guide item-by-item on the Access 1 handout to check their writing. Provide support to help them make changes as needed. **Intermediate & Advanced** **Use Drafting Guide.** Have mixed-proficiency partners read their completed drafts aloud to one another and use the Drafting Guide on the Access 2 and 3 handouts to check their writing. Remind them to check that they used transition words appropriately and make suggestions for how transitions could be improved or clarified.
	Extend **Critique.** Project on the board a draft of a story you have written using the unit prompt. (The draft can be very rough; the point is to give students an opportunity to see how a story goes through drafts, as well as to give them an opportunity to provide constructive feedback.) Then lead a class discussion to focus on one or two elements of narrative writing, such as descriptive details and transitions. Encourage students to point out strengths and weaknesses in those areas. After each bit of feedback, ask the class if the student's comment was helpful or not. Be sure to praise students for providing constructive comments or feedback. Encourage students to use similar approaches when they complete their peer reviews to ensure that their critiques are substantive but also supportive.

Please note that excerpts and passages in the StudySync® library, workbooks, and PDFs are intended as touchstones to generate interest in an author's work. The excerpts and passages do not substitute for the reading of entire texts, and StudySync® strongly recommends that teachers and students seek out and purchase the whole literary or informational work in order to experience it as the author intended. Links to online resellers are available in our digital library. In addition, complete works may be ordered through an authorized reseller by filling out and returning to StudySync® the order form enclosed in this workbook.

Teacher's Edition   405

BLAST:
Style

OVERVIEW

Students will learn how to recognize differences in writers' styles and revise for style when writing their own fictional narratives.

OBJECTIVES

1. Learn the definition of style for writing narrative text.
2. Practice identifying and analyzing style in narrative writing.
3. Participate effectively in a range of conversations and collaborations to express ideas and build upon the ideas of others.

ELA Common Core Standards:
Writing - W.6.3.A, W.6.3.B, W.6.3.D, W.6.4, W.6.6, W.6.10
Speaking & Listening - SL.6.1.A, SL.6.1.C, SL.6.1.D
Language - L.6.1.E, L.6.3.B

RESOURCES

Access 1 handout (Beginner)

Access 2 handout (Intermediate)

Access 4 handout (Approaching)

TITLE/DRIVING QUESTION

Core Path	Access Path
Discuss. As a class, read aloud the title and Driving Question for this Blast: "What style should you use to write your fictional narrative?" Ask students what they know about writing style. Can they think of examples of different styles of writing? Point out that style is composed of many different elements, including tone, word choice, and descriptive details. In a narrative, sometimes a writer might mix formal and informal writing, standard English and conversational English, in order to tell the story well. However, if a writer establishes a conversational style for a particular character, the writer needs to maintain that style for that character. If a writer establishes a formal style for a narrator, that style needs to remain consistent for that narrator. Remind students that they should not immediately reply to the Driving Question. They'll be returning to this question and responding after they've read the Background and explored the Model.	**English Learners All Levels & Approaching** **Share.** Have students backchannel using TodaysMeet (http://tinyurl.com/psef72j) to add their ideas about why writing style might be important. Have students revisit their notes after they have read the Background section of the lesson. Then have them compare their notes with what they have learned.
Draft. In their notebooks or on scrap paper, have students draft their initial responses to the driving question about the writing style that will best reach their target audience and fulfill their purpose. This will provide them with a baseline response that they will be developing.	**Beginner, Intermediate & Approaching** **Draft with Sentence Frame.** When drafting their initial response to the driving question, have students refer to this Blast sentence frame on their Access 1, 2, and 4 handouts: • The style I will use for my fictional narrative is _____. Point out that the prompt borrows language directly from the Blast driving question to provide a response.

Core Path	Access Path
	Extend **Tech Infusion.** **Draft.** Have students use a note-taking app, such as Evernote (http://tinyurl.com/2pmebl), to jot down their initial responses to the driving question. This will provide them with a baseline response that they can revise as they gain more information about the topic in the Background section of the assignment.

BACKGROUND

Core Path	Access Path
Read. Have students read the Blast background to provide context for the driving question about style in a fictional narrative.	**Beginner & Intermediate** **Read with Support.** Have students read the Blast Background to provide context for the driving question. When they encounter unfamiliar words or phrases, have students refer to the glossary on their Access 1 and 2 handouts. If there are unfamiliar words that are not included in their glossary, encourage students to check a dictionary or online reference tool, like http://tinyurl.com/6ytby. **Approaching** **Read and Summarize.** Have students read the Blast Background to explain the driving question. As they read, ask students to complete the fill in the blank summary of the background provided on their Access 4 handout. When they encounter unfamiliar words or phrases, have students refer to the glossary on their Access 4 handout.
Discuss. Pair students and have them discuss the following questions: 1. What connection does the author make between styles of clothing and writing? (Most people wear and even mix and match different styles of clothing. Writers do the same thing: They can mix and match formal and informal styles of writing.)	**Beginner & Intermediate** **Q & A.** Pair Beginning and Intermediate with Advanced (or Beyond) students and have them take turns asking and answering questions about writing style. Have students use the charts on the Access 1 and 2 handouts to record their answers.

Core Path	Access Path
2. How do you decide on the best style of clothing or writing? (In both cases, you need to figure out who your audience is and what you need to do—or your purpose. Once you know your audience and purpose, you can select your style.) 3. What are some of the things that affect a writer's style of writing? (the formality of the language used, the length and complexity of the sentences, the word choices, and the tone) 4. Why would a writer of a fictional narrative want to mix formal, standard English with an informal, conversational style? Explain. (A writer might want to use both. For example, the narrator of the story might use formal English, but the characters might speak using informal, conversational English.)	

Brainstorm. Remind students about the driving question for this Blast. Ask students to create a two-column chart, like the one below. The column labeled "Elements of Style" shows the different ways a writer can achieve his or her writing style in a fictional narrative. For the examples, ask students to write an original sentence or find one in the Student Model, "Taking the Shot." Have students meet with a peer to discuss their examples.

Elements of Style	Examples
Standard English	"He would dutifully stand in front of the net, try to line up his shot, and then wildly hurl the ball, which almost always landed in an entirely different part of the gym."

Please note that excerpts and passages in the StudySync® library, workbooks, and PDFs are intended as touchstones to generate interest in an author's work. The excerpts and passages do not substitute for the reading of entire texts, and StudySync® strongly recommends that teachers and students seek out and purchase the whole literary or informational work in order to experience it as the author intended. Links to online resellers are available in our digital library. In addition, complete works may be ordered through an authorized reseller by filling out and returning to StudySync® the order form enclosed in this workbook.

Teacher's Edition   **409**

Core Path		Access Path
Informal English	"They'd say stuff like 'Take cover, guys; Kyle is chucking the ball again. Your height is totally wasted on you, man. Your twin sister Celia has got all the athletic talent in your family, dude.'"	
Long, complex sentence	"So, the next time Kyle had to play basketball in gym class, we were both prepared, although Kyle didn't know it."	
Short, simple sentence	"He stared at me like I threw him for a loop."	
Precise language/ word choice	"Stunned, I tossed the ball and blew the shot."	

QUIKPOLL (UP TO 5 ANSWERS)

Core Path	Access Path
Participate. Answer the poll question. Have students discuss their reasons for their answers. Students should refer to evidence from the background and research links to defend their answer.	

NUMBER CRUNCH

Core Path	Access Path
Predict, Discuss, and Click. Before students click on the number, break them into pairs and have them make predictions about what they think the number is related to. After they've clicked the number, ask students if they are surprised by the revealed information.	

CREATE YOUR BLAST (140 CHARACTERS)

Core Path	Access Path
Blast. Ask students to write their Blast response in 140 characters or less.	**Beginner** **Blast with Support.** Have students refer back to the sentence frame on their Access 1 handout that they used to create their original Blast draft. Ask them to use this frame to write and enter their final Blast. **Intermediate** **Blast with Support.** Have students attempt to draft their Blast without the sentence frame on their Access 2 handout. If students struggle to compose their Blast draft without the sentence frame, remind them to reference it for support.
Review. After students have completed their own Blasts, ask them to review the Blasts of their peers and provide feedback.	
	Extend **Discuss.** As a whole class or in groups, identify a few strong blasts and discuss what made those responses so powerful. As a group, analyze and discuss what characteristics make a blast interesting or effective.

EXTENDED WRITING PROJECT:
Revise

OVERVIEW

This lesson asks students to revise the draft of their fictional narrative. Students are first asked to include any peer suggestions they previously received about their draft. Then they are asked to focus on revisions to include transition words or phrases that clarify shifts in time or setting and to move the events forward. They also are asked to evaluate the effectiveness of their organizational structure and their use of description and dialogue.

OBJECTIVES

1. Identify elements of a writing style appropriate to a fictional narrative.
2. Revise a narrative text or story to improve content and organization.
3. Participate effectively in a range of conversations and collaborations to express ideas and build upon the ideas of others.

ELA Common Core Standards:
Reading: Literature - RL.6.1
Writing - W.6.3.A, W.6.3.B, W.6.3.C, W.6.3.D, W.6.3.E, W.6.4, W.6.5, W.6.6, W.6.10
Speaking & Listening - SL.6.1.C
Language - L.6.1.E, L.6.3.A

RESOURCES

Grammar handout: Revising Dialogue

Access 1 handout (Beginner)

Access 2 handout (Intermediate)

Access 3 handout (Advanced)

Access 4 handout (Approaching)

1. WRITE

Core Path	Access Path
Discuss. Before students begin to revise, review with the class the writing prompt/directions. Ask whether students have any questions either about the prompt or the revision process. Respond to their questions, and explain the importance of thoughtful, focused revisions. Then read aloud the peer review instructions that students will use to comment on one another's work. Point out that understanding the peer review instructions can help students focus their writing on important features of narrative texts. The peer review instructions ask students to consider the following questions:	**Beginner, Intermediate & Approaching** **Review the Revision Checklist.** Read aloud the items within the Revision Guide with students. As the teacher reads each item in the guide, students should read along on their Access 1, 2, and 4 handouts. Encourage students to circle unfamiliar words and underline anything that is confusing or unclear. Then take a few minutes to clarify unknown vocabulary, answer questions, and provide examples for any items that students do not understand. Explain to students that they will need to check their own writing for each of these items.

Core Path (continued):

- Does the writer's sequence of events flow logically and naturally? How effectively do the events fall into a pattern of rising action and falling action?

- Which transition words and phrases does the writer employ to show sequence, make connections between (or among) events or ideas, and to indicate shifts in time and setting?

- How strong and precise are the writer's choice of words and use of language?

- Does the story contain a variety of sentence structures and patterns?

- What are some details that make the setting, the events, the characters and their problems seem vivid and interesting?

- How effective is the writer's use of dialogue? Does it sound natural? If the writer is using slang or dialect, is it used appropriately and clearly?

- How well does the story appeal to a particular audience?

- How well does the story convey a theme?

- What suggestions can you make to help the writer improve his or her narrative?

Access Path (continued):

Advanced
Read and Discuss. Pair Advanced students with an on-level partner and ask them to review the Revision Checklist. Allow time for them to discuss each item to ensure the students understand what they are being asked to do.

Beyond
Create Action Items.

1. Give small groups a writing sample and ask them to identify and underline the elements of a formal style.

2. Have students generate strategies they can use to ensure that their peer reviews are focused and substantive.

3. Ask them to create a list of action items for their revision to focus their efforts. Have them organize these items into a checklist.

4. Create a shared Google doc that all students in the class can add to, edit, and use to revise their work.

Please note that excerpts and passages in the StudySync® library, workbooks, and PDFs are intended as touchstones to generate interest in an author's work. The excerpts and passages do not substitute for the reading of entire texts, and StudySync® strongly recommends that teachers and students seek out and purchase the whole literary or informational work in order to experience it as the author intended. Links to online resellers are available in our digital library. In addition, complete works may be ordered through an authorized reseller by filling out and returning to StudySync® the order form enclosed in this workbook.

Teacher's Edition   413

Core Path	Access Path
Remind students that a peer reviewer's comments are most helpful when they are clear, constructive, and presented with a positive and supportive attitude. Make sure students understand your expectations for all aspects of the assignment before beginning their revision.	

Core Path

Highlight. Each student should start this activity with a copy of his or her draft, either printed on paper or open in a word-processing program. Students will conduct three rereads of their own paper, each with a different focus.

1. First, have students read through their draft to be sure they have included previous peer suggestions for improving their introduction, body paragraphs, and conclusions.

2. Next, ask students to look for places where they could add transition words or phrases to clarify the relationship between (and among) ideas and also indicate the order of events more clearly. Have them make a final evaluation of the order of events.

3. Finally, instruct students to read through their draft a third time. This time, students should look for opportunities to adjust the pacing of the story by adding some dialogue or description, or varying the structure of sentences. They might add a bit of vivid language to a description, or use slang and dialect if appropriate. Challenge students to find at least two places where they could add a detail that appeals to one or more of the five senses and highlight the details in yellow.

Access Path

Beginner
Reread with Support. Model for students how to reread their drafts looking for each focus. Help them to identify those important areas of their drafts where transition words can be used to clarify relationships. To help, ask students questions the reader may be thinking, which can be clarified or answered with the inclusion of transition words or phrases and other descriptive language. It may help to also demonstrate highlighting details from another text selection from the unit to further help students understand the task.

Intermediate & Advanced
Reread with Support. Pair Intermediate and Advanced students with more proficient and on-level students to help them with reviewing their drafts. Have pairs discuss what areas of the draft are most likely to require descriptive details to support or clarify the relationship between ideas and events. More proficient partners can use their own review as an example for Intermediate and Advanced students. Encourage students to write down questions they have about the details in their drafts that require more explanation. They can refer to this list when they are revising their drafts.

Core Path	Access Path
	Approaching **Reread and Analyze.** Have Approaching students work in pairs to reread and analyze their writing with one another. Have them work together to identify those areas in their drafts that will require transition words or phrases, as well as additional details. Remind students that asking questions about a detail is a good method for determining the need for more description or key transition terms to clarify the reading.

(G) **Grammar, Usage, and Mechanics.** Distribute the StudySync handout on revising dialogue. Remind students that variation is one way to create interest in a piece of writing. One way to do this is to vary the structures of sentences throughout a piece. Review with students the different sentence structures defined on the worksheet.

Another way to create interest is through the use of dialogue. Tell students that the dialogue spoken by their characters allows a reader to more fully understand the characters' ages, backgrounds, and personalities, along with the setting in which they live.

Explain that in a narrative, this often means varying from a more formal style of language—the style students might use to write an informative, explanatory, or argumentative text. Have students review the instruction on revising dialogue to more accurately portray characters before completing the practice exercise. (Answers for the practice exercise appear at the end of the lesson plan online.) After students have completed the exercise, point out these two pieces of dialogue from the Student Model and ask students to explain how the use of language gives the reader a better understanding of the character who is speaking. In addition, ask students to indicate whether they'd make any further revisions to the dialogue.

Beginner
Support Grammar Comprehension.

1. Read the grammar handout aloud with students, pausing to clarify concepts as needed. Review the table of wordy and revised sentences to explain the concept. Then have students explain why the revised sentences are stronger.

2. Work directly with small groups to complete the practice items by reading each sentence aloud and having students identify the redundancies.

3. Read students' drafts with them to help them identify areas that can be more succinct.

Intermediate
Support Grammar Comprehension. Have Intermediate students join with Beginning students for the instruction portion of the lesson. Then allow them to work with an Advanced or English proficient partner to complete the practice items and check their drafts for correct pronoun agreement.

Core Path	Access Path
1. They'd say stuff like "Take cover, guys; Kyle is chucking the ball again. Your height is totally wasted on you, man. Your twin sister Celia has got all the athletic talent in your family, dude." (Although the speaker is not identified in this dialogue, the use of idioms such as "Take cover" and "totally wasted on you" as well as slang words such as "chucking," "man," and "dude," indicate that he or she is a young person. The narrator's use of the informal word "stuff" indicates that he or she may be a friend or classmate of the speaker. The informal language suggests that the narrator and speaker are in not in a formal setting such as a classroom, and that an adult is not present. Eliminating one or two of the slang words—perhaps either "man" or "dude"—might make the dialogue feel more natural.) 2. "Hey," George said. "Hey," we answered. "I could use a little help," George said. (In this dialogue, the word "Hey" is used effectively. Although it's not a complete sentence, it's easily recognizable as a greeting in which the speakers aren't very excited to see each other. It makes it easy for the reader to visualize the meeting of the mean boy George and the narrator and her brother, and hints at the uncomfortable feeling in the air.) Finally, ask students to reread their stories to make sure that their dialogue reflects the way in which they want their characters to be perceived by readers. Encourage students to consider using a combination of standard English and informal language to make their characters more realistic, if necessary. Remind them to use a variety of sentence structures throughout the narrative, not just in dialogue.	**Approaching** **Partner Work.** Check in with Approaching students before they complete the grammar exercise. Ask them to explain what they understand about wordiness, and offer clarification as necessary. Allow them to complete the practice items with a partner. When they are done, have them check and discuss their answers. Have them continue working with their partner to check their drafts for wordiness together.

Copyright © BookheadEd Learning, LLC

Core Path	Access Path
	Extend **Tech Infusion** **Poll.** Project a writing sample on the board, and ask students to respond to three questions. • How effective is the introduction in getting readers' attention and setting up the story? • How well does the story resolve the conflict (or problem)? • How well does the writer use transitions to make the story's events flow logically and smoothly? • How well does the language match the tone and content of the story? Using Socrative (http://tinyurl.com/3bxbjpt), have students respond to each question on a scale of one to five, with five being best. Then discuss the poll results for each question, creating a list of possible revisions for the writing sample.
	Extend **Critique.** Project the Student Model on the board and ask the class to identify its use of dialogue and determine if the writer has a good balance of dialogue and narration or description. After students have had an opportunity to evaluate this aspect of the model, work as a class to generate strategies students can use to ensure that their peer reviews are focused and substantive.
Write. Ask students to complete the revision, making sure that they incorporate sensory details and transition words or phrases, that their dialogue suits their characters, and that their conclusion follows from the story's events. Once they have completed their writing, students should click "Submit."	**Beginner, Intermediate & Advanced** **Use Checklist.** Have all English Learners use the Narrative Writing Revision Checklist to help guide their revisions. Provide additional differentiated support as indicated on the following pages.

Please note that excerpts and passages in the StudySync® library, workbooks, and PDFs are intended as touchstones to generate interest in an author's work. The excerpts and passages do not substitute for the reading of entire texts, and StudySync® strongly recommends that teachers and students seek out and purchase the whole literary or informational work in order to experience it as the author intended. Links to online resellers are available in our digital library. In addition, complete works may be ordered through an authorized reseller by filling out and returning to StudySync® the order form enclosed in this workbook.

Teacher's Edition   **417**

Core Path	Access Path
	Beginner
	Focus on Condensing Ideas. Encourage students to review their drafts to look for places where they can condense ideas in simple ways, either by compounding verbs or adding prepositional phrases to improve the precision and detail of their writing. Provide students with the following example as a model:
	1. The first three sentences should read:
	• Lydia put her phone down. She let the news sink in. The first thing she wondered was if she was selfish for wanting to stay at school.
	2. Model for students how you can combine these sentences and revise them to be more precise and detailed.
	• Lydia put her phone down, letting the news sink in, and at once wondered if she was selfish for wanting to stay at school.
	3. Direct students' attention to the use of commas to set off an important detail, but not essential information to understand the sentence. Explain how this allows readers to infer that she must have been told something over the phone that was a serious issue. It also helps the reader to better understand the conflict suddenly facing the character.
	4. Also show students how the prepositional phrase "at once" reveals to the reader the instant reaction the character has to "the news." The rest of the sentence provides the reader enough information to guess at what is Lydia's conflict.
	5. When you finish modeling this practice for students, have them begin to read through their narratives to identify areas where they can condense ideas to improve the precision and detail of their writing.

Core Path	Access Path
	Intermediate **Focus on Textual Organization.** Remind students that when reading their narratives, they should pay close attention to ensure the text is organized. Have students form pairs and exchange their narratives with a partner. Have each student read the narrative and instruct them to identify the following elements: • elements of exposition • a hook • rising action • climax • falling action • conclusion/resolution Remind students to look for effective transition words to help them follow the text. If students have difficulty following the text's progression, ask students if the writing is too complex or lacks necessary transitions to indicate the sequence of events or relationship between ideas and events. Have students provide their partners with feedback, noting if they were unable to identify each of the elements listed above as well as any suggestions they have to improve the structure of the narrative. **Advanced** **Use Precise Language.** Ask students to work with an English-proficient partner to identify and underline places in their story where language could be made more clear or vivid. Then have them use the two-column Precise Language chart on the Access 3 handout to list words students underlined in their narrative that need revision, and brainstorm a list of new words to replace these words. Give them time to discuss which words are strongest (creating a feeling of tension) and choose the best to include in their story.

Please note that excerpts and passages in the StudySync® library, workbooks, and PDFs are intended as touchstones to generate interest in an author's work. The excerpts and passages do not substitute for the reading of entire texts, and StudySync® strongly recommends that teachers and students seek out and purchase the whole literary or informational work in order to experience it as the author intended. Links to online resellers are available in our digital library. In addition, complete works may be ordered through an authorized reseller by filling out and returning to StudySync® the order form enclosed in this workbook.

Teacher's Edition **419**

Core Path	Access Path
	Approaching **Practice Editing.** 1. Approaching students should practice identifying instances of sentences or paragraphs lacking transition words and phrases, words that could be replaced with more descriptive or precise language, and places where they need to vary the types of sentences using the exercise on the Access 4 handout. 2. After they edit the example paragraph, allow them to work with an on-level partner to read through their own drafts. They should focus on identifying and underlining instances of sentences or paragraphs lacking transition words and phrases, words that could be replaced with more descriptive or precise language, and places where they need to vary the types of sentences in their own writing. 3. Then have them make their revisions independently. Have them check their revised essay against the Narrative Writing Revision Checklist before they submit their revision.
Review. After completing their writing assignment, students should submit substantive feedback to two peers. Students should use the feedback they receive to improve their narrative.	**Beginner** **Review with Teacher Support.** As a small group, help students to go through the Revision Checklist on the Access 1 handout row-by-row to review one another's writing. Provide individual support to help them make changes as needed. **Intermediate & Advanced** **Use Guide.** Have mixed-proficiency partners read their completed drafts aloud to one another and use the Revision Checklist on the Access 2 and 3 handouts to check that their writing includes all of the required revisions. With teacher guidance as necessary, encourage them to suggest ways their partner could make any needed changes.

Core Path	Access Path
	Approaching **Use Revision Checklist.** Have partners use the Revision Guide on the Access 4 handout to make sure their completed revisions include all the necessary elements.

EXTENDED WRITING PROJECT:
Edit/Proofread/Publish

OVERVIEW

This lesson asks students to edit, proofread, and publish the revised and corrected version of their fictional narrative. Students are instructed to edit for final improvements in plot and character development and descriptive details, and to proofread for the correct use of capitalization, punctuation, spelling, grammar, and usage. Finally, students are encouraged to explore ways of publishing their story or presenting it orally to an audience of friends or classmates.

OBJECTIVES

1. Edit and proofread narrative text to finalize content, style, and organization, and to eliminate errors in capitalization, punctuation, spelling, grammar, and usage.
2. Use technology to produce and publish writing.
3. Participate effectively in a range of conversations and collaborations to express ideas and build upon the ideas of others.

ELA Common Core Standards:
Writing - W.6.3.A, W.6.3.B, W.6.3.C, W.6.3.D, W.6.3.E, W.6.4, W.6.5, W.6.6
Speaking & Listening - SL.6.1.C, SL.6.6
Language - L.6.1.B, L.6.1.C, L.6.1.E, L.6.2.A, L.6.2.B, L.6.3.A, L.6.3.B

RESOURCES

Grammar handout: Pronoun-Antecedent Agreement in Number and Gender

Access 1 handout (Beginner)

Access 2 handout (Intermediate)

Access 3 handout (Advanced)

Access 4 handout (Approaching)

Copyright © BookheadEd Learning, LLC

1. WRITE

Core Path	Access Path
Test. Have students submit their paper to PaperRater (http://tinyurl.com/ybf7o4l). This site checks for grammar and spelling errors. Students can also select from the dropdown menus to have the engine provide feedback for style, word choice, and punctuation. Invite students to do a round of edits on their own before submitting a section of their text to the Website. Make sure students understand that the application by itself might make suggestions that do not improve the paper. Students will need to exercise judgment as they review suggestions for changes. In particular, have them edit and proofread for the following: • correct use of intensive pronouns (e.g., *myself, ourselves*) and possessive pronouns • correct use of a variety of sentence structures • correct use of punctuation, particularly commas to set off nonrestrictive and parenthetical elements • use of conventional English, as appropriate; use of dialect and variations on standard English, as appropriate for individual characters or a narrator • errors in capitalization, spelling, and usage.	**All Levels** **Use Technology to Check Clarity.** Have students conduct a check for the clarity of their writing using Hemingway (www.hemingwayapp.com). This app is designed to make the writing clear and concise. It will suggest eliminating embellishments and revising syntax for readability. Emphasize, however, that the app's suggestions may not be consistent with what the writer wishes to say. There is no substitute for the writer's own judgment.
Discuss. Before students begin to edit, review with the class the writing prompt/directions. Have a volunteer read them aloud. Ask whether students have any questions either about the prompt or the process of editing and proofreading. Respond to their questions, and then review criteria that can help students make final adjustments and corrections to their text. Remind students of the following: • The text should reflect skill in narrative writing, including features such as an introduction, middle, and conclusion. • The text should use transitions effectively to make the sequence of events clear, and it should include description and dialogue to develop characters and events and to hold readers' interest.	**Beginner** **Use Writing Support.** Walk Beginning students through the Proofreading Checklist on the Access 1 handout item-by-item. Help them to identify and underline the sections of their essay they will need to edit. **Intermediate** **Use Checklist.** Have Intermediate students preview the Proofreading Checklist on the Access 2 handout before they begin their final editing process. Make sure they understand everything on the checklist. As needed, help individual students identify the items on the checklist that they need to pay special attention to as they edit their essay.

Core Path	Access Path
• The text should include a combination of different types of sentences to help vary the story's pacing. • The text should maintain a consistent and appropriate style. • The text should be free from all spelling errors. • The text should use commas and quotation marks correctly to set off dialogue. • The text should be free from other errors and include the correct use of paragraph indents and formatting, if using a computer.	**Approaching** **Support Proofreading.** Walk students through each item on the Proofreading Checklist on the Access 4 handout. Encourage students to circle unfamiliar words and underline anything that is confusing or unclear. Then take a few minutes to clarify unknown vocabulary, answer questions, and provide examples for any items that students do not understand. If you have identified individual students' challenges, circle those items on the checklist that they need to pay special attention to and provide individual support, or pair them with an on- or above-level student to make their final edits.

Before or after students make final adjustments to their essays, brainstorm publishing ideas with them. Students have already been using technology to create, revise, and submit their work on StudySync, as well as to collaborate with their peers. Now, students will want to share information with one another about additional appropriate online publication opportunities, as well as about possible print outlets for their work. Ask students to collaborate on creating a list of these opportunities and outlets for their own use to help them when they are ready to publish.

Once students have submitted the final version of their fictional narratives, you might also suggest that they adapt their writing to an oral format and tell their stories as a presentation to the class. Remind students that informal and conversational language should be used only for specific purposes, for example in dialogue or narration that suits a particular character. In general, formal language is used in presentations. To help students prepare and deliver their presentations, refer to the Presentation Skills in the Speaking & Listening Handbook.

Copyright © BookheadEd Learning, LLC

Core Path

(G) **Grammar, Usage, and Mechanics.** Distribute the StudySync grammar handout on pronoun-antecedent agreement in number and gender. Define *antecedent* as the word or group of words a pronoun refers to or replaces in a sentence. Then, explain that a pronoun must agree in number with its antecedent. For example, if an antecedent is singular, the pronoun that refers to it must be singular as well.

Next, explain that a pronoun must agree with the gender of its antecedent. If the antecedent is male, the pronoun used must be masculine ("he," "his," or "him.") Remind students that checking for correct use of grammar such as pronoun-antecedent agreement is an important part of the editing and proofreading process.

Have students review the information on pronoun-antecedent agreement on the handout before completing the practice exercise. (Answers for the practice exercise appear at the end of the lesson plan online.) After students have completed the exercise, point out these two passages from the Student Model and ask students to identify how the underlined pronouns agree in number and gender to their antecedents:

It seems that when Kyle isn't holding a real ball in *his* hands, *he* can line up a shot and make it. (The pronouns "his" and "he" agree with Kyle in number and gender. The pronouns refer to one person who is a boy.)

But it wasn't like the gang suddenly turned nice or anything. "Missed again," one of *them*—a boy named Trey—hissed just loud enough for Kyle to hear. (The pronoun "them" is the antecedent of "the gang." Assuming that the writer is using "the gang" informally to refer to all the members of the gang, the pronoun "them" replaces "the gang" in the second sentence. It is plural and agrees in number with the antecedent it replaces.)

Access Path

Beginner & Intermediate
Pronounce and Spell Words from Other Languages. Have students join in as you review the handout with the class. Then in small groups model each example aloud several times and have students repeat. Allow pairs or small groups to complete the exercises on their handouts. When their work is complete, check their answers. Review any incorrect answers by reading the words aloud and helping students to correct their pronunciation and understanding.

Advanced
Work with a Partner. After the instruction, have Advanced students complete the exercise with an English proficient partner. Encourage them to read each word aloud together, focusing on refining their pronunciation.

Please note that excerpts and passages in the StudySync® library, workbooks, and PDFs are intended as touchstones to generate interest in an author's work. The excerpts and passages do not substitute for the reading of entire texts, and StudySync® strongly recommends that teachers and students seek out and purchase the whole literary or informational work in order to experience it as the author intended. Links to online resellers are available in our digital library. In addition, complete works may be ordered through an authorized reseller by filling out and returning to StudySync® the order form enclosed in this workbook.

Teacher's Edition   425

Core Path	Access Path
Finally, ask students to reread their essays and revise if needed to make sure that pronouns they used agree in number and gender with their antecedents.	
	Extend **Tech Infusion** **Proofreading Groups.** Have students create a shared Google doc that they can proofread, with help from two other classmates. Before students review the document, talk as a class about strategies for effective proofreading, such as reading the text aloud or starting with the last sentence and working backward through the text. These strategies help the proofreader focus more on how the words appear and not on what they mean. Remind students that their suggestions for changes may not reflect what the writer wishes to say. The writer should have the final say in the changes. He or she can accept or delete the others' corrections.
Write. Ask students to complete the writing assignment. Suggest, if there's time, that they set the narrative aside for a few minutes, and that they then proofread it one more time. Once they have completed their writing, they should click "Submit."	**Beginner & Intermediate** **Check Spelling and Proofread.** Before students begin proofreading, remind them of the handout they just completed. Have them read through their essay with a partner and circle any words from other languages they may have spelled incorrectly. Then have them read the circled words aloud and try to use what they have learned to correct the spelling themselves before confirming it using a dictionary or spell checker. They can continue proofreading their essay with a teacher or partner using the Proofreading Checklist on the Access 1 and 2 handouts.

Core Path	Access Path
	Advanced **Read Aloud to Proofread.** Explain to students that reading their work aloud is a great way to check for errors they might have otherwise missed. After students have completed their editing using the Proofreading Checklist, have them read their essay aloud to an English-proficient partner. Tell them that if they stumble in their reading, it may indicate a place where they need to adjust punctuation or sentence structure. Have their partner listen for correct use of grammar and suggest corrections if needed. **Approaching** **Support Writing.** Have students check their final draft against the checklist on their Access 4 handout to make sure they made all the edits needed. Ask them if they have questions or found any part of the assignment challenging. If so, provide clarification and assistance so that they can make their final edits and proofread before submitting their work.
	Extend **Tech Infusion** **Publish Online.** Suggest that students search online for places to publish their stories. For example, they can pursue online publishers of student writing, such as Teen Ink (http://tinyurl.com/6qj8bft) or Merlyn's Pen (http://tinyurl.com/l4tqsf). They can also use Pen.io (http://tinyurl.com/3lsaa8u), Blogger (http://tinyurl.com/e67d), or Edublogs (http://tinyurl.com/ytgznw) to publish their stories online independently. Students can also share their stories via Facebook, Twitter, or other social media and invite friends and classmates to share their own ideas about when it is important to stand up for oneself or on behalf of others.

Research

Facing Challenges

TYPE

Research

TITLE

Grade 6 Unit 3: Facing Challenges

TIME

125 minutes (research and presentations)

OBJECTIVES

1. Complete topic-specific group research projects connected to the unit theme and driving question.
2. Practice and apply research strategies to produce presentations with multimedia features.
3. Participate in conversations and collaborations to express ideas and build upon the ideas of others.
4. Practice, apply, and reinforce the following Grade 6 ELA Common Core Standards for reading literature and informational texts, writing explanatory pieces, conducting research projects, providing bibliographic information for sources, and speaking and listening:
5. Practice the following Grade 6 ELA Common Core Standards:
   - Reading: Literature – RL.6.1, RL.6.2, RL.6.3, RL.6.7, RL.6.9
   - Reading: Informational Text – RI.6.1, RI.6.2, RI.6.3, RI.6.6, RI.6.7
   - Writing: W.6.7, W.6.8, W.6.10
   - Speaking & Listening - SL.6.1.A, SL.6.1.B, SL.6.C, SL.6.1.D, SL.6.2, SL.6.4, SL.6.5, SL.6.6

RESOURCES

Library, online resources, links to topics
StudySync Speaking & Listening Handbook

OVERVIEW

When should we stand up for others and ourselves? In order to better understand this question, students will research instances when individuals have confronted choices about defending themselves, their family, or their community. How do we judge if someone who takes action against perceived injustice or danger is responding courageously or acting rashly? What motivates people to stand up for themselves or others? Perhaps someone who is falsely accused of wrong-doing will fight for his or her honor, or someone else will

Please note that excerpts and passages in the StudySync® library, workbooks, and PDFs are intended as touchstones to generate interest in an author's work. The excerpts and passages do not substitute for the reading of entire texts, and StudySync® strongly recommends that teachers and students seek out and purchase the whole literary or informational work in order to experience it as the author intended. Links to online resellers are available in our digital library. In addition, complete works may be ordered through an authorized reseller by filling out and returning to StudySync® the order form enclosed in this workbook.

Teacher's Edition   431

face the challenge of standing up to correct social injustice. Others will take a stand to protect their beliefs. If introduced in the first half of the unit, this research project can serve as a resource for the Extended Writing piece students will produce at the unit's close.

As students work to complete their research projects, remind them of the skills they have practiced and applied during the unit. They should incorporate this knowledge into their project as they discuss, plan, research, write, and deliver their presentations. To help students plan and conduct their research and prepare and deliver their presentations, refer them to the relevant lessons in the StudySync Speaking & Listening Handbook.

Suggested topics for small-group research and presentations include:

- Ask students to view a section of one of the film versions of *Les Misérables*. It can be a section from the musical version or from one of the other available versions. How do the film and novel versions of the same story portray the society in which that story takes place? How do they present the ways in which individuals stand up for themselves or others against social injustice in the society? In what way are the presentations of the social challenges and issues faced by the characters different in the film and the novel?

- What events have challenged or inspired your friends and family members to stand up for themselves or their beliefs? Interview friends or family members. What challenge did they face? How did they stand up for themselves? What about the event pushed them to take a stance? Did their actions motivate others to stand up for themselves as well? If yes, how? What was the outcome?

- Throughout history, groups of people have united to take a stand against injustices. Choose a historical event in which a group was inspired to stand up for its members' rights or beliefs. Describe the challenge and discuss actions that they took against the injustice. In what ways have their actions had an impact on today's society?

- Research a current event in which people have joined together to take a stand against an injustice or in response to a challenging situation. What was the cause that brought the group of people together? How have they joined together to take a stance? What was the outcome after they took a stance? Did the strength of more people help achieve their desired outcome? Explain the events that motivated this group, the outcome of their stance, and the influence it has on society today or in the future.

- How might an individual motivate others to take a stance? Research an important historical figure who has helped others to stand up for their beliefs. Explain how the individual helped others to find their voice. In what ways was his or her influence positive? In what ways was it negative?

REVIEW AND DISCUSS (10 MINUTES)

1. **Revisit the Big Idea Blast and Unit Preview** *(SL.6.1.A–D, SL.6.2)*. As a group, reread the Big Idea Blast and watch the Unit Preview again. Use the following questions to guide a discussion prior to research:

   a. What is the most interesting or surprising lesson this unit has taught you about how people decide when to stand up for themselves and others?

   b. How have the actions of historical figures inspired people to stand up and fight for their rights or their own beliefs?

   c. What topics from the reading are you most interested to learn more about?

CONDUCT THE RESEARCH (80 MINUTES)

To help students conduct their research and prepare their presentations, refer them to the Speaking & Listening Handbook lesson, Using Various Media.

2. **Break Students Into Small Groups. Assign Each Group a Topic or Let Groups Self-Select. (40 Minutes)**

   a. **Make a Research Plan** *(W.6.7, W.6.8)*. Instruct students to formulate research questions for their topic. After students prepare questions, collaborate with them on the best places to search for information, the most useful keywords to use in their search, and the type of resources available to them during the research process. Remind students that their research should focus on how people decide when to stand up for themselves and others.

   b. **Gather Resources** *(W.6.7, W.6.8)*. Instruct students to gather a selection of the following: print and digital text resources, video, audio recordings, graphics, and photos. Remind students to evaluate the validity of a source before using information from that source.

   c. **Review and Discuss** *(SL.6.1.A–D, SL.6.2, W.6.7, RL.6.7, RI.6.7)*. Advise groups to assign each member a research task. Tasks should be completed and presented to the group by each member individually.

3. **Assemble the Research in Each Group (40 minutes)**

   a. **Share** *(SL.6.1.A–D, SL.6.2, SL.6.4)*. Instruct students in each group to share what they have learned about their individual research and why this information is important. As students develop their research presentations, they should remember to include relevant facts, definitions, and concrete details. They should use precise language and, when appropriate, domain-specific vocabulary. Remind students to use appropriate transitions to clarify relationships and ideas.

   b. **Focus** *(W.6.7, W.6.8)*. Ask students to review the information they have gathered and to select the information that is most relevant. Encourage students to revise their research questions, as needed. Each group should then create a bibliography of their resources. They should assess their sources and resources for credibility once again before including them in their bibliography.

   c. **Write Explanations of Facts** *(W.6.7, W.6.8, W.6.10)*. Instruct group members to write brief explanations of any facts they uncovered during their research. These facts can be included in the group presentation. Have students be sure to cite the sources of all information. Remind students to be sure as they write their explanations to paraphrase information, or use their own words, in order to avoid plagiarism.

   d. **Plan a Short Presentation** *(W.6.7, W.6.8, SL.6.1.A–D, SL.6.2, SL.6.3, RI.6.3)*. Ask groups to plan a short presentation of the information they compiled. Students should follow the format below:

      i. **Title:** Have students give their presentations a title that provides information about the topic.

      ii. **Introduction:** The introduction should include a general description of the topic and research questions.

      iii. **List of Top Facts:** The list should include five to ten key facts about the subject.

      iv. **Multimedia Elements** *(SL.6.5)*: Remind each group to include a visual resource (video, graphic, photo) or a recording in their presentation.

v. **Conclusion:** Provide a strong conclusion that explains how this topic is relevant today.

PRESENT THE RESEARCH (35 MINUTES)

To help students prepare and deliver their presentations, refer to Presentation Skills and the Informative Presentation Rubric in the Speaking & Listening Handbook.

4. **Group Multimedia Presentations (5–7 minutes per group)**

   a. **Present** *(SL.6.4, SL.6.5, SL.6.6).* Each group should take turns presenting their findings to the class. Remind students that a good presentation involves speaking clearly. This includes using appropriate grammar, adequate volume, a consistent and proper style and tone, appropriate eye contact, and nonverbal elements, such as meaningful gestures, to keep the audience's attention and to emphasize main ideas and key points. To introduce quoted material or specific facts, remind students that they can say, "According to," and follow this with the source of the information. Make sure that students have acquired and accurately use academic-specific words and phrases related to the skills they have learned. Remind students to use formal language appropriate to presentations. Encourage students to use available technologies to enhance their presentations, displaying any visuals so that everyone can see them, and making sure that any audio recordings are easily heard.

   b. **Summarize** *(SL.6.4)* Ask each group to briefly summarize their presentation.

   c. **Questions** *(SL.6.1.C).* If time allows, students in the audience should ask relevant questions.

EXTENSION: RESPOND TO AND POST THE PRESENTATIONS (10 MINUTES)

5. **Write** *(W.6.7, W.6.8, W.6.10).* Have students write about what they have learned from the presentations by:

   a. listing three things they know now that they didn't know before; and

   b. writing a paragraph explaining how the presentations informed their understanding of how people decide when to stand up for themselves and others.

Post the Research (10 minutes) Create an area in the room for students to review the research of other groups.

Full-text Study

Facing Challenges

Roll of Thunder, Hear My Cry

Mildred D. Taylor

INTRODUCTION

In Mildred D. Taylor's 1977 Newbery award–winning novel *Roll of Thunder, Hear My Cry,* nine-year-old Cassie Logan learns what it means to be African-American in the segregated South of the 1930s. While her family struggles to pay the taxes on their land, Cassie and her siblings become increasingly aware of growing racial tensions and the accompanying violence. Inequality seems to exist everywhere Cassie goes: at her school, in the nearby town of Strawberry, and at the Wallace store. As tensions between the Logans and the white community escalate, Cassie learns painful lessons about when to take action and when to hold her tongue.

Mildred D. Taylor's novels about the Logan family are based on stories she heard during her early childhood in Mississippi, where she was born in 1943. In addition to *Roll of Thunder, Hear My Cry,* the Logan family appears in four additional books including *Song of the Trees* and *Let the Circle Be Unbroken.* Her important contribution to young-adult literature earned her the inaugural NSK Neustadt Prize for Children's Literature in 2003.

As students read *Roll of Thunder, Hear My Cry,* ask them to think about injustice and risk. How do different characters weigh the risks of responding, or not responding, to injustice?

USING THIS READING GUIDE

This reading guide presents lessons to support the teaching of the book *Roll of Thunder, Hear My Cry.* Organized in sections of grouped chapters, the lessons preview key vocabulary words and include close reading questions tied to the Common Core State Standards. The lessons identify a key passage in each section that will help you guide students through an exploration of the essential ideas, events, and character development in *Roll of Thunder, Hear My Cry.* This passage will also serve as the jumping-off point from which students will engage in their own StudySyncTV–style group discussion.

Each section of the reading guide also includes a list of comparative texts—provided in the *Roll of Thunder, Hear My Cry* Full-text Unit on StudySync—that go along with that section. For each comparative text, the reading guide includes important contextual notes and ideas for relating the text to *Roll of Thunder, Hear My Cry.*

ROLL OF THUNDER, HEAR MY CRY

TEXT SECTIONS

AUTHOR'S NOTE AND CHAPTER 1: Trouble at School

The author precedes her novel with a tribute to her father, a fitting introduction to the strong character of the Logan family. In Chapter 1, on their first day back in school, Cassie and Little Man Logan refuse to accept the hand-me-down textbooks the white school donated to the poor black school. Although their teacher, Miss Crocker, punishes them for their "airs," Mama understands the insult implied in the old, soiled books.

CHAPTERS 2–3: Risking Revenge

Papa comes home from the railroad and brings Mr. Morrison with him, a big man who will stay with the Logans from now on. Cassie and her brothers seek revenge on the driver of the bus that passes them every day, splashing them with mud and ruining their clothes.

CHAPTER 4: The Wallace Store

Mama whips Stacey after she catches him with T.J.'s cheat notes during a test. After school, the Logan children break Papa's rule and go to the Wallace store in search of T.J. While T.J. and Stacey are fighting, Mr. Morrison shows up and brings the Logans back home.

CHAPTERS 5–6: A Bad Day in Strawberry

Cassie's trip to Strawberry with Big Ma goes awry from the moment she steps out of the wagon. After experiencing racism in Mr. Barnett's store and being manhandled by the white Simms family, Cassie comes home to find her Uncle Hammer visiting. When she tells him about her day, Hammer is enraged and heads for the Simms family, but Mr. Morrison—a cooler head—prevails.

ROLL OF THUNDER, HEAR MY CRY

CHAPTER 7: Protecting the Land

Big Ma transfers ownership of the family land from her name to Hammer and Papa's names. Mr. Jamison offers to back up the credit of the sharecropping families who decide to participate in the boycott of the Wallace store. Mr. Granger threatens to take the Logan family's land if the family goes through with the boycott.

CHAPTERS 8–9: A Question of Respect

After Papa gives Cassie advice about how to respond to disrespect, she gets revenge on Lillian Jean. Miz Logan loses her teaching job over gossip that T.J. spread, and a shopping trip to Vicksburg turns ugly when Papa gets shot.

CHAPTER 10: Calling the Note

With Papa's broken leg preventing him from working on the railroad, the Logans have a difficult time paying the monthly mortgage on their land. Then the bank tells Mr. Morrison that the rest of their mortgage is due immediately, and the family realizes the bank is targeting them for leading the boycott on the Wallace store.

CHAPTERS 11–12: Reckoning

The tension that's been building all summer seems to come to a head when the Simms and the Wallaces show up at T.J.'s house, looking to lynch him. Mr. Jamison tries to talk the men out of it, and Papa takes extreme action to distract the men.

AUTHOR'S NOTE AND CHAPTER 1: Trouble at School

KEY PASSAGE | Chapter 1, Paragraphs 172–173

In this passage we hear part of a conversation between Mama (Mary Logan) and Miss Crocker, Cassie and Little Man's teacher. Miss Crocker was dismayed to find Mama pasting brown paper over the inside covers of the textbooks to hide the racist book status list, and has warned Mama that someone from the superintendent's office might come down and see it. Here Mama scoffs at the idea that an official would bother to come down, then adds that if someone did, it would be good for him to see the school's out-of-date, hand-me-down supplies. Miss Crocker takes a be-grateful-for-what-you-have attitude.

WHY IT'S KEY

Character: Miss Crocker and Mama (Mary Logan) have opposite attitudes about the hand-me-down books their school is given to pass out among the students. Miss Crocker is a rule follower and thinks the teachers and students at Great Faith Elementary and Secondary School should be grateful for any kind of handout from the white school. Mary Logan, on the other hand, sees how insulting these books are and breaks the rules by gluing down the first page. While Miss Crocker is worried that Mary Logan will be found out for defacing county property, Mama knows the county doesn't care enough to check in on the school. She goes on to suggest that the school board should visit to see how poorly the school has been treated.

Theme: Not until the schoolbook was rated in very poor condition was it passed from the white school to Great Faith Elementary and Secondary School. The shame and indignity associated with segregation are themes throughout *Roll of Thunder, Hear My Cry*. While segregation was legal as long as public institutions were "separate but equal," it's clear from this passage that the schools are far from equal. The conflict between Miss Crocker and Mama indicates a larger rift in the black community about how to respond to the injustices of Jim Crow Laws.

YOUR STUDYSYNC® TV

Discussion Prompt: Compare and contrast Miss Crocker's and Mary Logan's attitudes towards the hand-me-down textbooks given to Great Faith Elementary and Secondary School. Why does each teacher react the way she does? How would you react if you were faced with the same situation?

Standards: RL.6.1, RL.6.3; SL.6.1.A, SL.6.1.C, SL.6.1.D

VOCABULARY

heritage
her·it·age *noun*
The accomplishments, values, and traditions of a culture, nation, or family
In Hawaii, third graders study local history in order to better understand their island heritage.

sustain
sus·tain *verb*
To support; encourage; assist
Cards from friends and relatives helped sustain me during my hospital stay.

exasperation
ex·as·per·a·tion *noun*
Irritation; annoyance; vexation
When she saw the long line, the child stamped her foot in exasperation.

emaciated
e·ma·ci·a·ted *adjective*
Unusually thin, often due to malnourishment or illness; skeletal
The survivors of famine are often emaciated.

underhanded
un·der·hand·ed *adjective*
Sneaky; secretive
The detective's methods were underhanded, often relying on threats and blackmail.

CLOSE READ

QUESTION 1: What did Mildred D. Taylor learn from her father?

Sample Answer: He taught her complex ideas, like the importance of heritage and her own family history, and he taught her simple skills like how to bathe a dog and how to skate.

Standards: RL.6.1

QUESTION 2: Why did Papa go work on the railroad?

Sample Answer: The price of cotton dropped and the Logan family could no longer rely on their crop to pay their mortgage. If they can't pay their mortgage, they'll lose their land and have to sharecrop.

Standards: RL.6.1

  Teacher's Edition

QUESTION 3: Based on the text, what can you infer about T.J.'s personality?

Sample Answer: T.J. is a troublemaker and a gossip. He suggests that Stacey help him cheat on tests, and he seems to relish telling the Logans information they don't know. He also lies and gets his younger brother Claude in trouble for going to the dancing room at the Wallace store.

Standards: RL.6.1

QUESTION 4: Why doesn't Cassie want her book?

Sample Answer: She gives her book back to Miss Crocker because it's "soiled and marred." On the front page of the book is a chart that documents the condition of the book. Only after the book was considered "poor" was it given to the black school. She's also supporting her brother Little Man because he refused to take a book first.

Standards: RL.6.1

COMPARATIVE TEXTS

Text: *Delta Blues* by Ted Gioia

Compare to: Author's Note, before beginning *Roll of Thunder, Hear My Cry*

Connection: In *Delta Blues,* Ted Gioia describes the people and the land responsible for some of America's most iconic music. Despite Mississippi's poverty, the high concentration of black residents in rural areas enable black culture—both storytelling and music—to thrive. Set in 1930s Mississippi, *Roll of Thunder, Hear My Cry* exists within the social, economic, and racial landscape Gioia so carefully describes. In fact, the book's title, taken from a spiritual sung by slaves, is a nod to the very musical legacy that spawned the blues.

Text: *Simeon's Story: An Eyewitness Account of the Kidnapping of Emmett Till* by Simeon Wright

Compare to: Chapter 1 of *Roll of Thunder, Hear My Cry*

Connection: In *Simeon's Story: An Eyewitness Account of the Kidnapping of Emmett Till,* Simeon Wright describes what it was like to farm as a black sharecropper in the Jim Crow South. Like many of the families in *Roll of Thunder, Hear My Cry*, Wright's father had to give a portion of his crop to the landowner each year. Though the Logan family has little money, their land gives them flexibility and freedom that most of their black neighbors lack.

Please note that excerpts and passages in the StudySync® library, workbooks, and PDFs are intended as touchstones to generate interest in an author's work. The excerpts and passages do not substitute for the reading of entire texts, and StudySync® strongly recommends that teachers and students seek out and purchase the whole literary or informational work in order to experience it as the author intended. Links to online resellers are available in our digital library. In addition, complete works may be ordered through an authorized reseller by filling out and returning to StudySync® the order form enclosed in this workbook.

Teacher's Edition   **443**

CHAPTERS 2–3: Risking Revenge

> **KEY PASSAGE | Chapter 3, Paragraphs 35–36**
>
> This passage narrates the end of the scene in which the driver of the school bus deliberately steers the bus so close to the Logan children as they walk to school that they are forced into the slimy water of the gully on the shoulder, trying to jump out of the way. Furious, Little Man steps out and hurls mud at the bus but it falls way short, earning roars of laughter and derision from the students in the bus. Little Man's rage turns to sobs of humiliation.

WHY IT'S KEY

Theme: The scene shows not only the inequality between the two schools—the white students have buses and the black students do not—but also how mean-spirited white students could be. Chasing down and terrorizing the Logans was a kind of sport for them, evidently spearheaded by the white bus driver. It's no coincidence that the troubles between white and black children are mirrored by the troubles between white and black adults. Children act the way they're taught. Later, this incident will be mimicked by the white Ku Klux Klan members who go riding that night.

Character: Of all the Logan children, Little Man is most concerned with his appearance. Though the bus forces all the Logans, and T.J., into the gully, Little Man is the most appalled about what happened. He also has no means of retaliation. His mud ball misses the tires, and there's no one in power he can report the white students to.

Language: The author's decision to use the highly offensive and inflammatory slur for African Americans is a choice anyone writing directly about racism and segregation in the Jim Crow South must grapple with. On the one hand, Taylor likely considered the sensibilities of her modern readership, many of whom are inclined to ban such taboos. On the other hand, she likely weighed the historical authenticity, the shock value, and the honesty of her message, and opted to include the word.

YOUR STUDYSYNC® TV

Discussion Prompt: Why do the bus driver and white students experience no repercussions regarding their treatment of the Logan children? What does this tell you about life in the Jim Crow South? What do you think the Logans' response should be, considering the times, and why?

Standards: RL.6.1, RL.6.3; SL.6.1.A, SL.6.1.C, SL.6.1.D

VOCABULARY

humiliation
hu·mil·i·a·tion *noun*
Feelings of shame; deep embarrassment
After I got caught cheating on the test, I had to experience the humiliation of telling my parents.

gully
gul·ly *noun*
A gorge or ditch carved by water
Each year, summer rains filled the gully at the bottom of the hill.

embittered
em·bit·tered *verb*
Caused a person to feel resentment or anger
The boy was embittered by his memories of being bullied in summer camp.

disgruntled
dis·grun·tled *adjective*
Dissatisfied; angry; fed up
The customers were disgruntled when the storekeeper refused their coupons.

coddled
cod·dled *verb*
Pampered; treated in a protective, indulgent way; spoiled
My grandparents coddled me, refusing to let me do dishes or help in any other way around their house.

CLOSE READ

QUESTION 1: Based on the text, what can you infer about Papa's decision to hire Mr. Morrison to stay on the Logan farm?

Sample Answer: Papa says Mr. Morrison is there to help pick cotton and do other chores on the farm. Because of Mr. Morrison's imposing stature and due to the recent burnings of African-American men, it's quite likely Papa also hired him to protect the family while Papa is away, working for the railroad.

Standards: RL.6.1

QUESTION 2: Why does Papa say that the Logans can no longer shop at the Wallace store?

Sample Answer: The Wallace store is owned by racist whites, and young black people have been hanging out there drinking. Because of recent violence, Papa is worried that the black folks who spend time at the Wallace store might end up victims themselves.

Standards: RL.6.1

QUESTION 3: Why is Mama happy that the bus broke down?

Sample Answer: The bus driver is paying dearly for bullying the Logans with his aggressive tactics. Until the bus is fixed, white children and black children will have to walk to school. For a few weeks, white and black students will have equal treatment. The bus driver will no longer be able to harass the Logans.

Standards: RL.6.1

QUESTION 4: What does Mr. Avery imply when he says, "They's ridin' t'night"?

Sample Answer: He's warning the Logans that the Ku Klux Klan will be out on the streets. This is dangerous. They've already burned the Berry boys, and it's clear they don't need much provocation at all to attack again.

Standards: RL.6.1

COMPARATIVE TEXTS

Text: "The Lynching" by Claude McKay

Compare to: Chapter 2 of Roll of Thunder, Hear My Cry

Connection: One of the most violent aspects of life during Jim Crow was the widespread practice of lynching. Black men in particular were at risk for being murdered, often by hanging, at the hands of angry white mobs. The Tuskegee Institute estimates that between 1882 and 1941, 4730 people were lynched in the United States. In Roll of Thunder, Hear My Cry, T.J. tells the Logan children about two men who were burned alive after one was accused of flirting with a white woman. Claude McKay's poem "The Lynching" calls attention to the horrors of racial violence.

CHAPTER 4: The Wallace Store

KEY PASSAGE | Chapter 4, Paragraph 157

This passage occurs shortly after Mr. Morrison came upon Stacey fighting with T.J. in front of the Wallaces' store. He picked up Stacey and ordered the Logan children into the wagon. Mr. Morrison has explained that he won't tell their Mama that they went to the Wallaces' store because he expects them to tell her. Here he goes on to say that the issue is not their fighting, but providing entertainment for racists, and that their Mama was justified in asking them to stay away from the store. He says that telling her is a matter of honor, but the decision is theirs.

WHY IT'S KEY

Character: Mr. Morrison surprises the Logan children by telling them he won't tell on them. This decision earns him Stacey's respect. Unlike the Wallaces, who laugh at "colored folks," he treats the Logan children as equals. Coupled with his immense size and build, Mr. Morrison shows immense self-restraint and the wisdom to allow the children to learn by doing the difficult thing themselves. He is a worthy exemplar in Papa's absence.

Theme: Throughout *Roll of Thunder, Hear My Cry,* characters must choose their battles wisely. Mr. Morrison acknowledges the importance of fighting back when he says, "sometimes a person's gotta fight." After all, Mr. Morrison lost his job at the railroad for getting into a fight himself. He objects to the fighting at the Wallace store because the Wallaces do not respect African Americans. Fighting with dignity, an idea Mr. Morrison and Papa share, would not be possible at the Wallace store.

Conflict: Stacey has been upset that Papa brought Mr. Morrison to the house to watch over the family. As the eldest son, he felt he could take care of this himself. Mr. Morrison's decision to "leave it up to y'all to decide" whether or not to tell Mama they were at the Wallace store is a kind of truce between Stacey and Mr. Morrison. Mr. Morrison isn't trying to act like a father. Instead, he treats Stacey like an adult and Stacey rises to the occasion and agrees to tell his mother where he was.

YOUR STUDYSYNC® TV

Discussion Prompt: Why do you think Mr. Morrison left it up to the Logan children to decide whether to tell Mama that they were at the Wallace store? How does his stance towards "tattling" impact his relationship with the Logan children? How would you characterize Mr. Morrison based on his words and actions?
Standards: RL.6.1, RL.6.3; SL.6.1.A, SL.6.1.C, SL.6.1.D

VOCABULARY

feign
feign *verb*
To give the appearance of; to fake
Despite my fatigue, I feigned interest in her boring story.

woefully
woe·ful·ly *adverb*
Sadly; full of grievance
My brother turned his pockets inside out and woefully pleaded that he was broke.

haughtily
haugh·ti·ly *adverb*
Proudly; snobbishly
The lead actress turned away haughtily and said she never signed autographs.

subtle
sub·tle *adjective*
Complex and understated; difficult to perceive
My grandmother has a subtle sense of humor that many people miss entirely.

yonder
yon·der *adjective*
Farther away; in the distance
The trail ended at the mountaintop over yonder.

CLOSE READ

QUESTION 1: Why is Cassie so upset when she's churning butter?

Sample Answer: She thinks that the KKK went riding because of the prank she and her brothers pulled on the white children's school bus. She can't tell any adult about her worries.

Standards: RL.6.1

QUESTION 2: What happened to Mr. Tatum?

Sample Answer: He was tarred and feathered by the night riders because he told the owner of the Mercantile, Mr. Jim Lee Barnett, that he'd been overcharged. Mr. Barnett accused Mr. Tatum of calling him a liar.

Standards: RL.6.1

QUESTION 3: How was Stacey treated unfairly by his mother, and why?

Sample Answer: Stacey's mother whipped him because she caught him with "cheat notes," but T.J. had foisted them on Stacey at the last minute. T.J. was the cheater, not Stacey, who had ripped up T.J.'s cheat notes earlier.

Standards: RL.6.1

QUESTION 4: Why is Big Ma offended that the Grangers want to buy her land?

Sample Answer: Unlike many of their sharecropping neighbors, the Logans own their land. If they lose it, they'll lose the profits from their crops. Owning land gives them independence.

Standards: RL.6.1

QUESTION 5: Why doesn't Mama want her neighbors to shop at the Wallace store?

Sample Answer: The Wallaces were responsible for burning Mr. Berry and his nephew. Because of racist law enforcement, they won't be held responsible for their crime. Mama wants her neighbors to boycott the Wallaces so that the Wallaces no longer receive income from the black community.

Standards: RL.6.1

Please note that excerpts and passages in the StudySync® library, workbooks, and PDFs are intended as touchstones to generate interest in an author's work. The excerpts and passages do not substitute for the reading of entire texts, and StudySync® strongly recommends that teachers and students seek out and purchase the whole literary or informational work in order to experience it as the author intended. Links to online resellers are available in our digital library. In addition, complete works may be ordered through an authorized reseller by filling out and returning to StudySync® the order form enclosed in this workbook.

Teacher's Edition   **449**

CHAPTERS 5–6: A Bad Day in Strawberry

This passage occurs as Mama tries to make Cassie understand the context of Big Ma's apparent passivity in the face of Cassie's humiliation in Strawberry that day. She has explained that Big Ma took the path of least resistance to protect Cassie, knowing the long history of racism in the Deep South dating back to when Big Ma's great-grandparents arrived in chains from Africa. Now Mama's history of slavery covers how white slave-owners justified slavery as a Christian value, not for the good of the slaves but to keep the slaves docile and faithful. Using religion as a ploy did not keep slaves from desiring freedom and becoming fugitives, however.

WHY IT'S KEY

Key Concept: Mama uses history to explain to Cassie why Big Ma didn't stand up for her in Strawberry. Although slavery is over, Jim Crow laws keep African Americans from being entirely free.

Theme: White Americans justified both slavery and Jim Crow laws as Christian acts. Mama points out that Christianity was misused as a tool to teach obedience and prevent slave revolts. The conflict between obedience and resistance to white supremacy continues to affect choices made by the Logans and their peers. Mama makes an important distinction between appearances and beliefs. Although slaves may have been loyal or obedient, they still wanted freedom. Similarly, although Big Ma acted subservient to Mr. Simms, she didn't feel that way.

Character: Mama's knowledge of history helps Cassie come to terms with the inequality of daily life in Mississippi. Although nobody in the Logan family likes Jim Crow laws, Mama helps Cassie understand their history and the dangers associated with protesting the existing racial order. Mama's commitment to education helps her and her family come to terms with the inequality of their day-to-day lives.

YOUR STUDYSYNC® TV

Discussion Prompt: Why does Mama take a historical approach when talking to Cassie about the events that took place in Strawberry? More generally, why is history important for understanding current events and our day-to-day lives?

Standards: RL.6.1, RL.6.3; SL.6.1.A, SL.6.1.C, SL.6.1.D

VOCABULARY

subdued
sub·dued *verb*
Quieted down; caused to feel less animated
The arrival of two police cars subdued the crowd.

bunion
bun·ion *noun*
An inflammation of a joint, usually in the foot
My grandfather wears special shoes to avoid irritating his bunion.

mercantile
mer·can·tile *noun*
A grocery or general store
The mercantile sold everything from ribbon to tractor hitches.

recoil
re·coil *verb*
To move away quickly
The child recoiled when she saw the dog approaching, but he wagged his tail and made friends.

aloofness
a·loof·ness *noun*
The state of being indifferent or distant
At first, the boy's aloofness made me think I'd somehow offended him.

CLOSE READ

QUESTION 1: Why is Cassie unhappy with where Big Ma sells her goods?

Sample Answer: Big Ma sets up her stall in the back of the market, behind the white sellers. Cassie is worried that no one will find the stall and that they won't be able to sell their goods.

Standards: RL.6.1

QUESTION 2: Which particular events ruin Cassie's day in Strawberry?

Sample Answer: Mr. Barnett ignores Cassie, Stacey, and T.J. in order to help white customers. When he helps a white girl, Cassie interrupts him politely and gets yelled at. Later she bumps into Lillian Jean Simms on the street, and Mr. Simms twists her arm and knocks her off the sidewalk. Instead of sticking up for Cassie, Big Ma makes Cassie apologize.

Standards: RL.6.1

QUESTION 3: Why doesn't Big Ma want Cassie to tell Uncle Hammer about her day in Strawberry?

Sample Answer: Big Ma is worried Uncle Hammer will react by seeking revenge.

Standards: RL.6.1

QUESTION 4: How does Mr. Morrison stop Uncle Hammer from seeking revenge for Cassie's humiliation?

Sample Answer: He talks to Uncle Hammer all night to distract him and defuse his anger.

Standards: RL.6.1

COMPARATIVE TEXTS

Text: *Rosa Parks: My Story* by Rosa Parks

Compare to: Chapter 5 of *Roll of Thunder, Hear My Cry*

Connection: In 1955, racial segregation on buses was common throughout the American South. When Rosa Parks challenged the bus law on December 1 in Montgomery, Alabama, by refusing an order to give up her seat, her arrest sparked a year-long bus boycott that left the public transit system financially crippled. In *Rosa Parks: My Story,* Parks explains that she was "tired of giving in." When Cassie Logan goes to Strawberry, Mississippi, in *Roll of Thunder, Hear My Cry,* she too—like Parks—encounters the humiliation and inequality of segregation.

Text: *The Warmth of Other Suns* by Isabel Wilkerson

Compare to: Chapter 6 of *Roll of Thunder, Hear My Cry*

Connection: Between 1910 and 1970, over 6 million African Americans migrated from the rural southern United States to the Northeast, Midwest, and West to escape racial oppression and pursue economic and social opportunities. Despite the hardship of life under Jim Crow, an even greater number stayed behind. Both *Roll of Thunder, Hear My Cry* and *The Warmth of Other Suns* consider how Southern African Americans in the 1930s and 1940s made the choice to stay or go.

Text: *The People Could Fly: American Black Folktales* by Virginia Hamilton

Compare to: Chapter 6 of *Roll of Thunder, Hear My Cry*

Connection: Although slavery is long over in *Roll of Thunder, Hear My Cry,* the repercussions of the American slave trade mark the Logan family and their land. In this folktale from Virginia Hamilton's book *The People Could Fly: American Black Folktales,* an old man explains why enslaved West Africans took off their wings and how an old man helped them to fly again.

CHAPTER 7: Protecting the Land

KEY PASSAGE | Chapter 7, Paragraph 188

In this passage, Harlan Granger, the one-time owner of the Logans' land, is warning the Logans that because of the depressed price of cotton, he might be forced to put a financial squeeze on the sharecroppers who work his land by charging them a bigger share of their crops. He expresses regret about having to do this, but he has just tried pressuring the Logans into halting their boycott of the Wallaces' store, only to find them united against him, including Big Ma.

WHY IT'S KEY

Conflict: Mr. Granger is angry that the Logans are supporting a boycott of the Wallace store. He knows that the only way nearby sharecroppers can afford the boycott is if the Logans back their credit, and the only way to do that is with their land. If Mr. Granger raises his prices, the sharecroppers who work his land won't be able to pay off their debt to the Logans and the Logans will lose their land. The Grangers owned the land before the Logans did, and Mr. Granger wants to use this opportunity to get his land back. On the other hand, Papa points out that the land was slave land, implying that he has as much right to the land as the Grangers do.

Character: Even though Mr. Granger already owns a considerable amount of land, most of which is sharecropped, he's selfish and doesn't like that the Logans own their own land. He also resents the power that comes with land ownership being conferred on the Logans.

Key Concept: Even though slavery is long over, Mr. Granger refers to the sharecroppers who work his land as "his people." This sense of ownership over people reflects the debt system of sharecropping. Farmers leased land in exchange for a portion of their harvests. Landowners made sure to keep sharecroppers in debt so that they had to farm each year to pay off the previous year's debt. Although this practice isn't slavery, it was a kind of financial manipulation that mimicked the plantation system.

Please note that excerpts and passages in the StudySync® library, workbooks, and PDFs are intended as touchstones to generate interest in an author's work. The excerpts and passages do not substitute for the reading of entire texts, and StudySync® strongly recommends that teachers and students seek out and purchase the whole literary or informational work in order to experience it as the author intended. Links to online resellers are available in our digital library. In addition, complete works may be ordered through an authorized reseller by filling out and returning to StudySync® the order form enclosed in this workbook.

Teacher's Edition   **453**

YOUR STUDYSYNC® TV

Discussion Prompt: Why is Mr. Granger so angry at the Logans, and how serious is his threat? If you were in the Logans' position, how would you respond?

Standards: RL.6.1, RL.6.3; SL.6.1.A, SL.6.1.C, SL.6.1.D

VOCABULARY

admonished
ad·mon·ished *verb*
Reprimanded; scolded
My father admonished me for spoiling my appetite.

flounced
flounced *verb*
Moved in an exaggerated way to express frustration or impatience
The judge flounced out of the courtroom, furious that neither lawyer was ready to present her argument.

collateral
col·la·te·ral *noun*
An item of value that backs up a loan and will be forfeited if a person or company defaults on the loan
The poker player offered his car as collateral and proceeded with his bet.

goaded
goad·ed *verb*
Pressured someone into doing something
I goaded the babysitter into finally agreeing to let us stay up late.

condone
con·done *verb*
To allow an action or attitude, often something morally troubling, to continue
My father didn't condone my going to the block party because he didn't like the neighborhood.

CLOSE READ

QUESTION 1: Why doesn't Stacey lash out at T.J. for bragging about his coat?

Sample Answer: Stacey restrains himself because he believes in Uncle Hammer's principle, "that a man did not blame others for his own stupidity."

Standards: RL.6.1

QUESTION 2: What new information does Cassie learn about Mr. Morrison's family?

Sample Answer: When Mr. Morrison was six years old, night men burned his house down, killing his parents and his sisters.

Standards: RL.6.1

QUESTION 3: What advice does Papa give Stacey about Jeremy?

Sample Answer: Papa advises Stacey not to become friends with Jeremy because, in the state of Mississippi, interracial friendships lead to trouble.

Standards: RL.6.1

QUESTION 4: Why doesn't Mr. Jamison want the Logans to back store credit with their land?

Sample Answer: He's afraid they'll lose their land. To help protect their land, Mr. Jamison offers to back the loans himself.

Standards: RL.6.1

COMPARATIVE TEXTS

Text: *The Color of Water: A Black Man's Tribute to His White Mother* by James McBride

Compare to: Chapter 7 of *Roll of Thunder, Hear My Cry*

Connection: In the memoir *The Color of Water: A Black Man's Tribute to His White Mother,* Ruth's indifference to racial categories determines the course of her entire life. As a Jewish teenager in Suffolk, Virginia, Ruth gets involved with a black teenager named Peter, before confronting the very serious danger that interracial relationships could spur in the Jim Crow South. Similarly, in *Roll of Thunder, Hear My Cry,* Cassie and her siblings must weigh the costs of befriending their white neighbor, Jeremy.

Please note that excerpts and passages in the StudySync® library, workbooks, and PDFs are intended as touchstones to generate interest in an author's work. The excerpts and passages do not substitute for the reading of entire texts, and StudySync® strongly recommends that teachers and students seek out and purchase the whole literary or informational work in order to experience it as the author intended. Links to online resellers are available in our digital library. In addition, complete works may be ordered through an authorized reseller by filling out and returning to StudySync® the order form enclosed in this workbook.

Teacher's Edition   **455**

CHAPTERS 8–9: A Question of Respect

This passage is part of a heart-to-heart talk between Cassie and Papa in the woods. Papa's message is basically that you have to choose your battles carefully. As an example, he explains having to weigh the outcome of choosing to confront Charlie Simms over his shoving of Cassie, or choosing to turn the other cheek. He concludes that letting it go served the greater good. On the other hand, he tells Cassie that other battles are indeed worth fighting. Those are the situations where one's self-respect needs to be defended. It is an individual decision as to what is worth going to the mat for, but earning others' respect hinges on how one stands up for oneself.

WHY IT'S KEY

Character: Papa is the moral compass throughout *Roll of Thunder, Hear My Cry*. While Uncle Hammer has a temper, Papa advocates more careful and judicious thinking before responding to racial injustice. His trust in Cassie is evident when he tells her that he knows she can make up her mind about how to handle her conflict with the Simms.

Key Concept: Navigating injustice is a tricky business. Papa's advice to Cassie is to proceed cautiously. He advises her to consider the potential harm that retribution could cause, in relation to the damage she would do to her own self-respect if she doesn't stick up for herself. This advice is relevant not only to Cassie's situation with the Simms, but also in thinking about Uncle Hammer's volatile moods and the Logan family's attitude towards the Wallaces. Though there are times when the family doesn't react to mistreatment, they risk their own land when they support the boycott.

YOUR STUDYSYNC® TV

Discussion Prompt: What does Papa's advice to Cassie reveal about his character? Apply his advice in the second paragraph of the Key Passage to a situation you've been in, or could imagine being in. Does his advice hold up? Explain why or why not.

Standards: RL.6.1, RL.6.3; SL.6.1.A, SL.6.1.C, SL.6.1.D

VOCABULARY

venture
ven•ture *verb*
To dare to do something or go somewhere challenging
I held my nose and ventured into the moldy basement.

sentinel
sen•ti•nel *noun*
A person who keeps watch
After the robbery, two sentinels stood outside the bank, on alert.

jovial
jo•vi•al *adjective*
Jolly; cheerful
The new principal was a jovial fellow who got along with both students and teachers.

flail
flail *verb*
To swing wildly; to wave
The drowning swimmer flailed his arms until the lifeguard took notice.

persnickety
per•snick•et•y *adjective*
Fussy; snobbish
The persnickety child refused to taste half the food on her plate.

CLOSE READ

QUESTION 1: How does Cassie know Lillian Jean won't tell on her after Cassie wrestled her into apologizing?

Sample Answer: Cassie threatens to tell all Lillian Jean's secrets if she tells anyone that Cassie beat her up.

Standards: RL.6.1

QUESTION 2: What can you infer about why Cassie's mom got fired?

Sample Answer: The school board fires her for teaching history that's not in the textbook. They learn from T.J., who complained about her at the Wallace store after she caught him cheating, that she's been ignoring and changing the books. Her firing is also a form of intimidation, because the Wallaces don't like her involvement in the boycott of their store.

Standards: RL.6.1

QUESTION 3: Why does Mr. Avery change his mind about participating in the boycott?

Sample Answer: Mr. Granger blackmailed Avery. He changed the price of cotton and told Avery that if he couldn't pay, then he'd end up working on a chain gang. To maintain his freedom and protect his family, Avery has to bow out of the boycott.

Standards: RL.6.1

Please note that excerpts and passages in the StudySync® library, workbooks, and PDFs are intended as touchstones to generate interest in an author's work. The excerpts and passages do not substitute for the reading of entire texts, and StudySync® strongly recommends that teachers and students seek out and purchase the whole literary or informational work in order to experience it as the author intended. Links to online resellers are available in our digital library. In addition, complete works may be ordered through an authorized reseller by filling out and returning to StudySync® the order form enclosed in this workbook.

Teacher's Edition   457

QUESTION 4: How does the feud between the Logans and the Wallaces continue to escalate?

Sample Answer: When Papa, Mr. Morrison, and Stacey are on their way back from Vicksburg with supplies, both wheels fall off their wagon. They suspect foul play. Before they can get back on the road, someone shoots at Papa, grazing his temple. The horses bolt and the wagon runs over Papa's leg, breaking it and preventing him from returning to his job with the railroad.

Standards: RL.6.1

COMPARATIVE TEXTS

Text: *Men We Reaped* by Jesmyn Ward

Compare to: Chapter 9 of *Roll of Thunder, Hear My Cry*

Connection: In Jesmyn Ward's memoir, *Men We Reaped,* Ward tells how, after her parents' separation, she learned to help her mother care for the whole family. Like Ward, Cassie Logan in *Roll of Thunder, Hear My Cry* must help her mother during difficult financial ordeals, particularly when her father is away, working on the railroad.

CHAPTER 10: Calling the Note

Copyright © BookheadEd Learning, LLC

KEY PASSAGE | Chapter 10, Paragraphs 133–138

In this passage, Papa has returned from the bank that loaned him the money to buy his land. He learned that the bank is demanding that he pay back the remaining amount due immediately. The man really responsible is Harlan Granger who, Papa explains to Mama, needs to assert his power over the Logans, and hopes to gain their land when they can't pay the loan. Big Ma protests that by the terms of the loan the Logans have four more years to pay it off. Pa asks wryly if he should take the bank to court.

WHY IT'S KEY

Plot: The white community has turned against the Logans to punish them for their boycott of the Wallace store, even though the boycott has ended. By claiming that their credit is no good and calling up the note on their land early, the bank is forcing the Logans to pay the rest of their mortgage all at once. If Papa and Uncle Hammer can't find the money, they'll lose the land, but the Logans don't have enough money to pay the note. Big Ma's argument that the mortgage has four more years is true, but Papa points out they can't delay payment of the note. The courts are just as biased as the bank. The Logans are in a terrible situation, and they have nowhere to turn.

Characters: Harlan Granger wants the Logan land. By getting the bank to force the Logans to pay their note early, he's betting that they'll default on their mortgage and lose the land. Granger is also upset at the Logans for the power they have in the black community, and he wants to take that away from them. Granger is motivated purely by greed and the need to hold sway in the community, a fire fueled by racist jealousy and the corruption of local officials

When times get tough, the Logan family loyally sticks together and talks candidly about their options. Their greatest asset, besides their land, is the love they have for one another. Although love can't pay the bills, the strength they find in one another helps them survive and navigate around great obstacles. They express their love with mutual respect and unflinching honesty.

YOUR STUDYSYNC® TV

Discussion Prompt: What drives the desires of Harlan Granger, and why does he set himself against the Logans? How does the Logan family respond to adversity? In times of crisis, what are the family's strengths and weaknesses?

Standards: RL.6.1, RL.6.2, RL.6.3; SL.6.1.A, SL.6.1.C, SL.6.1.D

VOCABULARY

lethargically
le·thar·gi·cal·ly *adverb*
Sluggishly; without energy
Every morning, I stumble lethargically into the kitchen and pour myself cereal.

deflated
de·flat·ed *verb*
Felt a loss of confidence or hope; weakened
I looked at my report card, and my good mood was completely deflated.

revival
re·vi·val *noun*
An evangelical Christian service or festival designed to cause a religious awakening
Each year, ministers come from far away to preach at the revival.

throng
throng *noun*
A crowd; a multitude
We wove our way through the gathering throng to the front of the stage.

condescending
con·de·scend·ing *adjective*
Displaying superiority in a way that makes others feel belittled
The hotel clerk asked us in a condescending way how we intended to pay for the room.

CLOSE READ

QUESTION 1: What do Mama and Papa mean when they talk about "Hammer's way" of doing things?

Sample Answer: Uncle Hammer has a quick temper. Hammer's way of doing things is to react aggressively. While that would feel good in the moment, the consequences of revenge would likely be dire and could even end in a lynching.

Standards: RL.6.1

QUESTION 2: Why does Mama want Mr. Morrison to go away?

Sample Answer: After defending Papa on the road back from Vicksburg, Mr. Morrison has caught the attention of the Wallaces. Mama is afraid they'll seek revenge, and she doesn't want Mr. Morrison to be hurt or killed.

Standards: RL.6.1

QUESTION 3: Why did Uncle Hammer sell his Packard?

Sample Answer: The Grangers convinced the bank to make the Logan mortgage note due early. Hammer sold his Packard to pay the mortgage and secure the family land.

Standards: RL.6.1

QUESTION 4: What is the nature of T.J.'s relationship with Melvin and R.W.?

Sample Answer: Melvin and R.W. give T.J. stolen clothes, but they don't actually like him. They're using him for their own purposes, so that he can take the fall if they get in trouble.

Standards: RL.6.1

CHAPTERS 11–12: Reckoning

Copyright © Bookhead Learning, LLC

| KEY PASSAGE | Chapter 12, Paragraph 150 |

In this passage, Cassie has just figured out that Papa set his land on fire to create a diversion that would interrupt T.J.'s lynching. Now she understands that she must not ever talk about what she knows—an understanding she shares wordlessly with Stacey.

WHY IT'S KEY

Plot: Cassie understands that her father set the fire in his own cotton field to prevent T.J.— and possibly himself and Mr. Morrison—from getting lynched. She also knows that if anybody suspects that the fire was intentional and not caused by a lightning strike, the Grangers, Wallaces, and Simms will seek revenge.

Theme: The land is the most important thing that Logans have, and yet Papa is willing to set it on fire to save T.J.'s life. Cassie understands that her father values human life more than his own cotton, and that by setting the cotton on fire he risked his own livelihood and, if he's discovered, his own life.

Character: Cassie has been growing up throughout the entire novel, but this is the moment when she understands the burden of racial politics and how important it is to maintain peace. Her father's sacrifice is enormous but must be kept quiet. Cassie's silent acknowledgment of her father's deed is a true coming-of-age moment. With the help of important role models of strength and wisdom—especially Papa, Mama, Big Ma, and Mr. Morrison—and by learning when to venture and when to yield,—as exemplified by Uncle Hammer, Stacey, Jamison, Jeremy Simms, and, by negative example, T.J.—Cassie is beginning to understand the terrible realities of the adult world that has so long been mysterious to her.

YOUR STUDYSYNC® TV

Discussion Prompt: How does the fire change Cassie's understanding of her family, her land, and the people of the community?

Standards: RL.6.1, RL.6.2; SL.6.1.A, SL.6.1.C, SL.6.1.D

VOCABULARY

finality
fi•nal•i•ty *noun*
The fact or impression of an irreversible ending
My mother spoke in a tone of finality, which indicated the matter was not open for discussion.

frenzy
fren•zy *noun*
A state of chaos; a period of wild behavior
Even after the deer leaped over the fence, the dogs ran around the yard in a frenzy.

despicable
des•pic•a•ble *adjective*
Detestable; deserving contempt
Today, most Americans agree that Jim Crow laws were nothing but despicable.

emerge
e•merge *verb*
To appear; to come into view
Grandpa emerged from the kitchen to tell us that breakfast was ready.

interminable
in•ter•mi•na•ble *adjective*
Never-ending (usually used in deliberate exaggeration)
Without a book to read or a movie to watch, the plane ride across the country felt interminable.

CLOSE READ

QUESTION 1: Why did R.W. and Melvin beat up T.J.?

Sample Answer: T.J. threatened to tell people that R.W. and Melvin attacked the Barnetts.

Standards: RL.6.1

QUESTION 2: Why does Mr. Jamison show up at T.J.'s house?

Sample Answer: He tries to convince the Wallaces and the Simms to let the police arrest T.J. He knows the men want to ignore the law and lynch T.J.

Standards: RL.6.1

QUESTION 3: What does Stacey mean when he tells Cassie, "I don't think Mr. Jamison can hold them"?

Sample Answer: The Simms and the Wallaces want to lynch somebody. Mr. Jamison is trying to talk them out of it, but Stacey doesn't think he has the power or influence to succeed. This is why Stacey tells Cassie to go home and tell Papa what's going on.

Standards: RL.6.1

QUESTION 4: Why is Cassie so excited when Jeremy tells her that Melvin, R.W., and Papa are all fighting the fire?

Sample Answer: If they're fighting the fire, it means that Papa is alive and that the Simms and the Wallaces stopped threatening to lynch T.J., Papa, and Mr. Morrison.

Standards: RL.6.1

COMPARATIVE TEXTS

Text: *A Mission from God* by James Meredith

Compare to: Chapter 11 of *Roll of Thunder, Hear My Cry*

Connection: While promoting voting rights through the 1966 March Against Fear, civil rights activist James Meredith was shot (wounded). In his memoir *A Mission from God,* Meredith describes the event and puts it into historical context. As with the threatened lynching of T.J. in *Roll of Thunder, Hear My Cry,* the attempted killing of Meredith was not an isolated event but instead part of the systematic violence used to maintain white supremacy in the American South.

Text: "I Am Prepared to Die" by Nelson Mandela

Compare: Upon completion of *Roll of Thunder, Hear My Cry*

Connection: During the 1964 Rivonia Trial in South Africa, Nelson Mandela was charged with plotting to overthrow the government. While on the stand, he famously said about apartheid, "The lack of human dignity experienced by Africans is the direct result of the policy of white supremacy. White supremacy implies black inferiority." Much like black South Africans during apartheid, African Americans in the American South were denied economic and educational opportunities.

Copyright © BookheadEd Learning, LLC

WRITE TO REVISIT

ARGUMENTATIVE WRITING

Prompt: From Cassie's treatment at the General Store in Strawberry to the attempted lynching of T.J., racial injustice is a theme throughout *Roll of Thunder, Hear My Cry*. Rather than being a hardship specific to people like the Logan family and their community, segregation, discrimination, and racially motivated violence were widespread in the American South from Reconstruction through the 1960s. Choose an instance of injustice in *Roll of Thunder, Hear My Cry* and research it. Potential topics include segregated schools, segregated buses, unequal customer service, unequal access to a trial, obstacles to African-American land ownership, sharecropping, lynching, etc. Evaluate Mildred D. Taylor's portrayal of your research topic, and refer to as many of the supplementary readings in the unit as seem relevant.

Standards: RL.6.1, RL.6.2; RL.6.1, RI.6.7, RI.6.9; W.6.1.A, W.6.1.B, W.6.1.C, W.6.1.D, W.6.1.E, W.6.7, W.6.8, W.6.9.A, W.6.9.B

CREATIVE WRITING

Prompt: Like blues music, which originates from the Mississippi Delta, blues poetry shares many themes with *Roll of Thunder, Hear My Cry*. Blues poems frequently reference themes such as struggle, perseverance, humble origins, land, and family. In addition, Blues poems are often written using three-line stanzas, with the last two lines repeating or mimicking one another. Imagery that references the five senses is used to make poems more vivid, and wordplay deepens the emotional impact of each line. Read Langston Hughes' poem "Weary Blues" and Sterling A. Brown's poem "Riverbank Blues". What do these two poems have in common, and what makes them both "blues poems"? Write a blues poem of your own that references the characters and events from *Roll of Thunder, Hear My Cry*. If you'd like, set your poem to music. Your poem should be at least a page long and should use the techniques and characteristics associated with blues poetry.

Standards: RL.6.4; RL.6.5; W.6.3.B, W.6.3.D, W.6.4, W.6.5

The Monsters Are Due on Maple Street

Rod Serling

INTRODUCTION

"The Monsters Are Due on Maple Street" is a teleplay written by Rod Serling for his classic anthology TV series *The Twilight Zone*. Over 150 episodes of *The Twilight Zone* aired between 1959 and 1964, including this famous episode about a small-town neighborhood torn apart by fear and suspicion. Every episode of *The Twilight Zone* has its own unique, self-contained narrative; however, all of them share paranormal or unusual subject matter, feature narration at the beginning and end (by Serling himself), and often conclude with a surprise twist at the episode's finale. True to Serling's socially conscious intent, "The Monsters Are Due on Maple Street" is also a metaphor about the panic that swept throughout the United States in the 50s as the Cold War intensified—in addition to a thrilling piece of TV drama.

Rod Serling (1924–1975) was a television writer and producer best known as the creator of *The Twilight Zone*. In total, he wrote 92 episodes of the series, which garnered critical acclaim and won numerous awards during its five-year run. He is remembered today as one of the early pioneers of the television medium.

As students read "The Monsters Are Due on Maple Street", ask them to think about some of its important themes, as well as its observations about human nature in the face of paranoia and suspicion. What could Serling be saying about life in 1950s America? What might the fictional, anonymous Maple Street and its residents represent?

USING THIS READING GUIDE

This reading guide presents lessons to support the teaching of Rod Serling's "The Monsters Are Due on Maple Street". Organized by sections of grouped scenes, the lessons preview key vocabulary words and include close reading questions tied to the Common Core State Standards. The lessons identify a key passage in each section that will help you guide students through an exploration of the essential ideas and events in "The Monsters Are Due on Maple Street". This passage will also serve as the jumping-off point from which students will engage in their own StudySyncTV–style group discussion.

Each section of the reading guide also includes a list of comparative texts—provided in "The Monsters Are Due on Maple Street" Full-text Unit on StudySync—that go along with that section. For each comparative text, the reading guide includes important contextual notes and ideas for relating the text to "The Monsters Are Due on Maple Street".

THE MONSTERS ARE DUE ON MAPLE STREET

TEXT SECTIONS

ACT I, PART 1: 6:43 PM

On a quiet suburban street, a mysterious flying object passes overhead and causes a mass power outage. Neighbors congregate in the street and discuss what to do. Steve and Charlie decide to go into town to investigate—until a neighborhood boy, Tommy, offers an ominous warning.

ACT I, PART 2: Fifth Columnists

Laughing off Tommy's warning as a comic book plot, the neighbors are suddenly alarmed when Les Goodman's car starts. They suspect Goodman of having something to hide, which Goodman emphatically denies, despite mounting accusations and suspicions of strange behavior.

ACT II, PART 1: Kangaroo Court

By night the situation has escalated even further, as Steve, Charlie, and the other neighbors now accuse each other of harboring dark secrets. Their argument is interrupted when they see a shadowy figure approaching. Charlie grabs his shotgun as the figure gets closer and closer.

ACT II, PART 2: The Monsters

Charlie fires at the shadowy figure, but when the neighbors finally come upon the body they realize it to be one of their own, Pete Van Horn. Hysteria settles in as the neighbors erupt into a full-blown riot. In the distance, two mysterious figures look on, providing ironic closure and a sobering lesson on human behavior.

ACT I, PART 1: 6:43 PM

> ### KEY PASSAGE
>
> In this passage, the Narrator's voice sets the scene on Maple Street, a picture-perfect 1950s suburban setting with children playing outside and the familiar sounds of a Good Humor ice cream truck. The camera pans over as two little boys purchase ice cream from the ice cream truck, then the Narrator gives the exact time—6:43 PM—at which point a bright flying object passes overhead. Several residents of Maple Street watch as it passes, including Tommy, Steve Brand, and Don Martin. Steve guesses it was only a meteor, and Don agrees, though he wonders why they didn't hear any crashing sound or impact.

WHY IT'S KEY

Dramatic Structure: Following the show's standard narrated introduction, we move to a nondescript suburban street that could almost be anywhere in the United States. With the guidance of the show's narrator, this passage introduces the setting, three of the principal characters, and the mysterious occurrence that sets the plot in motion.

Narrator: "The Monsters Are Due on Maple Street" uses a narrator for a couple of different purposes. First, the standard narration that begins each episode of *The Twilight Zone* sets the show's supernatural tone. Next, a sentence describes the setting: "a tree-lined little world of front porch gliders, hopscotch, the laughter of children, and the bell of an ice cream vendor." Coupled with the assorted images of the neighborhood, these details provide all of the necessary exposition in the first minute of the episode.

Setting: Maple Street is anonymized; that is, its attributes could belong to almost any neighborhood in the suburban United States of the 1950s. By framing the neighborhood this way, Serling is making a deliberate choice. We never know what city or state we're in, for instance, and there is a sameness to the neighborhood and its residents. This nondescript setting allows viewers to relate: after all, it could literally be anywhere.

Tone: Viewers of *The Twilight Zone* knew to expect the supernatural. When the flash of light passes over Maple Street, the neighbors at first suspect it was only a meteor. Their reassurances stand in direct contrast with the show's ominous tone, building mystery and suspense.

YOUR STUDYSYNC® TV

Discussion Prompt: Based on the descriptions in this passage, what are some other things you can infer about Maple Street? About the people living there? Discuss this setting as a group and talk about what it might have been like to live on Maple Street in the 1950s—as well as what a similar setting might be like today. Make sure you refer to passages from the text in your discussion.

Standards: RL.6.1, RL.6.5; SL.6.1.A, SL.6.1.C, SL.6.1.D

VOCABULARY

dimension
di•men•sion *noun*
An space or area of existence
In C. S. Lewis' The Lion, the Witch, and the Wardrobe, four English children discover a magical wardrobe that serves as a portal to another dimension.

intelligible
in•tel•li•gi•ble *adjective*
Clear; easy to understand
Her voice message was barely intelligible, so I wasn't sure what she wanted.

flustered
flus•tered *adjective*
Overwhelmed by confusion, anxiety, or excitement
Upset by some of the host's questions, the actress grew flustered and abruptly ended the interview.

murmur
mur•mur *noun*
The sound of low, indistinct voices
The Congressman's surprise announcement that he would resign drew a murmur of shock throughout the crowd.

assent
as•sent *noun*
An approval or agreement
Before downloading the software, you must give your assent to the terms and conditions.

defiant
de•fi•ant *adjective*
Resistant; uncooperative
Earl was defiant when the officers asked him for his license and registration, flatly refusing to cooperate.

CLOSE READ

QUESTION 1: How would you describe Maple Street? What are a few important or "telling" details in the script that help frame this setting?

Sample Answer: Maple Street is a quiet and peaceful suburban street. It is very "typical" in a number of different ways. Some telling details include bicycles, lawns, ice cream vendors, and children playing in the street.

Standards: RL.6.1

QUESTION 2: After the unidentified object passes overhead at 6:43 PM, the narrator states that this was "the last calm and reflective moment . . . before the monsters came." Why do you think this is included in the narration? What purpose does it serve to give vague hints of what's about to happen?

Sample Answer: This statement builds suspense and dread in the narrative. We aren't given enough information to know exactly what will happen, but we know that something bad is about to take place. This sets an ominous, foreboding tone.

Standards: RL.6.1

QUESTION 3: How does the script use dialogue to convey that something very strange is happening?

Sample Answer: The characters try to explain what's happening, but none of their explanations hold up. It can't be an electrical storm, because the sky is clear. It can't just be a power outage, because the radio doesn't work either. Cars won't start, yet they have plenty of gas.

Standards: RL.6.1

QUESTION 4: What is the crowd's initial reaction to Tommy's warning, and how is it different from Steve's reaction? Do you think this will change, and if so, how?

Sample Answer: The people in the crowd dismiss Tommy's warning as "crazy" and something likely out of the pages of a comic book. Steve is less dismissive and willing to listen, wanting to reassure Tommy that everything will be okay. (Answers to the final question will vary.)

Standards: RL.6.1

COMPARATIVE TEXTS

Text: *The Fifties* by David Halberstam

Compare to: Act I, Part 1 of "The Monsters Are Due on Maple Street"

Connection: When an unidentified object passes over Maple Street at 6:43 pm on an otherwise ordinary evening, many residents of the neighborhood reassure each other it was only a meteor. It's understandable why they'd be trying to quell each other's fears: in the late 1950s, paranoia ran deep. Tensions with the former Soviet Union had reached a fever pitch. Americans were growing more and more fearful of the capabilities of the Soviets as both nations were locked in a race for nuclear and technological superiority. This excerpt from author David Halberstam's *The Fifties* depicts a critical turning point in what was later dubbed the Space Race: the endeavor to launch the first artificial Earth satellite. It's something the residents of Maple Street and the viewers of the show probably shared: a fascination with the skies above.

ACT I, PART 2: Fifth Columnists

KEY PASSAGE

In this passage, Steve explains to Les Goodman that the neighbors suspect he's involved in the mass power outage because his car is the only one on the block that starts. With a little chuckle, Steve tells Les about the "monster kick" they're on, with some of the neighbors growing more suspicious of the true motivations of one another. Goodman is in disbelief, wondering if it's all a joke, but when his porch light suddenly goes out, the neighbors' suspicion only heightens. Les pleads with them, reminding them that the Goodmans have lived in the neighborhood for five years and are just like everyone else.

WHY IT'S KEY

Plot: The anxiety of the neighborhood intensifies when Les Goodman's car starts, bringing unspoken suspicions about Les and his behavior out into the open. Having taken the initial step "that changes people from a group into a mob," the neighbors confront Les Goodman and accuse him of having some kind of sinister involvement in the mass power outage.

Context: "Fifth columnists from the vast beyond," Steve chuckles, when describing the object of suspicion sweeping across Maple Street. "Fifth column" is a term that viewers in the 1950s would have been familiar with—code for a secret organization or group that seeks to undermine its enemy from within. This is one of many references in the script to contemporary fears and anxieties, and with the fear of communism spreading across the Western world throughout the 1950s, many Americans were already on high alert. A reference like this indicates that the fictional world of Maple Street depicts real-life concerns.

Character: At first, Les Goodman is in a state of disbelief, and soon thereafter, he pleads with the neighbors that he is "no different at all"—but the neighbors aren't so sure. The initial "sameness" of most of the characters in "The Monsters Are Due on Maple Street" has given way to the fear that any differences at all might threaten the stability of their very lives.

Theme: Already we see the group transforming into a mob, fueled by the destructive forces of suspicion and paranoia. "Mob mentality" is an ever-present theme in this episode, which offers a dramatization of a topical issue of the time: how the forces of distrust could tear a community apart. Suspicion and paranoia—two trademark behaviors of the "mob"—will remain important themes throughout.

YOUR STUDYSYNC® TV

Discussion Prompt: Why do you think members of a group are often afraid or disdainful of anyone who is "different"? How does this create pressure to conform? Using examples from this passage and others, discuss what it means to be a member of a community and the various forces that bring people together. Is it reasonable to fear people who are different? Why or why not? Where should you draw the line?

Standards: RL.6.1, RL.6.2; SL.6.1.A, SL.6.1.C, SL.6.1.D

VOCABULARY

taut
taut *adjective*
Pulled or stretched tightly
Make sure the strings on your guitar are taut, but not so taut that they will snap.

metamorphosis
me·ta·mor·pho·sis *noun*
A transformation of a person, animal, or object into a new stage and appearance
The actress lost more than thirty pounds and underwent a stunning physical metamorphosis in preparation for the role.

incisive
in·ci·sive *adjective*
Clear or direct; sharp
He is best known for his incisive weekly newspaper column, tackling contemporary issues with sharp, intelligent wit.

incriminate
in·crim·i·nate *verb*
To suggest proof of someone's guilt or responsibility for wrongdoing
Investigators found ample DNA evidence at the crime scene to incriminate Mrs. Banks for the murder of her husband.

insomnia
in·som·ni·a *noun*
A disorder marked by the inability to sleep
The doctor suggested that she try counting kangaroos to cure her relentless insomnia.

CLOSE READ

QUESTION 1: How do the neighbors respond when Les Goodman's car mysteriously starts? How does this shift the nature of the conflict?

Sample Answer: At first, the neighbors are baffled when Les's car starts. Then they start to suspect him of wrongdoing, wondering why he didn't come out to look at the flying object and accusing him of strange behavior. This shifts the nature of the conflict by redirecting the object of suspicion towards Les.

Standards: RL.6.1

QUESTION 2: In what ways does Steve stand out from the rest of the crowd? What can we infer about Steve in comparison to the other neighbors?

Sample Answer: When the group is ready to confront Les Goodman, Steve steps in front of them and tells them not to act like a mob. He talks to Goodman calmly while the others shout accusations. We can infer from this that he is more reasonable and level-headed than the other neighbors.

Standards: RL.6.1

QUESTION 3: What role does Charlie play in the group? Explain, citing dialogue or descriptions from the text.

Sample Answer: Charlie is an instigator. He is the first to suggest that Les has "always been an oddball," and he encourages the woman to come forward with her suspicions about Les. He quickly becomes the most aggressive and agitated member of the group.

Standards: RL.6.1

QUESTION 4: Why does the woman in the crowd speak out against Les? What does this tell you about the nature of their suspicion?

Sample Answer: The woman in the crowd speaks out because she has seen Les staring up at the sky in the middle of the night, and now that fear and paranoia are rising, this observation becomes the basis for her suspicions about Les's intentions. It tells us that fear and suspicion existed among the neighbors well before the power went out, and now all their fears and suspicions are coming out.

Standards: RL.6.1

COMPARATIVE TEXTS

Text: *The Rise and Fall of Senator Joe McCarthy* by James Cross Giblin

Compare to: Act I, Part 2 of "The Monsters Are Due on Maple Street"

Connection: As fears of Soviet influence spread in the 1950s, many people believed that the greatest threats to national security came not from abroad but from within, courtesy of communist agents supposedly infiltrating the highest levels of U.S. government. It was a time in which people's ideals and allegiances were called into question: co-workers, neighbors, and even friends and family were often suspected of ties to the communist party. A Wisconsin Senator named Joseph McCarthy became the face of fear-mongering when he gave a speech in 1950 claiming that he had the names of communist agents working in the U.S. State Department. As Act I comes to a close, the residents of Maple Street have begun to question Les Goodman's true intentions, exhibiting traits of "McCarthyism," a term used to describe any character attack intending to arouse suspicion without substantial evidence.

ACT II, PART 1: Kangaroo Court

KEY PASSAGE

In this passage, the neighbors' suspicion of each other has reached its highest point yet. Insisting that everything must come out in the open now, Don Martin steps forward and claims that Steve's wife has been talking a lot about her husband's odd behavior. Charlie pounces on this statement, encouraging Don to elaborate on this odd behavior. Meanwhile, an indignant Steve dares them all to talk. He sarcastically asks whether they should place the accused before a firing squad until every last suspect has been eliminated, wondering if that would make Charlie happy.

WHY IT'S KEY

Plot: As night falls and Maple Street plunges into darkness, the anxieties of the neighborhood continue to rise. No longer is Les Goodman the only focus of suspicion; slowly but surely, all of the men and women who have lived on Maple Street for years are beginning to turn on each other. Here, Steve Brand finds himself between the cross hairs when rumors about his own strange behavior are thrust out in the open.

Conflict: At the end of Act I, the group had directed its ire towards a particular target: Les Goodman. Now, however, the group has fractured, and it's every man for himself. The conflict shifts so quickly, it's hard to keep track of who's on top. As Steve Brand indicates here, losing his equanimity: life on Maple Street has become a game of asserting one's own innocence and deflecting blame onto another.

Central Idea: In a few hours, the mood on Maple Street has gone from tranquil to hysterical. The central idea of the episode has focused on how the unity and solidarity of a peaceful suburban neighborhood has come apart at the seams. We've yet to understand what's behind the mass power outage, or the mysterious flying object; these incidents have served only as the incitement for a character study of paranoia and suspicion.

Language: The author uses two terms in this passage that merit a closer look. "Kangaroo court" is a term for an assembly or other judicial gathering that blatantly ignores standards of fairness or justice, jumping to conclusions (perhaps this is where the "kangaroo" part comes from) without any regard for the due process of law. A "firing squad" is a method of capital punishment common in militarized nations or during a time of war. Understanding these references and their meanings help make Steve's insinuations more clear.

YOUR STUDYSYNC® TV

Discussion Prompt: In this passage, Steve suggests a couple of "solutions" to the neighborhood's suspicion, albeit sarcastically. Can you think of any *serious* ways to resolve this dispute and pacify the situation on Maple Street? Discuss as a class any proposals for peace that you can think of, and whether or not you think they might work. How would the characters respond? Who do you think would be the most difficult neighbor to manage, and why?

Standards: RL.6.1, RL.6.3; SL.6.1.A, SL.6.1.C, SL.6.1.D

VOCABULARY

legitimate
le·git·i·mate *adjective*
Reasonable; valid
It is entirely legitimate for people to be concerned about the ingredients in their food.

idiosyncrasy
i·di·o·syn·cra·sy *noun*
A distinctive behavior or characteristic
Sarita knew her sister's every idiosyncrasy, from eating two cloves of garlic every morning to sleeping with her favorite teddy bear from childhood.

dense
dense *adjective*
Thick-headed; not able to understand things easily
Mark can be so dense that I sometimes have to explain things to him several times over.

menace
men·ace *noun*
A person or thing that is threatening or harmful
Always ready to pounce at a moment's notice, her bulldog is a menace to any stranger who comes to her door.

scapegoat
scape·goat *noun*
A person or group blamed unfairly for something that others have done
The coach of the basketball team refused to be the scapegoat for the players' failures on the court.

CLOSE READ

QUESTION 1: What are the neighbors doing at the beginning of Act II? How much time can we infer has passed since the conclusion of the first act?

Sample Answer: At the beginning of Act II, the neighbors are all standing guard around the Goodman house, waiting for any sign of suspicious activity. It's suggested that a few hours have passed since the end of Act I.

Standards: RL.6.1

QUESTION 2: What does Charlie suggest they do about the problem? How is his suggestion indicative of his character?

Sample Answer: Charlie's suggests that they all stand around and wait for someone to "tip their hand," or in other words, to reveal their guilt. His suggestion reveals that he is consumed by fear and suspicion, and believes that the supposed "culprit" is one of his neighbors.

Standards: RL.6.1

QUESTION 3: What does Don reveal to the neighbors about Steve Brand? Why do you think he does this, and what does it imply about the general behavior of the neighborhood?

Sample Answer: Don reveals that Steve's wife has spoken to him about how Steve has been working on some kind of mysterious radio in his basement. A combination of peer pressure and suspicion probably causes Don to reveal this "secret." It implies that the neighbors probably do a great deal of talking behind each other's backs.

Standards: RL.6.1

QUESTION 4: How does Steve react after Don and Charlie begin to question his motives? What can we infer about his change in demeanor?

Sample Answer: Steve becomes increasingly frustrated and aggravated by the neighbors' suspicion, even provoking them by sarcastically "confessing" to his guilt. Although he is the most level-headed member of the group, this change in demeanor shows that even Steve is susceptible to the rising tension on Maple Street.

Standards: RL.6.1

QUESTION 5: How does the plot move toward a climax when Don grabs the shotgun? What do you think will happen next?

Sample Answer: The situation on Maple Street has grown more and more tense, and the tension increases even further when they see a shadowy figure approaching in the darkness. When Don grabs the shotgun, we can infer that there will be some kind of confrontation. (Predictions will vary.)

Standards: RL.6.1

COMPARATIVE TEXTS

Text: *Extraordinary Popular Delusions and the Madness of Crowds* by Charles Mackay

Compare to: Act II, Part 1 of "The Monsters Are Due on Maple Street"

Connection: As the episode reaches its climax, the neighborhood of Maple Street has been torn apart by fear and suspicion, without any explanation or understanding of the strange flying object that started it all. Although the episode's parallels to the fear of communism in 1950s America are strongly apparent, it's also easy to draw parallels to another notorious chapter in American history: the Salem witch trials of 1692 and 1693. This excerpt from journalist Charles Mackay's 1841 book *Extraordinary Popular Delusions and the Madness of Crowds* recounts how people in Salem and surrounding Massachusetts towns were driven into a mass frenzy by the suspicion that their neighbors and friends had fallen under the spell of the Devil.

ACT II, PART 2: The Monsters

KEY PASSAGE

In this passage, the two unidentified figures from another world, Figure One and Figure Two, discuss how the breakdown on Maple Street has all happened according to plan. Figure One explains to Figure Two that they are following a specific procedure, cutting off the power in various neighborhoods across the country and then watching the neighbors' quick descent into paranoia and violence. According to Figure One, this pattern always plays out the same, with almost no variations, because the world is "full of Maple Streets." It is ultimately revealed that these invaders plan to take control by causing groups of people to turn against each other, thereby destroying themselves from within.

WHY IT'S KEY

Plot: After Charlie mistakenly shoots Pete Van Horn, the whole neighborhood descends into chaos. Mass hysteria has taken over, and there's still no explanation for the power outage up and down Maple Street . . . until the camera pulls back and reveals two silhouetted figures standing alongside a spacecraft and watching the chaos unfold.

Resolution: Tommy was right all along! His "comic book" warnings, dismissed as nonsensical by the neighbors, were actually right on target. As mentioned in the introduction, episodes of *The Twilight Zone* often feature a surprise twist at the end, and the resolution of "The Monsters Are Due on Maple Street" is no different.

Dialogue: Discussing the hysteria in cold and clinical language, the two silhouetted figures offer a "recap" of what we've just witnessed: the power outage was all a part of their calculated plan to take over. Except, as Figure One explains, there's no need to engage the humans in a fight. As they've learned, all they need to do is sit back and "watch the pattern" emerge. The dialogue of the two silhouetted figures acts as commentary on the plotline of the episode.

Theme: Destruction from within is the theme of the hour on Maple Street and, on a more general level, the entire human race. It's easy to extrapolate from this conclusion that

Serling is offering a critique of the increasing suspicion of communism spreading throughout 1950s America. In the host's final narration, which immediately follows this exchange, the lesson is imparted even more directly.

YOUR STUDYSYNC® TV

Discussion Prompt: Do you agree with the two figures and their assessment of the human condition? Why or why not? Do people succumb to fear and paranoia as easily as it is depicted in this episode? Discuss these questions as a class, citing evidence from this passage as well as the others that came before it.

Standards: RL.6.1, RL.6.3; SL.6.1.A, SL.6.1.C, SL.6.1.D

VOCABULARY

apprehensive
ap•pre•hen•sive *adjective*
Showing hesitation or unease because of a concern that something bad will happen
Thanks to years of crushing losses, the fans were apprehensive even when their team was ahead.

contorted
con•tort•ed *adjective*
Twisted or distorted; not in its normal shape
You could read Jared's frustration in his contorted face as he struggled to assemble the bookshelves he had bought.

converge
con•verge *verb*
To come together or meet at a common point
During their annual pilgrimage, known as the Hajj, millions of Muslims from all over the world converge in the holy city of Mecca.

fallout
fall•out *noun*
The negative aftermath or repercussions of a situation
The Congressman knew that the fallout from the scandal would likely result in the loss of his job.

prejudices
prej•u•dic•es *noun*
Preconceived opinions or judgments formed before knowing the facts
If you show prejudices about religious or ethnic groups, you will probably not be asked to serve as a member of a jury.

CLOSE READ

QUESTION 1: Why do the neighbors turn on Charlie? How does Charlie respond to their accusations?

Sample Answer: The neighbors turn on Charlie because he shoots Pete Van Horn and, afterwards, because the lights in his house mysteriously turn on. Charlie breaks away from the mob as they chase after him and then attempts to blame Tommy for the whole incident.

Standards: RL.6.1

Teacher's Edition

QUESTION 2: Much of the dialogue in the climactic melee is spoken by characters named only *Man*, *Woman*, or even more simply, *Voices*. Why do you think Serling chose to keep certain speakers anonymous? How does this creative choice contribute to the meaning of the text?

Sample Answer: Answers will vary but should touch on how these anonymous voices represent the faceless and impersonal nature of the mob. They have lost their individuality and their capacity to reason by this point, so it's only appropriate that the dialogue is spoken by unidentified members of a crowd.

Standards: RL.6.1

QUESTION 3: How would you describe the nature of the mob at the end of Act II? Think of some words and descriptions that accurately characterize their behavior, and write them here.

Sample Answer: The mob is fickle, quickly shifting its rage from one person to the next as quickly as the wind blows. They don't possess the capacity to step back and reason; instead, they find a target as their anger and suspicion escalates.

Standards: RL.6.1

QUESTION 4: What do you think will happen next on Maple Street? Why do you think Serling chose to end the episode with this resolution?

Sample Answer: Answers will vary but should mention how the neighborhood has descended into complete chaos according to the aliens' plans. It will probably be very easy for the aliens to take over, now that the neighborhood has self-destructed. Serling chose this ending because this episode is a cautionary tale about how paranoia and suspicion can tear apart a community.

Standards: RL.6.1

QUESTION 5: What is the message or moral of this episode? How does the last paragraph of narration convey this message? Explain.

Sample Answer: The final message is that thoughts, attitudes, and prejudices can destroy a community just as bombs and weapons can. The last paragraph of narration explains how looking for someone to blame can tear a community apart. The final sentence drives home the message that even though this is fiction, the same thing can happen in real life.

Standards: RL.6.1

COMPARATIVE TEXTS

Text: *The Wisdom of Crowds* by James Surowiecki

Compare to: Act II, Part 2 of "The Monsters Are Due on Maple Street"

Connection: Finally, the surprise twist of "The Monsters Are Due on Maple Street" reveals itself as the episode draws to a close. "Their world is full of Maple Streets," says Figure One, as the two unidentified figures look upon a tight-knit neighborhood that has destroyed itself from within in the course of an evening. "Stop a few of their machines . . . throw them into darkness for a few hours, and then you just sit back and watch the pattern." As the two figures discuss what has transpired on Maple Street and the final narration commences, the lesson of the story is clear. But are all groups of people doomed to fail? Not so, according to author James Surowiecki, who argues in *The Wisdom of Crowds* that groups of people can be more intelligent than even their smartest members, given the right circumstances. His argument offers an interesting counterpoint to "The Monsters Are Due on Maple Street" and its conclusions about human nature.

Please note that excerpts and passages in the StudySync® library, workbooks, and PDFs are intended as touchstones to generate interest in an author's work. The excerpts and passages do not substitute for the reading of entire texts, and StudySync® strongly recommends that teachers and students seek out and purchase the whole literary or informational work in order to experience it as the author intended. Links to online resellers are available in our digital library. In addition, complete works may be ordered through an authorized reseller by filling out and returning to StudySync® the order form enclosed in this workbook.

Teacher's Edition **483**

WRITE TO REVISIT

NARRATIVE WRITING

Prompt: Think about a commonly held fear or adversary, whether it is in your own society or another society, real or imagined. It might be an irrational fear, like rumors of zombies or space invaders, or a plausible one, like a contagious disease. Ask yourself what the threat is, whether the fear is proportional to that threat, and what the dangers are of panic or hysteria. Then write a fictional blog entry or journal entry—or a series of entries—from someone who is experiencing the threat and the reaction of others to it. Think about the elements from "The Monsters Are Due on Maple Street", but without duplicating them.

Standards: RL.6.1; W.6.3.A, W.6.3.B, W.6.3.C, W.6.3.D

CRITICAL WRITING

Prompt: What is the precise "moral" of "The Monsters Are Due on Maple Street" that Serling and the show's creators want to impart? Is there a particular warning or message the episode contains, especially in context of the events of the 1950s? Write an essay explaining what you believe is Serling's specific message about real-life or contemporary events of the day, as well as about general human behavior. You must use direct citations from at least three of the supplementary readings in your analysis of the *content* and *context* of the episode's message.

Standards: RL.6.1, RL.6.2; RI.6.1, RI.6.2; W.6.1.A, W.6.1.B, W.6.1.C, W.6.1.D, W.6.1.E, W.6.4, W.6.9.A, W.6.9.B

PHOTO/IMAGE CREDITS:

Cover, ©iStock.com/CostinT, ©iStock.com/alexsl, ©iStock.com/aijohn784

p. iii, ©iStock.com/CreativeEye99,©iStock.com/TerryJLawrence, ©iStock.com/aijohn784, ©iStock.com/joshblake

p. v, Apic/contributor/Getty Images, ©iStock.com/gaiamoments, ©iStock.com/kertlis, ©iStock.com/ABDESIGN, ©iStock.com/technotr, ©iStock.com/poco_bw, ©iStock.com/Leonsbox, ©iStock.com/alexey_boldin

p. vi, ©iStock.com/skegbydave, ©iStock.com/alexey_boldin, ©iStock.com, ©iStock.com/Massonstock, ©iStock.com/RMAX, ©iStock.comprudkov, fair use, ©iStock.com/szefei, ©iStock.com/ gaiamoments, ©iStock.com/technotr ©iStock.com/Marilyn Nieves, ©iStock.com/welcome-to-carol-world, ©iStock.com/adisa, Yale Joel/Yale Joel/Getty Images, ©iStock.com/StephenSewell, Archive Photos/Archive Photos, ©iStock.com/DNY59, ©iStock.com/dblight

p. vii, Hero Images/Getty Images

p. ix, Apic/contributor/Getty Images

p. x, ©iStock.com/alexey_boldin, ©iStock.com

p. xii, ©iStock.com/MoreISO, ©iStock.com/bizoo_n, ©iStock.com/dtokar, ©iStock.com/gkuchera

p. xiii, ©iStock.com/gkuchera

p. xv, ©iStock.com/dtokar, ©iStock.com/Bunyos, ©iStock.com/ThomasVogel

p. xvii, ©iStock.com/Kamchatka, ©iStock.com/moevin

p. xviii, ©iStock.com/bizoo_n

p. xix, ©iStock.com/DNY59

p. xxi, ©iStock.com/kemie, ©iStock.com/belchonock, ©iStock.com/melissasanger, ©iStock.com/ErikaMitchell

p. xxiii, ©iStock.com/Toa55, ©iStock.com/sturti, ©iStock.com/IzabelaHabur, Stephen F. Somerstein/Getty Images

p. xxiv, ©iStock.com/TuomasKujansuu

p. xxv, ©iStock.com/Caval, ©iStock.com/kamonlai, ©iStock.com/ImagineGolf

p. xxvi, ©iStock.com/GeorgePeters, ©iStock.com/Aleksander, ©iStock.com/duncan1890, ©iStock.com/aniszewski, ©iStock.com/ExcellentPhoto, WIN MCNAMEE/Getty Images

p. xxvii, ©iStock.com/PhotoZidaric, ©iStock.com/neoblues, ©iStock.com/DaveAlan, ©iStock.com/stockstudioX

p. xxvii, ©iStock.com/makosh, ©iStock.com/m-imagephotography, ©iStock.com/sam74100

p. 1, ©iStock.com/aijohn784, ©iStock.com/vernonwiley, ©iStock.com/alexey_boldin, ©iStock.com/skegbydave

p. 2, ©iStock.com/vernonwiley

Text Fulfillment
Through StudySync

If you are interested in specific titles, please fill out the form below and we will check availability through our partners.

ORDER DETAILS

Date:

TITLE	AUTHOR	Paperback/ Hardcover	Specific Edition *If Applicable*	Quantity

SHIPPING INFORMATION

Contact:

Title:

School/District:

Address Line 1:

Address Line 2:

Zip or Postal Code:

Phone:

Mobile:

Email:

BILLING INFORMATION   ☐ *SAME AS SHIPPING*

Contact:

Title:

School/District:

Address Line 1:

Address Line 2:

Zip or Postal Code:

Phone:

Mobile:

Email:

PAYMENT INFORMATION

☐ CREDIT CARD

Name on Card:

Card Number: Expiration Date: Security Code:

☐ PO

Purchase Order Number:

StudySync Text Fulfillment, BookheadEd Learning, LLC
610 Daniel Young Drive | Sonoma, CA 95476